P9-AOI-437

Democracy and participation in Athens

Democracy and participation in Athens

R. K. Sinclair

Associate Professor of Ancient History,
University of Sydney

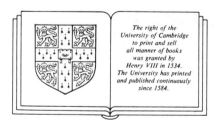

The right of the
University of Cambridge
to print and sell
all manner of books
was granted by
Henry VIII in 1534.
The University has printed
and published continuously
since 1584.

Cambridge University Press

Cambridge

New York   New Rochelle   Melbourne   Sydney

LIBRARY
COLBY-SAWYER COLLEGE
NEW LONDON, NH 03257

JC
79
.A8
S56
1988
c.1

Published by the Press Syndicate of the University of Cambridge
The Pitt Building, Trumpington Street, Cambridge CB2 1RP
32 East 57th Street, New York, NY 10022, USA
10 Stamford Road, Oakleigh, Melbourne 3166, Australia

© Cambridge University Press 1988

First published 1988
Reprinted 1989

Printed in Great Britain at the University Press, Cambridge

British Library cataloguing in publication data

Sinclair, R. K.
Democracy and participation in Athens.
1. Democracy 2. Athens (Greece) – Politics and government
I. Title
321.8'0938'5   JC75.D36

Library of Congress cataloguing in publication data

Sinclair, R. K.
Democracy and participation in Athens.
Bibliography: p.
Includes index.
1. Athens (Greece) – Politics and government.
2. Political participation – Greece – Athens. I. Title.
JC79.A8S56   1988   320.938'5   87–13174.

ISBN 0 521 33357 1

103352

VN

To Pat

Contents

Contents

ACKNOWLEDGEMENTS

The author and publishers wish to thank Penguin Books Ltd for permission to reproduce extracts from *The Politics* by Aristotle, translated by T. A. Sinclair, revised by Trevor J. Saunders (Penguin Classics, 1962, 1981), copyright © the Estate of T. A. Sinclair, 1962, revisions copyright © Trevor J. Saunders, 1981; from *The Athenian Constitution* by Aristotle, translated by P. J. Rhodes (Penguin Classics, 1984), copyright © P. J. Rhodes, 1984; and from *The Histories* by Herodotus, translated by Aubrey de Sélincourt, revised by A. R. Burn (Penguin Classics, 1954, 1972), copyright © the Estate of Aubrey de Sélincourt, revisions copyright © A. R. Burn, 1972; and the Trustees of the Loeb Classical Library and Harvard University Press for permission to reproduce extracts from Aristotle's *Politics*, translated by H. Rackham, 1932; from Demosthenes, Vol. I translated by J. H. Vince, 1930, Vol. II translated by C. A. and J. H. Vince, 1926, revised 1939, Vol. III, translated by J. H. Vince, 1935; from Isocrates, Vol. II, translated G. Norlin, 1929; from Lysias, translated W. R. M. Lamb, 1930; from *Minor Attic Orators*, Vol. II, translated by J. O. Burtt, 1954; from Plato, Vol. II, translated W. R. M. Lamb, 1924; and from Thucydides, translated by C. Forster-Smith, Vol. I, 1919, revised 1928, and Vol. III, 1921, revised 1931.

Preface

In the period from the middle of the fifth century to 322 B.C. the affairs of Athens were determined by a system of direct democracy involving thousands of citizens in the assembly, the courts and other institutions. The idea of participation or sharing is central to Greek thought and writing about citizenship and political life. Aristotle identified the distinguishing feature of a citizen as the possession of the right to participate in the exercise of power – in the courts, in the assembly, and in the offices of state. That definition of a citizen, he argued, applied especially to citizenship in a democracy.

The centrality of participation in the concept of citizenship is reflected in the lofty rhetoric of Perikles (as reported by Thucydides):

We find it possible for the same people to attend to private affairs and public affairs as well, and notwithstanding our varied occupations to be adequately informed about public affairs. For we are unique in regarding the man who does not participate in these affairs at all not as a man who minds his own business, but as useless. We ourselves decide matters or submit them to proper consideration, taking the view that debate is not harmful to action, but rather that it is harmful not to be informed, through discussion, before we proceed to take the necessary action.

Yet even Perikles' words imply that some Athenians were 'useless'. Three generations later, Demosthenes painted a very different picture from Perikles' vision. In a law suit in 355 he maintained that the outgoing Council of 500 had allowed itself to be dominated by 'a gang of orators'. He stressed the need for 'the majority not to leave matters in the hands of the talkers, but to offer the best advice themselves'.

The central interest of this book is the participation of citizens in the life of Athens in the period from the middle of the fifth century to 322 B.C. Both the possibilities and the realities – the manner and extent of participation, the cost and the consequences – are examined. Greek concepts and terms have been employed where appropriate, and the reader seeking clarification of an unfamiliar term may consult the index where an asterisk indicates where an explanation of the term may be found.

For Greek terms I have usually adopted direct transliteration from Greek (for example, *dēmokratia*), though occasionally I have used a form that has become firmly established in English (for example, chorus). Greek names, both personal and geographical, have long presented an intractable problem, for the goals of close transliteration, consistency, and the use of familiar forms cannot all be accommodated. The transliterated form of Greek names has been used as far as seemed consistent with reasonable ease of recognition. I have mostly preferred 'k' to 'c' (as in Perikles), 'kh' to 'ch' (as in Khalkidike), 'os' to 'us' (as in Dionysos), 'on' to 'um' (as in Sounion), 'ai' and 'oi' to 'ae' and 'i' (as in Aigospotamoi), 'ei' to 'i' (as in Peiraieus) and 'ou' to 'u' (as in Euboulos). In a few cases, usually place names, I have used the familiar anglicised form: for example, Athens, Corinth, Thebes. The spelling of the names of ancient writers presents special difficulties. Herodotos and Andokides are readily recognised as the historian and the orator. But I have retained forms which are firmly established in English and involve a loss or modification of the original ending (in particular, Aristotle and Plato) and on grounds of familiarity I have retained Thucydides and Aeschylus (despite the inconsistency with Aiskhines).

It is a pleasure to acknowledge my indebtedness to many people. First, to the numerous scholars who have contributed to the understanding of Athenian democracy. The bibliography testifies to this, and the lively interest which has been evident in the last three decades is reflected in discussions that have appeared since the completion of this manuscript. The book has benefited from comments and suggestions by Dr P. A. Cartledge, Sir Kenneth Dover, Professors Chr. Habicht, N. G. L. Hammond, M. H. Hansen, D. M. Lewis and R. S. Stroud, and particularly the late Mr G. T. Griffith. Professor W. Ritchie has read the proofs. I would also record my debt to the skill and interest of the staff of the Cambridge University Press.

I would express, too, my appreciation of the support of the University of Sydney, which granted me two periods of study leave to facilitate the writing of this book, and of the hospitality of the President and Fellows of Clare Hall in Cambridge.

My wife Pat has, with our daughters, given assistance and support at every stage: it is to her that this book is dedicated.

University of Sydney　　　　　　　　　　　　　　　　　　　　R.obert Sinclair
June 1987

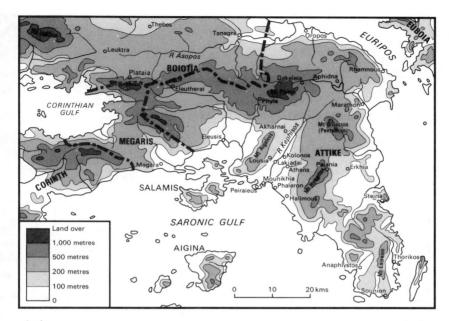

Attike

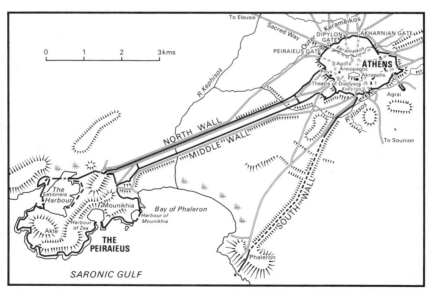

Athens and the Peiraieus

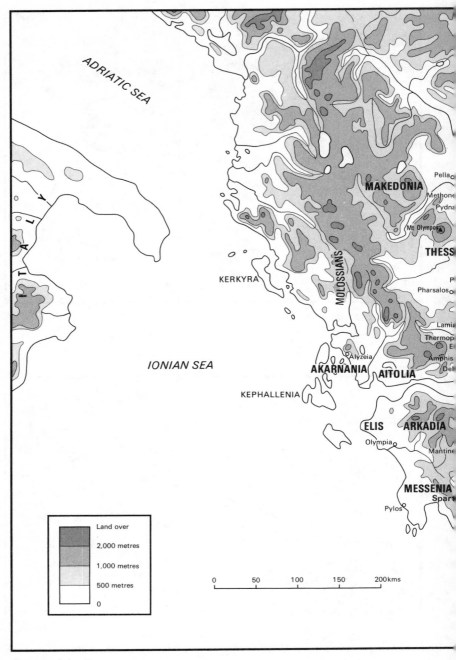

Greece and the Aegean

xiv

BLACK SEA

R Nestos

THRACE

ODRYSIANS

THRACIAN KHERSONESOS

PROPONTIS

Byzantion

Selymbria

Perinthos

R Strymon

Neapolis

Abdera

Maroneia

Amphipolis

THASOS

Krithote

Parion

Aigospotamoi

HALKIDIKE

Olynthos

Sestos

HELLESPONT

ASIA

Abydos

MINOR

daia

Torone

LEMNOS

Troy

TENEDOS

Methymna

Antissa

ATHOS

LESBOS

Mytilene

ARGINOUSAI
IS

Hestiaia
(Oreos)

SKYROS

aironeia

Khalkis

EUBOIA

AEGEAN SEA

KHIOS

Erythrai

Klazomenai

Eretria

BOIOTIA

IONIA

uktra

Thebes

Ephesos

Plataia

Magnesia

Eleusis

R Maiandros

Megara

Athens

Karystos

ANDROS

SAMOS

rinth

Peiraieus

Mt Mykale

ATTIKE

KEOS

AIGINA

Miletos

Iasos

os

Troizen

DELOS

PAROS

Halikarnassos

NAXOS

SIPHNOS

AMORGOS

ONIA

Knidos

RHODES

KARPATHOS

CRETE

The Athenian polis and the evolution of democracy

1.1 Athenian views of developments to *c.* 500 B.C.

At some time about the 460s an Athenian boy was given the name Demokrates, which would seem to signify approval of the *kratos* (rule or power) of the *dēmos* (the people). This is the earliest known occurrence of the name. The choice might appear somewhat surprising, for the father Lysis belonged to a propertied family wealthy enough to engage in horse-breeding and chariot-racing. Whatever the precise significance of Lysis' choice, the name at least suggests that the political role of the Demos in Athens was a matter of interest or perhaps of much debate at the time. To some the notion of the rule of the Demos was anathema. But the playwright Aeschylus probably reflected more accurately the attitudes of most Athenians in his play *The Suppliants* (produced *c.* 463). In anachronistic fashion not unknown in Attic tragedy he depicted – with evident approval – the need and the propriety for the king of ancient Argos to consult the people in assembly and win their support before giving refuge to the fugitive daughters of Danaos. Certainly by the mid-fifth century the power of the Demos was recognised in the public life of the Athenian state.[1]

Athenians of the later fifth century and the fourth century had differing views about the beginnings of democracy. Some even traced the origins back to their legendary king Theseus, but for most, Solon, the lawgiver of the late 590s, was a key figure. During the political dissension of the last years of the fifth century 'Solon's laws' were invoked by both oligarchs and democrats to give venerability and authority to their views.[2] Solon's primary aim seems to have been to restore stability to his native city when it was threatened by bitter civil strife and to prevent the seizure of power by a single individual. Some of his reforms guaranteed certain fundamental individual rights. In particular, they protected the personal liberty of Athenians against enslavement through debt

---

[1] Pl. *Lys.* 205c, *APF* 359–60, cf. Sealey 54–5 and Sealey (1974) 290–1; Aesch. *Suppl.* 397–401, 517–23, 600–24, 698–700, cf. Sealey (1974) 263–72, see ch. 1.4; see also the choice of the name Philodemos ('friendly to the Demos' or possibly 'befriended by the Demos') for an Athenian born by 480 (ML 33.35, Connor 101 n. 20).

[2] Isok. 10.34–7, 12.129, [Dem.] 59.75, 60.28 (cf. Paus. 1.3.3), Plut. *Thes.* 24; Webster (1969) 98–104, Boardman (1975) 228–9; Lys. 30.2, 26, Isok. 7.16–17, Dem. 18.6–7, 22.30–2; Arist. *Pol.* 1273b35–74a21, *AP* 35.2, 41.2; Fuks (1971) 14–25, 35–40, 95–6, 107–13, Ruschenbusch (1958) 398–424, Finley (1975) 39–40, 50–2.

default, they permitted anyone to seek redress on behalf of a person who had been wronged, and they provided for the right of appeal to the people against the decisions of arkhons or officials.[3] Solon also unlocked the door to leadership in Athens by breaking the aristocratic monopoly of office-holding. He divided the citizen body into four classes: *pentakosiomedimnoi* (those who produced at least 500 *medimnoi* or 'bushels' of grain a year), *hippeis* (knights or cavalrymen – 300 and more), *zeugitai* (hoplites, or perhaps 'teamsters' – 200 and more) and *thētes* (labourers – under 200). Using the census classes to determine eligibility for office, Solon provided for the various offices of the polis to be open to the highest class (in the case of the Treasurers of Athena), probably the top two classes (in the case of the arkhons), or the top three classes (the routine offices). The opening of the door was to be a slow process.[4] And the overall tenor of Solon's reforms is epitomised in some of the verses which he wrote to promote or to justify his views and his laws:

> I gave to the people as much privilege as is sufficient for them,
> Not detracting from their honour or reaching out to take it;
> And to those who had power and were admired for their wealth
> I declared that they should suffer nothing unseemly.
> I stood holding my mighty shield against both,
> And did not allow either to win an unjust victory.

And, as Solon also wrote:

> This is how the people will best follow their leaders:
> If they are neither unleashed nor restrained too much.
> For excess breeds insolence, when great prosperity comes
> To men who are not sound of mind.[5]

Another symbol of the spirit of the Athenian people was the tyrannicides. Around the figures of Harmodios and Aristogeiton there grew up or there was promoted the legend of champions of freedom who had rid the Athenian people of tyranny by slaying Hipparkhos in 514. The tyrant-slayers were the first men to have statues set up in their honour in the Agora or civic centre of Athens, and after the originals were removed by Xerxes in 480 new statues were dedicated. They had a striking impact, for not only were they placed in the centre of the Agora but they stood in splendid isolation.[6] The tyrannicides were commemorated, too, in drinking songs which proclaimed: 'they gave back to Athens fair laws to obey' and 'they made Athens a city of equal rights

---

[3] *AP* 9.

[4] *AP* 7.3–4, 8.1, 26.2, 47.1 (and *CAAP*), Plut. *Solon* 18; Hignett 101–2. On the primacy of military considerations or economic/occupational criteria, see Andrewes (1956) 87–9 and *CAAP* 138, 143.

[5] *AP* 12.1–2 (Penguin tr. adapted), Plut. *Solon* 18; Arist. *Pol.* 1273b35–74a21.

[6] Arist. *Rhet.* 1368a17–18, Arr. 3.16.7; Thompson and Wycherley 155–9, Taylor (1981) 10–50; Dem. 19.280, *AP* 58.1; free meals (*sitēsis*) in the prytaneion enjoyed by the descendants of the tyrannicides (*IG* i³.131.5–6, Dein. 1.101).

(*isonomos*)'.[7] The divergence between the myth and reality was recognised by Herodotos who noted that the murder of Hipparkhos made the rule of Hippias even harsher; more than that, he contended that it was rather the Alkmeonidai who freed Athens. Thucydides went out of his way to expose the myth, for he selected it to show how the Athenians like most people accepted traditions quite uncritically. Thucydides maintained that the origin of the slaying of the tyrant was a personal grudge, that the reigning tyrant was not Hipparkhos but his elder brother Hippias, that it was Hippias who was to be removed, but that in panic Harmodios and Aristogeiton killed Hipparkhos when they suspected that their plans had been revealed to Hippias.[8] Nevertheless, the tyrannicides remained the heroes of the Athenian democracy in the fifth and fourth centuries.

The Peisistratid tyranny, in fact, came to an end when the Spartans, accompanied by the Alkmeonidai and other Athenian exiles, expelled the tyrant Hippias in 510. Peisistratos and his sons, intent as they were on retaining their own position of power, had largely suppressed the rivalries between local aristocrats or 'local dynasts', and their rule from 546 to 510 had marked a period of stability and the encouragement of a sense of unity in Attike. The encouragement of city festivals in honour of Athena, the patron deity of Athens, and Dionysos provided not simply an alternative to local ties and loyalties but a potential focus on festivals held in the city and open to all Athenians. The Panathenaia and the City Dionysia were to prove powerful symbols of Athens and its people in the fifth century.[9]

However, in the early years after the expulsion of Hippias the Athenian polis was riven by the re-emergence of intense factional struggles between aristocratic families. Their strength lay in their ability to dominate the traditional four Ionic tribes which were the basis of the social, religious and political organisation of Attike. In the faction fighting the Alkmeonid Kleisthenes found himself being worsted. In an attempt to win the support of ordinary Athenians who did not belong to the traditional leading families, he took cognisance of the fears of many that their claim to be Athenians would be set aside,[10] for bitter disputes had arisen about who were entitled to be regarded as Athenians. These matters had been in the hands of the aristocratic families who controlled membership of the phratries (or brotherhoods) and thus admission to the tribes. Kleisthenes opposed rigid investigation of family backgrounds and favoured the recognition of those whose claim to being Athenians was in doubt, and in particular his reforms transferred control over these questions from the old aristocratic families to the demes or local communities in which all free Athenians were now to register. In this way Kleisthenes 'mixed up' the people, and locality replaced kinship or supposed

[7] Ath. 15.695a–b, Ostwald 121–36, Taylor (1981) 51–77.
[8] Hdt. 5.55, 62–5, 6.123, Thuc. 1.20.1–2, 6.53–9; *AP* 18.
[9] Andrewes (1956) 107–15, Parke 34–45, 125–35.   [10] Hdt. 5.66, 69, *AP* 20 (and *CAAP*).

kinship as the basis for political organisation.[11] Membership of the deme in which a man was living at the time became the vehicle for enrolment in the ten new tribes instituted by Kleisthenes: all Athenians enjoyed an equal status as citizens. Each of the tribes drew members from three regions: the City, the Coast and the Inland. No one local group could by itself dominate the affairs of a tribe. Moreover there were meetings and corporate activities not only at the tribal level, but also at the intermediate level of the 30 trittyes (or thirds) which formed the link between the demes and the ten tribes, and, most importantly, at the level of the demes. The adoption of the deme structure helped resolve the problems of disputes about Athenian status, while the trittys structure attempted to deal with the problem of local vested interests.[12] The prospect of extending political participation at various levels to ordinary Athenians who, as Herodotos put it, had earlier been pushed aside or spurned may well have been an important factor in winning support for Kleisthenes, whether (as is probable) he rallied support by adopting *isonomia* (equality of rights) as a slogan or not. The deme meetings in particular must have provided Athenians with the opportunity of interest and participation in matters with which they were more closely concerned, and thus, over time, have encouraged demesmen to challenge aristocratic dominance of local affairs, especially in the village communities of rural Attike.[13]

Kleisthenes' reforms, while dealing with the fundamental problem of the composition of the Athenian body politic, thus had some potentiality for circumscribing the political power of aristocratic leaders and limiting the effects of dynastic feuds. More important, by breaking up old ties and establishing new units for political and military organisation, Kleisthenes' arrangement succeeded in producing a greater cohesiveness among the Athenians. The disruptive or atomistic did prove unifying. For the ten new tribes, each drawing together citizens from different parts of Attike, were used as the basis for a new Boule (or Council of 500) and also for military organisation, with each tribal regiment of hoplites commanded by a *stratēgos* (general).[14] Kleisthenes' 'political' motive, however, was to strengthen his own faction and he expected that the Demos or Athenians at large would show gratitude and loyalty to his faction. Yet what was intended as a manoeuvre in aristocratic politics was to turn out quite differently as ordinary Athenians became conscious of their own political potential.[15]

---

[11] *AP* 13.5, 21.1–4 (and *CAAP*), Arist. *Pol.* 1275b34–9, 1319b19–27, Hignett 132–4.

[12] *AP* 21.4; Eliot (1962) 136–58, D. M. Lewis (1963A) 22–40, W. E. Thompson (1966) 1–10, Traill, Andrewes (1977) 241–8, Traill (1982) 162–71, Siewert (1982) 1–138, Whitehead 5–38.

[13] Hdt. 5.69.2; Ostwald 142–60; Headlam 165–8, Hopper (1957) 14–18; see ch. 3.1.

[14] *AP* 21.3–4 (and *CAAP*), Hignett 132–58, Rhodes 208–10; Bradeen (1955) 22–30, Siewert (1982) especially 139–53, D. M. Lewis (1983) 431–6; see Kearns (1985) 189–207; on ostracism see *AP* 22 and ch. 7.2.

[15] Woodhead (1967) 135–40; on Kleisthenes as the founder of Athenian democracy, see Hdt. 6.131, Isok. 15.232, 16.26–7, *AP* 29.3 (cf. Plut. *Kim.* 15), Larsen (1948) 12–15; see also Martin (1974) 5–22.

1.2 The growing power of Athens *c.* 500–*c.* 450

The possibilities for Athenians in general to assert some influence began to materialise in the course of the next two generations. In that period the Athenians passed from being rather subservient to Sparta to leadership of an alliance which enabled the city of Athena to win naval supremacy in the Aegean and to act independently and decisively. The Athenian hoplites who routed the Persian invaders on the field of Marathon in 490 created one of the great 'myths' of Athens. These 'Marathon-fighters', numbering probably some 9,000 men and assisted only by the full force of the Plataians (perhaps 600), demonstrated the ability, not of full-time soldiers such as the Spartans but of militia troops, to defeat the might of the Persian king who since 546 had loomed as a threat on the eastern shores of the Aegean. A generation later the Marathon victory was selected as the subject for one of the great paintings in what came to be known as the Stoa Poikile (Painted Portico). This stoa was erected, probably *c.* 460, in the Agora, where, as Aiskhines put it, 'the memorials of all our noble deeds are depicted'. The stoa was one of the main focal points of Athenian life, and here in this 'hall of victories' Marathon joined two of the most popular myths of the Athenians – the victory of Theseus and the Athenians over the invading Amazons and the sack of Troy, the subjects of two of the other paintings in the stoa.[16] The primacy of Marathon in time, a victory won virtually unaided, and the prestige of the hoplite assured the Marathon-fighters an aura at least equal to the renown won by the Athenians at large who in 480 chose to evacuate their country and played a crucial role in the Greek naval victory over Xerxes' fleet at Salamis. The magnitude of the defeat inflicted by the free men of Athens, slaves or subjects of no man, on the arrogant Persian king and his vast armada was captured in the tragedy by Aeschylus, *The Persians*, which was produced at the City Dionysia in 472.[17] In the victory at Salamis even those Athenians who could not afford to arm themselves as hoplites or heavily armed infantry had taken part as rowers in the fleet. After the Delian League was formed in 478 under Athenian leadership, it was these poorer Athenians who along with the hoplites formed the major part of the League forces which in the course of the next decade drove the Persians out of the Aegean and inflicted a crushing defeat on another Persian expedition at the Eurymedon. These remarkable military successes engendered in the Athenians in general a high confidence in their polis and in themselves, and also a recognition of the contribution of all Athenians to the security and safety of their polis. It was probably in the mid-460s that the Athenian polis assumed the responsibility for bringing the war dead back to

[16] Aiskhin. 3.181–90 (the roll call of great Athenians), Paus. 1.15.1–16.1; [Lys.] 2.20–6, Isok. 4.85–7, Pl. *Menex.* 240d–e, Lykourg. *Leok.* 104; Robertson (1975) 1.242–5, Thompson and Wycherley 90–3; Meiggs 471–2; see also *AP* 22.3. On Theseus see Tyrrell (1984) 2–22.
[17] Paus. 1.14.5; Loraux (1981), 157–74, 406–11; Aesch. *Pers.* 230–4, 241–2, 807–8, Pritchett 3.172–83. Athenian aristocrats like Andokides (3.38) preferred to date Athenian supremacy from Marathon and even to ignore Salamis (1.107–8).

Athens for burial. A practice which applied only to the leaders (for example, the Spartan kings) was being extended by the Athenian polis to all Athenians.[18]

The growing power of Athens and the confidence of the Athenians were clearly reflected in the 460s and 450s in the changing relations with other Greek states. In 465, for example, conflict between Athenian interests and those of Thasians in the north Aegean erupted in an attempt by Thasos to withdraw from the Delian League. The Thasians were besieged and were finally forced to surrender in 463. The Athenians not only enforced terms which deprived the Thasians of the capacity to contemplate secession but also took over from them their mining and trading interests in Thrace.[19]

More significant was the rupture in relations between Athens and Sparta in 462. Sparta had long been regarded as the most powerful Greek state. Indeed, it was to the intervention of the Spartans that the Athenians had owed their liberation from the tyrant Hippias in 510 (and perhaps this was no slight factor in encouraging fifth-century Athenians to attribute the liberation to Harmodios and Aristogeiton). In the following decades, though Spartan attempts to restore Isagoras failed, the Athenians had generally to acquiesce in the superior power of Sparta, and it was to the Spartans that the Athenians turned in times of crisis such as the pro-Persian stance of the Aiginetans in the late 490s or the Persian invasion of 490.[20] In 481, when faced with the invading forces of Xerxes, the Athenians acknowledged, as did other Greeks, the power of the Spartans by accepting their leadership in both land and naval operations. At the battle of Salamis in 480, it is true, the Athenians provided 200 of the 378 ships in the combined Greek fleet, with Corinthian ships numbering 40, Aiginetan 30 and Spartan 16. Herodotos depicted the Athenians as forgoing their claim to command the fleet in the interest of Greek unity: for a variety of reasons, Athenian leadership even at sea had hardly been a serious possibility.[21] After the Greek victories at Salamis, Plataia and Mykale, the Athenians accepted, and no doubt quietly encouraged, the invitation by other Greek states to lead an ongoing campaign against Persia. Whether the Spartans were quite as happy with that development as Thucydides represents may be doubted, not least because of their opposition to the rebuilding of the fortifications of Athens.[22] The Athenians, however, established their independence by pushing through the refortification. During the next decade or more they were willing to follow Kimon's doctrine of sharing the leadership of the Greek world with their 'yoke-fellow' Sparta while pursuing operations against the Persians. It was by an appeal to this doctrine that Kimon persuaded the Athenian assembly in 462 to send a hoplite force to help the Spartans put down a helot revolt.[23] The Spartan

---

[18] Paus. 1.29.4; Jacoby (1944) 47–55, cf. *HCT* 2.94–101, Clairmont (1983) 9–15; see R. Osborne (1985) 61; see *AP* 22.3, 27.1.
[19] Thuc. 1.100–1.   [20] Hdt. 5.49, 64–5, 72–6; 6.49–50, 105–6.
[21] Hdt. 8.1–3, 14, 42–8, Plut. *Them.* 7.2–3; cf. Amit (1965) 18–20.
[22] Thuc. 1.90, 95 and D.S. 11.50 for Spartan attitudes to the leadership question; de Ste Croix (1972) 170–1.   [23] See ch. 2.3.1.

dismissal of this force was the result of, but also increased, growing suspicion of Athens and Athenian policies. In Athens Kimon's doctrine was discredited.

The confidence of the Athenians was further encouraged by the conclusion of two alliances in 461/0 – an alliance with Megara which thus protected Attike from direct land invasion from the Peloponnese and an alliance with Argos, the old rival of Sparta in the Peloponnese. Athens became actively involved in the north-east Peloponnese (459), conquered its old rival in the Saronic Gulf, the island state of Aigina (458), and gained control of its northern neighbours, the cities of Boiotia (457). In 454, however, it suffered a serious setback with the defeat of an allied expedition which had been sent in 459 to help the Egyptian rebel Inaros in his attempt to throw off Persian rule.[24] In the late 450s and the early 440s Athens had to deal with disturbed conditions in, and problems in its relations with, its allies in the Aegean. These difficulties were precipitated by the 454 disaster, or by Persian interference in some of the cities or by internal dissension, or again by strained relations arising from allied perceptions of their ties with Athens and Athenian attitudes towards Persia.[25] One important element was the allied expedition against the Persians in Cyprus and Egypt (451). This seems to have had a catalytic effect: its success, coupled with the death of Kimon, the chief advocate of active operations against the Persians, may well have led Athenians to pay even greater attention to their relations with their allies. More so, because to the allies the need for a continuing alliance against Persia had been called into question by the success of Kimon's expedition. An indication of their restiveness has been seen in the payment of the annual *phoros* (tribute) by the allies. There is no evidence of the payment of phoros in 449/8, while in 448/7 some allies did not pay and some paid only part of their assessment. The payments seem to have been restored to a high level in 447/6 as the Athenians took various strong measures in their dealings with their 'allies'.[26] This restiveness is the more readily understood if the Athenians concluded in 450/449 a peace agreement with Persia recognising distinct spheres of influence, but even if no formal peace was concluded the Athenians, it would appear, did not again take up operations against the Persians.[27]

The Athenians may have overstretched themselves but their power was not to be underestimated, especially if they opted to concentrate their energies in Greece and the Aegean. Moreover, in 454 the Delian League funds had been transferred from the temple of Apollo on Delos to the temple of Athena in Athens. In the early 440s there was sharp controversy about the use of what represented a very large financial reserve – probably some 9,700 talents in 447.[28] The mere existence of this very large resource in Athens made the Athenian

---

[24] Thuc. 1.103–10, Meiggs 92–108.

[25] *IG* I³.14 (ML 40), 21; Plut. *Per.* 11.5, D.S. 11.88.3, Paus. 1.27.5; *IG* I³. 37 (ML 47); Meiggs 109–28, 152–74.

[26] Thuc. 1.112 (and *HCT*), Meiggs 124–8; ML 39, 50; Meiggs 152–74.

[27] Isok. 4.118, D.S. 12.4.5, Theopomp. *FGrH* 115 F134–5; Plut. *Per.* 17 (Congress Decree); Meiggs 129–56, 487–95, 512–15. [28] Thuc. 2.13.3 (and *HCT* 20–33); see ch. 2.3.1.

assembly less dependent on the allies but also less amenable to check by the Athenian upper classes, for the assembly could now be less concerned with the financial resources of the upper classes whether in the form of benefactions to the Demos or in support of warlike activities. The Demos might feel less dependent on the propertied classes. The vast reserve was drawn upon in a major way, in the first instance, to build the Parthenon which was begun in 447, but it was also available for the maintenance of Athenian power.[29]

In a matter of a few decades Athens' position had indeed been transformed. A vital element in that transformation was the development of naval power. The credit for that should be largely accorded to the Athenian leader whose farsightedness, judgement and ability to expound a case were much admired by the historian Thucydides. In the late 480s Themistokles had persuaded the Athenians to use the proceeds of rich silver finds in south-east Attike to build probably 100 triremes (warships), more modern and faster than pentekonters (50-oared galleys), thereby more than doubling the size of the Athenian fleet.[30] In 480 the Athenians had evacuated Attike before Xerxes' invading forces in accordance with an oracle which urged them to seek safety in their 'wooden wall'. That decision to accept the interpretation of Themistokles and other Athenians against the views of the 'professional' interpreters and to put their trust in their triremes was symbolic. In the next two decades the fleet and the mobility of power which it provided enabled Athens to spread its influence throughout the Aegean.[31] Vital for the fleet, it should be added, were the harbours of the Peiraieus. In the sixth century the open bay of Phaleron had been the maritime centre for Athens, but during his arkhonship in 493/2 Themistokles had initiated the fortification of the Peiraieus and in the early 470s had persuaded the Athenians to complete the walls of the Peiraieus. He recognised the potentialities of its three natural harbours and he took the view that the Athenians would gain a great advantage in the acquisition of power if they became a seafaring people. He was the first, according to Thucydides, to tell the Athenians to 'cling to' the sea. By making the Peiraieus easily defensible, Themistokles was able to give top priority to the fleet. In Thucydides' view, he played a key role in laying the foundations of their fifth-century empire. To Themistokles the Peiraieus was a more valuable place than the city of Athens: if ever the Athenians were hard pressed by land, he argued, they should go down to the Peiraieus and withstand all their enemies with their fleet.[32]

Attike indeed might still be vulnerable to invasion – to the invasion of Peloponnesian hoplites, for example, led by Sparta as had happened in 506 or as

---

[29] Davies (1978) 111; see ch. 8.2; Thuc. 2.13.3, Meiggs 154–5.

[30] Thuc. 1.14.3, 138.3; *AP* 22.7 (and *CAAP*), Plut. *Them.* 4, cf. Hdt. 7.144; Hdt. 6.89, 132.1.

[31] Hdt. 7.141–4; Thuc. 1.18–19, 96–101, [Xen.] *AP* 2.2–16; on Athenian naval power see Amit (1965) 18–26, Morrison and Williams (1968) 223–43.

[32] Thuc. 1.93.3–7 (and *HCT*), D.S. 11.41.2–4, Paus. 1.1.2–5; D. M. Lewis (1973A) 757–8, Dickie (1973) 758–9; cf. *AP* 24.1–2 (and *CAAP*).

had been promised in the mid-460s when the Thasians sought help in their revolt from Athens. However, the unexpected alliance in 461/0 with their western neighbours, the Megarians, held out the strong possibility that the Athenians could prevent direct Peloponnesian invasion, though the defeat of their army at Tanagra near the Attic–Boiotian border at the hands of the Peloponnesians in 457 was to serve as a reminder of the limitations of Athenian land power and the vulnerability of Attike.[33] And by 457, the Athenians were carrying through a plan to secure the city of Athens against one of the standard methods of fifth-century warfare – the siege of a city and the cutting off of its food supplies in order to force surrender. The plan was the 'Long Walls' which joined the Akropolis and the city area to the Peiraieus and their naval power. These walls linking the fortified city to the port of the Peiraieus and the Bay of Phaleron enabled the Athenians, even in the event of enemy invasion, to supply the city with food and other necessities brought in by sea.[34] The navy was the critical factor. Not only for this reason was it regarded as the symbol of Athenian power and Athenian democracy.[35]

1.3 Socio-economic changes *c.* 480–*c.* 450

Parallel to the transformation of Athens' standing in the Aegean world, and in many respects closely connected with it, were changes in the social and economic life of the Athenians in the first half of the fifth century – changes which probably accelerated in the 440s and 430s as resources were diverted from anti-Persian operations to public building in Athens and Attike. In the generation after Xerxes' invasion, for example, the population of Attike seems to have begun to increase considerably. Precise figures are not available, but between 480 and 431 the total population of Attike may well have doubled. There is general agreement that the largest increases were in the numbers of metics (foreigners permanently resident in Attike) (to perhaps 30,000–40,000 in 431 as a plausible 'guesstimate') and in the numbers of slaves (to perhaps 100,000 as a plausible guess). Athens offered opportunities which other Greeks had recognised since the early sixth century, and by the mid-fifth century they were beginning to flock to Athens. Moreover, prisoners captured in Delian League operations and a trade in slaves for sale on the lucrative Athenian market led to, and reflected, a much more extensive use of slave labour. Athenians – that is, men, women and children of citizen stock – may have numbered about 120,000 in 480 and 160,000–170,000 in 431. The number of adult male Athenians in 480 was perhaps approaching 30,000 and by 431 it probably was in the low 40,000s. These figures are modern estimates based on very limited evidence, but the

---

[33] Thuc. 1.107–8, de Ste Croix (1972) 187–96.
[34] Thuc. 1.107.1, 108.3, Plut. *Per.* 13.5. [35] [Xen.] *AP* 1.2, Arist. *Pol.* 1304a17–24.

broad trends may be accepted even though it is impossible to determine the rates of growth of the various elements in the population over the half-century from 480.[36]

Population movements were not, however, in one direction only. As early as the mid-470s Athenian settlers were sent to Skyros to replace the inhabitants who had engaged in piracy. In the mid-460s Athenian settlers sought to establish themselves on the river Strymon at the site of the later Amphipolis (founded in 437 by colonists from Athens and allied states). In the late 450s–440s many Athenians, while retaining their Athenian citizenship, went abroad as klerouchs or, so to speak, soldier-settlers in order to secure the loyalty of the area and its adherence to Athens. Some went to the Thracian Khersonesos at the southern entrance to the Propontis and the Black Sea. This was not a new area of Athenian interest, for in the mid-sixth century Athenians such as the Philaids, on their own initiative or with strong encouragement from Peisistratos, had left Athens and settled in this area (now known as the Gallipoli peninsula). Other klerouchs in the mid-fifth century went to the islands of Andros and Naxos and, on Euboia, probably to Karystos, Khalkis and Eretria as well as to Hestiaia where in 446 the population was removed and an Athenian settlement known as Oreos was established.[37] In the process not a few Athenians would have risen in status from the thetic to the zeugite class, for each klerouch (allotment-holder) received an allotment of land (*klēros*). But as well as the state-organised klerouchies, Athenian enterprise operated at the individual level. The Athenian merchants who in the 460s were active in the Thraceward area and were encroaching on Thasian interests were the successors in a sense of men like Peisistratos who in the mid-sixth century had exploited the mineral resources of that area. The long tradition of Athenian enterprise overseas may also be exemplified by the production of fine pottery beyond the needs of the local market and its export to widely scattered areas from the Black Sea to Italy and Sicily.

Other non-agrarian activity assisted in the Athenian recovery after the devastation caused by the Persian invaders. At Laureion in south-eastern Attike new rich veins of silver had been discovered in *c.* 483: these finds had been devoted, as we have seen, to the expansion of the navy. In the ensuing decades the mines were extensively exploited, providing a basic means of acquiring imports and being used particularly in the production of the Attic 'owls' – the coins which depicted the national types of Athena and her owl and which won wide acceptance, later with enforced measures by the Athenian polis, throughout the Aegean and beyond.[38] Furthermore, many Athenians were

---

[36] See Appendix 1A–C. On the proportion of thetes in the citizen population, see Gomme 12–16, 26, Jones 9, 177, Patterson (1981) 55–8.
[37] Thuc. 1.98.2, Plut. *Kim.* 8.3–6; Thuc. 1.100.3; Plut. *Per.* 11.5, D.S. 11.88.3, Paus. 1.27.5, Meiggs 121–3; Thuc. 1.114.3; see Green and Sinclair (1970) 515–27, but cf. Jones 161–80; Brunt (1966) 71–92. [38] Ar. *Frogs* 718–26, ML 45, Meiggs 167–72.

employed in Delian League expeditions, especially as the allies showed a propensity to commute their League obligations to money payments and to leave it to the Athenians to provide ships and men. As a consequence, the Athenians used the funds the allies had contributed, themselves served in the League's expeditionary forces and thus became in time the rulers of the very men who paid them, for the allies' lack of resources and their inexperience in war made revolt difficult and dangerous. At the same time, the Athenians derived most from the large amounts of booty won in operations against the Persians: the booty from the Eurymedon victory in the early 460s, for example, was used for various purposes including the building of a new south wall to the Akropolis.[39] Athens, and more particularly the Peiraieus, also attracted an increasing proportion of the trade and commerce of the Aegean (and beyond). The sheltered harbours of the Peiraieus, with improved port facilities for commercial as well as military shipping, provided the basis for these developments and also for an explosion in the population of the Peiraieus. So important did the Peiraieus become to the Athenians that in 457, as has already been noted, they completed the Long Walls which linked the fortifications of the city to those of the Peiraieus. Some indication of the vitality and the prosperity of the Peiraieus may be seen in the town-planning of Hippodamos about the middle of the fifth century.[40]

In the space of a generation, then, not only had the Athenians been highly successful as the leaders of the anti-Persian operations but they had also profited from economic changes of fundamental significance. Their military operations worked in varying degrees for Athenian interests, whether at Skyros or Thasos or the Thracian Khersonesos or elsewhere. Their naval power and their commercial interests symbolised by the Peiraieus had considerable geo-political consequences.[41] They were also potent factors within Athenian society. The benefits flowing from Athens' leadership of what in the 450s was becoming an empire or an alliance dominated by Athenian interests included tribute and booty, increased economic activity not least in shipbuilding and related industry, and internal revenues from harbour dues, mining concessions and royalties, and other sources. These internal revenues in the late 430s amounted to some 400 talents a year out of a total revenue of not less than 1,000 talents.[42]

The availability of these various revenues was an important factor in the emergence and maintenance of radical democracy. Behind both lay the expansion of Athenian naval power and the development of the Peiraieus. The Long Walls were highly symbolic. To some the Peiraieus was thereby 'kneaded

---

[39] Thuc. 1.98–9; Plut. *Kim.* 13.6, see ch. 2.3.1.

[40] Thuc. 2.38, [Xen.] *AP* 2.7; French (1964) 107–19, Amit (1965) 73–94; Arist. *Pol.* 1267b22–3.

[41] See, for example, from the latter half of the fifth century [Xen.] *AP* 2.2–7, 11–16, Ar. *Akh.* 533–4; see also Isok. 4.41–2.

[42] For the economic benefits of empire, more particularly in the 430s and 420s, see [Xen.] *AP* 1.17, Ar. *Wasps* 656–60, French (1964) 107–34, Meiggs 255–72, Finley (1978) 103–26; see Thuc. 2.13.3, Xen. *Anab.* 7.1.27; see ch. 8.2.

on to the city', but others saw the Long Walls rather as fastening the city to the Peiraieus and the land to the sea.[43] Ancient writers perceived a link between political power and those who safeguarded the military security of the state, and they associated the naval power of Athens with the increasing political power of the rowers.[44] Yet Corinth, which developed naval power in the seventh and sixth centuries, remained under oligarchic government until a short-lived takeover by Argos (392–386). One significant difference was the democratic framework established by Kleisthenes.

The inhabitants of the Peiraieus were, Aristotle noted in the latter part of the fourth century, more democratic than those of the city, and it might be suggested that the rapid development of the Peiraieus was a critical factor in the growth of democratic attitudes inasmuch as this new concentration of people produced a feeling of the need for, *and* the possibility of, asserting their political potential.[45] For the Peiraieus was, after all, only some 7 km from Athens. If distance alone were a consideration, inhabitants of the Peiraieus would, moreover, have found it easier to take part in political activities in the city of Athens than, say, the farmers or the charcoal burners from the most populous of the demes, Akharnai, which was over 10 km north of the Agora, or the inhabitants of Eleusis who lived some 20 km west-north-west and had to cross Mt Aigaleos. The demesmen from Marathon, living on the far side of Mt Pentelikon (or Brilessos as it was known in antiquity) with its marble quarries, would have taken six hours or more of fast walking to reach the city.[46] Thus, while Attike was in one sense compact with a total area of 2,000 square km and with the most remote part within a radius of 50 km from Athens, in practical terms much of the population was dispersed and some at considerable distances, and their capacity to participate in the life of the polis was thereby affected.

The shift towards non-agrarian activities was a significant factor in the development of Athens. The interest in these activities may to some extent have been intensified by the devastation of the Attic countryside in 480 during the Persian invasion, particularly in the case of olive growing and viticulture. Yet vines may send out shoots in the following spring and even olive trees which have been subject to 'destruction' may bear again within seven years: the extent and the consequences of the devastation should not be exaggerated.[47] Apart from trees and vines agriculture was not capital intensive and could quickly recover. In the mid-fifth century the majority of Athenian citizens still lived in the countryside. The basis of Athenian society and Athenian wealth remained agrarian. This is not to imply that Attike was self-sufficient: indeed it would appear that by the mid-fifth century, as the population increased, significant

---

[43] Ar. *Knights* 815, Plut. *Them.* 19.2–4.
[44] [Xen.] *AP* 1.2, Arist. *Pol.* 1304a21–4, Plut. *Them.* 19.4.
[45] Arist. *Pol.* 1303b10–12 and 1291b20–5.   [46] Hammond (1967) 216 n. 2.
[47] Hanson (1980) 51–71 (see also 148–55, 159–66; Plut. *Per.* 33.4, Soph. *OK* 698–702).

quantities of grain were being imported.[48] Farmers lived in numerous villages scattered throughout the countryside, some quite populous, while many of those who lived in the city went out to farm properties in the near vicinity.[49] There is little to suggest that landholdings were large. The largest known unitary holdings seem to have been about 70 acres, while it has been estimated that the plot of a zeugite was of the order of 9 to 14 acres and the average plot for those thetes who owned land was perhaps somewhat under 5 acres. Subsistence farming was probably widespread.[50]

1.4 Athenian perceptions and confidence in the 450s: dēmokratia

To the visitor to Athens, however, the city of Athens and the Peiraieus must have seemed thrusting, thriving places. One such visitor in the mid-fifth century was Herodotos, a man of perhaps 30 years of age and a refugee from his native city of Halikarnassos. A victim of exile at the hands of a tyrant, he was ready to agree with the Athenians in attaching great importance to freedom and in particular to the liberation of the Athenians from tyranny and the energising effects of freedom. The Athenian experience proved conclusively, Herodotos declared,

> how noble a thing *isēgoria* (in this context, 'freedom') is, not in one respect only, but in all; for . . . once they were rid of the tyrants, they proved the finest fighters in the world. This clearly shows that, so long as they were held down by authority, they deliberately shirked their duty in the field, as slaves shirk working for their masters; but when they had been freed, then every man amongst them longed to achieve something for himself.[51]

Welcome to Athenian ears also was the espousal by Herodotos of the view that

> Greece was saved (from submission to Xerxes) by the Athenians. It was the Athenians who held the balance: whichever side they joined was sure to prevail . . . Not even the terrifying warnings of the oracle at Delphi persuaded them to abandon Greece; they stood firm and had the courage to meet the invader.[52]

Marathon, Salamis and their experiences in the last two generations had developed in the Athenians of the mid-fifth century a certain pride, a belief that they were superior to the Persians, but also to other Greeks. One manifestation

---

[48] Garnsey (1985) 62–75; cf. de Ste Croix (1972) 45–9.
[49] R. Osborne 15–46, see Pečírka (1973) 133–7.
[50] Lys. 19.29, 42. Pl. *Alk.1* 123c, [Dem.] 42.5; Dion. Hal. on Lys. 34; de Ste Croix (1966) 109–14, Andreyev (1974) 5–25, Cooper (1978) 169–72, Davies 52–4; Kluwe (1976) 300–13.
[51] Hdt. 5.77–8 (Penguin tr. adapted): *isēgoria* (equal right of speech) was characteristic only of a democracy, and the term seems to have been used here by Herodotos to designate a wider concept, 'freedom' or 'democracy' (see Griffith (1966) 115). See ML 15, Thuc. 8.68.4; cf. Pl. *Menex.* 239a–b.   [52] Hdt. 7.139 (Penguin tr. adapted); Isok. 4.91–8.

of this was the myth of Athenian autochthony. Without any basis in fact, the Athenians cherished the belief that they were an autochthonous people, a people who had always occupied Attike and had not, like so many – or even all – other Greeks, dispossessed earlier occupants – 'autochthonous and free', as Lykourgos was to put it in 330 in his 'sermon on patriotism'. Or, in the words of a funeral oration of the early fourth century,

> in many ways it was natural to our ancestors, moved by a single resolve, to fight the battles of justice: for the very beginning of their life was just. They had not been collected, like most nations, from every quarter, and had not settled in a foreign land after driving out others, but they were born of the soil, and possessed in one and the same country their mother and their fatherland. They were the first and the only people in that time to drive out the ruling cliques in their state and to establish a democracy, believing the liberty of all to be the strongest bond of harmony.[53]

Another manifestation of Athenian pride or sense of superiority was their confidence in allowing easy access to their polis and they rightly stressed the openness of their society and their hospitable attitude towards foreigners. The growth in the metic population which has already been noted bears this out. These feelings of pride could also lead them to impose restrictions on admission to citizenship, while it may be argued that it was the exclusive and small-scale character of the polis that allowed Athens to become a direct democracy.[54]

The feeling of confidence showed itself most clearly in the Athenian willingness to innovate in the conduct of their public affairs. For pride and confidence were not confined to Athenian leaders of a limited group, but in the men of Marathon and the sailors of Salamis and their sons – that is, in the Athenian people at large – there was a growing political consciousness and sense of power. The political arrangements instituted by Kleisthenes provided some opportunities for Athenians other than the powerful and the wealthy – in the demes and the deme meetings, but also in the new Council of 500. From the deliberations of that body the fourth census class was excluded, but it must be presumed that all the hoplite members were equally free to express their views. In the course of the following decades, as increasing numbers of citizens gained experience and confidence in speaking in the Boule, they – and perhaps others – may have felt emboldened to speak in the assembly rather than leave it to officials or members of families with traditional claims to leadership. Whether established by custom or introduced as a legal right in the assembly about the

---

53 Lykourg. *Leok.* 41, [Lys.] 2.17–18 (Loeb tr. adapted); Hdt. 7.161.3; see Thuc. 1.2.5 arguing that the same people had always inhabited Attike because the poverty of its soil had caused it to be free of faction; Thuc. 2.36.1, Ar. *Wasps* 1075–80, Eur. *Ion* 29–30, 589–90, Xen. *Mem.* 3.5.12, Pl. *Menex.* 237b, Isok. 4.24–5, 8.49, 12.124–6, [Dem.] 60.4, Hyper. 6.7.

54 Thuc. 2.39.1, Soph. *OK* 258–62, Isok. 4.41; see ch. 2.1. See also the themes of Athens as an example and as benefactor, protector and teacher of Greece as developed in the latter fifth century and the fourth century: for example, Hdt. 9.27, Thuc. 2.37–41, Eur. *Suppl.* 187–92, Xen. *Hell.* 6.5.45–8, [Lys.] 2.7–16, 54–7, Isok. 4.26–40, 43–6, 52–4, 75–82, Pl. *Menex.* 237e–238a, Lykourg. *Leok.* 83–8, Hyper. 6.5.

time of Ephialtes' reforms or a little later, the equal right of speech in the assembly (*isēgoria*) belonged to all citizens in the second half of the fifth century.[55] The citizens were a small, exclusive group, and only to adult male citizens, who perhaps numbered in the mid 30,000s in *c*. 450, were accorded the political rights of the Athenian polis.

These citizens constituted in a political sense the Demos, the Athenian people. Yet there was in the word *dēmos*, like the word 'people', a certain ambiguity. In a technical sense it referred to the whole body of Athenian citizens or, in particular, to the Ekklesia or assembly, which all adult male citizens had the right to attend. Proposals accepted by the Ekklesia, for example, were designated by the formulas – 'it was resolved by the Boule and the Demos' or 'it was resolved (or voted) by the Demos' – while some Athenian decrees specifically refer to the introduction of foreign envoys 'to the Demos at the first meeting of the Ekklesia'.[56]

Yet to some Athenians, even when technically *dēmos* referred to the whole citizen body, it would have been conceived in the sense of 'the common people' or 'the masses', since the people were in the majority and *hoi polloi* ('the many' or 'the majority') might impose their wishes in a vote in the assembly. To these individuals who often referred to themselves as 'the better men' (*beltious*), 'the best men' (*beltistoi, aristoi*), 'the well-born' (*eugeneis, gennaioi*), 'the men of note' (*gnōrimoi*), or 'the good' (or 'useful') (*khrēstoi*), *dēmos*, even in a technical context, might well have a pejorative connotation. In non-technical contexts the Demos could all the more easily be referred to as 'the mob' (*okhlos*) or equated with 'the poor' (*penētes*) or with 'the worse men' (*kheirous*), 'the knaves' (or 'vulgar') (*ponēroi*), 'the mean' (or 'common or ordinary people') (*phauloi*), 'the common people' (*dēmotikoi*) in contrast to 'the wealthy' (*plousioi, euporoi*), 'the powerful' (*dynatoi*) or 'the good and true', 'gentlemen' (*kaloikagathoi*). While the dividing line could be drawn at various levels, *dēmos* could, and did, unmistakably carry the sense of the common people or the lower classes (and not infrequently with highly emotive force), and not only the sense of the whole people.[57]

In the course of the fifth and fourth centuries the word shifted in meaning and in its apprehension by particular groups within Athenian society. By the late fifth century, for example, *dēmos* may well have been used with increasing frequency in the sense of the poorer citizens. Yet those who were leaders in Athens in the sixth century and fifth century could still be referred to as *prostatai*

---

55 Griffith (1966) 115–38, Woodhead (1967) 129–40; cf. J. D. Lewis (1971) 129–40. On the question of freedom of speech in Athens, see [Xen.] *AP* 2.18, Radin (1927) 215–30 and *HCT* 1.387, and on Ephialtes' reforms see *AP* 25 (and *CAAP*) and ch. 1.5 below and n. 72.

56 See, for example, *IG* I³.40 (ML 52).1 (446/5 B.C.) and Tod 114.2, 6–7 (387 B.C.), and for the various enactment formulas and motion formulas see ch. 4 n. 52; Tod 124.8–9 (377 B.C.), 133.13–14 (368 B.C.). See ch. 3.5.

57 Hdt. 1.196.5, Thuc. 2.65.2, 6.53.2, [Xen.] *AP* 1.2, 4–9, Xen. *Mem.* 4.2.37, Arist. *Pol.* 1293b34–42, 1304b1; Neil (1909) 202–9, Connor 88–9, Dover 296–9.

tou dēmou (champions or leaders of the *dēmos*), with *dēmos* designating 'the people' in the wider sense. On the other hand, the author of the *Athenaion Politeia* or *Constitution of Athens* (in the mid-320s), drawing on the division between 'the common people' and 'the men of note', represented the political struggles of the sixth century and early fifth century in polarised terms as a conflict between the *gnōrimoi* or the *euporoi* and the *dēmos*, and characterised Solon, Kleisthenes, Xanthippos, Themistokles, Ephialtes and Perikles as *prostatai tou dēmou* and named Miltiades, Aristeides and Kimon as leaders of the *gnōrimoi*.[58]

Likewise, the term *dēmokratia* (the rule or power of the Demos) was neither unambiguous nor static. The basic notion of the Demos by its vote exercising sovereign power (*kratos*) may be discerned in Aeschylus' *Suppliants* which was produced in *c.* 463. The demands of the mythical setting and of the play could hardly allow Pelasgos, the king of Argos, to deny specifically and directly the chorus' statement that he held sole sway, but when Danaos later reported that the air bristled with right hands held aloft as, in full assembly, the Pelasgians resolved to give the Danaids refuge, the (anachronistic) reality was clear and the scene would have been immediately conjured up by Aeschylus' Athenian audience. The underlying tenor of the play is supportive of these democratic procedures and of the need and the propriety of involving all the citizens. It was probably in this decade or the next that the word *dēmokratia* was coined. Its first extant use is in Herodotos who was writing in the third quarter of the fifth century.[59] While *dēmokratia* seems to have been used mostly in a descriptive or neutral sense, its supporters seem to have felt that there were those, in particular among 'the better men', who deprecated the term and what it represented. For the supporters of demokratia are frequently reported as expounding it in public in terms of 'equality' of all citizens and especially in terms of isonomia. Perhaps, in part, they were countering, as Athenagoras specifically did at Syracuse in 415, the suggestion that demokratia meant domination by the common people. For isonomia was the principle of political equality – involving what is often called 'equality before the law' (that is, ruler and ruled are equally bound by the laws) and 'equality through the law' (that is, both ruler and ruled are afforded equal opportunity to rule, including the right to vote, to hold office, to participate in the assembly and the courts).[60] Similarly, the supporters of oligarchy advocated it in terms of the rule of 'the best men' (*aristoi*). But with the discrediting of

---

[58] Isok. 15.231–6; *AP* 28.2–3 (and *CAAP*), see Thuc. 8.89.4; Connor 108–15.

[59] Aesch. *Suppl.* 370–5, 397–401, 602–10, 698–700; Ehrenberg (1950) 517–24, cf. Sealey (1974) 263–72 (but contrast the vivid picture of the Athenian practice of voting by show of hands with the usual Spartan procedure of deciding by acclamation – see Thuc. 1.87.1–3), Kinzl (1978) 117–27, 312–26; Hdt. 4.137.2, 6.43.3, 6.131.1; Connor 199–206, Sealey (1974) 272 n. 19, Evans (1979) 145–9, cf. Fornara (1971B) 25–34 and (1981) 149–56.

[60] Hdt. 3.80.6, cf. 5.78, Thuc. 2.37.1, 3.82.8, 6.39.1, Eur. *Suppl.* 404–8, 433–41, *Phoin.* 535–48; see also Isok. 20.19–20, Dem. 21.67, 24.59, 51.11, Arist. *Pol.* 1301a25–35, 1308a11–13; Ostwald 107–20, Vlastos (1964) 1–35.

oligarchia/aristokratia by the conduct of the oligarchic regimes of 411 and 404/3 and the restoration of democracy in 403, demokratia (which oligarchs had recognised, or feigned to recognise, by 411 as acceptable) was the only practical form of government in Athens for decades to come. Thus, even the strongly conservative Isokrates, writing in the mid-fourth century, took democracy as the accepted form of government, though his conception of it was clearly Solonian, with the Demos receiving their due but no more.[61]

1.5 Characteristics of Athenian democracy *c.* 450

Dēmos and its derivatives were not the only terms used to describe the political situation in Athens. *Plēthos*, for example, seems to have been a virtual synonym for *dēmos*, indicating in many contexts 'the masses' or 'the multitude' and in some 'the citizen body' or 'the assembly'.[62] The rule or sovereignty of the people could thus be described as 'the *dēmos* ruling' or as 'the *plēthos* ruling'. In the well-known debate about the merits and defects of democracy, oligarchy and monarchy, Herodotos used both phrases. The debate, though attributed to Persian leaders, was cast within a framework of distinctively Greek ideas, and though reference is not made to any specific Greek poleis, Herodotos' analysis is of particular interest because he spent some time in Athens and knew Athens well, and because, as we have noted, he was writing in the third quarter of the fifth century. The historian declared that the rule of the multitude or people (*plēthos*) had the fairest name of all – isonomia – and singled out three features as distinguishing it from monarchical rule. These features were the selection of officials by lot, the accountability of officials, and decision-making by the popular assembly.[63]

The use of the Lot rejected the claims both of monarchy and aristocracy. It carried the implication that all citizens enjoyed an equal right to hold office and were capable of serving the polis by holding office, though it must be added that when, probably in 458/7, the Athenians extended eligibility for the nine arkhonships beyond the two highest census classes the thetes were not admitted, only the zeugitai.[64] Since 487 most Athenian officials had been selected by lot, not by vote. The major exceptions were the military officials, especially the strategoi who were in origin the commanders of the ten tribal regiments. These 'generals' were responsible for the military security of the Athenian polis and

---

[61] *AP* 29.3, Andok. 1.96, Isok. 7.20–2, 60–1, cf. 3.14–15.
[62] *AP* 2.1, 20.1, 28.2–3 (and *CAAP*); Hdt. 3.80–2, esp. 81.1–2; *IG* I³.14 (ML 40). 22–3, 27–9 (Erythrai decree of ? 453/2), Lys. 30.9, *Hell. Oxy.* 6.2, Pl. *Plt.* 291d.
[63] Hdt. 3.80.6, cf. 82.4, cf. 6.43.3; Arist. *Pol.* 1279b21–2; Ostwald 107–13, 178–9, Sealey (1974) 272–7.
[64] *AP* 26.2, but see 7.4 (indicating that the law excluding thetes from office had become a dead letter by the 320s, and perhaps much earlier); cf. 47.1. See Arist. *Pol.* 1294b7–9 and, for Sokrates' criticisms of use of the Lot, Xen. *Mem.* 1.2.9; cf. Isok. 7.23.

commanded not only land campaigns but also, more important as the Delian League developed, naval or combined operations.[65] Members of the Boule were also selected by lot. The use of the Lot meant also that an individual could make no assumptions from the fact of his appointment as an official or member of the Boule about the support that he enjoyed among his fellow-citizens.[66] The Lot was therefore an important element in limiting the opportunities for the emergence of a powerful state official or a powerful council that might challenge the sovereignty of the Demos. This was of particular importance in a society which was characterised by intense competition rather than by cooperative values. The attitudes of Athenian aristocrats fell within the prevailing Greek view of *aretē* (excellence) – that the individual should strive above all to win, to excel, whether in war, in athletic contests, or in public life. The Lot largely removed the electoral function from rivalries and animosities, though in some senses it intensified the rivalries for the Athenians stopped short of using the Lot to fill the crucial military offices. Nevertheless, among the various practices of the Athenian democracy the use of the Lot played a crucial part in limiting the advantages of social prominence and wealth and disrupting the influence of the old aristocratic families in the fifth century.[67] For it disturbed the *kharis* relationship – the continuing obligation to show tangible gratitude for benefits received – and helped to remove from the dispensers of benefits or protection one important means of gaining political return and advantage. One important avenue of 'helping one's friends' was to some extent limited.[68]

In contrast to the king who was responsible to no one, the Athenian official, whether selected by lot or by vote, had to answer to the people. In particular the 'responsibility' of officials was enshrined in the requirement that they undergo examination of their official acts and audit of any financial dealings at the end of their term of office. These processes, moreover, were carried out by officials appointed by the Demos, not by the Council of the Areiopagos which had earlier exercised some supervision of officials. This transfer seems to have been effected in 462/1 by the reforms of Ephialtes – reforms which aroused strong feelings. The Areiopagos was left with the jurisdiction of certain cases of homicide and wounding, poisoning, arson and certain religious offences, while the authority and the powers of the assembly, the popular law-courts and the Boule were enhanced. In archaic Athens the Council of the Areiopagos had

---

[65] *AP* 22.5 (and *CAAP*), 43.1 (including, in the mid-fourth century, the Commissioners of the Festival Fund); see ch. 2.3.3.

[66] On sortition as a feature of democracy, see [Xen.] *AP* 1.2–3, Xen. *Mem.* 1.2.9, Arist. *Pol.* 1294b7–9, 1300a32–b5, 1317b20–6; Dem. 39.10–11; Headlam especially 1–32, 191–2, and Hignett 228–31. In early times the method of sortition involved the drawing of beans from a container. In the later fourth century elaborate procedures involving the use of allotment machines (*klērōtēria*) were employed: see *AP* 63–6 and ch. 3 n. 103.

[67] Cf. Badian (1971) 17–30; cf. Kelly (1978) 1–17.

[68] See however the allegations of Aiskhin. 1.106, 3.62.

enjoyed more extensive supervisory authority, but it was now regarded as a symbol of the aristocratic ethos. For its members were a select group – those who had served as arkhons – and they retained their membership for life. Nor were their decisions subject to appeal. In matters political, therefore, the Areiopagos was an anomaly for it was in no sense responsible to the Demos nor was it drawn from the people at large.[69]

By these means the principle of the accountability of officials to the Demos was secured in Athenian practice by the middle of the fifth century. It should be added that an official could be removed at any time by decision of the assembly and that the power of officials was circumscribed in other ways.[70]

The third feature designated by Herodotos was decision-making by the popular assembly – that is, by the majority of the citizens attending the assembly. The Athenian Ekklesia decided on a vast range of matters from high matters of state to minor administrative details. It was open to all adult males of citizen birth: membership was not dependent on a property qualification such as pertained in oligarchic states. The Demos as embodied in the assembly held sovereignty or power (*kratos*).[71]

In short, by the mid-fifth century the three features named by the contemporary Herodotos as distinguishing the rule of the people were embodied in the Athenian political structure. From among other features of Athenian democracy two may be noted here as being of particular importance for an understanding of the mid-fifth century. First, the evolution of popular jury courts which dealt with all judicial matters, except for intentional homicide and a few other cases which were settled by the Council of the Areiopagos. Solon had, early in the sixth century, established the right of appeal to the people against the decisions of arkhons. When the Athenian people were meeting together to hear such appeals they were referred to as the *hēliaia*. In the decade or two before 462/1 it may well have been that appeals from the decisions of arkhons became increasingly frequent and that arkhons had tended to do no more than satisfy themselves that there was a matter which should be settled judicially and then to refer the case to the Heliaia. Whether it was a common practice or not, this procedure was probably made mandatory by a formal enactment of Ephialtes in 462/1.[72] By the mid-fifth century the determination of almost all judicial questions was thus no longer entrusted to officials nor to a narrow group, as was the case with the Council of Elders (*gerousia*) in Sparta, but to the Demos at large. The Heliaia had become a court of first instance. The Athenians by then had also adopted the practice of selecting 6,000 citizens by lot

---

[69] See ch. 2.3.1 and ch. 4.1; *AP* 25 (and *CAAP*), 35.2, 57.3, 60.2, Plut. *Kim.* 15, *Per.* 10, Aesch. *Eum.* 681–710, 858–69, 976–87, Thuc. 1.107.4–6; Arist. *Pol.* 1317b41–18a2; Hignett 193–213, Rhodes 201–6; cf. Sealey 42–58.

[70] See ch. 4.1; Arist. *Pol.* 1274a15–18, 1281b31–4, 1282a25–32, 1318b21–32.

[71] [Dem.] 59.88; see ch. 3.5.

[72] *AP* 9, 25.2 (and *CAAP*), Arist. *Pol.* 1273b35–74a21; Sealey 46–52, MacDowell 29–33, Forrest (1966) 217–18, Rhodes 204 n. 1.

each year to serve as heliasts and to divide this large group into jury panels (*dikastēria*).[73] It should be noted, moreover, that the dikasts (or heliasts, for like Heliaia the term did not drop out of use) voted by secret ballot, not by an open show of hands as was usual in the assembly.[74]

The other feature – state pay for public service – was closely connected with the dispensation of justice. At some time in the 450s, probably late in the decade, state pay for jury service was introduced.[75] If the jury courts were to draw on those who had to work for their living, some recompense had to be offered to the dikasts, especially at a time when judicial business was increasing with the growth of Athens and Athenian overseas interests. The rate was 2 obols a day. This measure was met with ridicule from the propertied classes: they charged that it made the people idle, cowardly, garrulous and greedy, and caused a deterioration in the courts.[76] And while ideological considerations were not lacking in the introduction of state pay and many of the other developments in the first half of the fifth century, those changes must rather be understood in a wider context. First, political rivalries within Athens and the issues and personalities involved in these rivalries, for many of the developments were part of the challenge by men like Ephialtes and Perikles to the political influence of Kimon and others and their policies. Secondly, we must recognise the crucial influence which the demands of foreign policy and the internal impact of these demands exercised, as we have seen, on internal political developments in the decades after the defeat of Xerxes and the formation of the Delian League.[77] Moreover, as is clear from klerouchies, domestic considerations could encourage particular foreign policy options. The interaction of all these elements determined the development of Athens and Athenian democracy.

1.6 Participation of citizens in the polis *c.* 450–322

The concept of the sovereignty of the Demos (or the sovereignty of the majority) continued to be regarded as fundamental to democracy in the fifth century and in the fourth century, though various writers, or the same writer in

---

73 Hignett 216–18, 223, but cf. Hansen (1981–2) 9–47, especially 27–39.
74 Aesch. *Eum.* 734–53, *AP* 68–9; Boegehold (1963) 366–74, Staveley 96–100; compare Xen. *Hell.* 1.7.7 with 1.7.9; Hansen 103–21; Ar. *Knights* 255, *Wasps* 891, 908, Antiphon 6.21, Lys. 10.16, Dem. 24.105.
75 *AP* 27.3–4 (and *CAAP*), Arist. *Pol.* 1274a8–11. See *AP* 24.3 and 62.2 (and *CAAP*) for others receiving payment, including bouleutai and officials: both received pay before 411 and probably by the 430s or earlier, but pay for civilian service (except for the nine arkhons and the prytaneis) was abolished by the oligarchs in 411 – see Thuc. 8.65.3, 69.4, 97.1, *AP* 29.5, 30.2, 33.1, Hignett 218–20. See ch. 2.3 and ch. 5.1.
76 *AP* 27.4, Pl. *Grg.* 515e.
77 See Ruschenbusch (1979A) (e.g. 76–82 on state pay), who denies or minimises the role of ideology in internal developments and exaggerates the (central) role of practical needs, especially foreign policy.

different contexts, might associate different features with this central concept. Freedom or liberty (*eleutheria*) was commonly held to be a fundamental characteristic of democracy, and in this Herodotos – and his contemporaries of the mid-fifth century – clearly concurred. Aristotle, who was writing his *Politics* in the years between 335 and 322, identified the sovereignty of the majority and freedom as the two things which were regarded as the defining features of democracy and noted that people asserted that freedom was the aim of every democracy.

One factor of liberty is to rule and to be ruled in turn. For the popular concept of justice is to have equality according to number, not worth, and if this is the concept of justice prevailing, the multitude must of necessity be sovereign and the decision of the majority must be final and must constitute justice, for they say that each of the citizens ought to have an equal share.[78]

But another mark of freedom, Aristotle argued, was 'living as one likes' or 'doing whatever one wishes': critics of democracy were quick to attack this 'licence' as they saw it in both the political and the social context.[79]

On the basis of equalitarian liberty Aristotle drew up a check-list of features which were democratic:

(1) election: all citizens eligible and to be elected by all; (2) rule: all over each and each in turn over all; (3) offices filled by lot, either all or at any rate those not calling for experience or skill; (4) no tenure of office dependent on the possession of a property qualification or only on a very low one; (5) the same man not to hold the same office (except the military offices) twice or only very rarely – or in the case of only a few offices; (6) short term of office for all offices or as many as possible; (7) judicial functions to be exercised by all citizens, that is by persons selected from all, and on all or on most matters and the most important and far-reaching, such as the examination of the official accounts, the constitution, contracts between individuals; (8) the assembly to be sovereign in everything, officials having no sovereign power over anything except quite minor matters. Or else a council is to be sovereign in matters of greatest importance, and a council is the most democratic of offices in states where there is not a plentiful supply of pay for all . . .; (9) payment for services, preferably in all areas, in the assembly, in the law-courts and in the offices, or if not for the offices, the law-courts, council, and the principal meetings of the assembly, or offices where it is obligatory to have meals together. Again (10), as good birth, wealth and culture are the marks of the rule of the few, so their opposites, low birth, poverty and vulgarity are regarded as typical of the rule of the people. (11) Life tenure of office is not favoured by democracy; and if any life-office remains in being after an ancient revolution, we note that it has been shorn of its power and its holders selected by lot instead of being elected by vote.[80]

---

[78] Arist. *Pol.* 1291b30–8, 1310a28–36, 1317a40–b7 (Loeb tr. adapted), 1284a19; Eur. *Suppl.* 349–53, 404–8, 438–41, Thuc. 8.68.4.

[79] Arist. *Pol.* 1317b11–13; [Xen.] *AP* 1.8–10, Pl. *Rep.* 557b–558c, 562b–563e, Isok. 7.20, 37, 12.131; cf. Thuc. 2.37.2–3, 39.1, 7.69.2; see ch. 8.3.1.

[80] Arist. *Pol.* 1317b17–18a3 (Penguin tr. adapted).

Not all of these features prevailed in Athenian democracy in the second half of the fifth century: payment for attendance in the assembly, for instance, was not introduced until the 390s. But in varying degrees most of these features – and in particular the sovereignty of the Demos and the equal right of all citizens to participate in the assembly and the law-courts – applied to public life in Athens from about the middle of the fifth century until the imposition of an oligarchic constitution, in particular a property qualification for citizenship, by the Makedonian Antipater in 322. There were two oligarchic interludes in 411–410 (as a result of intrigues within Athens) and 404–403 (with the help of the Spartan victors), but after 403 democracy was secure in a way that was no longer possible in the years after 322 when Athens effectively lost her ability to act independently. After 322 there were democratic interludes, but the continuance of democracy was patently and directly dependent on the play of external forces and even in those periods the determination of affairs seems largely to have been in the hands of the well-to-do. In many aspects of Athenian public life the same broad features and tendencies may be discerned throughout the period from *c.* 450 to 322, and this 'period' will therefore be encompassed in our examination of Athenian democracy.

It is, however, also true that in and after 403 some fundamental changes were introduced such as a regular procedure for the revision of the laws, and in some aspects of public life – not only in terms of institutions but also in terms of the political climate – it is appropriate to regard the fifth century and the fourth century as distinct.[81] Indeed, differences within each of these two periods, combined with problems arising from the character and the unevenness of the surviving evidence, provide grounds for a division into several periods within our span of about 130 years. A more definitive analysis of certain aspects of Athenian institutions would, for example, be possible if the discussion was confined to the 330s and early 320s, for it could then be mainly based on the description in the second part of the Aristotelian *Athenaion Politeia*, which was completed by the mid-320s. The problems of extrapolating from these two decades to earlier periods would thus be removed, but much of the evidence that we have about the democracy in operation could not, by the same token, be applied with certainty from earlier periods. Moreover, we would be restricted to a period when the victory of Philip at Khaironeia in 338 and his subsequent arrangements of Greek affairs had significantly limited the power of the Athenian Demos to conduct an independent foreign policy. Ironically, though,

---

[81] For example, see ch. 2.3.2 (on the trend to specialisation and on the Festival Fund Commission), ch. 3.5 (the Heliaia), ch. 4.2 (nomothesia), ch. 5.2 (ostracism; assembly pay), ch. 6.5 and 6.6 (use of the graphe paranomon and eisangelia), ch. 8.4 (financial problems; recourse to experts). On the features of the post-403 democracy, see Mossé 259–332, Rhodes (1980A) 305–23; cf. R. Koerner (1974) 132–46, Hansen (1974) 12–14; see ch. 8 n. 113.

it was in this period – in 333/2 – that the Athenians set up a colossal statue of Demokratia.[82]

The wider span of the period from the middle of the fifth century to 322 enables a keener appreciation of the central concept in the relationship between the individual citizen and democracy. That concept is the notion of sharing or participation. It was central to Athenian (and Greek) thinking and writing about citizenship and the life of the polis. As Aristotle observed, 'a citizen is simply defined by nothing else so much as the right to participate in judicial functions and in office'. In the term 'office' Aristotle included all those functions which entailed the exercise of power and he thus specified membership of the assembly as well as holding an official 'office' in the narrow sense. That definition, he argued, applied especially – and necessarily – to citizenship in a democracy.[83] And the focus of this investigation is the participation of citizens in democracy at Athens – not simply the institutions open to the citizens and their rights of sharing in the public life of their polis, but also the extent to which Athenian citizens may have realised the potential of equal participation. The privileges of Athenian citizens and the opening up of opportunities especially in the fifth century will first be considered.

---

[82]   *IG* II².2791, Raubitschek (1962) 238–43 (on the cult of Demokratia), Palagia (1982) 108–13; *IG* II².1496.131–2, 140–1, *SEG* 25.149.14; *IG* II².1604.24 (an entry in the first extant list [377/6 B.C.] of the series of fourth-century navy lists recording the name of a trireme [described already as 'old'] as Demokratia and the first of numerous listings of that and other triremes so named).

[83]   Arist. *Pol.* 1275a22–33, 1275b5–7.

2 The privileges and the opportunities of the citizen

2.1 Athenian attitudes to citizenship

The question of who were entitled to be Athenians in the fullest sense had, as we have seen, caused bitter controversy in the years after the expulsion of the tyrant Hippias in 510. Kleisthenes opposed the use of rigid investigation in settling disputes about an individual's origins and status and his reforms instituted a different mechanism for deciding acceptance as an Athenian.[1] Henceforth, Athenian citizens were those descended from Athenian men who had been registered in the Kleisthenic demes at the end of the sixth century, and it was the responsibility of the demes to keep a register of their citizen members.

In 451/0, the Athenian assembly accepted Perikles' proposal to require Athenian parentage in the female as well as the male line as the basis for citizenship. The motivations of this proposal and its acceptance have been much disputed.[2] Athens and its busy port Peiraieus were clearly attracting many foreigners to Attike – men in particular, it is likely, but women and families as well. With the marriage of foreign women into Athenian families, some Athenian fathers may have entertained fears of finding it difficult to marry their daughters to Athenian citizens, especially in the wake of Athenian war losses in the mid-450s.[3] Athenians at large may have felt themselves confronted by a flood of outsiders, and, in particular, may have been unwilling to share, on an unrestricted basis, the opportunities that Athens now offered. For Athenians were increasingly conscious of an Athenian identity. Perhaps, too, there had been laxity or even variations in the admission of citizens by the demes giving cause for concern. Whatever the reasons for this restrictive (but not retrospective) law, the offspring of foreign women (and Athenian men) were not to be accepted as Athenian. The citizen body was to be sealed off and self-perpetuating. Some relaxation of these exclusive attitudes was forced on the Athenians by the severe manpower shortages in the latter years of the Peloponnesian War, when Athens allowed the right of intermarriage to the

---

[1] See ch. 1.1.
[2] AP 26.4 (and CAAP), Plut. Per. 37.2–5; Hignett 343–7, Lacey (1968) 100–5, Harrison 1.25–9, Whitehead (1977) 149–54, Davies (1977/8) 105–21, Patterson (1981) 82–139.
[3] For the difficulty facing daughters of poor men (in the late 340s), see [Dem.] 59.112–13.

Euboians.[4] The Athenians had long had close ties with the Euboians, and the recognition of the children of an Athenian father and a Euboian mother as Athenian citizens was therefore more easily accomplished.

There might also be individual dispensations, as when Perikles, after the death from plague of his two legitimate sons, successfully sought citizenship for his son by Aspasia, the hetaira from Miletos.[5] But in 403/2 the restored democracy reaffirmed the Periklean citizenship law, though it did confirm the citizenship of those born to foreign mothers in the years when the law had been relaxed.[6] Thereafter eighteen-year-old boys born to a foreign mother might sometimes be admitted to the citizenship registers, whether through mis-representation on the part of an Athenian father or the exercise of influence or the inadvertence or negligence of deme members.[7] But Athenian citizenship was still in the mid-fourth century a jealously guarded privilege, in which Athenian women as well as, or perhaps more than, men took a keen interest. In the late 340s the jurymen hearing a case of the usurpation of civic rights were warned of the close questioning that they might expect from their wives or daughters or mothers when they learnt that the case involved Neaira who, though an alien, was living as the wife of an Athenian citizen and whose children had been passed off as Athenians.[8]

On the other hand, individuals who had rendered outstanding services to Athens or whose friendship the Athenians sought to cultivate might be rewarded with citizenship; and this commonly applied not only to the individuals themselves but to their descendants as well. Citizenship was conferred for example on the assassins of Phrynikhos, the oligarchic leader of 411, and on Kharidemos for his military services in the Khalkidike in the 360s, despite the fact, Demosthenes laments, that his native city Oreos in Euboia was not prepared to ignore his father's foreign origin and make Kharidemos a citizen.[9] In general, however, citizenship was not lightly awarded in our period. Indeed, following the latitude in applying the Periklean law in the latter part of the Peloponnesian War and the problems stemming from that period of laxity, the Athenians introduced, probably in the late 380s, a requirement that a grant of citizenship passed at one meeting of the assembly had to be confirmed at the next meeting, at which 6,000 were to be present.[10]

---

[4] Lys. 34.3. See also D.L. 2.26 who refers to a decree (after 413) allowing Athenian men to beget legitimate children from more than one wife: cf. Harrison 1.16–17.

[5] Plut. *Per.* 37.5.   [6] *AP* 42.1, Ath. 577b, Dem. 57.30, schol. Aiskhin. 1.39.

[7] Suspected irregularities presumably led the assembly in 346/5 to decree that every deme should review its register: see Dem. 57 for an appeal against a resulting exclusion from a deme register.

[8] [Dem.] 59.108–113.

[9] Citizenship decrees are collected and discussed in M. J. Osborne: the numbers (preceded by D) in the corpus of citizenship decrees in vol. 1 are cited in notes 10–16 below; see 1.17–18 for a list of citizenship decrees and 4.141–54 on eligibility for naturalisation; for grants of proxeny see Walbank (1978). Osborne D2 (*IG* i³.102, ML 85), Dem. 23.211–14.

[10] M. J. Osborne 2.56–7, see ch. 5.2.

From surviving inscriptions we can trace the wooing of Dionysios I the tyrant of Syracuse: an honorific decree of 393 did not dissuade Dionysios from continuing to assist the Spartans against the Athenians, but when better relations developed after the conclusion of an Athenian–Spartan alliance in 369, the Athenians in 368 granted citizenship to Dionysios, his sons and their descendants and in the next year made an alliance with him. Sometimes, too, Athens granted citizenship to those whose support of Athens had led or forced them to leave their native city.[11]

Even groups of people might be granted Athenian citizenship, though it was only extreme circumstances that induced the Athenians to offer citizenship to large groups. In 431 their old allies the Plataians were under attack by the Thebans and Spartans, but by 429 the Athenians decided they could offer no further help beyond leaving 80 Athenians to help the 400 Plataians withstand the siege after the rest of the population, apart from 110 women left behind to prepare the food, had been withdrawn to Athens. In 431 or, at the latest, by 429 the Athenians offered the Plataians citizenship rights in Athens. The latter were to share in all the privileges in which the Athenians shared, except that none was permitted to be drawn by lot for the office of the nine arkhons or for any priesthood. Their descendants, however, might be so drawn, provided they were born to an Athenian mother betrothed according to the law.[12] Again in 405, the loyalty of the Samians to Athens in the darkest days of the Peloponnesian War, encouraged no doubt by the presence of Athenian naval forces based on the island (though their presence itself implies support for Athens within Samos), was acknowledged by a grant of citizenship to all Samians, which was confirmed in 403/2.[13]

In general, however, the Athenians jealously guarded their citizenship. Consider, for example, 'the men from Phyle' and 'the men who joined in the return from the Peiraieus'. They assisted by force of arms in restoring the Demos to Athens in 403/2: among them were non-citizens as well as citizens and some recognition of their services was widely felt to be appropriate. A proposal sponsored by Thrasyboulos was blocked by Arkhinos – rightly so, in the view of the author of the *Athenaion Politeia*, because it proposed 'citizenship for all who joined in the return from the Peiraieus including some who were clearly slaves'.[14] 'Slaves' might indicate no more than free men of servile origin, but there seems to have been opposition to, or at least circumspection in, rewarding metics or resident aliens. Arkhinos himself proposed honorific awards for those

---

[11] Tod 108, Osborne D10 (Tod 133), Tod 136; see Osborne D14 (Tod 173) for three generations of Molossian rulers and Osborne D16 (Tod 178) for two Akarnanians, whose grandfather had apparently not taken up the Athenian citizenship granted to him and his descendants; Osborne D22 (*IG* II².222).

[12] Thuc. 2.78.3, 3.55.3 (and *HCT*), [Dem.] 59.98–106 (see Osborne D1).

[13] Osborne D4 (*IG* I³.127, ML 94), Osborne D5 (Tod 97). Cf. Hyp. 3.31–2 for a grant of citizenship to the Troizenians (who had received Athenian refugees in 480) expelled from their city in the 320s.   [14] *AP* 40.2 (and *CAAP*), Aiskhin. 3.195.

citizens who had survived, while a decree put forward by Theozotides restricted public support for orphans to the children of *citizens* 'who suffered violent death in the oligarchy'.[15] Yet in 401/0 a more generous attitude seems finally to have prevailed, for a mutilated inscription appears to enfranchise some 70–90 non-citizens who assisted in the restoration of the Demos and to grant to perhaps 850–870 others fiscal equality with Athenian citizens.[16]

In two grave military crises the Athenians are said to have relaxed the citizenship barriers. In 406, with a large part of their fleet blockaded at Mytilene, they not only melted down gold and silver dedications in the Akropolis temples to finance a new expedition, but also probably sought to overcome their manpower problems by offering citizenship to slaves and perhaps metics who served in the navy in this crisis.[17] Many scholars, however, have limited the offer to slaves to manumission and have been sceptical about any offer to metics and other foreigners. Then in 338, after Athens had been defeated by Philip II of Makedonia at Khaironeia and with 2,000 Athenians held prisoner, Hypereides proposed offering freedom to slaves, granting citizenship to metics and restoring their rights to disfranchised citizens. The Athenian assembly is said by Lykourgos to have accepted the proposal, but the military crisis was quickly over, peace was made and Hypereides' proposal was not implemented.[18]

In the classical period, in short, the Athenian attitude to citizenship – like that of Greek poleis generally – was exclusive, though loyalty or services to Athens might be rewarded with a grant of citizenship, whether to individuals or to groups of people. But most of the benefits of such a grant could only be exercised in Attike and some at least of those offered citizenship did not take it up.[19] What distinguishes Athenian attitudes (and the attitudes of other Greek poleis) from those of Philip II of Makedonia or the Romans is that there is no evidence to suggest that once the Athenian state had incorporated Salamis and the various areas of Attike, the Athenians seriously contemplated as a principle the incorporation in the citizen body of peoples over whom they exercised political power. They thereby denied themselves the opportunities of expansion supported by engaging the active involvement of other peoples in the manner of Philip II.

---

[15] Aiskhin. 3.187, Stroud (1971) 280–301 (*SEG* 28.46).

[16] Osborne D6 (cf. Tod 100) and 2.26–43; cf. Whitehead (1977) 114–16, 154–9 and (1984) 8–10, and Krentz (1980) 298–306. For the 'myth' of 'the men from Phyle' see Lys. 28.8, 12, Aiskhin. 3.187, 190–1 and *SEG* 28.45.

[17] Ar. *Frogs* 721–6; Ar. *Frogs* 692–4, Hellanikos *FGrH* 323a F25 (and Jacoby's commentary), Xen. *Hell.* 1.6.24, D.S. 13.97.1 (metics and other foreigners), Whitehead (1977) 153–4, M. J. Osborne 3.33–7, Davies (1977/8) 120; see also *IG* II².1951, Laing (1965) 107–19, 132–48 (argues for battle of Aigospotamoi); Welwei (1974) 81–101.

[18] Lykourg. *Leok.* 41, Hyp. fr. 18, [Dem.] 26.11, Dio. Chrys. 15.21.

[19] For example, most of the Samians and the Akarnanian Phormion mentioned in Osborne D16 (Tod 178): see n. 13 and n. 11.

2.2 Citizens, metics and slaves

What were the distinguishing marks of a citizen in Athens? Was it easy to tell whether a man was a citizen, a foreigner or a slave? Unlike Sparta, if we are to believe an oligarch of *c.* 430, it was impossible in Athens to distinguish a citizen from a slave (or a metic) by his dress or demeanour, and the slave would not even stand aside for the citizen in the street.[20] The economic and social situation in Athens, as the writer went on to explain, made for a less rigid control over slaves, and they are found working beside free men in activities ranging from small manufacturing enterprises to the building of temples. But these claims about the 'wantonness' of slaves must be set beside the reality that a slave in Athens was almost completely dependent on the goodwill of his master. For the owner could treat slaves like any other item of property, and could dispose of them by sale, hire, bequest or gift. The Athenian could beat or maltreat his slaves (and their only protection was to seek asylum at the shrine of Theseus or the altar of the Eumenides), while a master who killed a slave seems to have been required to do no more than submit to the ritual act of purification.[21] A slave could not take legal action himself, except in mercantile cases from the middle of the fourth century, and action on his behalf could be initiated only by his master, except in a few circumstances where the slave was dependent on the (unlikely) willingness of another citizen to take action.[22] For any wrongdoing a slave had to answer in his person or body, and according to Demosthenes this was the most important difference between a slave and a free man.[23] A slave might be allowed to hold money or other possessions but legally they remained his master's property. Domestic slaves were, in general terms, far better off than those who worked in deplorable conditions in the silver mines at Laureion in south-east Attike, and in some households they were well treated.[24] But in essence slaves lacked what the citizen most prized – freedom: they lacked the freedom to do what they desired to do and to go or live where they desired to go or live.[25]

Quite different was the position of the free foreigner. Not only was he free, but Athenians prided themselves on their open and hospitable attitude towards foreigners and contrasted this with the xenophobic practices of Sparta.[26] The

---

20 [Xen.] *AP* 1.10–12.   21 Harrison 1.171–2, MacDowell 80–1.

22 Harrison 1.166–71, MacDowell 81–2.

23 Dem. 22.55, 24.167. For a good example of double standards in punishment see *SEG* 26.72.16–32: a citizen who breaks the law with regard to accepting silver coinage has his goods confiscated and has to appear before the officials or the law-courts, whereas a slave is whipped.

24 Lauffer I (1955) 20–60. See also 'those who dwell apart' (Harrison 1.167), and the public slaves (like the archers who acted as police) who were owned by the state and whose legal and general situation seems to have been closer to that of a metic than a slave owned by an individual: Aiskhin. 1.54, 62, Harrison 1.177–8 and MacDowell 83; see ch. 8.2.

25 Westermann (1960A) 25–30. See Pl. *Rep.* 562b–563a on the consequences of excessive thirst for freedom, Harrison 1.171, 182–4 on the means of manumission, and [Dem.] 45.85, 59.2 and *APF* 427–30 on Pasion, the slave who became a citizen.

26 Thuc. 2.39.1 and see ch. 1.4.

foreigner who changed his home and settled in Athens was required to become a metic or resident alien. If he stayed in Athens beyond a limited period (perhaps a month), he had to register as a metic and pay the metic tax.[27] Metic status was essentially in the nature of a check on foreigners resident in Attike, as is further suggested by the need to obtain an Athenian citizen as one's 'champion' or 'protector' in order to secure registration and probably, at least until the early fourth century, to enable access to the Athenian courts. Metic status gave certain judicial advantages as compared with non-resident foreigners: in particular, it afforded in certain cases the privilege of resorting to the court of the polemarch. But the advantages of metic status have often been exaggerated, for it would appear likely that the premeditated killing of a foreigner attracted a lesser penalty than the killing of a citizen, and was treated in the same manner for metic and non-resident foreigner, while with changes in mercantile law in the mid-fourth century the advantages of the metic over the non-resident were largely removed.[28] Socially the metics could mix with ease with citizens, as may be inferred from the invitation to Glaukon and Adeimantos (Plato's brothers and citizens of a distinguished family) and (the humbler) Sokrates to the house of the metic Polemarkhos, brother of the orator Lysias, and the subsequent discussion depicted by Plato in the *Republic*. Indeed, many citizens may have felt a greater affinity with wealthy (or poor) metics than with poor (or wealthy) citizens, and some citizens clearly found congenial the company of sophists or other foreigners of intellectual or other ability who settled in Athens. Nevertheless, there remained very real differences between citizen status and metic status not least because, as we have seen, the children of a citizen and a metic were not citizens, and in social relations citizens could adopt a condescending attitude towards metics.[29]

But the great attraction of Athens for the metic was the economic opportunities which it provided, and not a few metics brought their wealth to Athens or acquired a fortune there. In two fundamental respects, however, the metic suffered a disadvantage compared with the citizen. First, metics – unless they had been specifically granted the right – were not permitted to own land or house in Attike. That was a serious restriction and it made metics dependent on citizen landlords, but ironically it led them to concentrate their energies in manufacturing, finance and trade which could be highly profitable. The vast majority of metics settled in the city and the Peiraieus: of 366 metics known from inscriptions of the late fifth century and the fourth, about 3 out of 5 lived in the urban and suburban demes of Athens and 1 in 5 in the Peiraieus deme,

---

[27] On the various aspects of metics and their status, see Whitehead (1977), who points out (7–10) that evidence for this pragmatic approach to foreigners coming to Attike relates with certainty (cf. Tod 139.30–6) only to the fourth century, but while the machinery may have been less rigorous in the second half of the fifth century there seems no reason to suggest a radically different approach on the part of the Athenians.

[28] Harrison 1.189–99, MacDowell 75–8, 221–4, Whitehead (1977) 89–97.

[29] Aiskhin. 1.195, Harrison 1.26–8, MacDowell 87, Whitehead (1977) 109–24.

while the others were scattered over more than 30 demes from all parts of Attike.[30] Secondly, in fundamental contrast to the citizen who paid no regular taxes on his income or his capital, metic men paid an annual poll-tax of 12 drakhmai and independent metic women 6 drakhmai. For those metics who were well-to-do the metic tax was trivial, but its real significance lay in setting the metic apart from the citizen.[31] For a building construction worker it represented about a day's wage or less each month. The building accounts of the Erekhtheion (409/8 and 408/7) show 1 drakhme a day as the usual wage irrespective of whether the workman was metic, slave or citizen, while in the Eleusinian accounts (329/8) unskilled labourers are recorded as receiving $1\frac{1}{2}$ drakhmai a day and semi-skilled and skilled workers 2 or $2\frac{1}{2}$ drakhmai.[32] The slave's earnings, it should be added, belonged to his master but the metic was free to dispose of his as he chose.

Wealthier metics undertook some of the liturgies or public services which wealthier citizens traditionally performed, but it is generally believed that they did not undertake the trierarchy, which involved the command of a trireme (though it was possible for this to be deputed to a metic in the mid-fourth century and perhaps earlier) as well as financial expense in the upkeep of the trireme and its equipment.[33] Again, wealthier metics were, like wealthier citizens, required to pay property tax (*eisphora*), a levy which was imposed from time to time as the need for finance, mainly for war, demanded.[34] Being free men, metics were also liable for other obligations laid upon citizens – in particular, maintaining the security of Athens. In 431 the Athenians had available a total number of 29,000 heavily armed infantry and it has been estimated that some 7,000 of these hoplites were metics.[35] Moreover, metics formed an important element among the rowers in the Athenian navy in the later fifth century: at that time rowers received regular pay and, for poorer metics, serving in the navy represented one of the real advantages of living in the Athenian polis.[36] Athens, and especially the busy port of the Peiraieus, afforded to the metic a vast range of opportunities in the second half of the fifth century. The benefits of living in the Athenian polis diminished, however, with the loss of prosperity which followed Athens' defeat in the Peloponnesian War.

Against the position of the slave and the metic we may more readily characterise the privileges of Athenian citizens. In a social sense, the differences

---

[30] Whitehead 82–4, noting the likelihood of some distortion from the accidents of the survival of inscriptions. [31] Whitehead (1977) 75–7.

[32] *IG* I³.475.54–7, 65–71, 250–6, 272–90 and 476.5–45, 59–62, 104–9 (5 obols), 124–40 (cf. *HCT* 2.45); *IG* II².1672.11–12, 26–34, 44–6, 60–2, 110–11, 159–60, 177–8.

[33] On metics and liturgies, see Whitehead (1977) 80–2, though in denying that a metic could undertake the trierarchy he depends too heavily on the usual means of designating a metic. The question remains uncertain for the fourth century; see Dem. 21.163. See *APF* 590–1 on 'Siphnians' who performed the trierarchy: the fact that they represent at least two generations suggests metics living in Attike rather than residents of Siphnos; see also Antimakhos the Khian (*IG* II².40.10–11 (and Addenda) and 1604.79).

[34] See ch. 3.4. [35] Thuc. 2.13.6–8 (and *HCT*), Jones 161–5. [36] Meiggs 439–41.

between these groups were not as marked as in states like Sparta, but in general we should assume the citizen as perceiving himself as a member of a privileged society within Athenian society. For only through Athenian citizen parents on both sides could an Athenian youth enter into the rights of Athenian citizenship. In the economic sphere we shall later consider his financial responsibilities, but two fundamental aspects have already been noted: his freedom from any regular direct tax and his right to own land. In the sphere of law adult male citizens alone enjoyed unrestricted capacity.[37] Women and minors, for example, were not qualified to make wills, nor were adult male citizens in the event of insanity or similar disabilities. Women remained under tutelage throughout their lives – to father, to husband, to a male guardian.[38] Athenian men lost their legal rights only if deprived of some or all of their civic rights by some specific act: a state debtor (and his heirs), for example, was subject to total loss of citizenship rights until he (or his heirs) paid his debts. The sharp distinction between citizen and metic status was reflected in the general notion that all those suits which were a matter for the eponymous arkhon in the case of citizens were in the case of metics a matter for the polemarch.[39] Above all, the citizen's person was normally protected and satisfaction had to be obtained from a citizen in terms of money, and it was only the citizen who could act as prosecutor in most 'public indictments' (*graphai*) for offences such as the embezzlement of public money.[40] These public indictments were as much a responsibility or obligation as a privilege and they will be considered below in Chapter 3.

It was above all in the political sphere that the citizen was distinctive: here, in particular, one might expect freedom and equality – the hallmarks of the Athenian citizen – to be seen most strikingly in operation. Once he had attained the age of 18 he was enrolled in the deme register: the Athenian male could – from the age of 20 in practice – attend all meetings of the Ekklesia or assembly and participate in the discussions and the voting.[41] When he turned 30, more opportunities were available to him – the right to offer himself for selection to the Boule (Council of 500) or to the various offices of state like the position of *stratēgos* (general) and the right to serve as a dikast or juryman on the jury panels (*dikastēria*).[42] In the intervening period he had the opportunity to gain political experience and knowledge within the limitation that the 20–29 age group was most liable to be called up for military service. Some premium was therefore placed on age and experience, but far less than in a conservative state like Sparta where the minimum age for the 28 members of the Council (Gerousia) was 60. In Athens public arbitrators were appointed in their sixtieth year.[43] An earlier law

---

[37] Harrison 2.82–5.   [38] Harrison 1.108–15.   [39] *AP* 58.3, Harrison 1.193–9.
[40] Dem. 22.55; MacDowell 56–61, 65.
[41] *AP* 42.1 (and *CAAP* – on the question of reaching eighteenth birthday or being in eighteenth year).   [42] Xen. *Mem.* 1.2.35, *AP* 63.3 (cf. 4.3), Dem. 24.151.
[43] *AP* 53.4. See *AP* 29.2, 42.2, 56.3 for 40 as a minimum age.

(attributed to Solon) giving precedence in addressing the Ekklesia to those aged 50 and over had fallen into disuse in the second half of the fourth century, if not long before.[44] In selecting envoys for a mission abroad the assembly occasionally decided that they were to be aged 50 and over, as for example the envoys to Perdikkas of Makedonia in 430/29, but usually the Ekklesia made no such stipulation or in fact specified that the envoys were to be selected 'from all the Athenians'.[45] Age, however, might still be useful as a criterion, as for example when envoys abroad experienced difficulty in deciding who of them should speak first or when there were no grounds for determining the order. One Athenian embassy in the mid-fourth century resolved the difficulty by giving precedence according to age – a procedure which Aiskhines found it convenient to argue seemed to be in accord with 'the orderly way of our city'.[46]

There were, then, some age limitations applied to those who aspired to leadership in Athens by holding official positions in the polis. But these were presumably derived in particular from an expectation that military service would devolve most on men in their twenties. The limitations were hardly severe and did not seriously impinge on the notion of equal right to hold office. Nor was poverty, Perikles claimed, a bar to active participation, but distinction in public life depended on a man's own ability, not his background.[47] How that worked out in practice must be considered later, but in a legal sense the office of arkhon had been opened in 458/7 to the third of the four Solonian census classes and by the 320s (and no doubt earlier) the exclusion of the thetic class seems to have become a legal fiction.[48]

Whether a man held office or not, the politically ambitious had to be able to exploit what was perhaps the most striking characteristic of Athenian democracy – the right of free speech (*parrhēsia*).[49] For the more conservative, it was this right of free speech in general and equal right of speech in the assembly (*isēgoria*) which gave the greatest cause for disquiet.[50] Though we should not be too ready to assume that large numbers of citizens availed themselves of the right, isegoria was practised in the Ekklesia throughout our period. As a regular procedure, when a matter was before the assembly for discussion, the herald issued a general invitation – 'Who wishes to speak?'[51]

On one celebrated occasion, according to Demosthenes, fear and uncertainty so gripped the Athenians that no one was willing to come forward and address the assembly: they had just heard (339/8 B.C.) that Philip II had moved into central Greece and occupied Elateia.

---

[44] Aiskhin. 1.23 and 3.2, 4; see Griffith (1966) 119–20.
[45] *IG* I³.61 (ML 65).16–18, Plut. *Per.* 17.2, Tod 123.72–5, 117.17–18.
[46] Aiskhin. 2.108.
[47] Thuc. 2.37.1.   [48] See ch. 2.3.2 and ch. 5.1; *AP* 26.2 (and *CAAP*), 7.4, 47.1.
[49] Eur. *Ion* 670–5, *Hipp.* 421–3, [Dem.] 60.26; but see Dem. 22.30–2, [Dem.] 25.25–8.
[50] [Xen.] *AP* 1.6, Pl. *Rep.* 557b; see ch. 1.4.
[51] Aiskhin. 1.23, 3.1–4; cf. Ar. *Akh.* 45, *Thesm.* 379, *Ekkl.* 130.

Evening had already fallen when a messenger arrived bringing to the presiding councillors (*prytaneis*) the news that Elateia had been taken. They were sitting at supper, but they instantly rose from table, cleared the booths in the Agora of their occupants, and unfolded the hurdles, while others summoned the generals (*stratēgoi*) and ordered the attendance of the trumpeter. The commotion spread through the whole city. At daybreak on the morrow the presiding councillors summoned the Council to the Council House, and the citizens flocked to the place of assembly. Before the Council could introduce the business and prepare the agenda, the whole body of citizens had taken their places on the hill. The Council arrived, the presiding councillors formally reported the intelligence they had received, and the courier was introduced. As soon as he had told his tale, the herald put the question, Who wishes to speak? No one came forward. The herald repeated his question again and again, but still no one rose to speak, although all the generals were there, and all the orators, and although the country with her civic voice was calling for the man who should speak for her salvation; for we may justly regard the voice, which the herald raises as the laws direct, as the civic voice of our country.[52]

On the day, Demosthenes claimed, he was recognised as the man to appreciate the needs of the hour and so at last he came forward and addressed the assembly. And though anyone might come forward, there were certain conventions and expectations. In matters relating to military security, for example, the strategoi, whether by right or by convention, would be among the first speakers. Or again, in normal circumstances, a matter brought before the assembly for decision should already have been discussed by the Boule, which would usually make a recommendation, either advocating a certain line of action or merely recommending that the assembly consider the matter.[53]

But among the citizens at large – the *idiōtai*, those who held no official position or those who were not habitual orators in the assembly – the desire to address the assembly was circumscribed.[54] It required some experience and skill to speak effectively in those large meetings, but it also required some familiarity with the issues being debated. The assembly might enjoy the entertaining speaker and it might habitually reject the advice of its leaders, as Plutarch asserted to be the case, but when it came to making crucial decisions like appointments to the office of strategos, the Athenians called upon the most rigorous and most sensible citizen. Thus Plutarch explained the selection of Phokion as strategos on 45 occasions, though the thrust of his account is that the Demos constantly opposed his advice.[55] And it is clear that the assembly, especially in the fourth century, did not accept advice uncritically, nor did it tolerate fools or the incompetent. Plato, it is true, makes Sokrates distinguish

---

[52] Dem. 18.169–70 (Loeb tr. adapted).   [53] *AP* 45.4; see Rhodes 52–63.
[54] The precise sense of *idiōtēs* (private person, individual) is determined, in the context, by an explicit or implicit contrast – for example, with state officials (*arkhontes* – Lys. 5.3, Tod 123.52–3), with habitual speakers in the Boule (see ch. 5.1) or the Ekklesia (see ch. 6.2), with dikasts (Antiphon 6.24), with physicians (Thuc. 2.48.3), with the polis (Thuc. 1.124.1).
[55] Plut. *Phok.* 8.

103352
LIBRARY
COLBY-SAWYER COLLEGE
NEW LONDON, NH 03257

between technical questions, such as ship construction where expert advice was demanded, and political questions, where the Athenians listened to anyone. In technical matters anyone who was not considered an expert, even if he was 'quite a gentleman, wealthy and well-born', was according to Plato, jeered and booed until he gave up or was removed from the speaker's platform. But it is clear from Xenophon that a similar intolerance of ill-informed speakers applied also in regard to larger questions: Sokrates endeavoured to bring home to the ambitious, young Glaukon who had been howled down several times that he needed to be well informed on such questions as revenues, expenditure, military strength and food supplies before he ventured to address the assembly.[56]

It is therefore fascinating to examine the types of people – their background and their personal talents – who were willing to seize the expanding opportunities for citizens at large and to seek power and influence with the Ekklesia and in Athenian life generally. In the sixth century Athenian public life had revolved around aristocratic factions, and in the first half of the fifth century members of the leading aristocratic families continued to play a leading role. In the course of the next hundred years the character of Athenian public life changed considerably with the working out of democratic trends and under the influence of external circumstances. Along with these changes can be discerned shifts in the types of people who aspired to leadership – shifts which may be sketched by investigating the background and talents of some of the leading figures in Athens in the fifth and fourth centuries.

2.3 Opportunities for leadership

2.3.1 Trends in leadership in the fifth century

Typical of Athenian leaders in the first half of the fifth century was Kimon, the son of Miltiades.[57] Sprung from an aristocratic family that had played a leading part in Athenian affairs for some generations and shown considerable enterprise in and beyond Attike, Kimon had the particular advantage of being the son of the hero of Marathon, though the glory of that action had been somewhat dimmed by Miltiades' unsuccessful expedition against Paros and his conviction on a charge of misleading the Demos (489).[58] In his youth Kimon was not highly regarded, but had a reputation as a wild young man and uncultivated – more in the Peloponnesian than the Athenian mould.[59] In 479 Kimon, then in his early thirties, was among the envoys sent, on the proposal of Aristeides, to

---

56 Pl. *Prt.* 319a–323c, see ch. 8.4; Xen. *Mem.* 3.6.
57 Detailed references to individuals in the sources may be found in the entries in *PA* and discussion of family background and wealth in *APF. PA* numbers are cited when there is some discussion of an individual and, where appropriate, page references to *APF* are added. For Kimon, see *PA* 8429, *APF* 293–307 and Plut. *Kimon.*
58 Hdt. 6.132–6, Plut. *Kim.* 4.3.   59 Plut. *Kim.* 4.3–4.

LIBRARY
COLBY-SAWYER COLLEGE
NEW LONDON, NH 03257

Sparta to ensure continuing Spartan participation in action against the Persians, who were led by Mardonios following Xerxes' withdrawal after the defeat at Salamis. In the next two decades he followed, as we have seen, a policy of cooperation with the Spartans, a policy which in the 470s was congenial to most Athenians in the wake of the joint Greek action in repelling the Persians.[60] In the military field he showed outstanding ability. The operations of the Delian League forces, led by Athenian strategoi, provided the opportunity for the deployment of Kimon's talents.[61] Most spectacular among his successes was the victory over the Persians at the Eurymedon River on the south coast of Asia Minor. That victory in *c.* 469 frustrated a determined attempt by the Persians to win control of the Aegean and brought vast quantities of booty to the Athenians. Kimon's prestige, popularity and ability as a commander are reflected in the fact that he was elected to the strategia on not less than ten occasions in the period between 478 and 461.

Kimon had his rivals in Athenian public life and they showed their hand in their (unsuccessful) prosecution of him on his return from the Thasos campaign in 463.[62] In 462 he managed with difficulty to persuade the assembly to respond to a Spartan request for help against the rebellious helots. The Athenians heeded his plea 'not to allow Greece to go lame, nor their city to be deprived of its yoke-fellow'.[63] Kimon, whose pro-Spartan sympathies had been recognised by the Spartans when they appointed him as their *proxenos* ('public friend') in Athens, was soon to appear as a man who could be represented as having put Sparta's interests before those of Athens. For the 4,000 hoplites sent to help Athens' 'yoke-fellow' were dismissed by the Spartans who had become afraid of their adventurous and innovative spirit.[64] The absence of Kimon and 4,000 hoplites had in the meantime given Ephialtes his chance to push through his reforms. Kimon's unsuccessful attempt, on his return, to overthrow the reforms added to the grave loss of influence and prestige which he suffered from the exposure of his pro-Spartan policy. With his influence and his popularity undermined, Kimon was vulnerable to a vote of ostracism and in 461 the Athenian Demos showed their rejection of Kimon and his policies by ostracising him.[65]

Kimon was essentially the aristocratic dynast, magnificent in his performance of liturgies and open-handed with his resources – in particular to assist his fellow demesmen. But by the funding of polis projects from his private fortune or from booty, Kimon's appeal and support passed over from his deme Lakiadai to the Athenians at large. Eurymedon booty was used to meet various public

---

[60] See ch. 1.2.
[61] Thuc. 1.98, 100. Notwithstanding the claims of Plutarch (*Kim.* 11), the preconditions of the Athenian empire were developing in the time of Kimon's prominence. Moreover, it was Kimon who commanded the forces which prevented the Thasians from breaking away (465–463 B.C.).   [62] Plut. *Kim.* 14, *Per.* 10, *AP* 27.1.
[63] Plut. *Kim.* 16.8.   [64] Thuc. 1.102.   [65] Plut. *Kim.* 16–17; see ch. 7.2.

expenses, including the construction of the south wall of the Akropolis, and Kimon is said to have laid the foundations for some sections of the Long Walls at his own expense.[66] Such magnanimity could be expected to bring political benefit, but the hoplites and the rowers who had shared Kimon's successes had become increasingly unwilling to accept his aristocratic style of leadership. Those successes had given them a great confidence and a stronger desire for asserting themselves against the established order and against aristocratic dominance.[67] The man who had named a son Lakedaimonios, the man who is said to have sung the praises of Sparta to the Athenians when criticising or inciting the Athenians, and even to have said 'But the Spartans (*Lakedaimonioi*) are not like that', the man who championed that symbol of aristocratic ways, the Areiopagos, was now out of harmony with the new spirit of Athens.[68] Alive to that spirit was Perikles who at some time in the 450s introduced state pay for jury service, 'offering the people what was their own'.[69] The day of the handout from the wealthy aristocrat was passing.

In many ways Perikles had much in common with Kimon, and some have seen Perikles as continuing the game under the old rules – that is, in terms of rivalry between the traditional families, with numerous small groups based on personal ties and liable to constant changes in alignments, but working within the family politics of the great houses, not going beyond them.[70] Many at the time may well have conceived it in this way. For, on his mother's side, Perikles came from one of the prominent aristocratic families, the Alkmeonidai, and the marriage of the Alkmeonid Isodike and Kimon, probably in the early 470s, is a reminder that rival aristocratic families might find reasons for reconciliation or even cooperation against other contenders for power, such as Themistokles.[71] Perikles' father Xanthippos had prosecuted Miltiades in 489, had been prominent enough to be ostracised in 484, and had commanded the Athenian fleet in the Greek victory at Mykale in 479. In 473/2 when he was in his early twenties, Perikles undertook one of the traditional responsibilities of wealthy Athenians when, acting as *khorēgos*, he defrayed the cost of equipping, paying and training the chorus for *The Persians* and the other plays in the trilogy written by Aeschylus.

Perikles was also the grand-nephew of Kleisthenes, who finding himself worsted in his struggles with his aristocratic rivals had turned to the Demos in 508/7 for support.[72] Kleisthenes no doubt regarded this as a manoeuvre in the

---

[66] *AP* 27.3 (and *CAAP*), Theopomp. *FGrH* 115 F89, Plut. *Kim.* 10.1–3; *APF* 311–12, Whitehead 305–11, cf. Connor 19–20. See Plut. *Kim.* 13.6–7.

[67] Plut. *Kim.* 15; see ch. 1.2.

[68] Plut. *Kim.* 16. See *APF* 306–8 for the political implications of the names of Kimon's three certain sons – Lakedaimonios, Oulios and Thettalos.

[69] *AP* 27.3–4, Plut. *Per.* 9.2–3 and, for another critical view, Pl. *Grg.* 515–17. On the problems of dating, see Hignett 342–3 and *CAAP* 338–40.   [70] Sealey 59–74, Connor 9–32, 66–75.

[71] *PA* 11811, *APF* 455–60 (and cf. 304–5), Plut. *Per.*; Westlake (1968) 23–42. The Alkmeonid connection may have been stressed more by his opponents than by Perikles – see Forrest (1960) 233.   [72] Hdt. 5.66, *AP* 20; see ch. 1.1.

game of aristocratic rivalry, but he had also revealed a readiness to take greater account of the Demos and, as we have seen, he confirmed this by the nature of his reforms. Perikles also showed a willingness to take the Demos into serious account, albeit in pursuit of his own ambitions. But the struggle for influence with the Demos was prolonged. The man whose father had prosecuted Kimon's father Miltiades in 489 probably pressed hard the attack on Kimon in 463, for the withdrawal of Themistokles from Athens by the late 470s and Perikles' own desire to win influence in the face of Kimon's great prestige would have counteracted any desire to continue such cooperation between the two families as had existed in the early 470s.[73] His association with the attack on Kimon and with the reforms of 462/1 did not assure him an immediate pre-eminence in Athenian public life, and there is reason to believe that for most of the 450s Perikles was not yet in the front rank of Athenian leaders. In the field of external affairs he seems to have played a limited role. Though he presumably played a part in stirring up feeling against Aigina when he labelled it 'the eye-sore of the Peiraieus', it was Leokrates who commanded the expedition against Aigina in 458.[74] By the late 450s, however, he may have been establishing a reputation in military and external affairs, for he is credited in the sources with the dispatch (in the late 450s or the 440s) of settlers to the Thracian Khersonesos, Naxos and Andros.[75]

In the 450s, however, Perikles was perhaps concentrating his efforts more on internal affairs, such as the institution of pay for jury service. With the development of democracy, increasing attention had to be paid to the ordinary citizens of Athens, but in the structure of Athenian democracy there was also inherent the need for *dēmagōgoi* (leaders of the Demos) or *prostatai tou dēmou* (champions or leaders of the Demos). There was a need for individuals whose standing or expertise or experience or ability enabled them to play an active role and take initiatives.[76] That need was recognised or anticipated by Perikles who recognised, too, that the ordinary citizens had to be taken into serious account. In the 450s (and 440s) Perikles sought support by using methods and adopting certain policies which were not well received by 'the best people' in Athens.[77] Their response was one element in the development of a pejorative connotation of the word *dēmagōgos*: another was the ambiguity of the word *dēmos* which, as we have seen, might be used to refer to the whole people (all the citizens) or the common people (the lower classes).[78] The next generation of 'the best people',

---

[73] Cf. Plut. *Per.* 10.5 and Sealey 59–74.   [74] Plut. *Per.* 8.5.

[75] Plut. *Per.* 11.5, 19.1; Green and Sinclair (1970) 518–19 and Meiggs 159–60.

[76] Finley (1974) 21.

[77] See Plut. *Per.* 11.2–3 for the view that the existence of two elements in the state – the popular (*dēmotikoi*) and the aristocratic (*aristokratikoi*) – was brought to the surface and made prominent by the conflict between Perikles and Thucydides the son of Melesias, the leader of the 'the good and true' (*kaloi kagathoi*). See ch. 1.4, and n. 69 above.

[78] The word *dēmagōgos*, when it first came into use, was probably neutral or even complimentary, except when used by those strongly opposed to the changing political situation, but the commoner term in the last third of the fifth century was *prostatēs tou dēmou*: see Connor 108–15, Ar. *Knights* 191–3; see ch. 1.4.

or at least some of them like the historian Thucydides, might see in the later Perikles a commendably strong leader who they believed was motivated by concern for the good of the state, not self-interest or factional interests.[79]

Apart from jury pay, the settlement of Athenians abroad as klerouchs was no doubt welcome to ordinary citizens but probably also to the well-to-do, if only for reasons of security or geo-politics. The citizenship law of 451/0 probably had support from the well-to-do and from citizens generally. There was, however, a marked division of opinion about Perikles' hard-headed recognition of the changed character of Athens' alliance with its Delian League allies and, in particular, his view that it was proper for Athens to use the resources of that alliance for the building of the Parthenon and other projects, as long as Athens kept the seas free, whether of Persians or of pirates.[80]

These issues involving the character and purposes of the Athenian alliance were at the centre of the celebrated conflict between Perikles and Thucydides, son of Melesias, a relation of Kimon and his successor as leader of Athenian conservatives.[81] An astute political leader who had his supporters sit together in the Ekklesia to give them more weight, Thucydides offered strong opposition to the imperialist and other policies of Perikles and his supporters over a period of several years.[82] The earlier issue of the use of the allies' money for the building programme and the wider question of the proper use of resources and foreign policy objectives seem to have developed or changed into allegations by Thucydides and his supporters of extravagant expenditure of public moneys.[83] In 443 the struggle and the issues were resolved by the ostracism of Thucydides. The building programme brought economic benefits (though explanations in terms of providing employment for a troublesome, unemployed mob should be regarded as anachronistic), but it powerfully influenced the Athenians' perception of Athens and its place in the world as well. Much of this activity which continued strongly in the 430s was associated with Perikles and would

---

[79] Thuc. 2.65; contrast the references cited in n. 69.

[80] See ch. 1.3 and n. 37; see ch. 2.1; Plut. *Per.* 12, and for the development of the empire see ch. 1.2 and Meiggs 68–204 (with bibliography).

[81] According to Plutarch (*Per.* 12) the building programme was fiercely attacked by Perikles' opponents on the grounds that Athens was acting immorally and misappropriating funds contributed by the allies. That an objection based solely on these grounds would have appealed to many Athenians, whether men of property or poor, may well be doubted (as by Andrewes (1978) 1–5), but there is no reason to doubt that a major issue in the conflict between Perikles and Thucydides was the use of League funds for the building programme in Athens. The objections probably centred on the question whether this was a sound use of resources and in particular whether it constituted a diversion of resources that should be used, or might be needed, against the Persians. In short, it may have been part of a wider debate about the propriety of making an accommodation with Persia: probably apposite is the remark attributed to Elpinike about the loss of Athenian lives against Samos (439 B.C.), not against the Phoenicians or the Persians (Plut. *Per.* 28).

[82] Plut. *Per.* 11; cf. Andrewes (1978) 2.

[83] Plut. *Per.* 12, 14.

have added to his popularity and influence.[84] An index of this is his re-election every year to the office of strategos from 443 to 429. He had already served as strategos on a number of occasions and he was a competent but not brilliant commander. In the eyes of some Athenians, therefore, he may have been worthy of re-election on grounds of military competence, but his constant re-election was also an index of his political power and influence.

In the last years of his life, Perikles' grip on Athenian affairs was such that the historian Thucydides declared that 'in what was nominally a democracy, power was in fact in the hands of the first citizen'. Nor can it be denied that Perikles exerted a pre-eminent influence in those years, but his dismissal from the office of strategos in 430 and indications of opposition to both him and his policies in the 430s bring home the fact that, while Perikles could and did take the initiative, he had to convince the Athenian people in assembly of the soundness of every proposal that he put forward.[85] Plutarch discerned a very stark contrast in leadership style between the period before Thucydides' ostracism and the later period. He depicted a demagogic phase in which Perikles deliberately sought the favour of the people and a firmer, more aristocratic or monarchical style.[86] There is much truth in this depiction, though the change was neither so simple nor so dramatic. In neither period could Perikles assume support from the sovereign Demos, but in the course of the 440s he clearly gained in confidence and in the light of past policies or achievements the Demos was more disposed to accept the proposals he put before them. And that predisposition was based on many factors – his recognised standing, his incorruptibility, his knowledge of Athenian resources, his command of the details of finance and administration, and the soundness of earlier advice.[87] But Perikles' political skills, the soundness of the particular proposal *and* his ability as a speaker in the assembly were crucial factors, for 'persuasion' of the mass assembly was increasingly perceived as the essential ingredient in political decision-making.[88]

This marked a change over the years since the reforms of Kleisthenes – a change which had gained momentum in the years since Perikles entered public life in the mid-460s. Among many factors at work, mention should be made of the increasing activity in, and importance of, the Dikasteria, the development of isegoria, the possibilities for individuals to play an active role in the Ekklesia and Dikasteria, the growing confidence of ordinary Athenians who listened to

[84] For an example of the transition from private patronage to public–imperial funding in the provision of public amenities, see *IG* I³.49.13–16 (440–432 B.C.) and Davies (1978) 108–9; see ch. 1.2; see Boersma (1970) 65–81 for works initiated by or associated with Perikles.
[85] Thuc. 2.65.9; 2.59, 65.1–3; Plut. *Per.* 13.9–10, 31–2 (attacks on friends and associates), *HCT* 2.184–9, Frost (1964) 392–9; Thuc. 1.44 (indecision in Athens about making an alliance with Kerkyra); Thuc. 1.140.3–5, Plut. *Per.* 29.5 (Megara), cf. *HCT* 1.464.
[86] Plut. *Per.* 15. [87] Thuc. 2.65.5, 8–9; see 2.13.2–9, 60.5–7.
[88] See Finley (1974) 11–18 on the element of unpredictability and the essential role of oratory. On persuasion (*peithō*) see Eup. fr. 94.5, Pl. *Grg.* 452e, Dem. 24.76, Buxton (1982) 10–24, 48–57.

the debates and voted in the assembly. And helping to meet the practical needs created by the changing situation were those sophists or teachers who in the second half of the fifth century offered instruction in the art of getting on in life, not least by eloquence and persuasive argument.[89] Speaking in public had long been important in the oral society that Athens was, but the development of the Dikasteria in the mid-fifth century and the need to win support in the Boule and the Ekklesia increased the self-consciousness of political and judicial eloquence, especially among those who aspired to leadership in public life. Those who could afford it were likely to seek instruction from those who taught the techniques of civic life. More widely, too, the advice and assistance of a professional speech-writer or a consultant came to be valued, as litigants, for example, had to speak in court on their own behalf, though they might also be supported by friends, especially those who were experienced speakers. Antiphon (the chief architect of the oligarchic revolution in 411) was described by Thucydides as a most able man in helping those who were engaged in the courts or the assembly and who sought his advice.[90]

Between Perikles and his successors the historian Thucydides saw a vast gulf. Whereas Perikles was perceived by the historian as leading the people rather than being led by them, his successors were seen to be more on a level with each other and therefore constrained to outbid each other for popular favour.[91] Certainly there was something of a vacuum after the departure from the scene of the dominant figure of Perikles, though his pre-eminence for almost fifteen years might well be seen as unusual for Athens and the transparent rivalries after his death as a return to a more common state of affairs. In any case, we exaggerate the contrast if we lose sight of the earlier career of Perikles and of his constant need to carry the Ekklesia with him. Among his successors, some differed very little from Perikles in regard to their family background. Alkibiades, for example, possessed many of the attributes associated with leaders of the traditional type. Born (probably in 451/0) into an aristocratic family and brought up by his kinsman Perikles, Alkibiades was a young man of extraordinary ability. Victories in the chariot races at the Olympic Games brought glory on himself and his family and, as he reminded the Athenians when he spoke in favour of his appointment as a commander of the Sicilian expedition in 416, also brought glory and profit to the Athenian polis. Alkibiades displayed similar magnificence in his performance of liturgies within Athens, thereby at his own expense benefiting both himself and the polis.[92] Birth and wealth, in short, still counted for much in Athens, and the insolence of

---

89 See Kennedy (1963) 3–14, 26–51 and Guthrie (1969) 35–51, 176–81; on the 'old' Athenian education and the sophists, see Marrou (1956) 36–60.

90 Kennedy (1963) 125–33, 154–7, 203–4; Thuc. 2.40.2; Ar. *Clouds* 458–75, Thuc. 8.68.1; see Xen. *Mem.* 1.2.12–31, cf. Dover (1968) 180–4.

91 Thuc. 2.65; Ar. *Knights* 128–49, 191–3, 1115–20; *AP* 28.1; cf. Plut. *Per.* 39.4–5 and Woodhead (1960) 294–6.

92 *PA* 600, *APF* 18–19, Plut. *Alk.*; Westlake (1968) 212–60; Thuc. 6.16.

Alkibiades was a reflection of that. Another indication of the continuing strength of traditional attitudes may be found in the figure of Nikias who shared with Alkibiades and Lamakhos the command of the great Sicilian expedition. A man of average abilities, Nikias nevertheless exerted great influence in Athenian life, through his respectability, his incorruptibility and his willingness to expend his great wealth in the service of the polis, not least in religious matters such as the purification of Delos. In many ways Nikias sought to accommodate or adopt the style, the values and the attitudes of the old aristocracy.[93] But in so far as the considerable wealth which he inherited was derived from mining interests and the employment of slaves in mining rather than agriculture, and in so far as there is no clear evidence of a relationship with the old aristocracy, Nikias represents some of the new influences operating in Athenian life.

With the increasing importance of the lower classes and the decline in the prestige of the older families in the third and especially the last quarter of the fifth century, there was coming to the fore what has been described as a new breed of politicians. Scorned by the aristocrats (and other Athenians) for their lack of birth, these men did not necessarily lack wealth.[94] But the basis of their wealth was not so much the traditional source – agriculture – as manufacture. Kleon, for example, seems to have inherited wealth from his father who owned a workshop of slave tanners, while Hyperbolos rose from poor circumstances by his success in lamp-making. Lyre-making proved sufficiently lucrative to enable Kleophon to participate actively in public life, though it should be noted that he was probably not of low socio-economic status and foreign birth (as portrayed in the literary sources), for it is very likely that his father is to be identified with the Kleippides who served as a general in 428.[95] In their style of leadership, too, these men were felt to be different from traditional political leaders. There is little reason, however, to believe that they broke with the past and did not make use of friends and associates. Yet they did appeal directly and unashamedly to the Demos and thereby demonstrated the crucial importance of isegoria in achieving full control by the Ekklesia over state affairs, with a minimum of restraint by Boule or officials. The character of their appeal was felt by men like Thucydides to be crude and uncouth.[96] And, though in this respect, too, the differences would not seem to be as great as the literary sources

---

[93] *PA* 10808, *APF* 403–4; Westlake (1968) 86–96, 169–211; Pritchett 3.47–153; Powell (1979A) 15–31, and (on the faith of the elite and not only of ordinary Athenians in religious prophecy) (1979B) 45–50; see Mikalson (1983) 3–12. Notwithstanding his apparent background, Nikias is described by *AP* 28.5 as 'a true gentleman' (*kalos kagathos*).

[94] Connor 87–175. See Davies (1975) 377 on the connection between the development of isegoria in the assembly and the (concurrent) development of *parrhēsia* (freedom of speech, outspokenness) in comedy (with its strong movement towards politicisation in the third quarter of the fifth century).

[95] *PA* 8674, *APF* 318–20; Westlake (1968) 60–85; *PA* 13910, *APF* 517; *PA* 8638, Ar. *Frogs* 675–85, ML 21; Connor 151–8.

[96] Griffith (1966) 127–30; Thuc. 3.36, Ar. *Akh.* 377–84, *AP* 28.3 (and *CAAP*), Plut. *Nik.* 8.3.

indicate, there were no doubt changes in political and oratorical techniques, and these may well be related to changes in the composition and character of the assembly as Athenians from the countryside took shelter in the city and the fortifications from the annual invasions in the early years of the Peloponnesian War. Moreover, as speakers in the assembly the 'new politicians' did not hold an official position and unlike a strategos or an arkhon they could not be held to account. They were in that sense 'irresponsible', but they did face, as we shall see, other legal challenges, and above all (it must be added) poor advice was likely to diminish their ability to carry the assembly in the future.

The most violent of the citizens (in 427) and the most influential with the Demos as Thucydides described him, Kleon was a man of no mean ability.[97] In the military sphere he had little or no background, unlike the traditional leader, and his early influence rested on his oratorical and political skills. The drain on Athenian resources in the early years of the Peloponnesian War was very heavy: in the first three years Athens probably expended over 3,500 talents, while in the years from 433 to 426 the Athenians 'borrowed' some 4,790 talents from the temple treasuries. Finance and financial management had clearly assumed critical importance.[98] It seems likely that Kleon took a strong interest in financial questions and that the trebling of the assessment of the tribute in 425/4 owed something to his influence.[99] For, trapped, or manoeuvring himself, into the command of the Athenian forces at Pylos in 425, Kleon proved that he also had capacity as a military commander, and it was in the wake of his triumph at Pylos that the assembly voted to increase the tribute.

Exasperation with the operation of full democracy and with the leadership of men like Kleon, Hyperbolos and Kleophon was one factor in the oligarchic revolution engineered by conservative forces in 411. With full democracy established in Athens for more than a generation and with the strong hand of Perikles removed, the implications of democracy had become apparent. Moreover, the increase in jury pay introduced in the mid-420s by Kleon would have antagonised wealthier citizens, who were also affected by levies of property tax necessitated by the war. There were, it should be noted, few men left who had had direct experience of political life in the years before 462/1. By some democracy was taken for granted, by others its alternative oligarchy was viewed favourably and uncritically. One of the safety-valves of democracy, ostracism, had been recently circumvented when the supporters of Nikias and Alkibiades had joined together to frustrate the (anticipated) ostracism of one or the other and to engineer the removal of Hyperbolos.[100] But lack of success in

---

97 Thuc. 3.36; Woodhead (1960) 289–317, Gomme (1962) 101–11, Andrewes (1962) 79–84, *APF* 319–20, Bourriot (1982) 404–35.

98 *ATL* 3.326–45, *HCT* 3.687–9, *IG* I³.369 (ML 72 and commentary).

99 Ar. *Knights* 312–13, *IG* I³.71 (ML 69 and pp. 194–7), Ar. *Knights* 773–6, 947–8, 312–13, 236–7, 255–7, but cf. *HCT* 3.500–2.

100 D. M. Lewis (1975) 90; Plut. *Nik.* 11, Thuc. 8.73.3 (and *HCT*), *PA* 13910.

the Peloponnesian War was the crucial factor which led to the overthrow of democracy.

The oligarchs' conduct in 411 and more particularly the excesses of the Thirty (Tyrants) in 404/3 discredited oligarchy as a practical alternative to democracy. Yet there were those who believed in some limitation of the franchise and openly advocated it. Phormisios, for example, proposed in 403 that while the exiles might return, the citizenship should be bestowed only on those who possessed land. The Spartans favoured the measure, which, it was claimed, would have excluded some 5,000 citizens (out of perhaps 22,000–25,000). But it was strongly opposed by at least some men of good birth and ample resources who recognised the divisiveness of such a proposal. The assembly did not turn its back on the artisans and sailors who had helped in the restoration of democracy, and the general mood in Athens in the years immediately after 403/2 seems to have inclined against oligarchic tendencies.[101]

2.3.2 Trends in leadership 403–322

In the years after the restoration of democracy in 403/2 there appears to have been an intensification of feeling against aristocratic families. Envy of the wealthy or the successful person was, as we shall see later, a fact which Athenian leaders encountered, and Alkibiades had complained of the envy felt towards any man who excelled in the glory of anything.[102] In post-war Athens anti-aristocratic feeling had perhaps become particularly strong if we may judge from the speech of Lysias written for Mantitheos at some time in the years 392–390.[103] Mantitheos had been elected a member of the Boule and at the scrutiny before taking up his position he defended himself against charges that he had been in Athens and served in the cavalry during the rule of the Thirty. He denied having served in the cavalry and claimed that he returned to Athens from Pantikapaion only five days before the men of Phyle returned to the Peiraieus. As Mantitheos rightly pointed out, in the case of scrutinies a man has a right to render an account of his whole life. But in his case it was essential, for he clearly laboured under a prejudice against him as a young aristocrat. Mantitheos made much of his zeal when serving in the army and he gave as the motive for his zeal the desire to protect himself against any unjust prosecution. He asked his hearers to judge him by his actions, not to hate him because of his long hair (an aristocratic fashion). Finally, he defended his action in speaking before the people at a comparatively young age, recalling how his ancestors had always participated in the affairs of the polis and observing that his hearers had a good opinion only of men of that kind.

Some intensification of anti-aristocratic feeling would be consistent with such information as we have about the origins of Athenian leaders in the years

---

[101] Lys. 34 (and the summary of Dion. Hal.), Jones 80; see ch. 8 n. 113 on the 'revision of the laws' completed by 400/399.   [102] Thuc. 6.16; see ch. 5.4.   [103] Lys. 16.

down to 322 when oligarchic forces, assisted by external circumstances, excluded probably some 22,000 of the 31,000 citizens on the basis that their property was less than 2,000 drakhmai. In the earlier part of the fourth century there seems to have been, unless we are to regard Plato as the exception, considerable disenchantment among the old families with the conduct of public affairs and a tendency to decide, against what would have been the expectation of most but not all men from aristocratic or very wealthy families, not to engage in public life.[104] The sons of aristocratic families did not entirely withdraw from public life: one of the few who attained to a leading position in fourth-century Athens was Lykourgos.[105] That however was in the years after the defeat at Khaironeia (338 B.C.) when there are signs of conservative tendencies in Athens, including a tendency for private funding of public utilities to re-emerge.[106] Belonging as he did to one of the old priestly families of Athens and with a grandfather who had been active in public life during the Peloponnesian War, Lykourgos was adept in financial management and in administration, and these qualities along with his oratorical ability rather than his family origins lay behind his prominence.

By the late fifth century and early fourth, then, it was clear that good birth was not necessary for an ambitious Athenian youth. But was Perikles right in claiming that poverty was not a bar? About the socio-economic position of many Athenians who appear on the scene in the fifth century and the fourth, whether as arkhons, strategoi or other officials, or as speakers in the assembly, we have no information. But for those about whom we have some information it would seem to be generally true that a measure of wealth, whether inherited or acquired, was necessary for those who aspired to leadership, both in the fifth century and in the fourth. Some have gone so far as to argue that in the fourth century political leaders were in terms of socio-economic origins drawn from the middle or propertied classes and formed a coherent social class.[107] Certainly there were leaders with substantial inherited wealth. Timotheos inherited not less than 17 talents from his father Konon, and Demosthenes should have received through his guardians an inheritance of not less than 10 talents.[108] A larger number are known to have belonged to the trierarchic class and came from families of moderate wealth. Such were Thrasyboulos of Steiria, who took a leading part in restoring democracy in 403/2 and who exercised considerable influence in Athens during the next fifteen years, and Kallistratos whose oratorical ability Demosthenes praised and whose financial expertise may be discerned in the 370s and 360s.[109]

But among political leaders there were some who came from poor

---

[104] See Appendix ID; Pl. *Ep.* 7.324b–326b, Finley (1968) 73–88; [Pl.] *Ax.* 368d–369b; compare, a generation earlier, Kharmides (Xen. *Mem.* 3.7); see ch. 8.1 and Connor 175–94; cf. MacKendrick (1969).   [105] *PA* 9251, *APF* 348–50.   [106] Mitchel (1970); Davies 91–2.

[107] Perlman (1963) 327–55; cf. Hansen (1983B) 151–80.

[108] *APF* 506–10, 118–35.   [109] *APF* 240, 280.

backgrounds. Demosthenes is far from a reliable witness for his rival Aiskhines, but there may be a grain of truth in the orator's claim that Aiskhines was a rich man who had been a beggar. He is said later to have inherited 5 talents from his brother-in-law and to have acquired a great deal of wealth through political bribes. Though some doubt may remain about Aiskhines' poverty and the extent of his later wealth, no doubt attaches to Demades who came from a poor family but acquired a considerable fortune, mainly through political bribes.[110]

What seems to emerge, then, is that whatever a man's socio-economic origins, an Athenian had to have inherited or himself acquired resources of some extent in order to sustain political ambitions. A similar situation seems to have pertained with those who tended to concentrate their energies on military activity. A background of a well-to-do family or a family with experience in the strategia was undoubtedly an advantage. Khabrias, the victor in the decisive naval battle of Naxos in 376, seems to have been one of those whose father had been wealthy enough to be called on to undertake the trierarchy. Iphikrates on the other hand was the son of a cobbler and was certainly self-conscious about his social origins, but the material rewards gained from his successes as a military commander, whether in Athenian service or not, must have been considerable.[111]

Apart from socio-economic background, the character of Athenian leadership was affected by the tendency to specialisation. By the mid-fourth century it appeared as if public men had distributed among themselves the work of the general and that of speaking in the assembly. One factor in this tendency, as we have seen, may be discerned in the second half of the fifth century – concentration on, and instruction in, the skills of public speaking. The tendency towards a separation of military and political leadership can clearly be traced in the careers of many of Athens' generals in the fourth century. Men like Iphikrates, Khares, Kharidemos and Diopeithes of Sounion, for example, concentrated their energies on military activity, and when there was no opportunity for the employment of their talents by Athens they would enlist in the service of the Persians, Thracian rulers or other foreign powers.[112] At the level of the rank-and-file the citizen hoplite found it more difficult to compete with the highly trained mercenary soldier, and at the level of command

---

[110] *APF* 547, 100–1.

[111] *APF* 560–1 (though Theophrastos named Khabrias and Iphikrates as examples of true leaders who would have been prevented by a property qualification from becoming strategoi – *De Elig. Mag.* Vat. Gr. 2306, fr. B.18–36 (Keaney and Szegedy-Maszak (1976) 231)), *APF* 248. On the qualities or qualifications desirable in strategoi, see Arist. *Pol.* 1309a33–b6 (experience more important than 'virtue' (*aretē*)) and Theophr. *De Elig. Mag.* Vat. Gr. 2306, fr. B.36–88, 105–29 (Keaney and Szegedy-Maszak (1976) 231–3) ('virtue', financial resources, experience, loyalty) and 172–8 (the desirability of serving as infantry commander (taxiarch) or cavalry commander (phylarch) before becoming a strategos); see Xen. *Mem.* 1.7.3, 3.1–5, especially 3.4.1.

[112] Plut. *Phok.* 7.3; Lys. 13.7, Isok. 8.54–5, Aiskhin. 2.184, 3.146, Dem. 18.170, 205; see ch. 2.3.1; Jones 128, Perlman (1963) 347 and n. 105, and (1967) 169–76, Hansen (1983A) 49–53; see ch. 6.5 and n. 77.

consistent employment was likely to engender a higher degree of competence and success.

It must be noted, however, that in the generation or two before Iphikrates there were 'professional' generals or certainly forerunners of the postulated fourth-century type. Phormion, the skilled naval tactician of Perikles' time, Demosthenes the dashing commander of the 420s and Lamakhos, the 'professional' appointed along with Nikias and Alkibiades to command the great Sicilian expedition, indicate that concentration on military affairs was not novel in the fourth century, though it did become more pronounced.

In the political sphere expertise in financial management might also, as in the case of Kallistratos, be a strong basis for political leadership. In the fourth century, the absence of imperial revenues which in the 430s had brought in some 600 talents each year meant that Athens was plagued by weakness in financial resources. In those circumstances the reform of the system of property tax in 378/7 was of fundamental importance, but it was not until the 350s that we have clear evidence of attempts to coordinate the various bodies responsible for expenditure of resources in the Athenian state.[113] Euboulos or his associates then established the Festival Fund Commission and carried a law that all annual surpluses be automatically paid into the Festival or Theoric Fund. This Commission, according to Euboulos' associate Aiskhines, acquired such power, because of the trust which the Athenians placed in Euboulos, that it had almost the whole administration of the state in its hands. In the next generation control of the purse strings was the foundation for the influence of Lykourgos, but for him, as for Kallistratos, ability to persuade the Ekklesia was of high importance.[114] But unlike him, there is no evidence to indicate that Euboulos, Demosthenes or Lykourgos was ever elected to the strategia.

Kallistratos, however, was not the only fourth-century leader to engage in both political and military activity. Another was Timotheos who was one of the most successful of Athens' commanders in the second quarter of the fourth century. But competent speaker though he may have been, he was less successful in the political sphere – because according to his teacher Isokrates, he failed or refused to curry favour with the Demos.[115] Phokion, who is said to have been elected general 45 times but who also participated actively in the Ekklesia, is another example which warns against exaggerating the fourth-century tendency for a separation between military and political leaders.[116] But the value of cooperation between those who concentrated on political affairs and those who were primarily generals can be demonstrated from the

---

[113] Polyb. 2.62.6–7.

[114] Aiskhin. 3.25; *AP* 43.1 (and *CAAP*); Buchanan (1962) 53–60, Cawkwell (1963A) 54–61, Rhodes 105–8, 235–40; [Plut.] *Mor.* 841b–c, Mitchel (1962) 213–29.

[115] Isok. 15.130–9; see ch. 7.1.

[116] Plut. *Phok.* 7.3 attributes to Phokion the intention of combining the work of the orator and general as Perikles, Aristeides and Solon had done.

relationships between Kallistratos, Khabrias and Iphikrates in the 370s and 360s.[117]

2.3.3 *Socio-economic factors; avenues for influence*

In summary, two things should be stressed about the ways in which Athenian citizens exploited their public opportunities in the fifth and fourth centuries. First, in socio-economic terms, it is clear that aspirants for leadership were drawn from wider sections of Athenian society as the implications of full democracy worked themselves out. In the early fifth century leaders were very much drawn from the old aristocratic families: family ties and marriage ties were important for would-be leaders. The deference shown to these families seems to have lingered, with something of a set-back in the period after the overthrow of the Thirty. But in the late fifth century men like Kleon could achieve political pre-eminence, to the chagrin of those who associated leadership with 'the better people' or 'the well-known people'. By now, inherited qualifications such as high birth or wealth were somewhat less important: as the comic poet Eupolis put it (in the last third of the fifth century), 'we old 'uns chose those . . . who were first in wealth and breeding'.[118] Non-inherited qualifications such as the ability to speak in public assembly and in court, skill in military command, administrative capacity, financial expertise or discernment in policy-making were not limited to those 'of good family'. These skills, largely supplanting 'expenditure', constituted what Davies has called 'the democratic power-base'. A measure of wealth nevertheless remained necessary for the man who wished to engage actively in public life, but for the able and ambitious among the poor there were means – whether political bribes or booty or high pay for military service in foreign employ – of acquiring resources. In the 340s Aiskhines could rightly assert that those who worked at a trade – and those who lacked ancestors who had served as strategoi – were not excluded from addressing the assembly, but the implication of his remarks was that it was unusual for such men to do so.[119]

Secondly, there were marked shifts in the avenues for exercising influence and these may be seen reflected in the development of the strategia in the fifth and fourth centuries. At the beginning of the fifth century the ten strategoi were the commanders of the ten tribal regiments and were subordinate to the polemarch (the commander in war).[120] From 487/6 the method of selection of the polemarch and the other arkhons was changed from voting to use of the Lot, while the strategoi continued to be selected by vote. That is, the polemarch could no longer be sure of the extent of his support among the people at large and in time the influence of holders of the office was certain to diminish, especially when command of the army passed to the strategoi.

---

[117] Sealey 133–63 and see ch. 7.1.   [118] Eup. fr. 103.
[119] Davies 114–22; Aiskhin. 1.27, Dem. 19.237.
[120] *AP* 22.2; Hignett 170–2, Fornara (1971A) 6, 72–3.

External events – the invasion of Xerxes and the assumption by Athens of leadership in the Delian League – not only made those responsible for the security of Athens more important but also widened the responsibilities of the strategoi. In particular, the navy – which at the beginning of the century numbered about 50 ships, was dramatically increased to 200 in the late 480s and stood at 300 ready for active service in 431 – was extensively used in the operations of the Delian League under the command of Athenian strategoi. The intimate connection of the strategoi with maintaining the Athenian alliance involved them in the management of large financial outlays, but also gave them considerable political importance.[121] The careers of Kimon and Perikles bear eloquent testimony to this. Prolonged absences from Athens, however, might adversely affect a general's political influence, leading him to concentrate on military affairs and/or to seek association with a person wielding political influence. This assisted the emergence of 'professional' generals.

The tendency for a separation of military and political functions, the growing 'professionalisation' of warfare and of political activity in the fourth century, and the crucial importance of finance and financial advisers seriously diminished the political significance of the strategia and encouraged a narrowing of its responsibilities. By the 320s five of the strategoi were assigned specific duties – one was appointed commander of the hoplites and led them on foreign expeditions, another commanded operations within Attike, two were responsible for the defence of the Peiraieus, another superintended the trierarchic symmories – while five were available to meet situations as they arose.[122]

In short, the character of the strategia had come almost full circle – from a military office, through a period in which it held great political potential, back to a role which was primarily military. And during these two centuries, depending on their backgrounds, their resources and their particular abilities, individual Athenians who sought to exploit the opportunities provided by citizen status might find the strategia more or less conducive in their pursuit of power and influence. But real political influence rested in all periods on the ability to carry the Ekklesia, not least through an individual's own ability to convince a mass assembly. Beside military command, financial expertise and cooperation with other leaders and their supporters proved important assets for exercising political influence.

---

121 See for example *IG* I³.71 (ML 69).44–50 (425/4 B.C.).
122 *AP* 61.1 (and *CAAP* on the symmories); cf. Dem. 4.26; see ch. 3.4 for the symmories instituted in 357.

3 The responsibilities of the citizen

3.1 Family and local interests and responsibilities

Certain obligations were specifically associated with Athenian citizenship, such as personal service in the armed forces and, in the case of the propertied classes, financial levies, but there was also a vast range of responsibilities which were implicit in membership of the polis. These might be interpreted in different ways by the individual. The friends of Sokrates, for example, when he had been condemned to death on a charge of impiety and corrupting the youth, urged him to escape and to live in exile. Not a few Athenians chose exile when under political or judicial attack, and, in fact, exile was a penalty which could be imposed by law. But Sokrates at his trial declined that legal alternative and also rejected the pleas of Kriton to escape from prison. He argued that all his life he had enjoyed the protection and benefit of the laws and that he must not now seek to evade them and so destroy them and the whole polis.[1] Not all Athenians would have fully shared the high-minded attitude of Sokrates, but in theory they would have endorsed the notion of obedience to the laws, for they shared with other Greeks a deep conviction that the laws, not the whim of a despot like the Persian king, were their master and that obedience to the laws was fundamental for the well-being of their polis.[2] In practice, conflicting demands might lead a citizen to disobey or set limitations on his legal obligations – or his wider responsibilities. For, while Athenians attached great importance to the fact that they had written laws, they were also conscious of the force of 'unwritten law'. In the relatively small community that the Athenian polis was, conventions and moral and social values continued to be very powerful forces, notwithstanding the challenge to many traditional values in the second half of the fifth century arising partly from the intellectual revolution associated with the sophists and partly from the pressures of life in Athens during the Peloponnesian War.[3] What is considered in this chapter, therefore, is the range of activities in which citizens felt moved to take part, albeit with varying degrees of 'compulsion' and with some marked differences in enthusiasm and in the degree of participation.

[1] Pl. *Kri.* 50a–54d.
[2] Solon fr. 3 (Diehl) (on *eunomia*), Hdt. 7.104, Thuc. 2.37.3, Dem. 24.210, Lykourg. *Leok.* 2–4.
[3] See, for example, Pearson (1962), Adkins (1972), Dover, and Fisher (1976).

Within the wide range of responsibilities, our concern will rest mainly with those which had a direct bearing on the role of the individual as a citizen (*politēs*) in relation to the polis. The maintenance of the *oikos* (the 'house' or the family living together in the house) was fundamental to the thinking of Athenians – a responsibility that owed its strength to the desire to continue the family and its property, to the respect for ancestors, to the devotion to the hearth and the household gods.[4] In the maintenance of the oikos Athenian women made a crucial contribution, and not simply in terms of what was regarded as their primary role – child-bearing and child-rearing.[5] In economic terms, women in well-to-do families supervised household affairs and the work of slaves, including the making of clothes and other necessities. In the case of the poor, Athenian women themselves carried out these household tasks, though they might also be forced by poverty to work outside the house – selling goods in the Agora for example.[6] In the political life of the city, Athenian women played no direct part, and their indirect influence, while not negligible, is very difficult to gauge.[7] The citizen family was, as we have seen, the vehicle for admission to the coveted citizenship, and on the well-being of the family depended the supply of citizens who could share in the life of the polis, and not least in its defence. The Athenian polis and its various agencies were therefore interested not only in the qualifications for citizenship and the enforcement of the law on that matter, but also in many matters relating to the family and to marriage.[8] The character of the obligations and responsibilities which related to the family might be illustrated by reference to two or three questions. A man's responsibility to preserve the family property, for example, is indicated by the possibility of legal action on the grounds of idleness or insanity which might diminish or dissipate the property. An Athenian was not required by law to give a dowry, though the sanction of custom operated very strongly in this matter, and the person controlling a woman's dowry was responsible for her maintenance. A citizen who as *kyrios* (lord) had control over a woman or a child assumed responsibility for their care and maintenance.[9] Plutarch attributed to Solon a law requiring a man to teach his son a trade on pain of not being supported by his son in old age, while Sokrates refers to laws requiring a father to instruct his son in *mousikē* (music and literary skills) and gymnastics.[10] The 'laws' referred to by Sokrates

---

[4] See *AP* 55.3 quoted in ch. 4.1.
[5] On the oikos and other aspects of family life, see Lacey (1968) chs. 4–7, and on the controversial question of the position of women see, for example, Gomme (1937) 89–115, Seltman (1957) 87–119, Pomeroy (1975) and (1973) 127–52, and Schaps (1979).
[6] Contrast the wife of the well-to-do Iskhomakhos (as portrayed in Xen. *Oik.* 7) and the mother of Euxitheos (Dem. 57.30–4, 45).
[7] See [Dem.] 59.108–13, 122.
[8] See *AP* 56.6–7, Harrison 1 (*passim*) and MacDowell 84–108 for obligations arising from the citizen's control of dependants and for questions relating to marriage, succession, orphans and *epiklēroi* ('notional heiresses').
[9] Harrison 1.45–60, 78–81; cf. Pomeroy (1982) 131–3.
[10] Plut. *Sol.* 22, Pl. *Kri.* 50d (cf. 45c–d).

would seem, however, to rely on the force of custom, not law. The Athenian polis as such appears to have taken little close interest in the upbringing or education of the young, and though wealthier citizens could afford to send their children for formal instruction by (private) teachers, in most Athenian families children were probably very largely dependent on what they learnt more or less informally from the father or the mother or others living in the house.[11]

The family and its well-being, or indeed its survival, may have largely absorbed the energies of some *politai*, but even those living close to subsistence level would usually have taken an active interest in their immediate locality – the deme. In the rural parts of Attike a pattern of nucleated settlement or village communities was well established by the sixth century, and Kleisthenes had been able to utilise these rural demes and indeed such identifiable 'villages' as existed within the area known as the City. For a great many Athenians these rural demes, which constituted relatively independent social groups, would in the fourth century have continued to be the centre of their life.[12] A rich and varied programme of festivals, for example, was provided in the demes, with sacrifices for local heroes and cults but also for cults of the Olympian deities. Among the Olympian deities Zeus and Apollo seem to have been prominent, more prominent in some demes than Athena who was the protecting deity of the polis as a whole, while among other gods and heroes Herakles and Pan were widely worshipped.[13] Particularly widespread and important in the rural demes was the Rural Dionysia in honour of Dionysos the god of wine: in origin it may well have been a fertility festival like the other widely celebrated festival of the 'ritual ploughing'.[14] These local cults and festivals continued to be focal points in the religious and cultural life of the demes, and the responsibility for maintaining many or most of them, whether from deme funds or through liturgies, rested with the demes as such.[15] The deme assembly also administered the property held by the deme and supervised deme affairs. The demes, and in

---

[11] Pl. *Alk.*1.122b, Aiskhin. 1.9–11 (laws of 'Solon' which were apocryphal or were no longer observed in the fourth century). On Athenian education in general, see Marrou (1956) 36–60 and Beck (1964) 72–146.

[12] Thuc. 2.16 (430s); D. M. Lewis (1963B) 724, W. E. Thompson (1971) 72–9, R. Osborne 15–46, 72–92, 127–53, Whitehead 5–38.

[13] See the sacred calendars of the demes (e.g., *IG* ii².1358 (Marathon), Daux (1963) 603–34 (and *BCH* 88 (1964), 676–7) (Erkhia) and Daux (1983) 150–74 (Thorikos)), Dow (1968) 170–86, Parke 175–82 and Mikalson (1977) 424–35; R. Osborne 154–82, Whitehead 185–208. Erkhia which may be regarded as a typical deme in the fourth century had 35 separate cult sites including altars and designated 25 days each year for annual sacrifices financed by or through the deme. Most of the local cults and festivals seem to have been separate and independent from the polis cults and festivals, and the demes do not appear to have normally provided local observances of the major polis festivals (Mikalson (1977) 428, cf. Whitehead 187 n. 63). The only 'polis' festivals which were observed at deme level may have been those which related to the family and were celebrated by women, to judge from the Theogamia (a festival of Hera as protectress of marriage and perhaps celebrated exclusively by women – Mikalson (1975B) 189).

[14] Mikalson (1977) 433–4; Ar. *Akh.* 247–79, Pl. *Rep.* 475d.

[15] Theophr. *Char.* 10.11 (the Mean Man serves small slices of meat when giving a feast for his fellow demesmen); Whitehead 176–222.

particular the demarchs, were moreover responsible for keeping the lists of citizens and a property register which served as a basis for establishing an individual's liability for property tax and for liturgies. From the 139 demes members of the Boule of 500 were drawn, broadly it would seem in proportion to their citizen population (or possibly their hoplite numbers). Many demes had only one or two bouleutai while the largest deme of Akharnai is known in the fourth century to have had 22. It was the bouleutai and the demarch who, along with men of property (with their greater opportunity to participate actively in the life of the polis), constituted the most important links with the polis as a whole.[16]

The vitality of Athenian life was, in short, directly related to the willingness of Athenian citizens to participate in the life of their deme and through it to accept also the wider responsibilities of the polis at large. Some were alleged by Euxitheos, the speaker in Demosthenes 57, to have been active in deme affairs for the sake of financial gain, others to have been negligent and incompetent, others to have adopted fraudulent practices in their pursuit of local rivalries and animosities.[17] Allegations in law suits are notoriously difficult to evaluate. So, too, are assertions which seem to be intended to win the support of the jurors. There may be some truth in Euxitheos' assertion that the deme of Halimous was at the time more corrupt than any other, though it is difficult to give any credence to his assertion that the malpractices directed against him were not known in large demes. On the other hand, Euxitheos seems, when demarch himself earlier, to have antagonised some of his fellow demesmen and in the interplay of local politics these men may have been willing to conspire with Euxitheos' enemy, the current demarch.[18]

The demes were also the basic units on which the structure of ten tribes was built by Kleisthenes. The ten tribes were still in the 320s the vehicle for the citizen to undertake some of his wider obligations and responsibilities. The hoplites, for example, were still organised in units according to tribes, with the taxiarchs (hoplite commanders) and phylarchs (cavalry commanders) being elected, one from each tribe. But they were now elected by the whole people, not the tribal assemblies, while the strategoi were similarly elected by the whole people who might, moreover, select two or more strategoi from one tribe to the exclusion of other tribes in that year.[19] The sense of cooperation and unity engendered by military service in tribal units was one of the important links in the integration of citizens from demes scattered throughout Attike into the

---

[16] *AP* 21.5, 42.1; cf. Rhodes 8–12, Traill 19, 56–8, 64–103, Davies (1979) 151–6, R. Osborne 72–92, Whitehead 17–23, 58–61, 86–175, 255–326. For the participation of citizens in other institutions, see, for example, three decrees of the phratry of the Demotionidai (*IG* II².1237).

[17] Dem. 57, especially 2, 6–8, 13 (probably 346/5 B.C.), and cf. *AP* 62.1 for a change (probably *c.* 370–*c.* 362) in electoral procedures to prevent selling of offices by the demes (see Kroll 91–4, Whitehead 287–90); R. Osborne 147–51, Whitehead 88–90, 106–8.

[18] Dem. 57.57–64; Dein. fr. A7, Anaxandrides fr. 4; Whitehead 292–301.

[19] *AP* 61.1 (and *CAAP*); Piérart (1974) 125–46, Hansen 119–21; cf. Fornara (1971A) 19–27.

polis. The tribes as such played a part in other areas. They shared for example in the (re)construction of the city walls and appointed Commissioners of Walls to supervise the work. The competitions for dithyrambs in both the men's and the boys' classes at the Dionysia and the Thargelia were between the tribes, and the successful khoregos, who had been chosen by his tribe to represent it and who selected his chorus from among the members of his tribe, received a tripod which he set up at his own expense. The 50 bouleutai from each tribe served in turn as a standing committee of the Council of 500, while from each of the tribes in turn were selected by lot the nine arkhons and their secretary.[20]

3.2 Religious cults and festivals

The obligations and responsibilities of the citizen at the polis level may be viewed, for convenience, under the broad categories of religious, military, financial, judicial and political. These categories, however, should not be given an existence or reality of their own, nor should the terms 'obligations' and 'responsibilities' be interpreted too narrowly. This may be seen, for example, in regard to cults and festivals. Most of these had developed in archaic Attike in close association with traditional agrarian pursuits and the inhabitants sought, by means of rites and ceremonies, to win the protection and aid of the gods against want, plague and enemies. For a whole complex of personal, religious and social reasons Athenians living in the countryside continued in our period to join in the celebration of local cults and festivals. Beyond the deme itself the demesmen might take part in the occasional festival involving a group of demes in one area, they might make a special expedition to Athens (as demesmen from Erkhia did in midsummer) to offer sacrifices on a specified day to a number of deities, or they might join in the sacrifice to Zeus Meilikhios at the Diasia in Agrai, where (somewhat unusually) all the demes gathered for the festival.[21] The local cults and festivals presumably engaged most Athenians living in the country to a greater extent than those festivals beyond their deme and even the great national festivals held in Athens such as the Panathenaic festival. On the other hand, no local religious activities are attested in the demes during major state festivals such as the Panathenaia, the Eleusinian Mysteries, the Anthesteria (the festival of flowers), the Lenaia (a festival in honour of Dionysos featuring dramatic performances) or, with some minor exceptions, the City Dionysia (featuring the performance of tragedies, comedies and lyric choruses).[22] With

[20] *IG* ii².1658.1 (394/3 B.C.) and 1660.1–3 (393/2); *IG* ii².244.28–36 (337/6): cf. Aiskhin. 3.14, 28–30. See *AP* 56.3, Pickard-Cambridge (1968) 75–8; *AP* 43.2, 55.1.

[21] Mikalson (1977) 429–32, Parke 176–7, Thuc. 1.126.6.

[22] Mikalson (1977) 428, Parke 29–169, Pickard-Cambridge (1968) 1–125; and for war festivals see Pritchett 3.154–229. On the number and the importance of festivals in Athenian life, see Thuc. 2.38, [Xen.] *AP* 3.2, 8, Xen. *Hell.* 2.4.20.

no local counter-attractions large numbers of country demesmen would have joined the inhabitants of Athens in the excitement and magnificent spectacle of the major festivals financed and supervised by the polis itself, but especially the Panathenaia. This was a festival of several days held in midsummer after the harvest when Athenians gathered to honour their protecting deity, Athena Polias, with a festival of singing and dancing, a procession, sacrifices and musical contests. The highlight was the procession which began at dawn from the Dipylon Gate and passed through the Agora up to the Akropolis, and it is this procession which was depicted on the 160-metre-long frieze of the Parthenon. Every fourth year the festival was celebrated with special splendour. At the quadrennial Greater Panathenaia the contests included foot-races, horse- and chariot-races, the pentathlon, wrestling and boxing: for the victors the prize was oil from the sacred olive trees stored in amphorae (jars) bearing a representation of Athena and a representation of the particular contest. The Panathenaic festival was especially promoted, and exploited, for religious–political purposes by the Athenians as they promoted Athens as the centre of their alliance in the fifth century.[23] The Panathenaia, in short, while growing out of the physical needs of an agrarian community, reflected the political and social significance of Athena who dwelt on the Akropolis and protected the polis.[24] Out of inherited myth and cult, a new official, somewhat 'secularised' worship had developed, evoking a pride in the city as well as reverence for the goddess. A whole range of motives might therefore lead the Athenian citizen – from Athens, the Peiraieus or even a remote deme in north-east Attike – to celebrate the Panathenaia, while there is a sense in which the magnificent spectacle and the lavish sacrifices may well be regarded as valuable for purposes of 'social control'. The meat distributed after the sacrifices was otherwise rarely included in the diet of most Athenians.[25]

3.3 The obligations of military service

Of all the citizen's responsibilities the military was in many ways paramount. Traditionally, the ability to arm oneself as a hoplite and to defend the polis –

---

23 *IG* I³.14 (ML 40).2–8 (Erythrai, 453/2 B.C. (?)), I³.34 (ML 46).41–3 (*c.* 447 (?)), I³.71 (ML 69).54–8 (425/4); Meiggs 291–305 and Barron (1964) 35–48.

24 The inextricable blend of 'religious' and 'political' matters is reflected in the fact that in the 320s (*AP* 43.6) three questions relating to sacred matters were to be discussed at two of the regular meetings of the Ekklesia each prytany and in the multitude of matters that came before the Ekklesia ranging from detailed regulations about the offering of first-fruits at Eleusis (*IG* I³.78 (ML 73)) to the election of 'religious' officials (*AP* 54.6–8; cf. 56.3–5, 57.1, 58.1, 60.1) and a major reorganisation of the temple treasures (cf. *IG* I³.52 (ML 58)).

25 See D. M. Lewis (1959) 239–47 (*SEG* 18.13) for a law of 336–34 providing regular funds for the celebration of the Lesser Panathenaia and *IG* II².334.25–7 (a decree relating to the same festival and inscribed on the same stone as the law) specifying that portions of the meat are to be distributed 'to each deme in proportion to the number in the procession provided by each deme'.

that is, the physical ability and financial ability – in a sense constituted the fully qualified citizen.[26] Military service was, in Greek poleis generally, the privilege as much as the obligation of those who possessed sufficient property. Hoplites were regularly drawn from the top three census classes of Athenian male citizens aged between 18 and 59. In the fifth century and the first half of the fourth century hoplite service seems to have been based on the notion of serving 'in turn', with the strategoi expected to conscript first those who had not already served on an expedition, but able also to include volunteers and the more experienced. In the second half of the fourth century citizens were called up by age groups: the age for active service was adjusted to the needs of the situation, with the 20–29 and 30–39 groups first to serve.[27]

In the 320s the Athenian polis was taking a direct interest in the training of eighteen- and nineteen-year-old youths (*ephēboi*). Presumably the epheboi had for long been required to do garrison duty within Attike and there had been some form of basic instruction in fighting together as hoplites. The *ephēbeia* (or systematic organisation of such training) as described by the author of the *Athenaion Politeia* cannot, however, with certainty be pushed back beyond the mid-330s.[28] In marked contrast to the control and supervision exercised by the Spartan polis over the life and upbringing of boys and girls from the age of seven, the ephebeia seems to have been the limit of the Athenian state's direct interest in the training of the young. What the polis expected of its epheboi (and citizen soldiers) is indicated in the oath sworn by Athenian epheboi of the later fourth century and preserved in an inscription from Akharnai:

I will not bring dishonour on my sacred arms nor will I abandon my comrade wherever I shall be stationed. I will defend the rights of gods and men and will not leave my native land smaller, when I die, but greater and better, so far as I am able by myself and with the help of all. I will respect the rulers of the time duly and the existing ordinances duly and all others which may be established in the future. And if anyone seeks to destroy the ordinances I will oppose him so far as I am able myself and with the help of all. I will honour the cults of my fathers. Witnesses to this shall be the gods Agraulos, Hestia, Enyo, Enyalios, Ares and Athena the Warrior, Zeus, Thallo, Auxo, Hegemone, Herakles, and the boundaries of my native land, wheat, barley, vines, olive trees and fig trees.[29]

---

26 This notion was particularly dear to the hearts of the moderate oligarchs of the late fifth century: Thuc. 8.65.3. See Ridley (1979) 510–22.

27 Lys. 9.4, 15, Aiskhin. 2.167–8, *AP* 26.1 (and *CAAP*), 53.7; Andrewes (1981) 1–3, Hansen (1986) 83–9; cf. Jones 163.

28 See *AP* 42 (and *CAAP* and Rhodes (1980B); cf. Ruschenbusch (1979B) and (1981A) accepting the implication of *AP* that thetes were included) and Marrou (1956) 105–7 for the organisation and (essentially military) content of ephebic training. In the second year the young men gave a public display of their military skill and received from the polis, it is interesting to note, shield and spear before undertaking patrol duties in the country. On hoplite training see Ridley (1979) 530–48 and on the date of the institution of the formal system of full-time national service see D. M. Lewis (1973B) 254–5 and Mitchel (1975) 233–43; cf. Pélékidis (1962) 7–79 and Reinmuth (1952) 34–50 and (1971) 123–38; see Mitchel (1970) 37–9.

29 Tod 204 (and commentary) (cf. Lykourg. *Leok.* 76 Loeb tr. adapted); Siewert (1977) 102–11 analyses the origins of elements in the oath.

The defence of the polis by citizens armed as hoplites was then a traditional obligation. While exemptions were allowed – for example, to officials, members of the Boule and those who had contracted to collect the 2% tax on grain as well as the unfit – avoidance of military service, desertion and cowardice were damaging charges against an individual.[30] Athens' power in our period was, however, based on its navy – the rowers and the smaller numbers of marines carried on a trireme – rather than on her hoplite army. Hoplites served as rowers when the need arose but most of the Athenian citizens who rowed in the fleet were from the thetic class. The developments of the fifth century, both external and internal, made them conscious of their increasing role and power in Athens and they are reported as ever eager for service in the fleet.[31] Apart from the crisis in 428 caused by the revolt of Mytilene and the crisis before the battle of Arginousai in 406, we hear of no real problems in manning the triremes during the fifth century and no other indications of a need to conscript crews. But from the fourth century there are reports – some of them perhaps exaggerated in order to highlight the efforts of a trierarch – of difficulties in recruiting sailors and in keeping them. In an emergency in 362 the assembly voted that 'the councillors and demarchs should make out muster-rolls (*katalogoi*) of the demesmen and hand in a list of sailors' so that the expedition could proceed without delay. After 362 the conscription of thetes seems to have become a common or perhaps a regular practice.[32]

By the mid-fourth century Athens was making considerable use of mercenary troops, not only peltasts or light-armed soldiers but also hoplites.[33] Some contemporaries made much of this. Demosthenes repeatedly contrasted the reluctance of citizens to serve in person with the attitudes of their ancestors. In the mid-350s Isokrates claimed that, in the good old days, 'when the Athenians manned their triremes they put on board foreigners and slaves but sent out citizens to fight as hoplites, whereas now we use mercenaries as hoplites but compel citizens to row the ships'.[34] True, Athens in the fourth century, as we have seen, did have to rely very heavily on citizen rowers, in part at least because of the decline in the number of metics. Yet Isokrates' assertion, with the rhetorical flourish of a writer not noted for his concern for historical exactitude, and Demosthenes' strictures, which were designed to stir the Athenians to

---

[30] Lys. 14. esp. 4–15, [Dem.] 59.27.

[31] [Xen.] *AP* 1.2, 2.14; Thuc. 3.18.3–4; Arist. *Pol.* 1274a5–21 and *AP* 27.1. See ch. 2.2 for metic rowers, but in the mid-fourth century the number of metics was much smaller than it had been in the late fifth (cf. Xen. *Poroi*).

[32] Thuc. 3.16.1, Xen. *Hell.* 1.6.24; [Dem.] 50.6–7, 16; Dem. 3.4, Aiskhin. 2.133; see also Thuc. 6.43; Amit (1965) 48–9, Jordan (1975) 102–3, 225–6, Hansen (1986) 22–4. On the contribution of Athenian hoplites see Ridley (1979) 522–7.

[33] Hoplites were hired during the Peloponnesian War, but almost exclusively by the enemies of Athens (Thuc. 1.60.1, 4.80.5; 6.43; 7.27.1, 29–30; Parke (1933) 15–18); see also Thuc. 1.31, 143.

[34] Dem. *Olynthiacs* and *Philippics*; Isok. 8.48 and see 8.41–8, but contrast 7.54.

adopt his policies, cannot be accepted as portraying fully or accurately the attitudes of citizens to their obligations to defend the polis. These attitudes have been much discussed and some aspects must be considered briefly here.[35]

First, Athenians' attitudes to military service were more than an aggregation or a balancing of their assessments of how war might affect them as individuals. At that level it was common to portray 'the poor' as having a vested interest in war in that it gave them employment, but it would seem rather to be the case that for 'the better men' who made these charges war was likely, but not certain, to be less welcome, for it might involve risk to those who had farms most vulnerable to invasions of Attike and it would involve them in heavier expenses through more frequent or more onerous terms as trierarchs or through levies of property tax.[36] As for the ordinary sailors and soldiers, the usual rate of pay in the Peloponnesian War period was probably 1 drakhme a day until after the Sicilian disaster when it was halved.[37] Some poor men thereby gained employment and support which they might otherwise have found difficult to obtain. Moreover, during the Peloponnesian War large numbers of Athenians often did not have access to their land and would have been eager to get out of the crowded city, especially if there was a prospect of booty in addition to military pay. Still, for many the neglect of their ordinary occupations, even when the rate was 1 drakhme, would have been a serious matter. The Athenian citizen serving as hoplite or sailor did not, however, conceive war purely or even predominantly in mercenary or immediate economic terms. In a sense he was habituated to war, for there were few periods of any length in which the Athenian state was not involved in war: the security and interests of Athens and her citizens were constantly protected or advanced by force rather than diplomacy. In consequence, though some sections of the citizen body, and at times even a substantial number, might desire peace in certain circumstances (for example, during the Arkhidamian War), citizens in general seem to have readily accepted personal service as hoplites or as rowers.[38] At the individual level and the level of decision-making in the Ekklesia, it is true that arguments based on advantage were advanced, but arguments based on a threat to Athens and on honour (*timē*) were of fundamental importance, not purely the

---

[35] See, for example, Jones 30–8 and Pritchett 2.104–112.

[36] Cf. [Xen.] *AP* 2.14.

[37] Thuc. 3.17.3–4, 6.8.1, 6.31.3; 8.45.2 (3 obols in 412 B.C., and for 407 see Xen. *Hell.* 1.5.4); Jones 30–2, Dover and Andrewes in *HCT* 4.293, 5.97–9. Cf. Gomme *HCT* 2.275–6 who argues 1 drakhme a day and 1 for their attendants was a special 'hardship' rate for the hoplites besieging Poteidaia, summer and winter, but admits to puzzlement as to why all the sailors at that time (as Thuc. 3.17.4 clearly implies) received the same rate. Pritchett 1.14–24 limits the drakhme rate to the sailors blockading Poteidaia and, like Gomme, regards the rate for the Sicilian expedition (6.31.3, 7.27.2) as a special rate (cf. 6.21–2 regarding the problems arising from a distant or protracted campaign or one involving special difficulties in obtaining food).

[38] Cf. Thuc. 1.70.6–9, 2.41.

ostensible grounds for action.[39] Moreover, decisions in the Ekklesia were not simply related to individuals' assessment of their personal interests, but were concerned with the soundness of the particular proposal in terms of Athens' security and interests and with the means of implementation.

Secondly, in the fourth century expeditions consisting solely or mainly of citizen hoplites were very common and, if the surviving evidence is a reasonable reflection of the actual situation, they were more numerous and more important than expeditions relying heavily on mercenary troops.[40] In the fourth century mercenary troops *were* employed by Athens (though mercenary considerations were not unimportant in the support that its allies gave to it in the fifth century, for example in the Sicilian expedition). Mercenary troops were freely available and were likely to be more highly trained, more experienced and more efficient, if less reliable, than citizen forces.[41] A decision to use mercenaries, while it relieved the citizen of the difficulties and danger of personal service, might on particular occasions be based on good sense and a recognition of the value of using mercenaries who were available, especially for year-long or distant campaigns.[42] The soundness of the decision should therefore be judged against the particular situation, though in the 340s the Athenians perhaps became increasingly prone to employ mercenaries. The orators were no doubt right in suggesting that at times the Athenians were careless of the consequences for their allies and friends and themselves of the use of mercenary troops who received little or no pay from Athens. These troops were therefore dependent on their commander's ability to secure money or supplies from friend as well as foe and to acquire booty and prisoners to be sold or ransomed.[43] These men felt no commitment to Athens' basic interests.

The strictures of Demosthenes also reflect different assessments of what were the appropriate policies for Athens from time to time. In the 350s and 340s citizens in the assembly did show some disinclination to commit themselves to personal service, for example in Thrace and the north Aegean and, in particular, in support of the Khalkidic city of Olynthos when it was threatened by Philip of Makedonia in 349/8.[44] In part this reluctance arose from a different assessment of the threat posed by Philip or the best means of effective opposition, for the

---

[39] See Thuc. 1.75; see also Dem. 24.183–5 dilating on the memory of the achievements of the Athenians of the fifth century and their readiness to expend all Athens' wealth for love of honour (*philotimia*), to pay property tax and to recoil from no danger for the sake of glory (*doxa*) and 18.63–7, 89, 97–101, 199–205, 207, 322 on the striving by Athens in every generation for primacy, honour and glory.   [40] See Pritchett 2.104–10.

[41] Isok. 4.167–8, 5.96, 120–1, 8.24; cf. 7.82–3.

[42] Cf. Dion. Hal. *Amm.* 1.9, Pritchett 2.108–9.

[43] For complaints about the conduct of commanders who were given few or no funds for their troops, see Aiskhin. 2.71–2, Plut. *Phok.* 14.2–3, Dem. 8.21–2, 26–8, and Pritchett 2.34–58, 82–5, 101–2 who argues that the assembly bore the ultimate responsibility for this and that it did supervise its commanders, though (it should be stressed) with varying degrees of seriousness and varying degrees of success; see ch. 6.4. See n. 52 and n. 54.

[44] Dem. 1–3.

protracted military campaigns in the area from the Strymon to the Thracian Khersonesos in the 360s had met with limited lasting success.[45] But when the threat was clear and near at hand, as when Philip seemed about to pass through Thermopylai into central Greece in 352, the Athenians could respond in force and to good effect.[46] Protracted or distant campaigns attracted less support from the citizens, who not only would have to leave their land or neglect their ordinary occupations, but could have little prospect of regular pay or financial recompense unless success gave access to booty.[47] This was a quite different situation from that during the Peloponnesian War. The reluctance to serve might, it is true, be attributed to the interest of the poor (and the Athenians generally) in the two-obol festival payments made to the citizens on some festival days. For the annual surplus which was used for these payments might in the event of war be diverted to military purposes. But the festival payments were of political or symbolic significance rather than of financial importance. In the words of one of the speeches ascribed to Demosthenes, 'the sum of money which you are discussing is small, but the habit of mind which goes with it is important'. For a time Demosthenes urged that the annual surplus of revenues which was paid into the Festival Fund and which made such payments possible should be diverted to the Military Fund. But he finally came to realise that what Demades called 'the glue of the democracy' was not the heart of the matter, or at the very least that his objections to festival payments were counter-productive.[48]

In the fourth century, however, some shift in the balance between devotion to the polis and the interests of the individual does seem to have been taking place and some loss of loyalty to the polis is therefore not to be denied. It is also important, however, to consider the Athenian attitude towards distant or protracted expeditions – not only in the fourth century but also in the fifth. 'Defensive' actions (such as the response to Spartan invasion of Attike as in 445 or in the early years of the Peloponnesian War) or certain 'reactive' expeditions (the suppression of the revolt in Euboia in 446 or the expedition to the island in 357 or the response to the revolt of Mytilene in 428) were undertaken because of compelling military and/or political considerations. The cost of such expeditions does not often seem to have weighed very heavily with the Athenian assembly, though funding could not be ignored, as is clear from the decision to raise 200 talents by a levy of property tax in 428 when Athens was confronted with the Lesbos revolt.[49] But as the character and purpose of an expedition became more 'aggressive' or might require a prolonged or distant campaign, the tendency to expect it to be self-supporting or at least to require a minimum of public money seems to have increased. Even with such expeditions, it is true,

---

45 Cawkwell (1962A) 122–40 and (1963A) 47–67.   46 Dem. 4.17, 19.84.
47 [Dem.] 50.10–14; Isok. 7.82–3; see Dem. 4.28–9 (Griffith (1935) 271–3); cf. Pritchett 1.24–9.
48 Dem. 1.19–20, 3.10–13, 31–3, [Dem.] 10.35–45, 13.2, 10 and 59.4–5, Plut. *Mor.* 1011b, Jones 33–5, Buchanan (1962) 53–74, 83–8, Cawkwell (1963A) 53–61.   49 Thuc. 3.19.1.

imperialist ambitions might lead the assembly to give strong support. The great Sicilian expedition was undertaken, *inter alia*, for dreams of conquest and the prospect not only of money for the present but also of additional dominion which would provide an inexhaustible source of pay (*misthos*).[50] Another critical factor in inducing the Athenians in 416 to give effect to what was not altogether a new ambition was the belief that the expedition could at least be initiated with the 60 talents brought by the Egestaians, who were requesting Athenian intervention and who spoke of an abundance of money in their temples and public treasury.[51]

With what we have called reactive expeditions there was normally an expectation that they would not in any case constitute a financial burden for the Athenian state. Disaffected allies would be required to pay heavy indemnities – Samos was required in 439 to pay back by instalments the cost of the campaign, quite apart from measures designed to limit or remove its capacity to resist Athenian demands in the future. Prospects of booty might for private and state reasons attract support for expeditions (whether reactive or aggressive), while a levy of property tax could, of course, be imposed as need arose, but despite all the complaints by taxpayers, and in a sense because of them, the assembly seems to have accepted limits to utilising this source of funding.[52] The more 'aggressive' the enterprise, the stronger the temptation throughout our period to grant a minimum of public funding. In the fourth century this tendency was strengthened by the almost constant shortage of public funds, for there were no imperial revenues and no reserves such as Athens had at the time of the outbreak of the Peloponnesian War. In some appointments the assembly clearly expected the commander to secure, by diplomacy or force, local support for his activities and to obtain booty.[53] In others the assembly seems to have presumed that the commander would use his own private resources to get an expedition under way and recoup the money by a successful campaign: the appointment of Timotheos in 373 to an expedition to Kerkyra and other appointments of Timotheos strongly suggest that the assembly, when it had inadequate funds or was lukewarm in support of a proposal, was willing to accept a proposal for an expedition but left the responsibility largely with the commander to find the means to give effect to the commission.[54] Citizens who served on such expeditions could therefore not count on regular pay as could their ancestors in the latter part of the fifth century, and they were more dependent on the ability and experience of their commanders, if they were to obtain pay from the proceeds of the sale of booty and prisoners or if they were to gain booty, whether seized by themselves or allotted to them.

---

[50] Thuc. 6.24.   [51] Thuc. 6.8.1–2, Plut. *Alk.* 17.2.
[52] Plut. *Kim.* 13.6; Lys. 28.3–7; Dem. 20.77; Polyainos 3.9.31; Pritchett 1.53–100. See ch. 5.5.
[53] Dem. 8.24–9; de Ste Croix 607 n. 37.
[54] See [Dem.] 49.6, 11, D.S. 15.47.2–3, 7, Isok. 15.109–11, [Arist.] *Oik.* 2.1350b4–15, Polyainos 3.10.5, 9; [Arist.] *Oik.* 2.1350a23–30.

After the frustration of their repeated efforts to regain Amphipolis and their loss of allies and prestige in the Social War (357–355 B.C.), the Athenians in the next generation – the generation when Demosthenes was warning of the danger of Philip – were more circumspect in undertaking military enterprises.[55] Many saw merit in policies like those of Euboulos which paid attention to the financial resources of Athens and perceived its vital interests with clear regard for the finance available. These and other developments therefore contributed to Athenian responses which may give an impression that Athenians in the mid-fourth century were less committed to the defence of the security and interests of their polis than they in fact were. Their responses tended to be less aggressive. Their perceptions of Athenian interests may have been somewhat restrictive.[56] Demosthenes thought so, but he did acknowledge the zeal with which the Athenians responded in 357 to the request of some of the Euboian cities to help them expel the Thebans from the island.[57] If it is objected that the adjacent island of Euboia was of crucial importance to Athens, as the Peloponnesian War had shown, it might be well to add that in 353/2 an expedition was sent to win the Thracian Khersonesos and klerouchs were established at Sestos. In that area, remote from Athens but for long important for the passage of its food imports, the Athenians judged that their interests required action and they so responded.

3.4 Financial obligations

Some citizens – men of wealth or background or ability, men motivated by love of honour or ambition (*philotimia*) or by other considerations – fulfilled their responsibilities by serving as company commanders, taxiarchs, phylarchs, strategoi, or as trierarchs. In the navy the trierarchs traditionally performed an important command role, but while they were responsible for the command of the trireme, they also had to meet the expenses involved in the upkeep of the trireme and its equipment.[58] In our period, the involvement of the trierarchs moved strongly from the personal element to the financial. About the end of the fifth century we hear of trierarchs expending approximately one-half to 1 talent in a year, but such expenditures, even if we accept the accuracy of the claims, may not be typical.[59] Nevertheless, the trierarchy clearly involved

---

[55] Cf. Davies (1978) 171 on a feeling, in the speeches of the 340s, of discontinuity with the past.

[56] The prohibition in 378/7 of land-owning by Athenians, whether by private individuals or by the polis, in the territory of allied states (Tod 123.25–46) materially assisted other factors such as the loss of imperial revenues in changing Athenian perceptions. Some klerouchs were in fact sent out (e.g., to Samos in 365), but there was a marked contrast with the fifth century with its numerous klerouchs and extensive landowning and the subsequent interest of both poor and well-to-do in strong policies abroad and the means (especially naval) of sustaining such policies.

[57] Dem. 8.74, 21.165; Aiskhin. 3.85.   [58] Amit (1965) 103–15 and Jordan (1975) 61–93.

[59] Lys. 19.29 and 42 (1¼ talents in 3 years – these may have been syntrierarchies), Lys. 21.2 (6 talents in 7 years). 1 talent = 6,000 drakhmai = 60 m(i)nai; 1 m(i)na = 60 drakhmai; 1 drakhme = 6 obols; see ch. 2.2.

heavy expense. About the beginning of the Peloponnesian War, when Athens had a fleet of 300 triremes, 400 men were designated as trierarchs each year, though the highest number of ships ever on active service in a single summer was 250. Before the end of the war the burden of frequent trierarchies had become such that pairs of trierarchs shared the responsibility for a trireme in some cases.[60] Syntrierarchs became much more common than sole trierarchs in the course of the first half of the fourth century, while the actual command or element of personal service could be deputed to a paid captain.[61] The problems of the trierarchy led in 357 to the reforms of Periandros, whereby the 1,200 wealthiest Athenians were grouped in 20 companies (*symmoriai*) in an attempt to distribute the burden in a more equitable manner.[62] These reforms fundamentally altered the character of the trierarchy or confirmed existing trends. For not only did they lessen the aspect of personal service by encouraging the hiring of captains, but they also largely removed the element of individual performance. In the past a trierarchy well performed brought not only personal satisfaction but also honour and the recognition of services performed in the interests of the polis.[63] These satisfactions were undoubtedly much less than in the mid-fifth century when the aristocratic ethos was more fully accepted, but men like the perhaps over-zealous Apollodoros (who was after all the son of Pasion, the slave who had finally become a citizen) still sought, by enthusiastic performance of a trierarchy, to bring honour to themselves.[64] The reforms of Demosthenes in 340/39 seem to have limited the number liable to the 300 richest Athenians.[65] The fourth-century developments had transformed the trierarchy into little more than an institution for collecting finance for the fleet and virtually left the trierarchs with the anonymity associated with the payment of tax.

Starkly financial in its character was the obligation of wealthier citizens (and, as we have seen, metics) to pay property tax (*eisphora*). This tax existed in the 430s but the date of its introduction is uncertain. The fact that it was levied as need for finance (almost always for war) arose added an element of unpredictability to the resentment of what was represented as a financial burden.[66] Although we know more about eisphora after it was reorganised in 378/7, many basic questions remain uncertain. Those liable to pay property tax

---

60 Thuc. 2.13.8, 3.17.2, [Xen.] *AP* 3.4, Davies 16–17, 21 n. 13, Rhodes (1982) 16 n. 17; Lys. 32.24.
61 *IG* ii².1609, Dem. 21.154 (syntrierarchs); Dem. 21.80, 51.7–8 (hired captains before 357); Dem. 21.163 (after reforms of 357).
62 Dem. 14.16–17, 21.155, 47.21; Rhodes (1982) 1–19, cf. Davies 15–20, see ch. 5.3.1.
63 Dem. 51.7; see Lys. 25.12–13.
64 [Dem.] 50.7, 10, 34–7 (362 B.C.). See Dem. 21.165 for gifts of triremes for the Euboian expedition in 357.
65 Aiskhin. 3.222, Dem. 18.103–4.
66 *IG* i³.52 (ML 58). B19 (and ML commentary in support of 434/3 B.C.); Lys. 19.29, Dem. 24.198, [Dem.] 47.54 and Davies 82–4.

after 378/7 probably numbered about 2,000, though the number has been put as high as 6,000.[67] The reforms of 378/7 involved the taking of a census of property owned by individuals in Attike, but as before there were possibilities for understatement and there were advantages in having certain assets in places outside Attike.[68] The total of the property liable for the assessment of payment of eisphora was recorded as 6,000 talents, and those liable paid in proportion to their capital.[69] In the mid-fourth century we hear of a levy of 1% which thus brought in 60 talents, and, whatever the precise means of calculating the levy, a total of this order is more plausible for the fourth century rather than the 200 talents which was raised in the crisis of 428/7. For the individual taxpayer a levy of 1% was the equivalent of an 8% tax on income, if the annual return on property was of the order of $12\frac{1}{2}\%$.[70] Difficulties in collecting eisphora led to the institution, probably *c.* 369, of *proeisphora* – advance payment of the tax by the 300 wealthiest Athenians who then collected their share from the other taxpayers.[71] It is interesting to note that in the period between 378/7 and 369 (if that date is correct) the arrears in payment of eisphora had amounted to 14 talents, and that it was not until the early 350s that a determined effort was made – by Androtion – to collect these arrears.[72]

---

[67] Ruschenbusch (1978) 275–84, Rhodes (1982) 5–11, cf. Jones 28–9, 83–4; see ch. 5.3.1. On eisphora in general, see de Ste Croix (1953) 30–70, Jones 23–30, Thomsen (1964) 195–206, Ruschenbusch (1978) 275–84 and (1985) 237–40, Rhodes (1982) 1–19.

[68] Dem. 27.8, 28.3–4, 42.22–3.

[69] Dem. 14.19, 27; cf. Polyb. 2.62.6–7.

[70] Within the limits imposed by variations in the component elements of a man's property and in rates of return, it may be suggested that an average rate of annual return was of the order of 10–$12\frac{1}{2}\%$. If the rates indicated in Isai. 11.42 are accurate and typical, the rental return on land and houses in the first half of the fourth century was about 8% (see de Ste Croix (1953) 39). But a farmer working his own land or a man working leased land would presumably expect to reap in produce rather more: the former might perhaps net on average 12% or $12\frac{1}{2}\%$. The estate discussed in Isai. 11.42 is said to have brought in an overall return (mostly from rent) of almost 10% (8% rent on land, $8\frac{4}{7}\%$ rent on houses, 18% on money). The rental return on workshops with slaves was higher (Dem. 37.5: 12% rent on a workshop at the silver mines and 30 slaves). Some wealthier Athenians hired out slaves on a regular basis: their return would have been much higher than from land leasing (Jones (1960) 5 suggests 35% or more; see *APF* 127–30; cf. the high theoretical maximum suggested by Markle (1985) 295–6 excluding the effects of the high-risk factors). Higher returns would have been enjoyed by those who had a larger proportion of their property in liquid assets (whether for reasons of concealment or political reasons: see *APF* 128–9, 134–5). For interest rates, see [Dem.] 53.13 (16% on a mortgage on a lodging house; see Dem. 34.23–4), Dem. 30.7 (10% represented as low), Dem. 27.9, 23 (12% represented as a very reasonable rate; see Dem. 37.5, Aiskhin. 3.104), [Dem.] 59.52 (18% the prescribed rate on money lent to repay a dowry) and Isai. fr. 23 ($33\frac{1}{3}\%$). On shipping loans see Dem. 35 and Michell (1957) 345–50.

[71] The earliest certain mention of proeisphora relates to 364/3 B.C. (Isai. 6.60). In 369 Athens made an alliance with her erstwhile foe, Sparta, in the face of the threat of Thebes. The Athenians decided, in Demosthenes' words (16.12), 'to pay eisphora and to risk their lives for the safety of the Spartans'. The situation required the urgent raising of money and was one in which the richest Athenians, many of them well known for their pro-Spartan sympathies, would have found the prepayment of property tax more acceptable.   [72] Dem. 22.42–4.

More acceptable, because they were annual and therefore regular, because they involved less expenditure, and because they retained the satisfactions – personal and political – of enthusiastic participation, were the annual liturgies or public services (*leitourgiai*), which each year in the mid-fourth century numbered more than 97 (and more than 118 every fourth year when the Great Panathenaia was celebrated).[73] These liturgies including the *khorēgia* enabled wealthy Athenian citizens, by their interest and their willingness to provide ample funds, to display their public spirit.[74] They belonged in concept to an aristocratic era and may have retained much of this character throughout our period. Like the trierarchy and the payment of eisphora, the regular or 'festival' liturgies were put forward by defendants in law suits as evidence of their public spirit and commonly with the admission that they were performed with enthusiasm in order to lay up a store of *kharis* (gratitude) to stand the person in good stead in court in the event of prosecution. Property power might also be employed in other ways to win honour and approval and to enhance a man's political influence – by voluntary contributions of various kinds or by ransoming Athenian prisoners-of-war.[75] These actions, and in particular the magnificent performance of a liturgy, were motivated by considerations akin to those of commercial sponsors that support modern cultural and sporting events in order to gain public approval, often political as well as commercial. The trierarchy, payment of eisphora and liturgies appear constantly in the orators as the 'standard' services performed by wealthier citizens with their property, while they helped to preserve the security of the polis by personal service.

In the fourth century men with property worth less than 3 talents were unlikely to be called upon to undertake the trierarchy or the other liturgies, while those with property in excess of 4 talents were unlikely to avoid these obligations in the long term.[76] For it was open to any citizen to whom a liturgy had been assigned to challenge another citizen whom he thought richer to exchange property or to perform the liturgy. This system of *antidosis* (exchange) helped to minimise the avoidance of performing liturgies as well as to take account of the changed economic circumstances of individuals.[77] The cost of most of the regular liturgies ranged, according to statements in the orators, from 300 to 2,500 drakhmai; most trierarchies were said to cost more than 3,000 (which may be the cost of a syntrierarchy) and less than 6,000

---

[73] Davies (1967) 33–40; compare the apparently conscious attempt of Demosthenes in 355/4 (20.21 – 'perhaps 60 or a little more') to minimise the number of annual liturgies.

[74] Xen. *Mem.* 3.4.3–5; see ch. 2.2.

[75] Lys. 19.56–7, 20.30–1, 25.12–13, Isai. 5.41–2, [Dem.] 25.76–8, Dem. 36.40–2, but cf. Lys. 26.4 and Dem. 21.169 for challenges to this line of defence. See Davies 91–7 on the translation into national and liturgical terms of what was a time-honoured form of spending for political purposes.

[76] *APF* xxiii–xxiv: Davies suggests the fifth-century figures may well have been rather higher.

[77] Lys. 24.9, Dem. 21.78–80, 28.17 (cf. Lys. 4.1–2). See also [Xen.] *AP* 3.4 and *AP* 61.1 for the adjudication of disputes about liturgical obligations.

drakhmai.[78] What expense was involved in the performance of public services by an individual over a lifetime is not easy to determine because of the difficulty of assessing the accuracy of the claims made by men who were anxious to impress their audience of jurors. The speaker of Lysias 19 said that over a period of fifty years (from *c.* 438 to *c.* 388) his father had undertaken khoregiai, served seven times as trierarch and made many, large payments of property tax and that the total cost of all these was 9 talents and 2,000 drakhmai. 'My father', he said, 'in all his life spent more on the polis than on himself and his family – twice the amount that we possess now, as he often reckoned in my presence.' Other indications point to very considerable wealth and the public services were hardly as burdensome as the son implies.[79] One other individual might be cited – the speaker of Lysias 21, who turned 18 years of age in 411/10 and in the course of the next nine years expended, on his account, 10 talents and 3,600 drakhmai. Most of these were critical war years and he said that he served continuously as trierarch for seven years, made two payments of eisphora (3,000 and 4,000 drakhmai) and performed a number of regular liturgies. He added that he would not have spent 'a quarter' of what he had spent if he had chosen to limit his public services to the letter of the law. Even allowing for exaggeration, this young man seems to have exceeded in frequency (and in level of expenditure) what was required, and he cannot be regarded as typical.[80] For there were in the fourth century provisions for an interval of one year between successive festival liturgies and two years between trierarchies: these provisions, or a general provision for a year's interval between liturgies, may have existed in the fifth century. The fourth-century prohibition of two simultaneous liturgies probably existed earlier, but it would have been over-ridden by the enthusiasm of a volunteer.[81]

3.5 Political and judicial fields

In the political and judicial fields there were some legal obligations placed upon the citizens, but far more important was the need inherent in the structure of Athenian democracy for widespread participation by the citizens. The Boule

---

[78] Lys. 21.2 (300 dr. for a dithyrambic chorus at the Lesser Panathenaia); Lys. 19.42 (5,000 dr. for two khoregiai). The cheapest recorded liturgy cost 50 or 100 dr. (*IG* II².417), while a dithyrambic chorus together with a commemorative tripod is said to have cost 5,000 dr. (Lys. 21.2). For other examples see *APF* xxi–xxii. For the trierarchy see ch. 3.4 above and Dem. 21.155 (6,000 dr. for a trierarchy leased out to a contractor).

[79] Lys. 19.9, 57–9; *APF* 200; cf. Lys. 19.42–3, *APF* 201–2; *APF* 135–8.

[80] Lys. 21.1–6. The speaker does not make the common claim about sacrificing his resources for the polis, but it may be that such a plea would have been laughed out of court because his wealth was very considerable or because the expenditure may have been a blatant attempt to overcome the political record of his father: see *APF* 592–3.

[81] Dem. 20.8, Isai. 7.38; Dem. 20.19, 21.155, [Dem.] 50.9; Rhodes (1982) 2–3, cf. Davies 17.

(Council of 500), for example, occupied a critical position in the operation of democracy and involved a considerable turnover in membership. In the 320s a man might serve no more than two terms on the Boule and it is possible that this applied from the institution of the Boule in the late sixth century. If, moreover, the terms could not be consecutive, an average minimum of 250 new men would be required each year, or in a ten-year period not less than 2,500 fresh councillors and not more than 5,000.[82] The supply of councillors was restricted by other factors. A man must have attained his thirtieth birthday, and it is often assumed that like arkhons bouleutai were drawn from the top three census classes, though that restriction would presumably have been ignored in the fourth century as it was in the case of arkhons.[83] The other major factor which would in any case have tended to make it very difficult for men of the thetic class to serve on the Boule was the heavy demands in terms of time. This would, in practice, have excluded those who were described as 'poor' or 'without (sufficient) resources' – those who depended for their livelihood on their own labour – until the level of bouleutic pay provided reasonable compensation. Bouleutic pay was probably introduced in the 450s (at the earliest soon after the reforms of 462) and in the 320s stood at 5 obols a day, though there is no evidence to indicate for how long this had been the rate.[84] Remuneration was essential for 'men without resources' as the bouleutai were summoned in the 320s to meet on some 260 days during their term of office and their normal activities might thus be seriously disrupted.[85] Though meetings may have been less frequent in the early part of the fifth century, the expansion of the Council's role as a result of the changes introduced by Ephialtes in 462 and the increasing administrative and other business in Athens from the mid-fifth century would have necessitated very frequent meetings.[86]

The Council of 500 therefore gave extensive opportunities for, and placed a clear responsibility on, Athenian citizens to become closely acquainted with the affairs of their polis. This was in part due to the large membership of the Boule

---

[82] *AP* 62.3; Rhodes 3–4, 242–3. The earliest evidence for two terms which can be dated with relative accuracy refers to Androtion, whose second term fell in or before 356/5; see also ch. 4 n. 61 for political leaders serving on the Boule. Larsen (1955) 10–11 was somewhat inclined to the view that originally only one term was permitted as with most Athenian offices and that the second term was found to be necessary because of the difficulty of finding 500 new councillors every year; see, however, ch. 5.1 for a 'reserve' of candidates. A rule against consecutive terms would be in harmony with Dem. 24.149 and has been inferred from the democratic constitution established by Athens at Erythrai in the 450s: bouleutic service was limited to one year in four (*IG* I³.14 (ML 40).12; Hignett 228 n. 3).

[83] *AP* 7.4; Rhodes 2–3 for other possible limitations.

[84] See ch. 5.3.1 on 'the poor'; Thuc. 8.69.4 (pay in 412/11); Griffith (1966) 125 re date; *AP* 62.2 (5 obols for a councillor, with an additional obol for the prytaneis). The rate of 3 obols proposed in 411 for the prytaneis and the arkhons (with no other officials to receive pay for the duration of the war – *AP* 29.5) may well have represented a reduction in pay.

[85] See Appendix 2A and ch. 5.1.

[86] [Xen.] *AP* 3.1–5; see *AP* 25.2 and Rhodes 16–19, 190–207, 209–11 who argues for limited powers and duties before 462.

and its changing composition, in part to the range of functions which it exercised. To understand these functions it is best to consider first the sovereign Ekklesia, the officials of the Athenian polis, and the Dikasteria or jury courts, for it was largely the Boule that provided whatever coordination there was between these entities.

Membership of the Ekklesia was open, as we have seen, to all adult male citizens. Apart from the reported device of using a vermilion-smeared rope pulled through the Agora to induce citizens talking or doing business in the Agora to go up to the Pnyx where the assembly usually met, there seems to have been no attempt to compel attendance.[87] The importance of attendance was, however, implied in the provisions that a quorum of 6,000 was required for certain types of decisions and for a valid vote of ostracism. In the fourth century attendance was encouraged by financial inducement: in the mid-390s 1 obol a day was offered, and within two or three years the amount was raised to 2, then to 3 obols. In the 320s 1 drakhme was paid for each of thirty ordinary meetings a year, and $1\frac{1}{2}$ drakhmai for the ten main meetings (one in each of the prytanies into which the Athenian year was divided).[88] In so far as individual citizens were anxious to see a particular proposal passed by the assembly they would, if they could, accept the responsibility inherent in their right to attend the assembly. In the extreme case in 411 the oligarchs engineered a meeting outside the walls, where only those with armour and weapons could safely attend, and thus brought about the overthrow of the democracy.[89] It was largely in order to deal with the problem of stacked meetings and snap votes that the Athenians instituted at the end of the century a specific procedure for the revision of the laws.[90]

The underlying assumption of Athenian democracy was the sovereignty of the Athenian people: 'the Athenian Demos has supreme authority over all things in the polis and it is in its power to do whatever it wishes'.[91] As well as the election of officials, the Ekklesia had complete authority over the whole range of 'legislative' and administrative matters. The great matters of state came before it: whether to reject the Spartan demands in 432/1 and face the threat of war, whether to expand their alliance in 378/7 by issuing a general invitation to join the Second Athenian League.[92] Minor matters also came before it – matters of regulation or administrative detail which in the modern state would be

---

[87] Ar. *Akh.* 17–22, but cf. *Ekkl.* 378–95; see ch. 5.2.

[88] *AP* 41.3, 62.2. In the 320s a main meeting and three other meetings were held each prytany (*AP* 43.3–6, listing certain regular items dealt with at the four meetings); the denial by Hansen 41–3 of the possibility of additional (emergency) meetings is difficult to accept. Nor is it clear that we should deduce from Dem. 24.21, 25 (indicating three meetings in the first prytany) that in 353/2 only three meetings were held in each prytany (see Hansen and Mitchel (1984) 13–19). The frequency and regularity of meetings may have been somewhat less subject to prescription in the period before 403. See ch. 5.2–5.3.2 for attendance levels.

[89] Thuc. 8.67.2.   [90] See ch. 4.2 for nomothesia.

[91] [Dem.] 59.88; Andok. 2.19–20, Arist. *Pol.* 1298a3–11.   [92] Thuc. 1.139–45, Tod 123.

delegated to ministers or to civil service departments. The volume of business before the assembly and the importance of much of it carried considerable responsibilities for the Boule and the officials directly concerned with the meetings of the assembly, and also for individual citizens.[93] The assembly's decisions, for example, were not to contravene existing law. The responsibility for ensuring this had in the early fifth century rested with the Council of the Areiopagos. At some time before 415 (and perhaps as early as the 450s) this responsibility devolved upon the officials presiding at the meeting of the assembly, and also upon every individual citizen. For a proposal which, though passed by the Ekklesia (or the Boule), contravened existing law or which had been passed by an irregular procedure could be blocked by lodging an indictment for an illegal proposal (*graphē paranomōn*).[94] This indictment could be brought by any citizen against the proposal itself at any time, but clearly if it was to achieve anything in that regard it was normally lodged more or less immediately. The charge was heard by the Dikasteria. Within the year of the passing of the proposal, the proposer could also be prosecuted. The presiding officials, too, could be subject to prosecution. Herein is revealed one of the central tenets of Athenian democracy – the personal responsibility of those who put forward proposals and those who presided over the meeting, but also of every individual Athenian. There was no public prosecutor to lodge a graphe paranomon or to prosecute the presiding officials, but it required the watchfulness and initiative of individual citizens. Presiding officials, however, had a special obligation to ensure that there was no contravention of the laws and they might thus be called upon to frustrate the will of the Demos: Aristotle, not particularly sympathetic to democracy, drew particular attention to this fundamental dilemma for democratic states – the conflict between the rule of law and the will of the people as expressed in decrees or resolutions.[95]

If we turn from the operation of the Ekklesia itself to officials or magistrates, several features figured strongly in involving considerable numbers of citizens in the working of democracy and in giving them experience and a measure of authority and responsibility. The first was the principle of limited tenure and rotation. Apart from the military offices and probably the handful of other elective offices, a citizen might hold an office for one year and one year only: this prohibition on re-election ensured rotation in office-holding, spreading the

---

[93] See ch. 2.2 for the provision that a matter which was before the assembly for decision should already have been discussed by the Boule. For the clauses of the bouleutic oath see Xen. *Mem.* 1.1.18 ('to take counsel in accordance with the laws') and Rhodes 194–9.

[94] Andok. 1.17.22 (re 415 B.C.); Thuc. 8.67.2, *AP* 29.4, 45.4; Hignett 210–13, Griffith (1966) 130–1, Wolff (1970) 12–28, Hansen (1974) especially 55–61, Sealey (1982) 297–301; see ch. 6.5. Prosecutions on the grounds of 'making an unsuitable (or inexpedient) law' are known from the fourth century (*AP* 59.2, Dem. 20.144, 24.138); see ch. 6 n. 87.

[95] Dem. 23.92–3; *AP* 59.2 (and *CAAP*); Rhodes 194 n. 13 for a probable clause in the bouleutic oath not to put anything to the vote that was contrary to the laws. See Xen. *Hell.* 1.7.12–15; Aiskhin. 2.84; Arist. *Pol.* 1292a4–37.

responsibility more widely and also making it more difficult for an individual to acquire influence through repeated tenure of one office. The second principle – the notion of collegiality – likewise increased the opportunities and responsibilities of citizens and militated against individual influence. With few exceptions, most officials were members of a board (commonly of ten) and the differing opinions and rival ambitions of colleagues made it more difficult for any individual to acquire a position of leadership. Both these aspects of holding office materially assisted the maintenance of the sovereignty of the Demos *vis-à-vis* officials – sovereignty which was based on the fundamental notion that all officials were 'answerable' or 'responsible' to the Demos and must render an account of their term of office. Willing to allow extensive opportunities for citizens to hold office, the Athenians were nevertheless concerned about the individual's ability to resist the temptations of irresponsible power.[96]

These features meant that considerable numbers of Athenians participated in the holding of office – several hundred officials in Attike each year (apart from bouleutai and officials abroad), for Athens was a large polis and the Athenians went further than other poleis in the multiplication of official positions.[97] Even larger numbers were involved in dispensing justice in the Dikasteria. Not all cases, it is true, came to the Dikasteria. Officials, for example, dealt with certain minor offences, particularly offences (such as disorderly conduct at a festival) which prevented the official from carrying out the duties of his office, but they could not impose a fine above a certain limit (probably 50 drakhmai at most) and had to refer more serious cases to the Dikasteria.[98] Many minor matters in dispute between individuals were probably settled by the thirty 'deme judges' and, after 403/2, by the Forty or (if more than 10 drakhmai was involved) by public arbitrators, but a disputant could appeal against an arbitrator's decision to the Dikasteria. The Areiopagos dealt with cases of the intentional homicide of an Athenian citizen and cases of poisoning and arson.[99] But judicial decisions were typically a matter for the Dikasteria. Though there was a preliminary hearing of a charge by one of the arkhons, it was a formal affair checking that the matter was admissible and enabling the case to be heard by a particular court. The arkhon subsequently presided over the court in a purely formal sense, for the jurors themselves had to decide on questions of fact and law, 'guided' by the parties involved, and to determine any penalty. The Dikasteria and the dikasts were *the* distinguishing feature of Athens: at least, when

---

[96]   *AP* 43.1 and 62.3 (and *CAAP*); Arist. *Pol.* 1279a8–11; Jones 61.

[97]   With regard to the fifth century the text of *AP* 24.3 refers to about 700 officials at home and about 700 abroad. The latter figure is rejected by most scholars as careless repetition by a scribe. Hansen (1980B) 153–73 believes the first figure is about right, while Rhodes (*CAAP* 304–5) notes that the (incomplete) lists of fourth-century officials in *AP* 43, 47–56, 60–1 approach 300 officials at home without including arbitrators or officials who were also bouleutai.

[98]   *IG* i³.82.24–30, Dem. 21.179, Aiskhin. 3.27; Stroud, *Hesperia* 43 (1974) 158, lines 23–6 (10-dr. limit); *AP* 61.2 (strategoi in the field); MacDowell 235–7.

[99]   *AP* 26.3, 53.1–3 (cf. 42.1), 57.3; Harrison 2.4–68.

Strepsiades was shown a map of the world in Aristophanes' *Clouds* and Athens was pointed out to him, he retorted: 'What do you mean? I don't believe it, for I see no dikasts in session.'[100]

Throughout our period the Heliaia was in a sense distinct from the Ekklesia, for each year several thousand citizens who had to be in possession of full citizen rights were selected by lot as dikasts or heliasts. Moreover, there was an age limitation: citizens under the age of 30 were not eligible to serve as jurors. In the fifth century the number of jurors was 6,000 and each dikast was allotted to one court for the whole year. We hear of references to courts of 1,000, 1,500, 2,000 and 6,000, but ordinary cases may have been heard by 500 dikasts.[101] Corruption of juries led early in the fourth century to the introduction of a new system in allocating jurors to courts: dikasts were distributed at the beginning of the year among a number of panels (designated by a letter of the alphabet and, in the 320s, numbering ten) but each day the Lot was used to determine the allocation of a particular panel to a particular court.[102] Whether each panel numbered a maximum of 500 or 600 (the latter would make more likely the presence of about 500 despite absenteeism) cannot be established with certainty, but the sources refer to 500 and multiples of 500. The continuing possibility of bribery, the problems of ensuring adequate numbers in the panels or other problems led to further changes, known in some detail from the 320s but probably introduced about the 370s. By a complicated procedure involving the use of a juror's ticket bearing the name of the dikast, individual dikasts (not a whole panel as before) were assigned each day to a particular court.[103] From the second half of the fourth century we have references to courts of 500 or 501 and multiples of 500 (1,000, 1,500, 2,500 or (probably more accurately) stated as 1,001 and so on, with the odd number designed to avoid a tied vote), and an occasional reference to 201 or 401.[104] The Athenians then took great pains in an attempt to ensure fairness and to prevent corruption, but most important from the point of view of citizen responsibility are the large number of dikasts hearing any one case (500 being common in the fourth century for ordinary cases) and the large number of dikasts involved each year in the dispensation of justice.

These two facts and the notion of a random sample achieved by the extensive use of the Lot indicate that in many senses the Heliaia was regarded as a cross-

---

[100] Ruschenbusch (1957) 257–74; Ar. *Clouds* 206–8.

[101] *IG* I³.281.60–1, Plut. *Per.* 32.2, Lys. 13.35, Andok. 1.17 (cf. Hansen (1981–2) 21).

[102] Ar. *Ekkl.* 681–90.

[103] See *AP* 63–9 on the operation of the Dikasteria in the 320s; MacDowell 35–40. See Dow (1937) 198–215 and (1939) 1–34, Bishop (1970) 1–14, Staveley 62–9 and *CAAP* 706–9 for the *klērōtēria* (allotment machines) and Kroll for the system of jurors' tickets. See also Wycherley 144–50 and Thompson and Wycherley 52–72 (on buildings and furnishings such as allotment machines and water clocks); cf. Hansen (1981–2) 16–27.

[104] *AP* 68.1, Dem. 21.223, Dein. 1.52, 107, Dem. 24.9 (and scholiast on avoidance of a tied vote, but cf. Antiphon 5.51, Ar. *Frogs* 684–5, Aiskhin. 3.252, *AP* 69.2 on acquittal in the event of a tied vote); *AP* 53.3, Tod 200.206–8.

section of the Demos at large or virtually the same as the Demos. The orators, though they sometimes drew a distinction between a jury and the Demos as a whole, often identified jury and the people at large and occasionally addressed the jurors as if there was no difference between the Ekklesia where the citizens met to make decisions of all kinds (ranging from high matters of state to relatively minor administrative matters) and the Dikasteria where they met to decide on alleged breaches of the laws of Athens.[105] Furthermore, largely as a result of the origins and development of the Heliaia there was overlapping in the character of the functions of the Heliaia and the Ekklesia. In some respects, the line between the two institutions remained fluid: for example, some of the more serious charges laid by means of the procedure known as *eisangelia* (impeachment) might be heard by either the assembly or the jury courts.[106] More than this, the Dikasteria were very frequently faced with cases which were really political in character rather than judicial. The celebrated case of the gold crown proposed for Demosthenes was concerned technically with the question whether the proposal which had been passed was in strict compliance with the laws. Aiskhines' attempt to block the proposal by the use of the graphe paranomon was motivated by the political desire to deprive Demosthenes of honour and the recognition of his policies, while Demosthenes' speech *On the Crown* played down the technical aspects and presented a detailed account of his career and policies. Such a line of defence was clearly acceptable to the jurors. The political character of the great public trials is also indicated by the fact that Aiskhines let the charge of making an illegal proposal lie for some six years and then in 330 he clearly judged the political climate was right to press his charge against Ktesiphon, or in reality against his old rival Demosthenes. However, he misjudged the political climate, or possibly the skilful oratory of Demosthenes was the critical factor in the overwhelming rejection of Aiskhines' charge.

One other factor must be mentioned which was important in encouraging as many citizens as possible to accept the responsibilities implied in the Athenian judicial system. Payment for dikastic service, which is generally accepted as the first case of state pay for public service, was designed to encourage service on the jury panels as well as to recognise the demands caused by the increasing volume of business coming before the courts in the bustling Athens of the mid-fifth century.[107] In the mid-420s the daily rate of 2 obols was raised to 3 by Kleon and it is important to note that 3 obols remained as the fee throughout our period. Pay was available only for those days when the dikast was required and not all the dikasts were required every day. Jury pay was therefore not as attractive to the poor as has sometimes been supposed, though pay did make it feasible for a wider range of citizens to contemplate leaving their normal occupations.[108]

[105] Aiskhin. 3.8 but 1.176; [Dem.] 43.72; Lys. 13.10, Andok. 1.66, Isai. 4.17; cf. Hansen 139–60.
[106] Rhodes 162–71 and (1979) 103–14; cf. Hansen (1975) 51–4; see ch. 6.6.
[107] See ch. 1.5.
[108] Ar. *Knights* 51, 255, *Wasps* 88 (with scholia), *AP* 62.2; see ch. 5.4.

The operation of the judicial system necessitated the involvement of large numbers of Athenians as jurors. One of the incentives was the substantial power of the Heliaia and in particular its political potential through the imposition of fines (sometimes very heavy), exile or the death penalty. Against the decisions of the Heliaia there was, essentially, no appeal.[109] The system also depended on the willingness of individuals, whether leading public figures or private individuals, to take action against wrongdoers. Officials did have some responsibility in this matter, for they could take action, as we have seen, against those who committed offences which related to the performance of their office. So, too, did the Boule, in relation, for example, to its supervision of the conduct of officials and state administration generally.[110] If the offence was serious and was presumed to merit a fine beyond the power of the official (limited probably to 50 drakhmai) or the Boule (limited to 500 drakhmai), these bodies took steps to have the matter heard by a Dikasterion. There were no permanent officials similar to the public prosecutors known in modern states. The prosecution of an official on a financial charge at his examination (*euthynai*) was however regularly launched by the ten *synēgoroi* (advocates) appointed annually by lot, while on a particular matter brought before them the Ekklesia or the Boule could appoint an individual or individuals to prosecute.[111]

Legal action could therefore be launched by officials or the Boule while the Boule or the Ekklesia could appoint prosecutors, but most 'public cases' were initiated by individual Athenians. Public cases included treason and embezzlement of public money and also offences such as the maltreatment of an orphan or the seduction of a free woman. Voluntary prosecution by individuals was permitted or indeed encouraged in those cases which were regarded as affecting the community as whole, but not in 'private cases'. The maintenance of democracy and the prosperity of the polis depended, Lykourgos argued, on three essential elements: the code of laws, the vote of the dikasts and individuals prepared to prosecute transgressors of the law. But, he added, prosecuting was a thankless task and resulted in a reputation for being meddlesome, not patriotic. Yet he felt impelled to prosecute Leokrates for treason since he had left Athens after the defeat at Khaironeia in 338: impelled, he declared, not by enmity nor by a desire to be contentious, but by justice and the feeling that crimes which affect the public offer public grounds for enmity.[112]

Prosecutors usually emphasised, with or without sincerity, that they were motivated by a desire to help and protect the laws, while personal enmity was

---

[109] *AP* 9, Arist. *Pol.* 1274a2–15. The view of Hansen (139–60 and (1974) 15–21) that the ultimate sovereignty lay with the courts, not the assembly, has rightly been challenged – for example, by MacDowell (1976) 231–2 and Caven (1976) 227–8. On remedies against judgements, see Dem. 24.54, schol. Pl. *Laws* 937d, Harrison 2.190–9.

[110] *AP* 45.2, 46.2, Rhodes 144–62.

[111] *AP* 54.2; cf. Ar. *Akh.* 713–16, *Wasps* 482–3; Hyp. 5.38, Dein. 2.6; Harrison 2.208–10, MacDowell 53–66.   [112] Lykourg. *Leok.* 3–6; cf. Ar. *Plout.* 898–919.

also frequently advanced as a (proper) ground for launching a prosecution in a public case. 'What is frequently said about public suits is no mistake,' Aiskhines claimed, 'for very often private enmities correct public abuses.' These explanations were commonly offered by speakers so that they would not be thought by the jurors to be contentious or meddlesome or to be inspired by hope of financial gain.[113] For the Athenian polis offered financial inducements in certain types of cases – the reward for a successful prosecution, for example, on a charge of giving a foreign woman in marriage to a citizen was one-third of the offender's property, while the rest was confiscated.[114] These inducements were not the only cause but they were the major cause in the emergence of *sykophantai* (or malicious accusers) – men who harassed their fellow-citizens in order to obtain the financial rewards offered by the state, or on the paid instructions of a third party, or in the hope of extorting silence money from the victims.[115] The ancient sources indicate that the practice of *sykophantia* flourished in Athens, despite widespread public disapproval, despite the provision for bringing a charge that a man was a sykophantes, and despite penalties which in general attempted to prevent malicious or frivolous prosecutions by individuals.[116] These latter penalties did not relate only to cases involving a reward. They mostly provided for a fine of 1,000 drakhmai and the loss of the right to bring the same type of charge again if the prosecutor withdrew before the trial or failed to receive one-fifth of the dikasts' votes.[117] Thus, when Aiskhines in 330 failed to get one-fifth of the votes in favour of the graphe paranomon which he lodged against Ktesiphon's proposal, he left Athens (because, it was said, he was not willing to pay the fine but in essence because of the lack of public support which the vote indicated) and disappeared from political life. Aged 60 at the time, Aiskhines fled to Ephesos, went to Rhodes in 323 and then to Samos. Nevertheless, the deterrents seem to have done little to check the abuse of the graphe paranomon and other abuses of voluntary prosecution such as sykophantia.

3.6 The role of the Council of 500

We must now return to the Boule and consider the range of functions which the 500 councillors exercised, particularly in relation to other bodies. Public cases, as we have seen, were in many instances brought before the Dikasteria by the Boule. But the indispensable link in the Athenian democratic system was the

---

113 Aiskhin. 1.1–2; Lys. 14.1–2 (cf. 7.27), 24.24–5.   114 [Dem.] 59.52.

115 Lys. 7.27, Pl. *Kn.* 45a; Lofberg (1917) ix–x, 1–10, 26–59.

116 Ar. *Akh.* 818–29, 899–958, *AP* 43.5, Lys. 13.65, Aiskhin. 2.145; Bonner and Smith 2 (1938) 39–74, Lofberg (1917) 19–25, 86–95.

117 Some public cases were partially or fully exempted, and in general the provisions do not seem to have been effective; see MacDowell 64–5.

relationship between the Boule and the Ekklesia, which had authority in all matters except 'judicial' cases. In the decision-making process the Council played a key role. For it was to the Boule (or the prytaneis, the committee of the Boule) that states or individuals normally made their first approach – whether foreign envoys with their requests or protests, messengers from abroad, Athenian officials with their reports, or individuals with their proposals.[118] Not only did the Boule consider the detailed aspects and implications of these various matters and decide whether or not (and in what form) to pass them on to the Ekklesia, but it also gave prior consideration (*probouleusis*) to all matters, whatever their origin, that were to be decided by the Ekklesia.[119] In the decision-making process, therefore, these probouleutic functions of the Council were crucial.

In the implementation of the assembly's decisions, whether major policies or minor administrative arrangements, the Boule played a supervisory and coordinating role. The details of that role are best known from the description of Athenian constitutional and administrative arrangements in the 320s.[120] In the course of the years since the mid-fifth century there had undoubtedly been changes in the functions and powers of the Boule and its relative importance among Athenian institutions.[121] The increasing complexity of Athenian life in the second half of the fifth century may have given particular importance to the work of the Boule, not least through its involvement in the assessment and collection of allied tribute. By the late fifth century it had acquired a general responsibility for the supervision of public finances through its involvement in the sacred treasuries as well as the collection of tribute and its supervision of the financial officials who received and made payments on behalf of the polis. This routine financial supervision through a number of committees enabled the Boule to advise the Ekklesia whether money was available for a particular purpose or project, but the degree of supervision did not lead to the development of anything like a modern budget coordinating the various financial sources or needs of the polis. In the fourth century there may perhaps have been limitations imposed on its competence, but the major factor affecting the Boule was the emergence in the late 350s and 340s of the Festival Fund Commission, which came to exercise a strong supervisory role in the administration of the polis.[122]

The basis for the supervisory role of the Council of 500 probably rested on its judicial powers in dealing with officials. For each prytany officials submitted their financial accounts to a committee of bouleutai and at the end of the year the Boule participated in the euthynai of officials. Though it had more limited

---

[118] Tod 131.8–16, 133.6–40, Xen. *Hell.* 6.4.20; Dem. 18.169–70; Tod 143.6–19; Dem. 24.47–8; Rhodes 42–6.   [119] Isok. 12.144, *AP* 45.4.   [120] *AP* 43–69.
[121] Rhodes 209–21, and especially 218 for certain fourth-century changes (marginally) affecting the Boule; cf. 82–5, 184 rejecting the view that for a brief period at the beginning of the fourth century the Boule enjoyed greatly enhanced powers.   [122] Aiskhin. 3.25.

powers of punishment than previously, the Boule could in the later fifth century and in the fourth impose fines of up to 500 drakhmai.[123] Over the wider area of state administration the Boule was likely to be involved in some way at almost every point, as may be illustrated from inscriptions as well as literary sources. So we find it taking a part in financial matters, in the building of temples, in the offering of first fruits at Eleusis, in making appointments for religious purposes, in the keeping and publication of public records.[124] The Council conducted the scrutiny of the cavalry and above all it had considerable responsibility for the navy – in its supervision, for example, of the dockyard superintendents and the dispatch of expeditions, but also in the building of new ships.[125] The Athenians attached considerable importance to the building of new ships for the navy, and a Boule which failed in this responsibility was not entitled to receive a crown of honour, no matter how effective it had been in the discharge of its other duties.[126]

Members of the Boule could thus acquire considerable knowledge of day-to-day affairs which should have contributed significantly to its probouleutic function and the advice it might offer the Ekklesia. But its relationship with that body, which will be further examined in the next chapter, was conditioned by the fact that the Council was not an ongoing executive with a strongly developed corporate sense, for it is probable that at the end of a year not one of the Council of 500 could continue as a member. Yet the Boule occupied a crucial position in the operation of democracy because of its links with all the other agencies and it was vital that large numbers of citizens be willing and able to fulfil the responsibilities of membership.

In summary, two points should be stressed about the responsibilities of Athenian citizens and their involvement in those responsibilities. First, the need for leaders was met by a perceptible widening in the course of the fifth and fourth centuries in the range of socio-economic groups from which they came. The second matter, and perhaps more striking, is the extent to which more modest citizens could, and for the mere operation of democratic institutions needed to, participate in public life. Not content to leave the affairs of the polis simply with the traditional elite, Athenians were inclined moreover to limit any dependence on 'experts', though their value in the military and financial fields was more widely recognised by the mid-fourth century. The military security of the polis was not in the hands of permanent armed forces. It had resided traditionally with the hoplites who were called up as need arose but, because of the dependence of Athens on her navy, members of the thetic class also shared in these responsibilities while trierarchs made a special contribution to the security of Athens. Nevertheless, there was a trend towards the employment of

---

[123] *IG* I³.78 (ML 73).57–9, [Dem.] 47.43, *AP* 45.1, Rhodes 179–207.
[124] *IG* I³.52A (ML 58A). 18–21; I³.35 (ML 44). 15–18; I³.78 (ML 73).21–4, 30–2; I³.40 (ML 52). 57–67; see [Xen.] *AP* 3.1–5; *AP* 43–9; Rhodes 88–143.
[125] *AP* 49.1–2, 46.1, [Dem.] 47.33, 41–3.   [126] Dem. 22, especially 12–16.

mercenary forces. In the sphere of public finance provided from within Athens, while indirect taxes, mining royalties, rents and other charges provided the major sources of actual 'revenue', the wealthier groups carried a considerable burden through liturgies and the payment of eisphora. But it was in the political–judicial area that Athenian democracy was probably most distinctive. The very structure and a variety of factors worked strongly in favour of the involvement of considerable numbers of citizens, and in chapter 5 the question of the extent to which Athenians actually participated is considered.

The sovereignty of the Demos, officials and the Council

4.1 The accountability of officials to the Demos

While the citizen (*politēs*) shared in all the facets of the life of the polis, his citizenship (*politeia*), his membership of the community of citizens, was most distinctively worked out in what we have called the political–judicial area. Attention may therefore be focussed on various political–judicial institutions and, in particular, on the question of how they were related to the central feature of Athenian democracy, the sovereignty of the Demos. These institutions were not static throughout our period and some were directly affected by the developments that have already been discussed. Quite apart from actual changes in the constitutional structure and procedures, developments such as the tendency to specialisation in the fourth century or shifts in the character of the strategia affect any evaluation of the structure of Athenian democracy. Changes in the socio-economic origins of leaders and other changes also had an impact on the actual operation of democratic institutions. Yet despite all the changes which affected, directly or indirectly, the supreme authority of the Demos, certain devices or factors contributed more or less constantly to the maintenance of that sovereignty in our period.

Rotation and other factors worked strongly, as we have seen, in encouraging the involvement of large numbers of citizens. These factors combined with the involvement of large numbers of citizens to make it more difficult for men from aristocratic families to retain their pre-eminence and for powerful individuals or groups to emerge that might challenge the control of the Demos. Of prime importance, too, was the subordination of all officials to the Demos: this was encapsulated in the principle of the accountability of officials. Before they took up office, all officials, whether they had been selected by lot or elected by show of hands, underwent a preliminary scrutiny (*dokimasia*) – for most officials, before a jury court.[1] The questions asked in the scrutiny of the arkhons were:

'Who is your father and to what deme does he belong? And who is your father's father, and your mother, and your mother's father, and to what demes did they belong?' Then

---

[1] The dokimasia of the three arkhons and the six thesmothetai (statute-setters) and of the 500 bouleutai involved in the 320s a scrutiny before the Boule and also before a jury court; in an earlier period the decision of the Boule was final (*AP* 45.3, 55.2; Dem. 20.90; cf. Hignett 205–8; Rhodes 176–8).

they ask whether he has an ancestral Apollo and a household Zeus and where their sanctuaries are, whether he has family tombs and where these are, whether he treats his parents well and pays his taxes, and whether he has served on the military expeditions. Having asked these questions (the presiding official) says: 'Call the witnesses to these statements.' Then, when he has presented his witnesses, he asks: 'Does anyone wish to bring a charge against this man?' If there is an accuser, (the presiding official) allows the charge and the defence to be heard, and then he has the Council vote by show of hands, or the law-court by ballot.[2]

The preliminary scrutiny, then, established that the individual was a member of the citizen body and had fulfilled financial, military and other responsibilities. There is, however, little to suggest that any real consideration was given at the scrutiny to the ability or experience of the officials or, for the vast majority of them, at any other stage since most were selected by lot. For most individuals the dokimasia was probably little more than a formality, but there was the opportunity for an individual to bring a charge against a would-be official, as happened in the case of Mantitheos.[3] The latter was particularly concerned to refute the suggestion that he was a man of oligarchic sympathies and had associated with the Thirty, and presumably it was the question of his military service which enabled his enemies to challenge him. The doubt related to his past associations, not to his ability or administrative experience. Dokimasia, then, was intended as a check on the accuracy of the deme lists, as a safeguard against irregular candidature, not against the caprice of the Lot. It applied whether the selection was by lot or by voting. In the political climate after the oligarchic revolutions (and possibly at other times) it was capable of a wider interpretation of what constituted legal disqualification, unless we are to regard the arguments about oligarchic associations as completely irrelevant, though prejudicial.[4]

At the end of their year of office all officials had to account for their conduct. Before 462/1 complaints about the conduct of officials (as distinct from individual decisions against which there could be an appeal to the Heliaia) had been heard by the Council of the Areiopagos. That council was composed of

---

[2] *AP* 55.3 (von Fritz and Kapp tr. adapted).   [3] See ch. 2.3.2.

[4] See Adeleye (1983) 295–306. The arkhons in the 320s were selected by a double sortition: ten men were first selected by lot from each of the ten tribes, and from each of these groups one was selected (*AP* 8.1, 55.1; cf. 22.5). The first stage in the process had employed voting as late as 458/7, but this opportunity of excluding unsuitable candidates was eliminated by the adoption (at some time before *c.* 430 – [Xen.] *AP* 1.2) of the Lot for the first as well as the second stage: see Hignett 227. Thereafter, informal processes, such as the consequences of the demonstration of gross incompetence, would seem to have been the only means of discouraging unsuitable aspirants. Members of the Boule were selected by lot in their demes (*AP* 62.1; cf. Whitehead 266–70 for the suggestion that the process may have been completed at tribal level); some demarchs and others may have seen fit to employ informal means of deterring aspirants. See Lys. 16 (cf. 26.9–15); Headlam 96–102, 202, Hignett 232, Rhodes 6–8, de Laix 149–54. See *AP* 56.1 (and *CAAP*), [Dem.] 59.72–8 and Bonner 13–14 for the two assessors or assistants *chosen* by each of the three senior arkhons: perhaps a survival from the archaic period.

ex-arkhons who might better understand the difficulties faced by an official but who might be unduly sympathetic and thus reluctant to punish offenders. But in our period officials were required to undergo a radically different, public examination of their term of office. In the 320s this examination (*euthynai*) involved both the submission of financial accounts to ten auditors (*logistai*) and ten advocates (*synēgoroi*) appointed by lot from the whole citizen body and a public hearing before examiners (*euthynoi*) when any citizen was able to lay a complaint. Failure to render proper accounts resulted in prosecution before a Dikasterion, while complaints which seemed to the euthynoi to be well founded were referred to the deme judges in private suits and to a Dikasterion (via the *thesmothetai* – statute-setters) in public suits.[5] In these ways all officials including the 500 bouleutai were fully answerable or 'responsible' for their actions. Serious offences came before the Dikasteria which were held to be a cross-section of the Demos. Faced with the prospect of being called to account for decisions, officials would have tended to prefer to have clear, detailed directions rather than rely too much on their own initiative. It is less surprising, then, to find the assembly making, and in many cases presumably called upon to make, decisions about trivial administrative details. Thus the sovereignty of the assembly was reinforced.

Furthermore, in sharp contrast to the magistrates at Rome, Athenian officials were not immune from attack or prosecution during their term of office. In each prytany the financial accounts of officials were examined by ten auditors selected by lot from the Boule, and this was one of the major means by which the Boule exercised a general supervision over officials.[6] But the accountability of Athenian officials went far beyond this, for at the main meeting in each prytany a vote was taken to confirm officials in their office if they were held to be governing properly. If the Ekklesia voted against confirmation, the official was tried before a Dikasterion.[7] The procedure of *eisangelia* (impeachment) might also be employed against officials. In 430 the reaction against Perikles' defensive policy in the early years of the Peloponnesian War led to his deposition from the strategia, his trial and the imposition of a fine. In that there was a definite element of justice, so to speak, for the man whose policy had permitted the devastation of the Attic countryside, quite apart from the complications of the plague, was being held responsible for his leadership. But the possibility of deposition in mid-term was disruptive of continuity and, for the individual, not necessarily conducive to conduct which in the long term might prove its value. In a matter of weeks or months Perikles was re-elected to the generalship: to Thucydides that was typical of the crowd. In chapter 6 the

---

[5] AP 54.2 (for the logistai and synegoroi and the penalties that might be imposed by the Dikasteria for embezzlement, bribery or maladministration), 48.4–5 (ten examiners, each with two associates, selected by lot) and 53.1 (deme or local judges selected by lot; cf. 16.5, 26.3); Aiskhin. 3.17–22 (for the universality of audit); Hignett 203–5.

[6] AP 48.3; Rhodes 111.   [7] AP 43.4, 61.2.

supervision and control of strategoi in the fourth century will be examined when the hazards of leadership are analysed.[8]

The ambitious individual, therefore, if he sought office at all, had to work within this framework of accountability, but the possibilities of using office to acquire power and influence were also restricted by other devices. The related notions of limited tenure and rotation and the principle of collegiality severely curtailed the opportunities for individuals, in the case of most offices, to use office to acquire a position of leadership.[9] These notions were not, of course, novel to our period nor peculiar to Athens. The limitation of the term of office to one year, for example, applied to the arkhons in Athens in the early sixth century, ensuring as it did the distribution of power among the ruling elite. Similarly, the principle of dividing power between officials pertained to the arkhons in Solonian times, and to officials in Sparta. The five ephors at Sparta were not only annual appointments but they also exemplified the concept of collegiality – the sharing of power among colleagues within the field of their competence. But in Athens in our period the extent to which these devices were applied and the multiplicity of official positions were important factors in making Athenian democracy distinctive. Moreover, the judicial powers of officials in our period were considerably reduced and the duties of most officials were of a limited, routine character.[10] Overshadowing these devices and peculiar to Athenian democracy was the extent to which lot was employed in the selection of office-holders, including members of the Boule. The Lot was, as we have seen, an important element in limiting the opportunities for the emergence of a powerful individual or a powerful council that might challenge the sovereignty of the Demos.[11]

Voting was used, however, to select some officials concerned with the civilian administration as well as all the military officials (including the strategoi). It was, for example, used in the 320s to select the Treasurer of the Military Fund, the Commissioners of the Festival Fund and the Superintendent of the Water Supply.[12] These positions were felt to require a measure of competence as they needed particular expertise or were of critical importance: towards the end of our period, as we have already seen, the Festival Fund Commissioners assumed a very important role. It was, however, primarily

[8] Thuc. 2.59–65, HCT 2.182–3, Plut. Per. 35.4–5, Hansen (1975) 71–3; see ch. 6.4.
[9] See ch. 3.5.
[10] The reduction of the judicial powers of officials is probably to be associated mainly with the period of Ephialtes' reforms and the development of Dikasteria. It may have been a continuing process as well, though references to the powers of the strategoi are not conclusive in this respect. The strategoi were not competent to impose the death penalty in the 320s (AP 61.2), but it is by no means clear that the instances cited from the late fifth century (Xen. Hell. 1.1.15 and Lys. 13.67) refer to the execution of citizens (as opposed to foreigners or slaves). Cf. Hignett 221–3.   [11] See ch. 1.5.
[12] AP 43.1. Voting was also used for a few positions requiring technical expertise like naval architects (AP 46.1) and for the appointment of envoys to visit foreign states on a particular mission. See also AP 42.2, 49.2, 54.5, 57.1.

the strategia where the method of election helped to give a special importance to the office thoughout most of our period. A strategos could assume from his election that he enjoyed a measure of popular support: this was one of the very few offices which permitted re-election and thus the accumulation of experience and influence. Yet in Athens there was much less room for powerful, independent officials than in republican Rome where, during the Late Republic, the Senate lost its grip on affairs and magistrates *qua* magistrates exercised (and exploited) great power and influence. Athenian officials did not possess the power enjoyed by Roman magistrates and, unlike the consuls in Rome, the strategoi did not preside over the Ekklesia or the Boule.[13]

Some scholars, however, have argued that the strategoi held certain specific powers beyond the area of military command and, in particular, that they were ex officio members of the Boule and that they could themselves convene a meeting of the Ekklesia.[14] Clearly their advice was a crucial (but not the only) element in the deliberations of both the Boule and the Ekklesia on matters relating to the security of the polis. On matters of defence and foreign policy they must have had priority of access, whether by custom or by legal right.[15] When enemy forces were operating or likely to operate in Attike, the strategoi could presumably oppose or indeed prevent a meeting of the assembly being held, and in wartime or at any time the prytaneis were hardly likely to deny a request from the strategoi to convene a meeting.[16] It is probable, though, that their relations with the Boule in these matters were rather based on close cooperation, as they were in other matters. The Boule and the strategoi very frequently, and then usually with some others, swore the oaths to a treaty and the two were often called upon to protect those who were honoured by Athens.[17] It was this close contact with some of the central activities in the Athenian polis, combined with their exercise of authority in actual operations, that helped leaders like Perikles to build up their influence through repeated tenure of the strategia. Moreover, on the annual board of ten strategoi Perikles enjoyed considerable prestige and thus a greater influence than other, less experienced colleagues. Nevertheless, their interrelationships were those of colleagues with equal power and responsibility. No one strategos possessed a constitutional supremacy over his fellow strategoi, though for a particular campaign the Ekklesia might give the commanders authority to act and

---

[13] In the sixth century presidency of the Ekklesia rested with the eponymous arkhon, but scholars have been divided about the date of the transfer of the presidency to a chairman drawn from the Boule. The transfer may well have been made by Kleisthenes, but may have been as late as Ephialtes, with some scholars suggesting a period (487–462) when the strategoi presided. See Hignett 151, 175; Rhodes 21 n. 4.   [14] Cf. Hignett 245–7.

[15] *IG* I³.61 (ML 65).55–6. Cf. *IG* I³.89.55–9 (417–13?) and Walbank no. 65 (*IG* I³.92).5 (*c.* 416/15) for decrees based on proposals of the strategoi; Tod 143.6–9 (362 B.C.), 168.6–9 (346 B.C.); Rhodes 43–6.

[16] Thuc. 2.22.1, 2.59.3, 4.118.14; Plut. *Phok.* 15.1; Gomme *HCT* 2.76, Dover (1960) 74–5.

[17] Tod 103.10–12, 147.14–16, 173.7–15.

designate them *autokratores* (having full powers).[18] Generals could make treaties with foreign states in the wake of military operations, but these arrangements had subsequently to be approved by the Ekklesia. The treaty, for example, made by Alkibiades and his fellow generals with Selymbria on the northern shore of the Propontis was ratified in 407 by a decree of the assembly and duly inscribed on a marble *stēlē* (pillar).[19] But the power of generals, even when they were given specific authority to act, was essentially the power to carry out the decisions of the Ekklesia, and in all matters they were personally and directly responsible to the Demos. Decisions of detail as well as decisions of policy were made by the assembly.

Strategoi in matters of defence and foreign policy, or men like Euboulos in financial matters, or men, whether officials or not, with interests in specific matters, enjoyed the advantage of close acquaintance with those matters when they were debated in the Ekklesia. The Demos, as we have already seen, might become more disposed to accept the advice of a Perikles, but the soundness of each proposal and the effectiveness with which it was advocated in the assembly on the day were perceived as the essential elements in decision-making.[20] Thucydides in particular and the ancient sources in general give the impression that it was only the assembly debates that mattered.[21] Nor can that be denied in so far as the final decision on an issue was made by the sovereign assembly and in so far as the crucial element was not the status of a strategos as such, but rather his ability or the ability of his supporters to exploit the equal right of free speech (*isēgoria*).[22]

There was therefore a certain compactness in space and time in the final stage of Athenian decision-making and a directness which in a sense imparted extreme influence to individuals. A leader of the Demos could and did derive his influence directly from the Demos. The secret of his power lay in his continuing ability to persuade and the success of the policies he advocated. His power was therefore starker, and at the same time more fragile, than in modern states where countervailing forces clearly play a part in defining and limiting the role of individuals. In Athens there was nothing comparable to the small cabinet in modern governments, nor to ministers with considerable power and an individual as well as a collective responsibility, nor to permanent civil service departments. The tension between the sovereign Demos and ambitious individuals, and between individual leaders, was considerable and was exacerbated by the relative weakness of countervailing forces. The supreme

[18] Thuc. 6.8.2 and 6.26.1 (the three commanders of the Sicilian expedition in 415), Xen. *Hell.* 1.4.10, 20 (Alkibiades); Dover (1960) 61–77, Fornara (1971A) 28–39, 79–80; cf. Hignett 247–50, 348–54, Jameson (1955) 63–87.

[19] Walbank no. 86 (*IG* i³. 118, ML 87) (cf. *IG* i³.119 (ML 88) for the treaty made by Alkibiades and his colleagues with the Klazomenians at Daphnous).

[20] See ch. 2.3.1. [21] See ch. 4.3.

[22] See Dem. 19.182–6 on the serious consequences of telling lies to an assembly and on delays in making and executing decisions.

authority of the Demos and the all-embracing character of that authority are also highlighted by contrast with many modern states, where in varying degrees and with varying degrees of success an attempt is made to keep the legislature and the judiciary (or the legislature, the executive and the judiciary) independent.

4.2 The assembly and the making and revision of laws

There were, it is true, some restraints on the power of the Ekklesia. The requirement that its decisions should not contravene existing law has already been noted.[23] Furthermore, specific procedures for the revision and making of laws (*nomothesia*), whereby all proposed changes were submitted to *nomothetai* (lawmakers), were instituted in the last years of the fifth century, largely in order to prevent snap votes in the assembly, such as had led to the repeal of key democratic institutions in 411 and 404. Henceforth, at a meeting in the first prytany of each year the Ekklesia was asked to vote whether the laws, grouped together in four categories, were adequate and, if any were not so judged, these were discussed at a later meeting in the same prytany. In the interim, any citizen who wished could propose a law and was required to write it on a white board and exhibit it in front of the Eponymous Heroes. The subsequent meeting determined the time to be allowed to the nomothetai to decide what changes should be made to the laws. The nomothetai, who were appointed at the second meeting, were drawn from among the dikasts.[24] This annual procedure or Review Law did not allow the immediate passage of a law which was felt in the course of a year to be urgent. Other procedures, however, are indicated in the fourth-century evidence, and various reconstructions have been offered by modern scholars.[25] It may well be that a law was introduced (perhaps *c.* 370) amending the Review Law by specifying other times for legislation than the annual review, whether a new law was being proposed or an old law was being repealed and replaced by a new law – and perhaps not spelling out the requirements of the Review Law about publicity and the recruitment of nomothetai from sworn dikasts. A need for urgent action and the deficiencies of the new law (if it was silent about publicity and recruitment) could be exploited to secure what was alleged by Demosthenes in 353 – the immediate appointment of nomothetai by combining the bouleutai and 1,001 dikasts.[26] The new law seems to have included the requirement that, in the event of conflict between a proposed law and an existing law, a proposed law could not be enacted by the nomothetai unless the existing law was concurrently

---

[23] See ch. 3.5.   [24] Dem. 24.19–23; Harrison (1955) 26–35.
[25] Dem. 20.89–99, 24.32–3 (cf. 3.10), Aiskhin. 3.37–9; MacDowell 48–9 and (1975) 62–74, de Laix 52–68, Hansen (1971–80A) 87–104, Sealey (1982) 289–97, Rhodes (1985) 55–60.
[26] Dem. 24.27–8.

repealed.[27] A citizen, however, might represent a new law as urgent and as not conflicting with any existing law: if such assertions were not challenged, new laws might be enacted which had not been subjected to the same close scrutiny as at the annual review and which conflicted with existing laws – as was alleged in the mid-350s.[28] Such conflicts were, or could be, referred to *ad hoc* commissions, but at some time between the mid-350s and 330 an Inspection Law was introduced requiring the thesmothetai each year to inspect the laws and bring any conflicts to the attention of the assembly which would refer them to the nomothetai.[29]

Nomothesia has sometimes been regarded as a serious diminution of the sovereignty of the assembly, but it should rather be seen as a brake on the making of decisions which might affect the fundamental laws and institutions of the polis. Nomothesia did not prevent constitutional or legal changes but it did slow down the process and sought to prevent change through snap votes or a single stacked meeting. Moreover, it would seem that the Ekklesia could prevent any proposals going forward to the nomothetai. In any case, the procedures applied only to 'laws' (*nomoi*) whereas most decisions of the Ekklesia were 'decrees' (*psēphismata*) relating to temporary or specific circumstances. The general view is that nomoi were conceived to be not only superior to psephismata, but more fundamental, more universal and more permanent. Some of the nomoi which have survived, however, especially those concerned with money, deal with specific questions arising from particular circumstances and illustrate the difficulty of drawing a neat distinction between 'laws' and 'decrees'. Most laws, it might be suggested, tend to deal with questions of an ongoing rather than a 'temporary' character, though decrees too may deal with ongoing questions.[30] Furthermore, the nomothetai could be regarded, like other large bodies, as a cross-section of the whole Demos.

4.3 The Council of 500 and the decision-making process

Apart from these constraints on the power of the assembly there was one agency which might seriously limit its decisions and lessen the stark contrast between the assembly and individual leaders. For the Council of 500, as has been seen, exercised extensive probouleutic functions in regard to business coming before the Ekklesia: in particular, the assembly could not vote on a decree unless it had

---

[27] Dem. 24.33. [28] Dem. 20.91. [29] Aiskhin. 3.37–9.

[30] On nomoi and psephismata, see Ostwald 1–3, Rhodes 49–52 and Hansen 161–206. For inscribed nomoi which have come to light see Stroud (1974) 157–88, especially 162–3, 185–7 (*SEG* 26.72; silver coinage, 375/4), Clinton (1980) 258–88 (*SEG* 30.61; Eleusinian Mysteries, 367–348 (?)), *IG* II².140 (and Alessandri (1980) 1131–61; Eleusinian first-fruits, 353/2), 244 (rebuilding of the walls, 337/6), *SEG* 12.87 (law against tyranny, 337/6), *IG* II².334 and *SEG* 18.13 (Panathenaia, 336–334), *IG* II².333 (sacred rites, 335/4); Rhodes 276. On decrees dealing with general, 'permanent' matters see the minimal list in Hansen 187–91.

been previously discussed by the council and placed on the agenda by the prytaneis.[31] It would appear, however, that while the Boule was in general left to determine what should be discussed in the assembly a matter could be raised in the Ekklesia and the council could be directed to discuss it and make a recommendation. In any case it was clearly possible to find one councillor among 500 who would bring before the Boule a matter of any real significance.[32] The provision for prior discussion (*probouleusis*) therefore enabled discussion of details and consideration of the ramifications of a proposal but did not, in view of the frequency of meetings of the Boule, necessarily involve more than a brief delay. It should also be noted that in the 320s, and presumably earlier, certain regular items of business were set down for each of the assembly meetings in a prytany. At the main meeting, for example, a vote was to be taken to confirm the officials in their office if they were thought to be carrying out their duties satisfactorily, and discussion of the food supply and the defence of the country was also prescribed. Moreover, other procedures and conventions, such as the privilege of priority of access granted by the assembly, also constrained the prytaneis in drawing up the agenda.[33] At the same time, however, its probouleutic functions would seem to have given the Boule the potential to exercise a decisive influence on the assembly. Yet some scholars have argued that serious discussions seldom or never took place in the Boule and that it was a processing body more like a secretariat than a body whose deliberations had a decisive effect on the decision of the Ekklesia.[34]

The Boule's role in the decision-making process was, like its supervisory and coordinating role in the implementation of the assembly's decisions, subject to change in the course of our period.[35] Its probouleutic role, for example, may have been affected by institutional changes such as the introduction in the 390s of pay for attending the assembly. Aristotle, at any rate, argued that the power of a council, in particular in regard to its probouleutic functions, was weakened in those democracies in which the people in assembly dealt with everything and that this latter situation usually arose when there was a plentiful supply of pay for those attending the assembly. Being at leisure, Aristotle maintained, they would meet frequently and decide all things themselves.[36] In the case of Athens, however, it is important to note that from the fifth century as well as the fourth there are examples of the Ekklesia dealing with detailed matters that might have been expected to be delegated to a council or officials.[37] Nor is it clear that the propensity for this increased significantly in the fourth century, but the evidence does not admit of a secure answer.

Investigation of Boule–Ekklesia relations shows up in sharp relief some of the methodological problems involved in the use of evidence relating to Athens in

---

[31] See ch. 3.6.   [32] *IG* II².152; *AP* 29.1, Aiskhin. 3.125.
[33] *AP* 43.4–6 (and *CAAP*), Rhodes 52–60; Tod 131.15–16, see 167.55–7.
[34] Headlam 57–63, Gomme (1962) 181–8, Jones 110–22.   [35] See ch. 3.6.
[36] Arist. *Pol.* 1299b39–1300a4; cf. 1317b30–4; 1293a2–11.   [37] *IG* I³.84.11–28.

our period. In the first place, there is in the literary sources little information on the Boule's role in decision-making for the fifth century and by comparison a reasonable amount for the fourth. What is more, we might be led to conclude from Thucydides' narrative that in the late fifth century the Boule played an insignificant role in the decision-making process, for he locates all debates in the Ekklesia and only once mentions deliberations in the Boule.[38] Secondly, most of our literary evidence for the fourth century comes from the orators. They had an axe to grind, for they were endeavouring to establish that a particular action, often involving themselves, was right or wrong. Thirdly, the statements of the orators do not relate to a representative sample of assembly debates, for the orators were dealing mainly with controversial issues. The picture which they present is that debates in the assembly tended to be lively and that motions were frequently proposed in the assembly by non-councillors.[39]

On controversial issues the recommendations of the Boule were least likely to be adopted without amendment by the assembly, and it is therefore important to examine the wider sample provided by a study of inscriptions recording the decisions of the Ekklesia and the Boule. Four major problems should, however, be noted in the use of this epigraphical material. First, it is well known that many decisions of the assembly were recorded on stone. But bronze stelai or wooden tablets were also used, while some decrees were probably recorded only on papyrus.[40] It is likely that decisions where public display was considered important tended to be inscribed on stone – in particular, alliances with foreign states. Secondly, in the case of decisions inscribed on stone, the element of chance which affects the survival and the discovery of inscriptions may produce an unrepresentative sample of decrees no less serious than the bias towards controversial issues reflected in the orators. Thirdly, the fragmentary character of the stele on which the particular decree is inscribed may lead to error or compound the difficulty. Fourthly, there were differences in formulas and in recording techniques in the course of our period: where clear patterns have been discerned by scholars, these can help with dating and other questions, but the significance of some of these differences has not been established. Sometimes, indeed, carelessness on the part of the mason or the secretary may be assumed or suspected as the cause of variations.[41]

These problems may be illustrated by the stele which records the Athenian

---

[38] Thuc. 5.45 (cf. Plut. *Nik.* 10, *Alk.* 14); see 8.69–70 for the only other mention of the Boule of 500 (its dismissal by the oligarchs in 411); Rhodes 57 and n. 3. See also Thuc. 3.36.5 for the action in 427 by the Mytilenaian envoys and their supporters in getting 'the authorities' to convene another meeting of the assembly so that the question of the punishment of Mytilene could be put to a second vote. 'The authorities' were probably the prytaneis (or the Boule), or the initial approach may have been made to some of the generals (*HCT* 2.298; cf. Hignett 246–7).

[39] Rhodes 52–64.   [40] Connor (1974) 33–4 and Stroud (1963) 138 n. 1.

[41] See Henry (1977) 31 and n. 40, 104–5 for secretaries' discretion and carelessness (or inconsistency) in framing prescripts. See also Appendix 3A.

alliance with Eretria in 394.[42] The stele is now in two fragments covering the first 21 lines of a decree. The preamble contains the formula 'it was resolved by the Boule', not the usual formula for assembly decrees of this period – 'it was resolved by the Boule and the Demos'. Now the Boule could take certain action on its own authority, and on the basis of this decree and others an increase in the Boule's powers has been postulated for a brief period in the early fourth century. Yet the dangers of making deductions from recorded formulas are strikingly shown by a decree dated to 385/4.[43] This decree also includes in its preamble the formula 'it was resolved by the [Boule]', but the end of the inscription contains a rider or amendment of the common type ('[all the rest] as resolved by the Boule, [but] . . .'). The rider establishes that the Boule's decision was ratified by the Ekklesia, even though the enactment formula as recorded is 'it was resolved by the [Boule]'. It is possible that the last part of the stele recording the Eretria alliance contained a similar amendment: the recovery of the missing fragments would then provide proof that the secretary had failed to change the enactment formula when the Boule's proposal for an alliance with Eretria was accepted by the Ekklesia. On the other hand, the Boule's proposal may not have been amended and proof of oversight might be impossible. But while speculation in terms of human error in recording is very hazardous, the view of most scholars that the Eretria alliance was ratified by the Ekklesia rests fundamentally on the reasonable assumption that the Boule could not commit the Demos, particularly to an alliance with a foreign state.[44]

On the same grounds, the widely accepted notion that there was a secret pact in the early 350s between the Boule (or Athenian envoys) and Philip, that Athens would hand over Pydna in exchange for Amphipolis, has been challenged.[45] A binding commitment could not, it may be agreed, be made by the Boule, but there may have been some 'understanding' between Philip and Athenian envoys who consulted the Boule 'off the record'. The Boule did occasionally hold secret meetings, though it is hard to conceive of absolute secrecy with a body of 500.[46] Consultation with the Boule (with its members drawn from a wide cross-section of Athenian citizens) was a useful means of sounding out public opinion. Demainetos at any rate thought so in 396 when he was planning, in line with recent anti-Spartan activities, to seize a trireme from the state dockyards and join Konon who was encouraging the Persians to challenge Spartan naval power in the Aegean. The commotion which followed his departure led the Boule to call a meeting of the assembly and to deny any participation in the affair: in fear of Spartan retaliation against Athens, the assembly advised the Spartan governor of Aigina that Demainetos had acted without its authority.[47]

[42] Tod 103.   [43] *IG* II².32.   [44] Jones 114, Rhodes 82–5.

[45] Theopompos *FGrH* F30, Dem. 2.6; de Ste Croix (1963) 110–19.

[46] Andok. 2.19–20, Lys. 31.31, [Dem.] 25.23, Aiskhin. 3.125–6, de Ste Croix (1963) 115 n. 1; Rhodes 40–2, de Laix 80–1.   [47] *Hell. Oxy.* 6.1–3.

The Boule's handling of the Demainetos affair would seem to be a close reflection of Athenian feeling in 396. There was growing resentment of Spartan power and policy and an increasing readiness to assert a measure of independence for Athens, but this readiness was neither universal nor very strong (since Athens still had no walls and only a token naval force) and it could evaporate if pro-Spartan elements raised the bogey of Spartan retaliation. Twenty-five years later the Boule reflected the antipathy towards Thebes which, Athenians felt, had been making no contribution to the anti-Spartan cause, especially in regard to naval activities, and which rather had been consolidating its control over the other Boiotian states to the disquiet of Athens: the council dismissed the Theban herald bringing the news of the Theban victory at Leuktra over the Spartans without so much as a reply to the Theban request for help, let alone the usual invitation to hospitality in the *prytaneion* (town hall).[48] This negative power of the Boule, probably exercised rarely in matters of substance and only when the Boule felt confident about current attitudes, is one element in the assessment of the Boule's role. Somewhat more frequently, the Boule may have declined to raise in the Ekklesia minor matters brought before it, and some such matters may well have been set aside by the prytaneis before reaching the Boule. This, however, was probably a screening of the trivial, not a serious blocking even of matters that we might regard as minor from reaching the assembly for debate.

4.4 The decrees of the assembly

4.4.1 Probouleumatic decrees

What, then, do the decrees of the Ekklesia which are known from being recorded on stone reveal about the relations between the Boule and the Ekklesia and in particular about the influence of the Boule's recommendations on the decisions of the assembly? Some decrees may certainly be interpreted as accepting the substance of the recommendation of the Boule (*probouleuma*). In 377, for example, the Boule resolved as follows. '*With reference to what the Khalkidians say, bring them* (the Khalkidians) *before the Demos at the next assembly and communicate the resolution of the Boule that it seems good to the Boule* to accept the alliance of the Khalkidians, with good fortune, as proposed by the Khalkidians. . . .'[49] The Ekklesia approved the recommendation of the Boule, and the assembly decree began with the 'probouleumatic formula' (that is, the italicised words quoted above). Another generally useful criterion for identifying the contribution of the Boule is the rider or amendment which employed the formula: 'all the rest as resolved by the Boule, but . . .'. One of the friends

---

[48] Xen. *Hell.* 6.4.20; cf. Hdt. 9.5; Aiskhin. 2.58–9, Dem. 18.28; see Wycherley 166–74 and Thompson and Wycherley 46–7 for the prytaneion.   [49] Tod 124.7–13.

of Oiniades (who came from the island of Skiathos and was honoured in an Athenian decree in 408/7) used this formula to move his amendment that the designation of Oiniades be changed from 'Skiathios' (as in the Boule's recommendation) to 'Palaiskiathios'. The assembly responded to Oiniades' wish to be known as coming from 'old' Skiathos.[50] 'All the rest' was in this case clearly the probouleuma or recommendation of the council, though in some decrees we cannot be as confident that all the earlier part of the decree was simply the recommendation of the council.[51]

In both the decrees cited, the substance of the Boule's recommendations was approved and the actual words of the probouleumata were adopted. In the second half of the fourth century the Athenians seem to have made a distinction between decrees which thus ratified verbatim a probouleuma, whether or not there were amendments to it, and decrees which were enunciated in the assembly, and they seem regularly to have employed different formulas for the two types.[52] For the sake of analysis, the former may be called 'probouleumatic decrees' and the latter 'non-probouleumatic decrees'. The distinction is based purely on the form of the final motion. For non-probouleumatic decrees may in varying measure owe something to specific proposals by the Boule. Probouleumatic decrees, however, give a clearer basis for some evaluation of the Boule's contribution to the formulation of policy and should be considered first.

The focus of any analysis of decrees is likely to rest on fourth-century decrees which are more numerous, but fifth-century decrees display some common features as well as differences between the two broad periods. At all times the Ekklesia might, of course, accept the recommendation of the Boule as presented and did so on substantial matters such as the committal of Athens to foreign alliances as well as on minor matters. In 356, for example, the assembly approved the recommendation to accept an alliance with Thracian and other kings and authorised the Boule to make any necessary addition.[53] Sometimes more or less routine additions were made in the assembly to rectify oversights or accidental (or in some cases perhaps intentional) omissions, such as instructions for the publication of the decree or some specification about defraying the cost of inscribing the decree or the invitation (to envoys or honorands) to hospitality in the town hall on the following day.[54] In the light of discussion in the assembly (or realisation of omissions after the debate in the Boule) these additions might be proposed by a citizen who was not a member of the Boule or by any of the bouleutai including the councillor who put forward the probouleuma in the assembly. In 405 the proposal to grant Athenian

---

[50] Walbank no. 87 (*IG* i³.110, ML 90). 26–31. Though the change was made in lines 7–8 in the decree as inscribed, the rider was still formally recorded and inscribed.

[51] See ch. 4.4.2 below.   [52] See Appendix 3B.

[53] Tod 157.34–5 and (more cautiously) 200.264–9; cf. Tod 123.31–5 and *IG* ii².204.85–6 for other specific authorisations by the Ekklesia.   [54] *IG* ii².232.18–27; Rhodes 278–9.

citizenship to all the Samians was put forward in the assembly by 'Kleisophos and his fellow prytaneis', and it was they who moved a rider providing for the immediate enrolment in the ten tribes of the Samian envoys then in Athens, inviting Eumachos to hospitality as a citizen, and providing for the publication of the decree and the payment of the cost thereof.[55]

Riders moved by other people ranged from minor corrections to patently contentious amendments. Sometimes an amendment simply provided for the publication of the decree and the specification of the amount to be spent.[56] In 369/8 a probouleuma recommending the award of the titles 'public friend and benefactor' to Pythodoros of Delos was amended on the motion of Epikrates (who had been one of the administrators of the Delian temple properties from 377 to 373) by adding provisions for publication and payment of the cost and for protecting the honorand. The last provision was of some importance and may perhaps have had an element of contention in it, though it may have been merely a sensible precaution and may have been accepted as such.[57] Yet there could be no mistaking the amendment moved by Kephalos in 386 to the probouleuma giving a reward to Phanokritos of Parion and granting him the title of 'benefactor'. In itself the proposal by Kephalos to upgrade the honours by granting the two titles of 'public friend and benefactor' was of some significance, but not unusual, while the specification that the Receivers (of public moneys) were to pay the reward could be regarded as a minor or (less likely) a major matter. But there was nothing routine or innocuous in the grounds advanced for upgrading the honours: 'since he (Phanokritos) passed on information to the strategoi about the movement of the ships and, if the strategoi had paid heed, the enemy triremes would have been captured'. Clearly Kephalos, who had a reputation for abuse in the assembly, was being contentious and seized the opportunity in an endeavour to discredit the strategoi involved or their political associates.[58]

Sometimes the amendments passed in the assembly went well beyond the probouleuma and fundamentally changed it. In 418/7, for example, a rider by Adousios who moved the Boule's recommendation about the leasing of a temple's land not only increased from 1,000 to 10,000 drakhmai the penalty for failure to carry out the provisions of the decree in the current bouleutic year, but also provided that the cost of fencing the temple be met by the lessee, not from the revenue from the land, as recommended by the Boule, and added details about the removal of the mud from the ditch as well as administrative details.[59] In 409 Erasinides moved on behalf of the Boule that the assassins of

---

55   Osborne D4 (*IG* I³.127, ML 94).32–40; the unique formula which associates all the prytaneis with the formal mover Kleisophos in both the probouleuma and the rider has been widely interpreted as a desire to emphasise unanimity. Cf. *IG* II².206.26–36.

56   *IG* I³.82.42–4.

57   *SIG*³.158.15–27 (cf. Tod 125.10). Cf. Tod 125.134–42 and *IG* II².373.

58   Tod 116; Ar. *Ekkl.* 248–51.   59   *IG* I³.84.11–28.

Phrynikhos be rewarded with a gold crown. A long amendment by Diokles granted Thrasyboulos citizenship (with lesser honours for others) and a share in some property or award and envisaged further benefits, while a second rider by Eudikos ordered an inquiry into allegations of bribery in the matter.[60]

In short, in the case of decrees which may, on the basis of format, be designated 'probouleumatic', the assembly's response to the Boule's specific recommendation might range from complete acceptance to transformation of the proposal. Some but not all probouleumatic decrees may therefore seem to carry the implication that the real debate was conducted in the Boule and that the assembly 'merely' ratified the probouleuma. Moreover, there can be no doubt that the Boule discussed matters of policy and that leading political figures served on the Boule.[61] Yet while complete acceptance is an index of the seriousness and thoroughness of the debate in the Boule and its sense of current attitudes among Athenians at large, it is an insecure basis for denying that on the particular matter there was a lively and serious debate in the assembly. It may well be that it was only after considerable debate that the assembly came to the view that the Boule had achieved the best formulation.

Again, on some matters of substance there should have been little need for discussion in the Boule beyond the exact wording to be adopted since the tenor of Athenian policy was clear. In 377, for example, the year in which a general invitation was extended to states to join the Second Athenian League, the question of whether to recommend an alliance with Khalkis should not have required extensive discussion, especially when the principles of admission had been laid down.[62] That is, in endeavouring to establish the contribution of the Boule, we should take account of several variables including the importance of the issue covered by a probouleuma, the current policies (if any) on that or

---

[60] Osborne D2 (*IG* I³.102, ML 85).14–47.

[61] Dem. 8.4, Aiskhin. 3.125; Pl. *Menex.* 234a–b. Political figures who are known to have served on the Boule (probably, at least in some cases like Demosthenes in 347/6, choosing to stand in a year that was expected to be critical) included Kleon, Hyperbolos, Androtion, Demosthenes, Demades and Lykourgos; see Rhodes 3–4 and Tritle (1981) 118–32 (possibly Phokion in 336/5). The shortness of the list, it must be noted, is an index of the paucity of information about councillors: councillors known for the years down to 322/1 do not number enough to fill a single Boule, despite the thousands who would have been councillors (between 1,000 and 2,000 different citizens in every four years). For the same reason deductions should not be drawn from the fact that only 12 (or at most 22) can be identified with any confidence as having served twice on the council in the period from 403/2 to 322/1, and all of these apparently after a gap of some years: see Rhodes 242–3 as modified in Rhodes (1980B) 197–201 and (1981) 101–2, and Meritt and Traill (1974) 349–469. See also Hansen (1986) 51–5 for an analysis of the limitations of the evidence and for the view that not less than one-fifth of all bouleutai served twice: the number could easily have been as high as one-quarter and still ensured observance of the (probable) rule that a man could act as chairman of the prytaneis only once in his life (*AP* 44.1 and *CAAP*).

[62] Tod 124 is essentially a 'machinery' recommendation from the Boule, which applied to this particular alliance with Khalkis the provisions laid down in Tod 123: see, for example, lines 21–6 on the 'freedom and autonomy' of Khalkis. Tod 122, if it is a probouleumatic decree, is very much a 'machinery' motion since it simply provided for Methymna, which was already

related issues and the degree of support for, or controversy surrounding, the current policies or the issue under debate. The evidence unfortunately does not often enable detailed analysis or permit certainty in concluding that a probouleuma was essentially a formal or 'machinery' recommendation, albeit on an important issue, or that it was the Boule that initiated the fundamental discussion of a substantial question or developed new initiatives of significance.

Nevertheless, the subject matter of decrees and the extent and character of amendments provide a rough index of the role of the Boule in policy formulation and development. The index is tentative not only because it is based on a limited sample of recovered inscriptions but, in particular, because the form (or the fragmentary character of many inscriptions) frequently makes it difficult or impossible to assess whether the council made a specific recommendation on all points or not and to determine the extent and nature of amendments. From the 50–60 years down to 404/3 there are some 20 decrees which are clearly probouleumatic and of these about half may be held to relate to 'substantial' matters.[63] In foreign affairs, for example, the Boule's recommendations were accepted, with or without amendments, in regard to an alliance with Egesta in 458/7 (?), relations with Methone in 426/5 and an alliance with Carthage in 407/6.[64] The very important decree providing for the reassessment of the tribute in 425 was based on the Boule's recommendation, as was the 405 decree granting citizenship to the Samians.[65] Substantial questions also seem to have been dealt with in decrees relating to the superintendents at Eleusis (*c.* 449–7), the temple of Athena Nike (*c.* 448 (?)), access to Eleusis, regulations for the festival of Hephaistos in 421/0 and the assassins of

an 'ally of Athens', to become an 'ally of Athens and the other allies' (that is to join the Second Athenian League). Nor could the Boule in 375 have been in any doubt about the acceptance of Kerkyra, Akarnania and Kephallenia as new allies into the Second Athenian League, though the end of the decree (now fragmentary – Tod 126.25–8) may have referred to problems raised in the Boule but not resolved; cf. Cargill (1981) 68–75 who argues that the treaty of 375 was partially aborted (cf. Tuplin (1984) 544–66). Even where Athenian overall policy was clear, negotiations for a particular alliance might raise unexpected fundamental difficulties. Nor could the Boule in 394 (in view of the anti-Spartan coalition of 395) have been in any doubt that the assembly would make an alliance with Eretria, though Tod 103.8–11 may conceal some serious problems yet to be resolved between the two states. But the first two cases, while they relate to a substantial question (an alliance), appear to have proved to be straightforward matters. In so far as there is nothing to suggest that the recommendations required fundamental and difficult discussion by the Boule, the resulting decrees may therefore be differentiated from other decrees which are described here as 'substantial' on the criterion of content as suggested by Rhodes 78–81, especially 78 n. 3.

63 See Rhodes 246–7 and also *IG* I³.89.1–8 (but cf. Hoffman (1975) 92–104). Other decrees may well be based on specific probouleumata (for example, *IG* I³.40 (ML 52) on relations with Khalkis in 446/5; see de Laix 92–4; cf. Rhodes 71 n. 2) but are excluded here since they cannot be securely designated 'probouleumatic' on the basis of format. For other decrees such as the Kallias financial decrees of 434/3 (*IG* I³.52A (ML 58A)) and a decree relating to Methone (*IG* I³.61 (ML 65).3–32 of 430/29) there are no real indications in the form of the decrees whether they are based on specific recommendations by the Boule. Cf. de Laix 87–108.

64 *IG* I³.11 (ML 37), 61 (ML 65).32–56, 123.

65 *IG* I³.71 (ML 69), Osborne D4 (*IG* I³.127, ML 94).

Phrynikhos.[66] There appears to have been a tendency for the Ekklesia to accept the formulation of the Boule, but the sample is too small to define this more precisely and in any case it may be rather a secretarial reliance on, or even the assembly's inclination to retain, the Boule's wording.[67] The impression, however, is that in the later fifth century the assembly showed a certain readiness in its decisions to be guided (but not dominated) by the recommendation of the council.

Slightly more than 100 decrees known from the period from 403/2 to 322/1 are probably probouleumatic and of these some 9 (or possibly more) may be regarded as dealing with substantial matters.[68] The Boule's recommendations were accepted, with or without amendment, in decrees relating to Eretria (394), the Eteokarpathians from the island of Karpathos (*c.* 393 (?)), Thebes in 378/7, Kerkyra, Akarnania and Kephallenia in 375, Mytilene in 369/8, Dionysios I of Syracuse in 369/8, Siphnos, and Thracian and other kings in 356.[69] Regulations of *c.* 335/4 for the Panathenaic festival, by the luck of survival, seem to be the only other significant decree clearly based on a probouleuma.[70] The small proportion of 'substantial' probouleumatic decrees is a reflection of many factors, including the fact that many honorific decrees have survived due to the desire of honorands to have a permanent record on stone of the honours and their willingness, in not a few cases, to bear the expense involved. While these awards were clearly important for the honorands, it is probably best not to regard them singly as 'substantial' in terms of overall Athenian policy, though it is well to remember that pro-Athenian elements in other states represented in varying degrees an important element in Athenian relations with those states.[71] The proportion of 'substantial' probouleumatic decrees is not markedly different, given the chance factor in survival and the difficulties of interpretation, from surviving non-probouleumatic decrees if some 15 (or less) out of

---

66 *IG* I³.32, 35 (*SEG* 31.9, ML 44), 58, 82, 102 (ML 85). See also a decree about the important subject of the water supply (*IG* I³.49) which is too fragmentary to rank as dealing with a substantial matter.

67 See, however, ch. 4.4.1 for Adousios' decree; see de Laix 104.

68 Rhodes 247–50, but the numbers may be inflated since (as Rhodes notes) some decrees from the first half of the fourth century are classified as probouleumatic on the sole basis of the enactment formula 'it was resolved by the Boule and the Demos'. See ch. 4.4.2 re 'crossbreeds'.

69 Tod 103, 110 (dated by Jameson to the fifth century: cf. D. M. Lewis (1977) 144 n. 55), *IG* II².40, Tod 126, Tod 131.35–60, Tod 133, *SEG* 17.19, Tod 157. The second of these decrees honouring the Eteokarpathians shows that there was serious discussion in the Boule (if the enactment formula does in this case indicate a probouleumatic decree), but the reverse of the stone is badly preserved and may have recorded a rider (which might permit an assessment of the significance of contributions in the assembly) or a second decree. For three other decrees ranked as substantial by Rhodes 247–9, see n. 62 above re alliances with Methymna and Khalkis (Tod 122, 124), and the fragmentary decree of 355 relating to Neapolis (Tod 159).

70 *IG* II².334; cf. *SEG* 18.13.

71 See Walbank (1978) 7–8 and 29 nn. 33–4 for publication of a proxeny decree as probably an additional privilege and an indication of the willingness (or otherwise) of the Athenian polis to take the further step of paying the cost of recording the grant on a stone stele.

about 100 are held to deal with 'substantial' matters.[72] The proportion of 'minor' matters in both categories is also an index of the interest of the Ekklesia in matters of minor importance as well as great matters of state.

4.4.2 Non-probouleumatic decrees

Now 'non-probouleumatic decrees' are those decrees which do not identify any of the clauses as incorporating the actual words of specific recommendations by the Boule. They do not necessarily imply that there had been no serious debate in the Boule. Two broad possibilities may be assumed. First, the Boule made a purely open or formal recommendation – that the Ekklesia discuss the matter – because, for whatever reasons, there was no serious discussion of the issue in the Boule or the Boule was unable or unwilling to make a specific recommendation. The reasons for an open recommendation might relate to any one or more variables: lack of time to formulate a view on an urgent matter or in a crisis (as, for example, on receipt of the news of the capture of Elateia in 339), an attempt to avoid prosecution for making a proposal contravening an existing law (as when Apollodoros invited the Demos to decide whether surplus moneys should go to the Military Fund or, as currently required by law, the Festival Fund), or an inability to formulate a clear recommendation because of the controversial character or novelty of a proposal or deep divisions about an appropriate response.[73] One aspect of a recommendation might be left open – for example, in regard to matters involving the expenditure of money, since in the fourth century any addition to the funds or budget which had been allocated by the assembly in the annual *merismos* (allocation) had subsequently to be approved by the nomothetai. Councillors (like citizens in the assembly) were therefore likely to be circumspect in proposing changes relating to finance, sometimes because the matter raised a general question of financing or a new obligation, sometimes because expenditure beyond the current year was involved.[74]

The second possibility is that the Boule made specific recommendations which were rejected in entirety or in substance by the assembly. Or the 'rejection' may have amounted to a question of format and recording practice rather than of substance, for the format of a motion as put to the assembly for voting depended on the interaction between the councillor who moved the council's recommendation, an individual in the assembly who might be anxious to emphasise particular matters or to move a motion in his own name, and the chairman of the assembly on that day (and chairman on that day only). The point at which a probouleuma had been so amended that a reformulation or a new motion was deemed necessary would have been determined by that

---

[72] Rhodes 79, 259–62.

[73] Dem. 18.169–70 (see ch. 2.2), [Dem.] 59.4, Rhodes 58, 59 n. 3, 271–2.

[74] *IG* II².223A13; see *IG* II².222.41–6, II².330.15–23, *SIG*³ 298.35–41; cf. Tod 167.39–44, 53–9; Jones 102–3, D. M. Lewis (1959) 245–7, Rhodes 50 n. 1, 73 n. 3, 101, de Laix 133, Hansen 191–5, W. E. Thompson (1979) 149–53.

interaction. Moreover, the words of the motion as recorded and inscribed might not be exactly the same as the words of the motion as put: there is evidence that it might sometimes be left to the mover and the secretary who prepared the decree for publication to work out the exact words of the motion, the assembly being content sometimes to vote, for example, that an individual be made an Athenian citizen and leave some of the usual phraseology to be added.[75] Variations of practice or 'inconsistencies' might result at one or both of these stages.[76] Consequently, a decree that is probouleumatic in terms of its format may, as we have seen, in essence go far beyond the probouleuma, while a decree that is non-probouleumatic in form may be closer to the substance of the probouleuma.

The final format of a non-probouleumatic decree does not therefore provide a secure criterion for regarding it as a complete or substantial rejection of the Boule's recommendation, let alone for assuming that the Boule did not discuss the matter seriously. Only rarely is there information that would enable an assessment of the extent to which the provisions of a specific probouleuma may have been subsumed in a 'non-probouleumatic' motion as passed by the assembly. There are special difficulties which arise from the lack of information and the reliance on the format of the assembly's decree. Where, for example, a rider is introduced by the formula 'all the rest as moved by X' (where X is presumed to be an individual citizen who had moved the motion in his own name in the assembly and not as a recommendation of the council), it is assumed that the Boule's recommendations have been rejected or at least superseded. In 346 when he was not a member of the Boule, the well-known Androtion moved a decree in the assembly to honour the Bosporan rulers Spartokos and Pairisades; another leading political figure Polyeuktos wished to crown their brother Apollonios also and moved an amendment which is recorded as 'all the rest as moved by Androtion, but . . .'.[77] Yet the motion of Androtion contains language appropriate to a probouleuma. An attempt has therefore been made to distinguish clauses in Androtion's motion which may derive from a pro-bouleuma and clauses which may be 'concealed riders', but the variety and the possibility of lack of care in drafting and recording Athenian decrees rather frustrate arguments based on logical cohesion.[78] Nevertheless, it is clear that

---

[75] Ar. *Thesm.* 431–2; M. J. Osborne (1972) 138. See Aiskhin. 2.64, 68 for the submission of written motions to the presiding officials to put to the vote; *AP* 54.5, Jones 114–15.

[76] Changes in the secretaryship (see p. 228) and the fact that a chairman presided over the assembly for only one day increase the likelihood of variations in practice in the putting of proposals to the vote and also in the recording of proposals, and consequently make analysis based on the format of the published decree more difficult.

[77] Tod 167.65–8; see Tuplin (1982) 121–8.

[78] Laqueur (1927) 58–63; Billheimer (1938) 466–9, refuting Laqueur's theory that any clause recorded after the instruction for the publication of the decree must be an amendment. On the other hand, it is not to be assumed that every rider (for example, amendments immediately accepted by the mover) is scrupulously identified as such nor that each published decree is simply a transcript of the minutes, completely uniform in style and in meticulous recording of details. See n. 76; cf. de Laix 91, 167–9.

Androtion subsumed in his motion at least something from the Boule's recommendation.[79]

It is also rare to have information to identify decrees on matters where the recommendation was purely 'open'. The Kitian merchants who in 333 were granted permission by the assembly to acquire land for a temple of Aphrodite were anxious to set out the precise details of their legal claim and, at their own expense, had not only the assembly's decision but also the probouleuma inscribed. The Boule, after making reference to 'what the Kitians say about the foundation of a temple to Aphrodite', used its regular formula 'that the presiding officials (*prohedroi*) who are selected by lot to preside bring them (the Kitians) before the next assembly and raise the matter for discussion, and communicate to the Demos the resolution of the Boule that it seems good to the Boule that . . .'. In this case the Boule's opinion was 'that the Demos hear the Kitians with regard to the foundation of the temple and any Athenian who wishes (to speak), and decide what seems to it to be best'.[80]

Usually, then, there is no means of deducing from a non-probouleumatic decree whether the Boule was acting rather like a secretariat by making a completely open recommendation or whether the decree represented a rejection – total, partial or largely apparent – of the specific proposals of the Boule. Sometimes a probouleuma seems to have been specific with respect to some aspects of a question but to have left others for discussion by the assembly.[81] Again, a recommendation which is open in form might by its formulation or the mere fact of its existence anticipate a favourable response, but might for a variety of reasons stop short of offering a firm proposal.[82]

In the format of some of the most important surviving Athenian decrees there is nothing to indicate whether the Boule seriously discussed the matter or what its recommendation was. Among six decrees from the fifth century which are clearly non-probouleumatic in form, one is very fragmentary but appears to deal with a minor aspect of a matter (the lease of public property) while the other five deal with substantial matters.[83] Two of these five (relating to tribute collection and coinage) are very fragmentary but were probably similar to two of the others (relating to the Brea settlement and tribute) which are detailed proposals such as we might expect to have been discussed in the Boule, whether the matters were initially raised in the council or the assembly, rather than

---

[79] Rhodes 73–4. See also the analysis of *IG* II².360 by Rhodes 66–7 for the subsuming of probouleumata in assembly decrees which reveal no indication of their origin; cf. 72–3 on *IG* II².276.

[80] Tod 189.   [81] Tod 173.33–5.

[82] Tod 133 where the Boule recommends the grant of citizenship to Dionysios I, his sons and descendants, but leaves the Council of the Allies to convey its views on certain matters raised by Dionysios direct to the Ekklesia (lines 8–17).   [83] *IG* I³.44, Rhodes 259.

enunciated in the assembly.[84] But even if that was the case, the council may have been content with making an open or formal recommendation.

About 100 decrees from the period from 403/2 to 322/1, as has been noted already, have been regarded as non-probouleumatic: of these some 15 have been held to deal with 'substantial' matters.[85] But in at least one case there is every reason to believe a decree which is technically non-probouleumatic was in line with the council's recommendation. For the assembly in 362/1 accepted in effect the recommendation of the Council of the Allies (*synhedrion*) and the Boule to make an alliance with the Arkadians and other Peloponnesian states but it was subsumed in a motion moved in the assembly.[86] This decree is the same as five others (of the 15) in that they are 'crossbreeds' or contain an enactment-formula which would point to a probouleumatic decree and a motion-formula indicating a non-probouleumatic decree. The (new) motion-formula ought to be the more reliable guide to their technical classification.[87] But apart from this doubt, these five decrees seem to have involved substantial discussion on substantial questions such as we might expect to have been first aired in the Boule. This is particularly the case with the 377 decree inviting other states to join the Second Athenian League. Yet with one possible exception there is nothing in the format of that decree to suggest that the Boule seriously discussed the question.[88] It is true that the broad principles at least had earlier been determined, but it is a detailed, complex and substantial decree.[89] It is not impossible that the formulation was worked out *ab initio* in the assembly, but it is far more likely that Aristoteles of Marathon, a man with a reputation as a

---

[84] *IG* I³.60 (tribute collection), 90 (coinage); I³.46 (ML 49) (Brea – cf. de Laix 94–5) and 68 (ML 68) (tribute decree of Kleonymos); I³.89.55–9 (alliance with Arrhabaios). The tribute decree of Kleonymos, if it originated in the assembly, would be a striking example of details of policy being worked out there or drafted before the meeting was held, for it may be that Kleonymos (if a councillor as seems to be the case –Rhodes 71 n. 2) drew up the motion himself, being dissatisfied with the probouleuma. But the decree may have been probouleumatic, for the rider formula is not an infallible guide (the speaker rather than the Boule may have been uppermost in the amender's mind – see ML p. 188) or another rider formula may have stood in a fragmentary part of the decree (see de Laix 96–8).

[85] Rhodes 79, 259–62; de Laix 109–42.

[86] Tod 144.15–16 indicates that the Boule supported the conclusion of an alliance: it would seem that a speaker in the assembly took over the recommendation(s) but began with his own suggestion for a prayer for the blessing of the gods. [87] Rhodes 75–7.

[88] The provision to send an embassy to Thebes (Tod 123.72–5) may possibly have been added as an amendment to a probouleuma (cf. Laqueur (1927) 40–1, Billheimer (1938) 457–8). Lines 91–6 (which are fragmentary) record another motion by Aristoteles but without enactment formula or, it would seem, rider formula. The poor quality of the lettering suggests that the stele had already been set up when these lines were inscribed and hence that this was a later motion or a belated effort to include either an omission from the text of the main motion or a motion passed at much the same time as the main motion. Cf. Cargill (1981) 39.

[89] Tod 123.23–5 specifies that the terms for future admissions are to be 'the same as for Khios, Thebes and the other allies'. Byzantion was accepted as an 'ally of the Athenians and the other allies . . . on the same terms as Khios' (Tod 121.6–7), while the Khian alliance of 384 was on the basis of 'freedom and autonomy' and adherence to the provisions of the King's Peace of 387

speaker, brought his proposal before the Boule or subsumed the Boule's recommendation in a motion which he put in the assembly.[90] Aristoteles may also be an example of Athenians who took a special interest in particular areas of policy or in particular foreign states. Connections with an Aegean state or states might, for example, have been considered important in selecting the embassy to Thebes (as proposed in the decree) and might have balanced the pro-Theban sympathies of the other two envoys, Thrasyboulos of Kollytos and Pyrrhandros of Anaphlystos.[91]

The other four decrees probably involved substantial discussion on important matters: relations with Ioulis on Keos in 362 after the suppression of the revolt of Keos, the dispatch of klerouchs (Athenian settlers) to Poteidaia in 361, an alliance with Thessaly in 361/0 and the renewal of the alliance with Mytilene in 346.[92] But there is no real basis for determining how much, if any, of this discussion took place in the Boule with respect to these four or the other nine 'substantial' non-probouleumatic decrees. Eight were probably 'substantial' in regard to both the nature of the business and the character of the discussion: these were the decrees concerning relations with Klazomenai in 387, the klerouchs on Lemnos in 387/6, the alliances with Khios in 384 and Dionysios I of Syracuse in 367, relations with Sidon and with Eretria, the renewal of Khabrias' treaty with Keos, and the dispatch of a colony to the Adriatic in 325/4.[93] The alliance with Messenia and other states in the late 340s may perhaps have engendered less debate in view of the direction of Athenian policy at the time.[94]

4.4.3 *The indications of the epigraphical evidence*

The overall indications of the epigraphical evidence are that throughout our period the Boule was not concerned simply with routine, non-controversial matters. Many probouleumatic decrees show that the council did discuss major issues in a serious, thorough manner and that its recommendations were accepted, with or without amendment, by the assembly. Probouleumatic decrees, however, acknowledge the same fact as non-probouleumatic decrees, that the final decision was made by the Ekklesia, but if the format of the latter highlights this, it should not be used to infer that the Boule had declined to give serious attention to the particular issues and thus had played no part in the formulation of policies. Sometimes the Boule did make a purely open or formal recommendation that the Ekklesia discuss a matter. A probouleuma which was

---

(Tod 118.19–24; cf. Accame (1941) 9–14, 32–7). The alliance with Thebes may have enunciated in detail the meaning of 'freedom and autonomy' as set out in 123.20–3 (cf. the phrases in a decree of 387: Tod 114.23–5) but hardly the clauses prohibiting Athenian land-holding in allied states (123.25–46), and all these detailed clauses may have been drafted at the time of Tod 123.

[90] D.L. 5.35. The other possibility is that Aristoteles moved the motion as a member of the Boule of 378/7.   [91] Aiskhin. 3.138–9.   [92] Tod 142, 146, 147, 168.

[93] Tod 114, *Hesperia* 40 (1971), 162–73, no. 23 (new text of *IG* ii².30), Tod 118, 136, 139, 154, *IG* ii².404, Tod 200.170–271.   [94] *IG* ii².225.

formally open could, nevertheless, indicate a preference.[95] Sometimes the Boule acted rather like a civil service department in examining alternatives and leaving the matter open for the Ekklesia to decide, but mostly it seems likely that it made specific recommendations to the assembly.

The Ekklesia, however, was clearly not a rubber-stamp in major matters, and even in minor matters its approval was not to be taken for granted. Almost no matter seems to have been so insignificant as not to invite amendment or rejection in the assembly. Some of these amendments, such as the rectification of minor oversights, might have aroused little or no discussion, and sometimes, as we have seen, the Ekklesia was content to authorise the Boule to attend to any omissions. In any case, on some routine questions the Boule seems to have been competent – for example, to order the publication or re-publication of decrees which had awarded to individuals the honour of 'public friendship' (*proxenia*).[96]

The epigraphical evidence, in short, provides an invaluable supplement and correction to the literary evidence. The two taken together reveal a complex of factors which interacted in determining the tenor of the Boule's recommendations, how specific the recommendations were, and the Ekklesia's response to them. Some of the variables were general and long term, others related to the immediate circumstances and the personalities involved. The selection of Athenian envoys provides an instructive example of the probouleumatic role of the Boule. The regular procedure seems to have been that the decree passed by the Ekklesia, with or without a specific recommendation by the Boule about envoys, laid down the number of envoys (usually ten, five or three) and any specific requirements, leaving the Boule to consider nominations and present a list to a subsequent meeting of the Ekklesia. That meeting 'voted' or 'appointed' the envoys. Acceptance of the names recommended by the Boule was probably usual, but it was not automatic. In the case of the controversy about the appointment of Aiskhines or Hypereides as a delegate to the Delphic Amphiktyony *c.* 343, Briant has suggested that the Ekklesia rejected a recommendation for Hypereides' appointment as one of three delegates and that Demosthenes intervened to have the matter referred to the Areiopagos which decided to reject the Ekklesia's choice, Aiskhines, and appointed Hypereides.[97] As with other items of business, the consideration of the selection of envoys ranged from the highly controversial to simpler cases: the chief value of the Boule's role was that it was fully informed about relations with foreign states and it could consider the question in detail in the light of the debate in the Ekklesia, but with less restrictions in terms of time, weighing the various considerations – the qualifications, experience and availability of particular individuals (especially the mover of the decree) and the range of opinions on

---

[95] See Rhodes 61.   [96] *IG* ii².13 and Tod 98.
[97] Aiskhin. 2.18–19, 94, Dem. 19.121–2; *IG* i³.61 (ML 65).16–18, Tod 117.17–18; Dem. 18.134; Briant (1968) 7–31, Mosley (1965) 255–66.

relations with the state concerned. In two instances the Ekklesia might seem to have delegated its authority to the Boule – when it instructed the Boule to 'select immediately . . . ten men, five from the Boule and five *idiōtai*' (that is, ordinary citizens holding no official position) to take the oaths of alliance from Eretria in 394, and to select 'a herald from among all the Athenians' to protest to the Aitolian Confederacy in 367 about the arrest of two Athenian heralds. Both instructions, however, are probably to be interpreted as relating to the 'selection' process, with the final 'appointment' still in the hands of the Ekklesia.[98]

When the Boule's recommendation was presented to the assembly, it appears to have been possible, at least in the fourth century, for the matter to be dealt with expeditiously. The procedure was known as *prokheirotonia* ('pre-vote'). There is uncertainty about the precise nature of this procedure, but it seems to have had the effect of presenting to the Ekklesia the option of accepting a specific recommendation from the Boule without further debate or discussion of the proposal. If that was the effect of a pre-vote, frequent acceptance by the assembly without debate would be highly significant. There is, however, very little information about prokheirotonia and information about only one specific instance of its use, and the notion of the assembly accepting a probouleuma without debate has aroused much scepticism among scholars. If however, as Hansen has plausibly suggested, a probouleuma was ratified only if no hands were raised against acceptance in the pre-vote, some probouleumata may well have been passed in this manner.[99] Yet one is left with the impression that even routine matters and uncontroversial issues were far from being assured of immediate passage in the Athenian assembly. The circumstances in which 'they sometimes take business without a preliminary vote' may perhaps relate to completely open probouleumata in which the Boule simply advised that the Ekklesia discuss a particular matter.[100] The final decision in the assembly depended, as did the processes of formulating policies, on persuasion. A change of mind in the course of the assembly debate should not occasion surprise. In 369, if we may believe Xenophon's account, the assembly favoured the Boule's recommendation that the terms of the alliance with Sparta should provide for the Athenians to command by sea and the Spartans on land, but was persuaded by Kephisodotos to accept his proposal that each side hold the leadership in turn for periods of five days.[101]

In the later fifth century the assembly, we have suggested, seems to have shown a certain readiness to be guided by specific recommendations of the Boule. In the fourth century that readiness did not disappear, but in so far as it is

---

[98] Tod 103.17–20, 137.14–18; Briant (1968) 10–12.
[99] Harpokration s.v. *prokheirotonia*, *AP* 43.6 (and *CAAP*), Dem. 24.11–13, Aiskhin. 1.23; Hansen 123–30, de Laix 182–3, Rhodes 58 n. 4.
[100] *AP* 43.6; as an example of a purely open recommendation, see Tod 189 discussed above.
[101] Xen. *Hell.* 7.1.1–14.

possible to judge from the format of the assembly's decrees the Ekklesia seems to have been slightly more ready to do what it could and did do in the fifth century – make substantial amendments to the council's recommendation, direct the council to make a recommendation on a particular matter, and in particular approve motions which were enunciated in the assembly (subsuming the probouleumata or adopting a different view).[102] There is little to suggest, however, that the introduction of assembly pay seriously eroded the power of the Boule or that the range of matters dealt with by the assembly expanded significantly.[103] One factor was the adequacy or attractiveness of assembly pay, but there was the added factor that, even with four meetings each prytany, the assembly did not meet frequently enough to rely on itself alone to deal with all matters.

One of the important elements in the Boule's probouleutic role was its close acquaintance with the day-to-day administration of the polis, not least in the field of finance and its supervision of officials. The Boule was well placed to examine issues and to assess the needs of the polis. In the second half of the fifth century and the first half of the fourth the Boule was the major agency of such coordination as existed within the Athenian polis. In the second quarter of the fourth century, as we have seen earlier, the importance of financial expertise became more apparent and in the 350s to 320s Euboulos, working through the Festival Fund Commission, and Lykourgos were acquiring a knowledge of the day-to-day administration of the state which affected the position of both the Boule and the Ekklesia.[104]

4.5 A crucial role?

The Boule was, therefore, much more than a secretariat in regard to the preparation of items for discussion by the Ekklesia. Its deliberations were important not only in the fact that they played a crucial role in the investigation and formulation of policies and thus facilitated serious debates in the Ekklesia, but also in the influence that they exerted on the final decisions of the Demos. The strong doubts which have been expressed by some scholars about the power of the Boule are based mainly on the impressions conveyed by the literary sources and on the character of the Boule.[105]

With respect to the literary sources, we have seen how the indications

---

[102] *IG* II².40, 334, 360 (see n. 79 above), Tod 167.

[103] Connor 70 (1974) 34–5, drawing attention to the problem of periodisation and the dangers of generalisation, notes that the ratio of probouleumatic to non-probouleumatic decrees exceeds 3 in the period down to 404/3, varies between 1.4 and 2 in the years between 403/2 and 338/7 and drops to 0.5 in the period from 337/6 to 324/3 (and in the years from 323/2 to 301/0).

[104] Andok. 2.19; see chs. 2.3.2 and 3.6, and Rhodes 105–8. On changes in financial organisation, see Rhodes 102–5.   [105] See n. 34.

provided by probouleumatic decrees supplement and correct the impressions gained, for example, from Thucydides who relates only one (dramatic) episode involving the deliberations of the Boule. Alkibiades is represented as having discredited the Spartan envoys in 420 by tricking them into denying before the assembly what they had told the council about their authority to negotiate with the Athenians. The story seems to have been included by Thucydides primarily for its bearing on Alkibiades.[106]

The decree of 425 concerning the assessment of tribute and other decrees are enough to show that the explanation for the apparent discrepancy between Thucydides and the epigraphical sources is to be sought in terms of Thucydides' interests and focus of attention: he was not concerned with the various stages in the decision-making process. Given the concentration of the population in the city during the invasions (and later occupation of parts) of Attike, it would not be surprising if the meetings of the Ekklesia developed some special characteristics during the Peloponnesian War. Thucydides frequently depicts the speaker's ability to persuade the mass assembly as the paramount factor in decision-making in Athens at the time. It is very likely that the full consequences of the assertiveness of the Demos especially through the Ekklesia became apparent and were intensified during the Peloponnesian War and that this made a dramatic impact on Thucydides' perception of the Ekklesia. Moreover, throughout our period decision-making in Athens *was* based on discussion, but it is not enough to ask with Gomme: 'Where were the great speeches made?'[107] The *final* decisions were made in the assembly, and certainly this was the one place where failure to persuade was (usually) final. But the processes of initiating, discussing and formulating policy must also be examined without assuming that serious discussion took place only or mainly in the assembly. A fifth-century *Athenaion Politeia* (wrongly ascribed to Xenophon and probably written *c.* 430) recognised the very important role of the Boule, not only in administration but also in discussion of policy.[108] This is in line with the general indications of the epigraphical evidence which shows that the difference between Thucydides and the orators is not related to fundamental differences in the role of the Boule but to the focus of their writings or speeches.

The character of the Boule was determined in large measure by its size, its changing composition and the use of the Lot in selecting councillors and in its procedures: it consisted of 500 citizens serving a one-year term as councillors – serving for the first or second (and last) time. It could not become a cohesive group exercising power over a number of years such as the Spartan council (Gerousia), with its twenty-eight members (over the age of 60) appointed for life and the two kings, might (but did not necessarily) become. Yet the very factors

---

[106] Thuc. 5.45; Plut. *Nik.* 10, *Alk.* 14; Brunt (1952) 65–9, Andrewes *HCT* 4.51–3.
[107] Gomme (1962) 178.   [108] [Xen.] *AP* 3.2.

which prevented the Athenian council from becoming an ongoing executive with a strong corporate sense would have engendered in the citizens at large a measure of confidence in the Boule. It was, as one ancient commentator put it, 'the polis in miniature'.[109] The councillors were, moreover, recruited from throughout the citizen body: each year 50 councillors were selected by lot from each tribe, and they were drawn from all the demes, and broadly, it would seem, in proportion to the numbers of demesmen. In consequence, knowledge of the issues being discussed by the Boule would usually be available to all those citizens who were interested.

In its day-to-day operation, moreover, the Boule exemplified many of the fundamental aspects of the Athenian democracy. For one-tenth of the year (a prytany) the 50 councillors of each tribe served as prytaneis and exercised functions characteristic of standing committees. Foreign envoys and others would normally bring their business first to the prytaneis who met every day in the Tholos or Skias (a circular building near the Bouleuterion or council hall) and ate there.[110] Among their duties the prytaneis summoned meetings of the Boule and the Ekklesia and were responsible for publishing the agenda.[111] The meetings of the Boule and the Ekklesia were presided over by the prytaneis in the fifth century and the early fourth, and later by prohedroi.[112] The chairman, whether of the prytaneis or the prohedroi, acted as chairman of the meetings of the Boule and the Ekklesia for but one day. In consequence, with some 260 meetings of the Boule in the course of a year, each councillor had a more than even chance of chairing a meeting.

The organisation and vast range of the work of the Boule gave its members the potential for acquiring a close acquaintance with the issues in hand. Thereby the Boule had a distinct advantage over most of the ordinary citizens in the assembly. The latter, it is true, had the opportunity to be politically knowledgeable and experienced through terms as officials or as members of the council and through participation in the assembly. But the importance of up-to-date, detailed knowledge and experience is not to be underestimated, for it was this close acquaintance which helped to make the Boule powerful. Its relationship with the Ekklesia and with officials and its range of executive and judicial activities made the Boule, in Gomme's words, a 'lynch-pin of the democracy', but it was not simply indispensable.[113] It was dynamic, influential and powerful, but not so powerful as to challenge the sovereignty of the Demos. For the Demos made the final decision both in the assembly and the law-courts, the Boule was in no position to prevent the discussion of an item in the assembly, and the councillors were themselves accountable or responsible to

---

[109] Schol. Aiskhin. 3.4.
[110] Wycherley 128–37, 150–60, 179–84 and Thompson and Wycherley 29–36, 41–6 for the Bouleuterion, the Metroon (or State Records Office) and the Tholos (or Round House).
[111] *AP* 43.2–4. [112] See Appendix 3C. [113] Gomme (1962) 186; Rhodes 214–15.

the Demos.[114] For the same reasons the assembly could have a measure of confidence in the Boule without, of course, feeling bound to accept its recommendations. The assembly also had the power to appoint special commissions to deal with specific questions such as the repayment of sacred moneys to Athena in 410/09, while some assembly decrees specify that the strategoi made the recommendations which were being approved.[115]

Above all, the assembly also received advice directly from individual citizens who held no official position in the state but who with their supporters could exercise considerable influence. For, if (as is likely) a councillor was limited to (two) non-consecutive terms, each year's Boule had among its members not one citizen who had served on the Boule of the previous year and, in the absence of an independent entity able over a long term to shape the policies of Athens, a greater opportunity was afforded to individual Athenians (and their supporters) to shape those policies. At the same time, leading Athenians might find considerable value in attending meetings of the Boule and participating, directly or indirectly, in its deliberations. Some, in fact, are known to have served on the Boule, and at times when they were not councillors, political leaders regarded some of its discussions as potentially decisive in the formulation of policy and therefore listened to or participated in those discussions.[116] The identification and evaluation of the central issues in a question could be significantly influenced by the Boule's discussions. At its worst, participation in a debate of the Boule could be regarded as a useful trial run, at its best persuading the Boule could be a decisive step in a process of persuasion that culminated in the Ekklesia. It must also be stressed that the Boule would not itself be easily convinced. Nevertheless, failure to convince the Boule was not final. The issue could be debated in full in the assembly and the skilful leader might win over the Demos, though the assembly was less of an easy prey to 'persuasion' than has sometimes been supposed.

The final test, therefore, was in the Ekklesia, and while the Boule did in various ways impinge upon the relationship between the Ekklesia and individuals, whether 'private' citizens or officials, in the last resort the starkness and directness of that relationship remained. Aristotle's analysis of the Boule as

---

[114] Cf. Andok. 2.19–20, who points out the value of the Boule (which can be called to account) having the time to examine proposals which he has already put to the Boule 'in secret', but who also acknowledges that 'it is rightly in your power (the citizens in the Ekklesia) to order your affairs well or badly at will'. See also *IG* I³.71 (ML 69).28–38.

[115] *IG* I³.99.8 (and see I³.21.3 (arrangements at Miletos, 450/49), 78.3–4 (Eleusinian first-fruits, *c.* 422 (?)), 135.3); I³.89.55–9, Walbank no. 65 (*IG* I³.92).5 (cf. Tod 143.6–19); Rhodes 267.

[116] See n. 61; Dem. 19.10, Aiskhin. 3.62, 3.125–6 (allegation that Demosthenes took advantage of the inexperience of a councillor who moved a motion (in a secret session) to overturn Aiskhines' proposals about Amphissa in 340/39); Dem. 22.36–7; cf. Plut. *Per.* 7.5 and 7.7, *Nik.* 5.1; cf. Xen. *Hipparch.* 1.8 (with particular reference to the Boule's responsibilities in respect to the cavalry).

being supreme among the offices of state may be applied to the Athenian polis, but its supremacy was among the offices of state.[117] For like individual officials, the councillors, by virtue of their oath of office and their accountability, were subordinate to the Demos.[118]

[117] Arist. *Pol.* 1322b12–18.   [118] Cf. Dem. 19.296–7.

5 Citizens and participation

5.1 The Council of 500: active participation or manipulation?

Democracy (*dēmokratia*) in Athens rested on the power or sovereignty (*kratos*) of the Demos. This sovereignty was exercised, as we have seen, in the making of policy decisions and administrative decisions in the Ekklesia which all citizens were entitled to attend, while at least in the fourth century matters of an ongoing or universal kind were discussed in the Ekklesia but finally determined by the process of *nomothesia*. In the dispensing of justice, decisions rested with citizen juries which, by their size and the use of the Lot in their selection, might be expected to represent a cross-section of the sovereign people. Similarly, size, use of the Lot and recruitment from all the demes provided grounds for applying the description 'the polis in miniature' to the Boule – the council which played a vital role not only in the decision-making process, but also in the supervision of the implementation of the assembly's decisions. Finally, apart from the few officials who were elected (by the Demos), the use of the Lot, rotation and limited tenure provided the citizens with enhanced opportunities for serving as officials and for engaging in the ruling of the polis.

The very structure and the leading features of Athenian institutions therefore worked strongly in favour of involving large numbers of citizens; but did the citizens avail themselves of their opportunities? To what extent did the various institutions in their actual operation involve the whole Demos or at least reflect a cross-section of the whole citizen body?

First, the Boule. If we consider the composition of that body, it may properly be described as 'the polis in miniature' in the (important) sense that its 500 members were each year drawn by lot from the demes of the whole of Attike. But in socio-economic terms the description is not apt if, as is very likely, the Boule in the fifth century, like the other offices of state, was not open to members of the thetic class. It is very likely that by the 320s the question of census class was ignored, as it was in respect to the election of arkhons, and that thetes were members of the council.[1] With this legal fiction the thetes were apparently content, which may suggest that few of them aspired to these positions. Again, such limited evidence as we have indicates that men of

[1] See ch. 3.5.

property were more strongly represented in the Boule than their numbers in the citizen body would justify. An incomplete list of members of the Boule, probably belonging to the year 336/5, appears to include among the 248 names an undue proportion of men who were either trierarchs themselves or whose families had provided trierarchs.[2] The more conservative tendencies of the 330s may have accentuated this bias, but a council which implied the constant availability of members for the 35 or 36 days of their tribe's prytany and attendance at meetings of the Boule on about 260 days throughout the year must have favoured men of sufficient wealth to have the opportunity of some leisure. Such citizens would, moreover, be more likely to contemplate a second term.[3]

The demands made by membership of the Boule must have borne more heavily on citizens from rural demes, though attendance would not necessarily be a burden for *all* members even of remote demes. For deme affiliation is not a certain guide to the usual place of residence in, say, 431, let alone in 355. A citizen belonged to the deme in which his ancestor was registered at the time of Kleisthenes' reforms in the late sixth century. The fourth-century leader Timotheos, for example, whose name appeared on the register of the coastal deme Anaphlystos, had a house in the Peiraieus which was probably, when he was not abroad, his usual place of residence.[4] And though there was much less mobility in Attike than in many modern communities, there was undoubtedly some migration, not least from rural demes to the city of Athens. Many of the rich with political or other reasons for being frequently in the city probably had a house in or near Athens or in the Peiraieus where they might spend a significant part of the year.[5] For them bouleutic service was clearly feasible.

And what of those who continued to reside in their ancestral demes? Athenians, it is true, were accustomed to walking considerable distances. A

---

[2] SEG 19.149 (=Meritt and Traill no. 42); Rhodes 4–6; cf. Sundwall (1906) 1–18; Larsen (1955) 11. [3] See Appendix 2A.

[4] [Dem.] 49.22. Cf. Lys. 20.11–12 and Gomme 38–9 for a trend (most evident by the fourth century) for a higher proportion of men in public life to come from coastal or inland demes rather than the city – a trend which suggests some movement from the country to residence in the city; see n. 118 and R. Osborne 60–3.

[5] Gomme 37–48 exaggerates the movement from rural areas in the fifth and fourth centuries. The undoubted movement of many well-to-do or enterprising citizens (see n. 4) is not to be assumed to apply to the wide range of Athenians who were very much attached to their ancestral land (see Thuc. 2.14–17). Moreover, his analysis of the manumission inscriptions (which show that nearly all the ex-slaves lived in Athens or the Peiraieus) overlooks the probability that many ex-slaves moved away from the area where they were known as slaves. It also assumes that artisan occupations indicate city residence, yet the women textile workers, as Gomme 42 n. 9 notes, would mostly have worked at home, while manufacturing, distributive and other occupations which he describes as urban were pursued not only in Athens and the Peiraieus but also in rural demes: 'industrial' activities were, for example, carried on at Thorikos in south-east Attike. See Randall (1953) 204–6 for an analysis of the deme registration of citizens and metics and actual residence of metics working on the Erekhtheion between 409 and 405 (IG I³.474–9). On migration to the city see also Whitehead 353–7, and on possession of a house in or near Athens or in the Peiraieus see R. Osborne 50.

distance of 12–15 km (2–3 hours) or even more might well be contemplated by a citizen anxious to attend an important meeting of the assembly, but the demands of bouleutic membership were heavy and constant.[6] The exercise of a man's functions as a bouleutes really involved staying in Athens, unless perhaps he lived in one of the closest rural demes. Wealthy citizens who normally lived elsewhere in Attike – at Sounion, say, in the far south-east – would have been relatively little inconvenienced by spending long periods in Athens during a term of office on the Boule. Men of moderate wealth, too, could afford time away from their usual occupations. Most other men would have been dependent on the availability of hired help (made financially possible, if it was available, by the payments they received as councillors, if not from their own resources) and especially on the willingness of relatives and neighbours to help with their labour at critical times during a councillor's term of office, though such help would have been limited at the height of the harvest. It is also worth noting that there were recognised areas of the city where demesmen from a particular deme tended to stay or to congregate.[7] A similar phenomenon is known in Athens in modern times. Accommodation with relatives or friends in such circumstances would not entail much expense, but even that was likely to be beyond the resources of a poor man who was eking out an existence at some distance from the city and who in any case could ill afford long periods away from his work, particularly the periods implicit in membership of the Boule. Only driving political ambition would induce him to ignore the problems associated with unsupervised hired labour or even the help of relatives and friends. In short, in the case of outlying demes in particular, it may well be that most of the councillors who still resided in their ancestral demes stayed in Athens only during their tribe's prytany (when they lived and ate in the Tholos at the expense of the polis) and for the rest of the year were much less regular in attendance or indeed rarely attended at all.[8]

As far as bouleutic service is concerned, therefore, some bias in favour of the well-to-do is not surprising, and wealth combined with other variables in affecting the feasibility of a term of office so that residence in the city would push lower down the socio-economic scale the point where membership of the Boule and whole-hearted participation in its affairs became possible. Moreover, payments to the bouleutai or to officials were regular (as opposed to the element of luck involved in allocation to jury service with its payment of 3 obols a day) and in the course of a year totalled much more than payment for attendance at the 40 meetings of the Ekklesia (1 drakhme for each of 30 ordinary meetings and 1½ drakhmai for each of 10 main meetings in the 320s). To the poorer citizens, it might be thought, the receipt of 5 obols a day for some 260 days (with an additional obol for the 35 or 36 days of one prytany) would be attractive.[9] But

---

6 See Hansen (1983c) 233–6, R. Osborne 69.
8 Hansen (1983c) 235–7.

7 Lys. 23.3 (and 6).
9 *AP* 62.2; see ch. 3.5 and ch. 5.4.

though Demosthenes complained about passive bouleutai, it was not quite so easy to be passive in the council as in the assembly, while in the law-courts the individual juror could easily avoid displaying his inexperience. A man from a family with limited experience in polis affairs and without the means for some formal tuition in public speaking would therefore have needed ambition or strong political instincts to risk exposing his inexperience in the deliberations of the Boule, the activities of the prytaneis, or as a presiding official at meetings. It was this last prospect that may have been somewhat daunting. During the fourth century, in the course of each prytany of some 36 days a new board of 9 *prohedroi* (presiding officials) was selected by lot on any day when the Boule met (some 260 days in the course of a year) or the Ekklesia met. One of the 9 was selected by lot to act as *epistatēs* (chairman), but no one could act as epistates on more than one day in the year. Each prytany, an average of 234 bouleutai were thus involved, and gained some experience, in presiding over meetings of the Boule and the Ekklesia, and in the course of a year a bouleutes had a more than even chance of being selected by lot to chair one of some 260 meetings of the Boule. During the year some 40 or more bouleutai were required to act also as chairman at a meeting of the Ekklesia. In the fifth century these presiding functions in the Ekklesia and the Boule had been exercised by the 50 *prytaneis* (presidents) – the 50 bouleutai from each tribe serving in turn for one tenth of the year as the committee of the Boule; every bouleutes was involved in presiding over meetings of the Ekklesia during his tribe's prytany, while one of the prytaneis was epistates at a meeting of the Boule or of the Ekklesia. At all times the councillors who were presiding were subject to jeers and pressure at meetings but also to penalties if they were convicted of offences relating to their presiding functions.[10]

For similar reasons, an inexperienced man might be reluctant to hold one of the other state offices, though this would have varied according to the character and the demands of the office. As an unskilled worker on a construction site he could in any case earn up to $1\frac{1}{2}$ drakhmai a day, at least in times when that or other work was available.[11] For some, nevertheless, 4–6 obols might have been sufficient recompense to participate. Still, the 4 obols paid to the arkhons in the 320s for their maintenance had to cover the expenses of maintaining a herald and a flute player.[12] It is therefore not surprising to hear of an Athenian citizen of respectable but impoverished family who in the 350s seems to have been induced to serve as basileus (the arkhon primarily concerned with religious matters) by an offer of financial aid from one of his friends.[13] Yet the old

---

[10] *AP* 44.2, 59.2 (and *CAAP*); IG i³.105, Thuc. 6.14, Xen. *Hell.* 1.7.12–15, Dem. 24.50, Hyp. 2.4–6; Rhodes 16–28, 194–6; see ch. 3.5.

[11] See ch. 2.2 and n. 32 and Appendix 2B.

[12] *AP* 62.2; Hansen (1979A) 5–22 and (1971–80B) 105–25, Gabrielsen (1981) 57–87 and D. M. Lewis (1982) 269.

[13] [Dem.] 59.72: the friend is alleged to have wormed his way into the favour of the basileus who is described as inexperienced in affairs.

arkhonships were probably more demanding than most offices in the character of the duties as well as in the expense involved. In general, it would seem that ordinary citizens may have been more attracted to the offices selected by lot than to elective offices. But the impression that these offices were eagerly sought by 'the poor' is open to doubt: poverty (that is, lack of sufficient resources) and the consequences of poverty *were* for many Athenians a bar to holding office in the polis.[14]

This is not to deny the widely held view that by the later fourth century thetes were members of the Boule. Indeed, it has even been argued that thetes – and the citizens of the other three census classes – were automatically regarded as candidates for the Boule, unless they had already served twice or were serving in the current year. The argument depends in part on estimates of the citizen population about which there is much room for divergence of opinion, but there is no compelling reason to believe that the thetes had to be included in order to provide a sufficient pool of candidates.[15] Whatever population estimates are adopted, it must be added that while the number of citizens reaching their thirtieth birthday is an index of the number of new potential candidates, account must also be taken of a considerable 'reserve' or back-log. For when the first council was selected towards the end of the sixth century, there would have been at least 20,000 (and probably closer to 25,000) citizens of whom perhaps about 10,000 belonged to the top three classes.[16] Citizens under the age of 30 should be excluded, but even if we limit the number of 'serious' candidates for bouleutic service at that time to a much lower figure (for example, 5,000), this represents a continuing reserve which would build up as the numbers of men of hoplite census and above increased (as happened by the mid-fifth century as a result of general prosperity). In the last thirty years of the fifth century the number of citizens dropped dramatically, but even at the generally assumed low point (*c.* 400 B.C.) there were probably some 11,000 men of zeugite census and above, and in this group not less than 250 may be assumed, on the basis of demographic models, to have reached their thirtieth birthday each year. That number would have just sufficed by itself to provide candidates for the Boule, irrespective of whether the rule of two terms was original or whether it marked a change at whatever date from no (or a less severe)

---

14 [Xen.] *AP* 1.3 (asserting that the Demos seeks office for the sake of pay, but avoids the (elective) military offices), Dem. 24.112 (poor officials selected by lot are contrasted with wealthy, elected ambassadors), cf. *AP* 47.1; cf. Thuc. 2.37.1; Jones 104; see ch. 7.4.

15 Ruschenbusch (1979C) 177–80 and (1981A) 103–5, Rhodes (1980B) 191–201; R. Osborne 43–5. For bouleutic alternates or deputies, see Meritt and Traill no. 492, Rhodes 7–8, Traill (1981) 161–9, Whitehead 267–9.

16 The 30,000 of Hdt. 5.97.2 (and 8.65.1) is to be regarded as a conventional figure: Gomme 3, Patterson (1981) 51–6; see Appendix 1A. A considerable reserve of potential bouleutai is also consistent with the tentative suggestion made by Hansen (1986) 55–6, 80–2 that the average age of 62 bouleutai from the period 403–322 was at least 40, which would indicate that it was not imperative for citizens to volunteer once they had reached the minimum age of 30 or soon after.

limitation on re-election or from a one-term limitation.[17] And there remained the 'reserve'. Citizens were, of course, also needed to serve as officials and dikasts, but the total pool of candidates for the state offices and the Boule was potentially adequate throughout our period.

But did it become necessary, or had it long been the case, that all eligible citizens were automatically treated as candidates for the Boule? The logic of numbers does not compel this conclusion, and in the absence of evidence to the contrary it seems best to assume that citizens 'volunteered' for selection by lot as bouleutai. That is, some were eager to serve, others may have been persuaded by the demarch or their fellow-demesmen that it was time to accept this responsibility, others may have had their names put forward and did not persist in objecting.[18] Nevertheless, for some demes there may well have been difficulty in supplying councillors. The deme of Halimous, for example, seems to have been 'under-populated' for a deme providing three bouleutai. Perhaps the citizens of Halimous had suffered exceptionally heavy casualties on some campaign in the past, but each year only two of its demesmen (on average) would have been in their thirty-first year – from all the census classes – if we interpret literally the statements of a litigant in a case in *c.* 346/5. For he declared that at a deme meeting which had voted on the claims to citizenship of those who were registered in the deme's list, 'more than twenty' cases had still to be decided after his, which was 'about the sixtieth case'. Taken literally, that would mean a total of 80–90 demesmen, but the statements were perhaps sufficiently elastic not to provoke incredulity or challenge if in fact there were, say, 110 demesmen (probably including some who were living abroad). If there were 110 demesmen, there would have been three new potential candidates for the Boule each year.[19] In any case, the drain on what we have called the 'reserve' would have been considerable in the case of Halimous if the number of bouleutai was unusually high in proportional terms. But even in this case, after allowing for the political apathy of some from the top three classes and reluctance on economic and other grounds especially among the thetes, the

---

[17] See Appendixes 1A, 1C, n. 35 below, and ch. 3.5.

[18] Lys. 31.33, cf. Isok. 15.145, 150, Ar. *Georgoi* fr. 1 for a farmer willing to pay his way out of being pressed into office and the Arrogant Man (Theophr. *Char.* 24.5) who, when he is being elected (by vote) to office, excuses himself on oath, saying he does not have the time. On the process of selecting bouleutai see Staveley 52–4, Whitehead 320–1.

[19] Dem. 57.9–13, 15 (probably 346/5 B.C.). It is interesting to note a further implication of Euxitheos' figures – the very high proportion of demesmen present: 73 out of 80–90 demesmen – if the figures are taken literally. Admittedly the business of this particular meeting was of vital importance – voting on the claims to citizenship of all demesmen – and it is very likely that this voting was part of the general revision or check of the deme lists which was decreed by the Ekklesia in 346/5. But the figures given by Euxitheos, who alleged that conspiracy lay behind the meeting's rejection of his claim to citizenship, should be interpreted widely and should certainly be treated with caution; see Hansen (1986) 10–12 (assuming 30-year-old males represented 2.7% of all males over 18 on the basis of a model life table with mortality level 4 (life expectancy at birth of 25.26 years) and annual increase of $\frac{1}{2}$%), 62–4; see Appendix 1C.

deme could have managed, though perhaps with not a little pressure being applied to some 'volunteers'.

Apart from the problems of recruitment and the probability that the bouleutai were not fully representative of the whole spectrum of Athenian citizens, was the actual working of the Boule manipulated by an elite or by certain elements among the councillors? Were the ordinary members (*idiōtai*) of the Boule apathetic, for example, and were they dominated by political activists or 'orators' or 'talkers' (*rhētores, hoi legontes*) as Demosthenes alleged against the Boule of 356/5?[20] Indeed, Demosthenes urged a jury to deny the council a crown as a mark of recognition of its services and argued that this would not affect the whole council but only Androtion and a few others who had tried to impose their wishes on the council. 'For', Demosthenes asked, 'who suffers disgrace if, when he makes no speech and moves no resolutions, and perhaps does not even attend most of the meetings, the council does not receive a crown?'[21] The implication of the rhetorical question and the wider context seem to suggest that passivity and non-attendance were typical of the 'ordinary members' of the council, and typical furthermore not only of the council of 356/5.

The circumstances in which these statements were made need to be considered more closely in assessing the value of the statements and they are, moreover, illuminating for the character of political prosecutions. For they were made by Demosthenes or Diodoros, the client for whom he composed the speech *Against Androtion* and who declared that he was seeking revenge for unjust judicial attacks on himself and his uncle by Androtion and his supporters. The prosecution against Androtion arose from the fact that at the end of 356/5 Androtion had proposed and carried a motion in the assembly granting a crown to the outgoing council (of which he was himself a member). Such an honour was contingent at that time on the outgoing council having had a specified number of triremes built. The council of 356/5 had, according to Demosthenes, failed to do so. Moreover, Androtion had proposed his motion in the assembly without a council recommendation (*probouleuma*) which we have seen was legally required. Diodoros and Euktemon, who had himself been removed, through the agency of Androtion, from office as collector of arrears due to the state, took their opportunity to attack Androtion by entering a prosecution for an illegal proposal (*graphē paranomōn*).[22]

Demosthenes in his attack on Androtion sought, as speakers commonly did, since there was no cross-examination in Athenian courts, to meet arguments that were likely to be advanced by the defendant: among these was the argument that the condemnation of Androtion on this charge would mean that the whole council would be unjustly deprived of the honour of a crown.

---

20 Dem. 22.35–7; on the term *rhētōr* see Hansen (1983A) 33–55, especially 43–9.
21 Dem. 22.35–7. On the date see Sealey (1955) 89–92, Cawkwell (1962B) 40–5; cf. D. M. Lewis (1954) 43–4.　　22 Dem. 22, especially 1–11, 16, 47–8.

Demosthenes countered that the loss of the crown would concern only those few who had dominated the council (not the majority who had been passive members and had shown little interest), but that if it did affect the whole council, great advantage would flow to the state from the condemnation of Androtion. For it would demonstrate to the citizens at large the importance of the affairs of the Boule being in the hands of the ordinary members, not the talkers.[23] Demosthenes was therefore anxious to exaggerate the contrast between the political activists and the rest of the 500.

Yet there is no need to deny the central point that a few men like Androtion could exercise very great influence on the activities of the council. Androtion, for example, came from a family with sufficient wealth to enable his father Andron to associate with the sophists and Androtion himself to be given formal instruction in oratory by Isokrates. Androtion, when governor of Arkesine on Amorgos (at some time between 362/1 and 357/6), had lent money to that state free of interest and in other ways helped Arkesine from his own financial resources: the total outlay would probably have amounted to something like a talent. Androtion is said by Demosthenes in 356/5 to have been active in public life for over thirty years, and his first term as a member of the Boule may have been as early as 387/6. Demosthenes' depiction of Androtion as a skilful speaker is to be accepted, though it was principally designed to warn the jurors not to be misled. In the mid-360s Androtion played an important part in the reorganisation of the temple treasures, and it was probably in his second term as a councillor in 356/5 that Androtion had Euktemon removed from office and had an *ad hoc* commission of ten (including himself) appointed to collect arrears of property tax.[24] In any case, there can be no doubt that Androtion played a prominent role in the activities of the Boule of 356/5.[25] 'Ordinary members' with little or no experience and with no great ambition might well play less than an active role in the Boule and might be depicted, with some justification, as apathetic and unwilling to become deeply involved. It should be stressed, however, that we do not hear of anything in the rules of selection or administration of the Boule that favoured men like Androtion. Indeed, as we have seen, 'ordinary members' were given, or indeed impelled into, opportunities of presiding at meetings and gaining experience.

And how seriously should we take the claims of poor attendance? At any session some members might be absent on business arising from membership of

---

[23] Dem. 22.35–7.

[24] Dem. 22, especially 4, 35, 42–8, 66, 69–73, and 24, especially 160–2, Tod 152 (see Cawkwell (1981) 51), IG ii².61.6–7; PA 915, APF 33–4, D. M. Lewis (1954) 34, 43–7, Harding (1976) 186–200. See Dem. 24.12–16 for Androtion's appointment in 355 as one of three envoys to Mausolos, Tod 167 for his decree in honour of the Bosporan rulers, and Jacoby FGrH 324 for the *Atthis (History of Athens)* which he is said to have written in exile in Megara and which was published *c.* 340.

[25] See R. Osborne 68–9, and compare the Boule of 405/4 in which Satyros and Khremon are said (Lys. 30.14) to have had the greatest influence.

the Boule or on state business: Demosthenes in 347/6, for example, served on two embassies to Philip.[26] Some would occasionally have been ill or had urgent private reasons which might be regarded as legitimate, while others no doubt were not regular in attendance, whether through the demands of their livelihood, the location of their home or lack of interest. It has already been suggested that councillors from outlying demes may have tended to be irregular in attendance except during their tribe's prytany. The same tendency may well have operated in varying degrees in the case of councillors living in the nearer rural demes and, for that matter, in city demes. The intention of the Four Hundred (in 411) to impose fines on councillors who did not attend and had not obtained leave of absence was consistent with oligarchic attitudes but also with the possibility that there had been problems under the democracy.[27] The payment of 5 obols a day for councillors and a drakhme for the prytaneis would not of itself have induced full attendance but would have been a help, as would the pressure of councillors from the same tribe and the fact that bouleutai were held to account at the end of their term of office.[28] Towards the end of the fifth century, a new Council Hall (*bouleutērion*) was begun and though there was a very slight reduction in the size of the actual chamber, the new Bouleuterion, on the basis of half a metre of bench per person, provided seating for 500 or slightly more. The old building (probably erected early in the fifth century) had provided for about the same number.[29] We have no means of telling how often the chamber in the old or the new Bouleuterion was filled to capacity nor what the 'average' attendance was. Demosthenes' claims about poor attendance on the part of the 'ordinary members', despite their rhetorical cast, are not to be discounted entirely but perhaps reflect something of the reality of participation in the Boule.

5.2 Attendance levels in the assembly

Important as the Boule was, the essential character of Athenian democracy nevertheless depended on the sovereign Demos and *inter alia* on the size and composition of meetings of the assembly. In our period the number of citizens probably fluctuated between the low 20,000s and the low 40,000s. But at many stages there were considerable numbers of Athenian citizens living abroad, so that the number of citizens living in Attike probably never reached 40,000 and may at most stages have been rather of the order of 30,000 or less.[30] The

---

[26] Dem. 19.13, 154–5.

[27] *AP* 30.6 (a fine of 1 drakhme a day); cf. Lys. 20.14–16; Arist. *Pol.* 1297a17–24.

[28] Dem. 22.39.

[29] See H. A. Thompson (1937) 115–224, especially 132–5, 153–60, McDonald (1943) 171–9, Rhodes 30–5, especially 31 n. 1, and Thompson and Wycherley 29–36. For restorations of the interior arrangements, see Rhodes, Plans E and F.

[30] See Appendix 1A, D, E.

Athenians, by implication, regarded 6,000 as an appropriate level of attendance for the exercise of certain powers of the sovereign Demos. For a total attendance of 6,000 was required for decisions relating to individual privilege such as the confirmation of a grant of citizenship (in the fourth century at least), grants of dispensation (for example to a citizen proposing a levy of property tax), or for a vote of ostracism. Apart from these particular cases, there is no clear evidence of quorum requirements for the Ekklesia, that is the meetings of the Demos for deliberative, legislative and electoral purposes.[31] 6,000 was also, as we have seen, the number of dikasts selected by lot each year to be available for the exercise of judicial functions (and use of the Lot made acceptable a further delegation of power to the jury panels of 500 or multiples of 500), but this represented a higher proportion of the eligible citizens for, at least in the fourth century and probably also in the fifth, dikasts were required to be thirty years of age or more.[32]

How many citizens did in fact attend meetings of the Ekklesia? Was Athens in this respect a participatory democracy to the extent believed by some modern writers? The envoys sent by the Four Hundred in 411 to reassure the Athenian forces at Samos were, according to Thucydides, instructed to point out that, 'what with their expeditions and employments abroad, the Athenians had never yet assembled to discuss a question important enough to bring 5,000 of them together'.[33] Some have disregarded this statement as a tendentious claim by the oligarchic conspirators. The statement does at least suggest that in peacetime (not altogether a common state) the attendance may not infrequently have been over 5,000. As far as the period of the Peloponnesian War is concerned, in many years Athenian forces were away from Athens beyond the 'campaigning season' from about March to October–November, though the effects of overseas expeditions might be expected to have been offset to some extent by the concentration of population in the city as a result of Peloponnesian operations in Attike, especially after the occupation of Dekeleia in 413. There were, however, very large numbers of Athenians on active service overseas, not least in Sicily in 415–413, and engaged later in naval operations in the Aegean. The effects of overseas activities might perhaps be seen in regard to ostracism. The institution seems to have continued in the fourth century, but as a 'dead letter': presumably each year the assembly voted not to hold an ostracism. According to Plutarch, no one was ostracised after Alkibiades and Nikias joined forces, probably in 417,

---

[31] Andok. 1.87; [Dem.] 59.89–90, Dem. 24.45–6; *IG* I³.52 (ML 58B).12–19; Plut. *Arist.* 7.6; Rhodes 196–8, W. E. Thompson (1979) 149, Hansen 7–8, 25–6, 212–13.
[32] See ch. 3.5. The origins of the notion of a quorum of 6,000 are obscure, and the usual assumption that that requirement for ostracism was instituted at the outset by Kleisthenes is not certain. Patterson (1981) 51–5, who argues that the citizen population did not reach 30,000 until the 460s, has suggested that in the late 460s–early 450s a concern for a representative assembly and courts may have arisen and that it may have been then that a quorum was adopted (or fixed at the level of 6,000). See Meiggs (1964) 2–3 on the quorum as a fifth of the total.   [33] Thuc. 8.72 (Crawley tr.).

to bring about the removal of Hyperbolos.[34] That is, there was no further resort or 'successful' resort to ostracism. The demise of the institution may perhaps be attributed to difficulties that may have arisen in obtaining a quorum in the last years of the Peloponnesian War (and in the immediate post-war years), partly because of overseas activity, partly because of a serious decrease in the number of citizens during the war. For Athens had suffered heavy casualties in the war which had dragged on (with some intermission) since 431, especially in the disastrous defeat at Syracuse in 413, while the ravages of plague had carried off perhaps as much as a quarter of the population in the early years of the conflict. The effects of war and plague were devastating, cumulative and long-lasting. The number of adult male citizens (the vast majority of them then living in Attike) may have been as low as 22,000–25,000 about the end of the fifth century.[35] In the demise of ostracism, however, the circumvention and discrediting of ostracism by the alliance against Hyperbolos would also seem to be critical factors, and they were highlighted by the disaster in Sicily which flowed in part from the manipulated ostracism and the failure to resolve or reconcile the differences between Alkibiades and Nikias.

Some indication of Athenian attitudes to attending the assembly may be gleaned from the introduction in the 390s of payment for attendance. According to the author of the *Athenaion Politeia*, the reason for instituting assembly pay was that 'men did not come and many skilful attempts by the prytaneis to bring the masses [or the citizen body] (*plēthos*) in for the sake of ratifying the voting' failed.[36] This would imply that at various times measures which required a quorum were frustrated by low attendance rather than that all the work of the Ekklesia had come to a halt. What devices were tried by the prytaneis we do not know, but perhaps they had tried concentrating all measures requiring a quorum at one meeting each prytany or, as was the case in the mid-fourth century with the vote for the confirmation of a citizenship grant, they had placed them first on the meeting agenda.[37]

It should not be assumed, though, that this attendance problem had been serious in, and characteristic of, the second half of the fifth century. It is true that we have reference in Aristophanes' play *The Akharnians*, which was presented in 425, to a vermilion-smeared rope which seems to have been used to 'drive' the citizens dallying in the Agora up to the Pnyx. The context suggests, however, that this reflects starting-time problems rather than attendance

---

[34] *AP* 43.5; Plut. *Alk.* 13, *Nik.* 11; see ch. 2.3.1.

[35] Connor and Keaney (1969) 313–19. For the demographic effects of the Peloponnesian War (including losses due to battle and plague), see Strauss (1979) 73–91, 92 n. 4, 94 n. 11. The number of Athenian citizens living in Attike may have dropped to *c.* 20,000 by the last months of the Peloponnesian War, but was then swelled by the klerouchs and other Athenians whom Lysander forced back to Athens: the siege of Athens and the civil war of 404–3 took their toll, while in the years after 403 some Athenians left Athens – for example on military employment (Xen. *Hell.* 3.1.4). See Gomme 26, Ehrenberg (1969) 33, Strauss (1979) 81–2, 89, Hansen (1986) 68. [36] *AP* 41.3. [37] [Dem.] 59.89–90; cf. Hansen 11–13, 21–2.

problems: the citizen not wishing to attend could presumably keep out of the Agora at these times.[38] If it was also an attendance problem, it might be traced to the extensive overseas operations in the early years of the Arkhidamian War. If that had been a problem of long standing, the gap of some sixty years between the introduction of state pay for jury service and pay for the assembly is difficult to explain. And the gap is curious, unless we assume that the Athenians in the fifth century were not so concerned about widespread participation in the assembly as in the courts or unless the attendance problem noted in the *Athenaion Politeia* was a comparatively recent phenomenon, at least in acute form. After the oligarchic revolutions there may have developed greater concern about participation in the assembly, but in particular the absolute numbers attending are very likely to have been a problem. For in the impoverished conditions in Athens in the years after its surrender in 404 it is hardly likely that very many in the greatly reduced ranks of citizens could afford the time from their daily pursuits. A quorum of 6,000 would have represented the (high) figure of 24–27% of the 22,000–25,000 citizens estimated for the end of the fifth century. In short, there is good reason to believe that citizen support had recently emerged as an acute problem. With some improvement in Athens' fortunes in the course of the 390s, assembly pay became a possibility. For some the pay might have been of the character of poor relief. The token sum of 1 obol was increased to 2, then to 3 obols in a matter of a few years. The rapid increase would seem to indicate competition for political support by Agyrrhios and Herakleides (originally from Klazomenai) as well as the inadequacy of the rate. By the 320s, as we have seen, the rate had increased to 6 obols for the 3 ordinary meetings each prytany and 9 obols for the main meeting. Meantime, jury pay remained constant at 3 obols.[39]

Another clue to attendance may be sought in the size of the Pnyx, the hillside (about 400 metres south-west of the Agora), where the assembly most often met.[40] It has been estimated that during the fifth century some 6,000 citizens could be accommodated seated on the Pnyx. The meeting area was restructured at some time *c.* 400, though the precise period has not been established. The restructuring probably did not appreciably increase the accommodation.[41] We may presume that there were no political imperatives requiring much more

---

[38] Ar. *Akh.* 19–24, but to judge from *Ekkl.* 376–88 the rope was used in the late 390s to keep the latecomers separate from those who arrived early and would receive pay (cf. *Ekkl.* 282–4, 289–92, *Thesm.* 277–8); cf. Hansen 27–8, 34, 131–8; see *RIG* 466 for a third-century decree from Iasos limiting payment to those who arrived within a specified time after sunrise (as determined by the use of a water-clock).

[39] See ch. 3.5 and nn. 88 and 108; Buchanan (1962) 26–7.

[40] For other places where the assembly met in our period (the theatre of Dionysos and the Peiraieus, but probably not the Agora), see McDonald (1943) 44–59, Staveley 79–80, Hansen 3–7, 21.

[41] Kourouniotes and H. A. Thompson (1932) 90–217, Dinsmoor (1933) 180–2, McDonald (1943) 70–6, Travlos (1971) 466–75, Hansen 16–18, 23, 27–8, Moysey (1981) 31–7, H. A. Thompson (1982) 133–47.

space, unless these were overridden by economic considerations, and that when the oligarchs in 411 claimed that no meetings had exceeded 5,000 they were not grossly misrepresenting the case, though they were no doubt citing the experience of current attendance patterns to suit their argument. Yet in considering the capacity of the Pnyx, allowance must also be made for the possibility that at particular meetings, or during parts of meetings, citizens may have packed into the meeting area and there may have been standing room only. In such cases well over 6,000 could have crowded in. For most meetings the natural limitations of space on the Pnyx would suggest a maximum attendance of the order of 6,000 if all the citizens were seated.

In the fourth century, Hansen has argued, the attendance was higher than in the fifth and, in particular, 6,000 was a normal attendance. His view is based in part on his estimate of the capacity of the restructured Pnyx and in part on the procedures for citizenship grants.[42] From at least *c.* 369/8, but probably since the 380s, a second vote was required to confirm such awards, while in a speech delivered to a court in the early 340s a speaker declared that the confirmation required a quorum of 6,000 at the next meeting after the grant was passed. Two decrees which have survived on stone record grants passed at a main meeting of a prytany. That is, in these instances, the confirmation vote was presumably taken at one of the ordinary meetings.[43] Hansen argues that the Athenians scrupulously observed quorum requirements in citizenship and other cases and therefore concludes that there was a general expectation that the normal attendance at all meetings in the fourth century was 6,000.[44] Yet the very requirement of a second vote and the stipulation of a quorum suggest that the Athenians were deliberately attempting to tighten up in regard to citizenship and to ensure that only deserving individuals likely to win general support in Athens would be proposed. The later 380s is a likely period for these changes. The requirements of Perikles' citizenship law had come back into force in 403/2, and by 385/4 children born in the period when citizenship qualifications had been relaxed in the last years of the Peloponnesian War would have attained the age of 18 and been admitted as citizens. Thereafter exemptions from the law were not necessary. The implication, in my view, is that in the later 380s (or whenever the changes were introduced) the attendance for ordinary meetings at least was below 6,000 either commonly or not infrequently. At the very least, 6,000 should be regarded as simply the traditional figure for a quorum – with no necessary implications for high attendance levels at normal assembly meetings in the fourth century. It might therefore be the case that after the introduction of the changes, a proposal for a citizenship grant was potentially fraught with the risk of a lack of a quorum, and that sponsors would usually seek to arrange for the award to be made at the meeting before a main meeting (though there

---

[42] Hansen 10–20, 22.

[43] M. J. Osborne (1972) 138–40 and *Naturalization* 2.56–7, [Dem.] 59.89–90, *IG* II².336, 448.

[44] Hansen 12–16, but Hansen (1986) 18 admits the possibility of the relaxation of the quorum requirements in time of war.

may perhaps have been some difficulty in establishing the exact dates of meetings).[45] Otherwise it would require very determined efforts by the sponsors and their supporters to induce others to attend the next meeting of the Ekklesia.

The level of attendance in general may have been materially assisted by the provision of pay for the assembly, as Hansen suggests, but the increase in the rates of pay rather indicates continuing difficulties in securing support for the assembly.[46] While the Athenians, it may be assumed, recorded the amounts of money paid out for each meeting of the assembly, no records have survived from which we might calculate the number of citizens who received pay for attending a particular meeting of the assembly. Dikasts voting in the courts cast ballots (*psēphoi*), and we have from our period a few inscriptions recording voting figures and statements in the literary sources about the margin of acquittal (or condemnation) in a number of cases. Citizens in the assembly, however, used ballots only in special circumstances (such as the confirmation of a grant of citizenship). Ordinary proposals were accepted or rejected by a show of hands and there is no clear evidence that an actual count was a regular procedure. How precisely the presiding officials 'judged' or determined the result when the vote was close is not certain.[47] We have therefore no secure basis for calculating the levels of attendance in the assembly. Granted that attendances probably fluctuated from period to period, from season to season, and from meeting to meeting, it may be that the principal meeting each prytany was likely to attract about 6,000 citizens and the other meetings might attract appreciably fewer.[48]

5.3 The assembly and the courts

5.3.1 *Aristotle and leisure*

There is a further question. Did the meetings attract a cross-section of the citizen body? One famous meeting was certainly dominated by hoplites and men of

---

[45] The demands of the festival calendar, however, would have severely restricted the range of days available for assembly meetings; see Mikalson (1975B) 186–93; cf. Hansen 15–16, 23, 89–90.   [46] Hansen 18–19; cf. Kluwe (1976) 295–333; see ch. 5.4.

[47] *AP* 44.3, Hansen 103–21 especially 110–13; cf. Staveley 81–7, Boegehold (1963) 372–4. For voting figures in court cases, see *IG* II².1641B.30–3 (100 votes for condemnation, 399 for acquittal: mid-fourth century), Pl. *Ap.* 36a (a transfer of 30 votes would have resulted in the acquittal of Sokrates), Aiskhin. 3.252 (Leokrates acquitted on a tied vote), and other instances cited by Hansen 110, 118. For the Athenian assembly in the Roman period, see *IG* II².1035.3 (3,461 votes for, 155 against), 1051B.26–7, 1053.11–13. For other cities, see the evidence cited by Hansen 112, 118: the three figures for Magnesia on the Maiandros (2,113, 3,580 and 4,678), the low figure of 600 (584 votes for, 16 against) at Miletos and the contrast between (the probably rounded figures of) 1,200 and 4,000 at Halikarnassos underscore the variables (including date and circumstances) affecting attendance and the difficulties in estimating 'average' attendances in any polis.

[48] Cf. Jones 109 (normal peacetime attendance may have been well over 5,000) and Staveley 78 (2,000–3,000 was probably normal at the ordinary meetings).

property. That was the meeting convened in 411 at Kolonos, outside the walls of Athens. The operations of Peloponnesian forces based at Dekeleia made it dangerous for those who were not armed to attend, and the dominance of citizens of hoplite status was made possible by the absence of large numbers of thetes serving with the fleet at Samos. But those were disturbed times and the situation was deliberately exploited by the oligarchic extremists who pushed through the measures to overthrow the democracy.[49]

Perhaps Sokrates was describing the character of a 'typical' meeting of the assembly when he spoke of the assembly as being composed of fullers, shoemakers, carpenters, smiths, farmers, merchants and shopkeepers. Certainly there was a sharp contrast between Athens and oligarchic states in this respect. The people named by Sokrates seem to represent a wide range in economic terms: the shopkeepers, for example, were in both economic and social terms inferior to the merchants. But while merchants might be away from Athens for extended periods, shopkeepers and artisans, in so far as they were their own masters or owned the goods they produced, might feel from time to time that they could leave their business for a day or a good part of a day – often in the hands of a member of the family or a slave – and attend the assembly.[50] But the characteristics of the fullers and the others which Sokrates had particularly in mind were their lack of wisdom or knowledge and their insignificance in terms of individual power (though the latter was, of course, closely related to wealth). And for those who believed that experts rather than amateurs should govern the polis, the presence of artisans and others who were not among 'the prudent' or 'the powerful' would have bulked large and assumed exaggerated proportions. Another witness, even more strongly partisan, was the author of a critical analysis of the Athenian democracy about the time of the outbreak of the Peloponnesian War. Known in modern times as the Old Oligarch, this writer detected the impact of the lower classes in the making of alliances, and not only in the decisions of the Dikasteria.[51] More soberly, Aristotle argued that the economic character of a polis played a part in determining the character of its political institutions: he exemplified this by pointing to the prominence of the trireme crews in Athens. Aristotle's point, however, was a comparative one – at Tenedos, for example, ferrymen represented a significant element – and in any case his description of Athens does not necessarily imply the numerical dominance in the assembly of the thetes who largely supplied the Athenian element in the crews of the triremes.[52]

In another section of the *Politics*, Aristotle recognised the importance of sufficient leisure or freedom from economic preoccupations to attend the assembly and serve in the law-courts. In many states, he argued, such leisure was

[49] See ch. 3.5.
[50] Xen. *Mem.* 3.7.6; Pl. *Prt.* 319c–d; see Kluwe (1976) 314–21.
[51] [Xen.] *AP* 1.14, 16–18, 2.17; cf. Isok. 5.116.
[52] Arist. *Pol.* 1291b14–30; cf. 1303b10–12 and 1327a40–1327b13.

restricted to men of property whose resources allowed them time to participate, whereas in democracies which developed in large states with considerable revenues, state pay provided the opportunity for leisure and for participation. Indeed, in such democracies – and among these Aristotle, it might appear reasonable to presume, would have included Athens – the multitude (*plēthos*) had a great deal of leisure and were not hampered by attention to their private affairs, whereas the rich were and so in many cases they did not take part in the assembly or in the law-courts. Thus the poor, Aristotle concluded, displaced the laws as being sovereign over the state.[53]

What did the Athenians understand by 'the rich' (*hoi plousioi*) and 'the poor' (*hoi penētes*)? Generally the terms were vague and subjective and often emotive. They could be used in a public speech to excite prejudice by dubbing someone as 'rich' or to arouse sympathy by describing someone as 'poor', though there was sometimes felt a certain unease in introducing a 'poor' witness. The main cause of such unease was related to the notion that the poor were vulnerable to bribery and the fear that the credibility of a poor witness might therefore be suspected. Yet it must be added that a background of poverty could be used by an orator to the prejudice of an individual and even to vilify him.[54] Sometimes a middle group (*hoi mesoi*) was distinguished, but the more common categorisation was rich and poor.[55] The terms *plousioi* and *penētes* did not by themselves cover the whole spectrum, for the Athenians also spoke of 'beggars' (*ptōkhoi*), nor were they mutually exclusive. They were frequently used in a relative sense, to be interpreted by reference to the speaker or writer and the audience. Demosthenes, for example, when discussing the 1,200 richest citizens who, between 357 and 340, were responsible for undertaking the trierarchy, felt that he could speak of all but the richest 300 as being 'poor' (*penētes*) or 'men without resources' (*aporoi*) and oppressed by their trierarchic obligations.[56]

Much of the debate about the socio-economic composition of the assembly and the law-courts has utilised these concepts 'rich' and 'poor'. And for a variety of reasons, not least the use of such terms by the Athenians of our period and the paucity of evidence in general, the concepts have to be used despite their notorious vagueness. Yet, for all their elasticity, the various Greek terms might also be used with some precision. There was, for example, a widely accepted notion that *hoi penētes* were those who had to work for their living, more specifically with their hands, and had little or no leisure.[57] It might appear from this that Athenian citizens in general had assimilated the aristocratic attitudes towards manual labour, though such an inference must be qualified by the fact

[53] Arist. *Pol.* 1292b23–1293a11.
[54] Lys. 6.48, 27.9–10, Dem. 21.98, 213, 20.18, Hyp. 4.32; Dem. 21.83, 95; 57.30–6, 45; cf. 18.127–31, 258–65, 19.199–200; cf. Thuc. 2.40.1; cf. Dover 109–12.
[55] Arist. *Pol.* 1295b26–1296b2, 1296b35–1297a8, Eur. *Suppl.* 238–45; cf. de Ste Croix 71–6.
[56] Dem. 18.104, 108.
[57] Ar. *Plout.* 552–4, Isok. 8.128; Davies 10–11, Markle (1985) 268–71.

that large numbers of citizens engaged in such labour.[58] *Aporoi*, too, especially when contrasted with *euporoi*, connoted those without sufficient resources rather than men with no property at all. And a measure of precision is implied in the term *hoi euporoi* ('those well endowed with resources', 'those with resources') when they are defined by Aristotle as 'those who serve the polis with their property'. In 'those who serve the polis with their property', Aristotle certainly included those who were liable on the basis of their wealth to undertake the *khorēgia*, the trierarchy and other liturgies or public services, but it may well be that he also had in mind those who paid property tax (*eisphora*).[59]

In contemporary Athenian usage (as is clear from the Attic Orators) 'the rich', 'those with resources', 'the men of property' were identified more particularly with those who were liable to perform liturgies. The liturgists seem to have possessed not less than 3 or 4 talents in property.[60] The average return may have been of the order of 3,000 drakhmai a year from 4 talents. With perhaps $1\frac{1}{4}$ obols or less as the approximate daily amount required to maintain a slave (some 75 drakhmai a year), 'those with resources' patently had sufficient property to employ, and rely on, the labour of others and to 'serve the state with their property'.[61]

Those who volunteered for liturgies or were caught up in the liturgic net may have numbered 1,000–1,200 in the 380s to 360s.[62] Between 357 and 340 the 1,200 richest citizens were enrolled in the trierarchic symmories or companies. The number of those who paid eisphora was probably of the order of 2,000 rather than 6,000, though the question of the patterns of property distribution and our lack of information about the organisation of eisphora even after the major reform of 378/7 make certainty impossible.[63] In either case those who paid eisphora possessed at least a moderate amount of property in Athens and the richest of them were responsible also for performing liturgies, while the term 'poor' may be applied in general to the rest of the citizen body.

It might be thought that in view of their numbers 'those with resources' would have found it difficult to exercise any influence on the voting, whether in the assembly or the law-courts, and would therefore have been discouraged from taking part. Aristotle clearly implied that, and if he had in mind (in the Athenian case) the richest 1,200–2,000, there would seem to be an element of

---

[58] See Appendix 2c.

[59] Arist. *Pol.* 1279b18–19, 1291a33–8, 1320a33–b4. It may be that in the passage cited (1291a33–8) Aristotle was not using 'to serve (the polis)' (*leitourgein*) in the technical sense of the agonistic and military liturgies performed in Athens, but in a wider or general sense. For, having defined the seventh class or element in the polis as 'those who serve the polis with their property – we call them *euporoi*' (see Lys. 31.12), he defined the eighth class as 'the class of public officials, that is, those who serve in the offices of state'. If Aristotle was using *leitourgein* in the wider or general sense, he may be understood to have been including among 'those with resources' (*euporoi*) men who paid eisphora.   [60] Dem. 21.208; Davies 11–28.

[61] See ch. 3 n. 70. Markle (1985) 296 suggests 1.1 obols a day; cf. 3 obols allowed to public slaves for maintenance in the 320s (*IG* II².1672–3).

[62] Davies 133–50, Rhodes (1982) 11–13.   [63] See ch. 3.4.

truth in his view.[64] Moreover, in Athens 'those without resources' may well have had more leisure than elsewhere. But we should not too readily accept this paradox of the poor displacing the rich in Athens in having leisure to participate in the Ekklesia and the Dikasteria. For individual or other reasons, the men of property might devote their time to their private affairs or, like Plato, to philosophy. Nevertheless, they were probably over-represented in the Council of 500, while most leading political figures possessed a measure of wealth, whether inherited or acquired.[65] As far as a more passive role in the assembly and the law-courts is concerned, we should not necessarily infer from Aristotle that there was widespread abstention by the men of property in Athens. If Aristotle had in mind the payers of war tax, and if they numbered 6,000, 'those with resources' represented 20%–25% of the adult male citizens, and Aristotle's paradox would be even less convincing.

5.3.2 The implications of extant speeches

In fact, if we examine the extant speeches which were delivered or said to have been delivered in the assembly, it is clear that orators were at times particularly conscious of the presence in the assembly of those who paid property tax (*eisphora*) or, as it is also described in view of its most common use, war tax. Demosthenes, for example, in several of his speeches urging the Athenians to take resolute action against Philip, rebuked them for shrinking from taking part in military expeditions and begrudging the payment of war tax and exhorted them to pay their tax willingly and to serve in person. Often Demosthenes distinguished himself from his hearers as the man who recognised the need for urgent action and so used the second person 'you', but at other times, in order not to antagonise his audience, he declared 'we refuse to pay war tax or to serve in person'.[66] Demosthenes' skill in alternating 'we' and 'you' demonstrates the care which had to be exercised in the application of this line of argument.

A great many extant speeches contain no such arguments since the particular question being debated did not involve the possibility of a levy of eisphora or did not lend itself to an appeal to the taxpayers. This specific recognition of the presence of taxpayers in the assembly is found mostly in speeches delivered in what seem to have been the great debates, but the number of assembly speeches surviving represents a small sample even from the great occasions and it may be that the taxpayers were less prominent in run-of-the-mill meetings. But in so far as the surviving speeches give a general indication of the composition of assembly meetings it would seem that it was important to win the support of the taxpayers in the assembly. Jones therefore concluded that they usually were, if not a majority, a substantial part of the audience and that it was only in moments of crisis that the poorer classes came in force and might outvote the

---

[64] Arist. *Pol.* 1292b23–1293a11.
[65] See ch. 2.3.2.   [66] Dem. 1.6, 2.24 (cf. 2.23, 27), 8.23 (cf. 8.21).

taxpayers.[67] Such was the crisis which arose in 354 when Athens was beset with rumours of a Persian attack.[68]

Yet arguments directed to payers of war tax probably indicate no more than that they represented a significant part of the assembly. Significant not so much in purely numerical terms, but more particularly because they had to be persuaded to the speaker's viewpoint by arguments of special interest as well as general considerations, or because, without their more or less willing support, the proposal might falter or fail through refusals or delays in the payment of eisphora when the proposal was implemented.[69] Against this interpretation it might be argued that it implies that the poorer citizens, if they were the majority in the assembly, did not usually use their numbers to milk the rich. Yet on balance the poor do *not* seem to have exploited fully their numbers or potential numbers in the assembly, despite the complaints of eisphora-payers who were, or felt they were, exploited by the poor.[70] The complaints for the most part would seem exaggerated and to be like modern complaints from those who would prefer to pay no income tax at all.

As far as the assembly is concerned, then, the statements of Aristotle (and other contemporary writers) about the predominance of the poor should not be interpreted too narrowly, nor should they be discounted as much as Jones' view would require. Those who paid property tax would seem to have constituted a significant element in the Ekklesia: on certain issues their support could be, or had to be, invoked and was worth invoking. If they numbered 6,000 as Jones believed, it is perhaps conceivable that they occasionally represented a majority of the meeting of the assembly, but if they numbered 2,000, the possibility of their constituting an actual majority is seriously diminished.

Though the proportion of taxpayers in meetings of the assembly must remain open to doubt, there would seem to be a clear and striking contrast with their significance in the law-courts. This emerges most clearly in certain speeches of Lysias, especially *Against Ergokles* (no. 28) and *Against Philokrates* (no. 29). These two speeches belong to the same year – 388 – and were principally concerned with the misappropriation of public funds by the associates of Thrasyboulos. At a meeting of the assembly Ergokles had been found guilty of treason, misappropriation and taking bribes. Another meeting of the assembly was held to fix the penalty: the speech *Against Ergokles* was composed for this occasion. Ergokles was condemned to death and his property was confiscated.[71] Subsequently, when no trace could allegedly be found of his property of more than 30 talents, Philokrates (who had served as Ergokles' treasurer on the expedition) was prosecuted before a Dikasterion on a charge of

---

[67] Jones 35–6, 109–10; cf. Harrison (1959) 60–1.
[68] Dem. 14.24–8; cf. 19.291.   [69] See Dem. 14.25–6.
[70] Lys. 19.29, Dem. 24.198, [Dem.] 47.54, Jones 55–8, Davies 82–4; see ch. 8.3.2.
[71] Lys. 29.2; cf. Roberts (1980) 108–11 and Roberts 96–102.

withholding 30 talents from the state. The speech *Against Philokrates* was written in support of that prosecution.

The charges against Ergokles were more serious than those against Philokrates, and this difference should not be overlooked. Lysias, for example, stressed Ergokles' conduct at Halikarnassos, but he gave particular weight to his misappropriation and the serious financial consequences of that. Furthermore, in his speech *Against Philokrates*, Lysias stressed the defendant's association with Ergokles and demanded the death penalty so that Philokrates could not live to enjoy the proceeds of misappropriation and bribery.[72] Any difference, therefore, in the socio-economic composition of the assembly which dealt with Ergokles and the court which heard the charge against Philokrates should be related not so much to the character and importance of the issues as to the Athenians' perceptions of the two institutions and their attitudes to participating in their proceedings.

The speech *Against Ergokles* made a strong appeal to those who paid property tax. The Athenians were addressed as 'being oppressed by the levies of property tax' and the speaker implied that the conduct of Thrasyboulos and his associates 'has made you poorer through the levies of property tax and made Ergokles and the other cronies of Thrasyboulos the wealthiest of the citizens'. It is clear from other sections of the speech that the wealth which these men had appropriated was derived from funds obtained from foreign states which should have been paid to the public treasury.[73] The loss of such revenue would, of course, have increased the likelihood of Athens' wealthier citizens being called upon to pay property tax if the state's funds were not adequate for military and naval activities such as those conducted by Thrasyboulos and his associates.

The central issue of the retention of 'your own money' was repeated in the speech *Against Philokrates*, but in it the speaker made no identification of audience and taxpayers. In fact he referred to the latter in the third person.

It would be strange, gentlemen of the jury, if you should be angry with those who are not able to pay the levies of tax on their own property and should confiscate their property on the grounds of default, but yet should fail to punish those who are keeping your own property.[74]

It is not, of course, to be inferred that the jury included no taxpayers, but the clear implication is that the taxpayers did not constitute a significant element in the court.

The speech *Against Philokrates* was composed for delivery to a Dikasterion, the speech *Against Ergokles* to a meeting of the assembly. That fact appears to be highly significant, for though we do not know a great deal about the detailed circumstances of the two speeches, there seem to be no grounds for invoking other factors such as differences in the character of the issues to explain the

---

[72] Lys. 29.11–14; Cohen (1983) 31–3.
[73] Lys. 28.3, 4, 5, 6, 10, 13.　　[74] Lys. 29.8, 13, 14 and 9.

difference in argumentation utilised by one of the most skilled speech-writers in Athens. We must conclude that Lysias judged it useful to appeal to the taxpayers in the assembly but not in the law-courts. In the assembly he sought to win over taxpayers who might otherwise be more sympathetic to an Ergokles than less well-to-do citizens were. He could not afford to ignore, let alone antagonise, other groups in the assembly, but he might well assume that they would be persuaded by the misappropriation of funds and by Ergokles' conduct on campaign.[75] A specific appeal was therefore directed to the taxpayers who were reminded of the likelihood of increased demands for funds arising from Ergokles' misappropriations and of the hardships imposed by levies of eisphora. In the court hearing the charges against Philokrates, no such specific appeals to taxpayers were judged to be necessary.

That the taxpayers constituted a significant element in the Ekklesia but not in the Dikasteria can be corroborated by two other speeches of Lysias – *On the Property of Aristophanes: Against the Treasury* (no. 19 – belonging to 388 or 387) and *Against Epikrates* (no. 27 – probably to be dated to 390). These two speeches – both composed for jury courts – in their different ways confirm the contrast between the speeches *Against Ergokles* and *Against Philokrates*.[76] Where the circumstances of the case allowed the possibility of appealing to the taxpayers, Lysias judged it a useful line of argument in the assembly but not in the law-courts. That is, in the years about 388 those who paid eisphora seem to have constituted a significant element in the Ekklesia but to have been of little significance in the Dikasteria.

This difference would also seem to have applied in the time of Demosthenes. In particular, four speeches which have been interpreted as indicating the numerical strength of the taxpayers in the law-courts seem, on the contrary, to indicate what Lysias recognised.[77] In the speech *Against Leptines*, Demosthenes could not ignore the effect of Leptines' law on the liturgists, but his argument is very strained and he was forced to overlook the poorer liturgists who would once again be liable for liturgies if Leptines' law was annulled. About the effect of the law on the masses he said very little.[78] This was not, as suggested by Jones, because non-liturgists were not in the majority, but rather because the consequences of annulling Leptines' law and thus limiting the number of liturgists *were* likely to be adverse for the wider range of citizens. In the speeches *Against Androtion* and *Against Timokrates*, Demosthenes wished to arouse the indignation of the dikasts against the high-handed methods used by his opponents in collecting arrears from payers of war tax: trespass on private houses and against the persons of citizens – as if they were slaves – not simply against their property.[79] He therefore sought to win the jurors' sympathy for

---

75 Cf. [Dem.] 60.14.
76 See Sinclair, 'Lysias' Speeches and the Debate about Participation in Athenian Public Life', *Antichthon* 21 (1987); see also Markle (1985) 281–92.
77 Jones 35–7; cf. Perlman (1967) 163–5.   78 Dem. 20.18–23, 28.
79 Dem. 22.53–5, 24.197 (cf. 24.193).

the defaulters by appearing to identify the defaulters with the jurors at large, but at the same time he was careful to distance the defaulters and the jurors. He added: *'they* (the taxpayers) pay double'.[80] In the speech *Against Meidias* (which was not delivered and which was probably published by someone other than the orator), Demosthenes exploited the antipathy towards very wealthy, arrogant men like Meidias, but also recognised the problems in introducing a 'poor' man as a witness.[81] These indications and the general tenor of the speech would seem to point neither to a jury consisting mainly of well-to-do citizens nor to a very poor audience, but rather to a range of citizens most of whom were either well removed from real poverty or were not averse to being regarded by the orator as removed from that status.[82]

5.4 The character and the attraction of the courts

In short, it would seem that for much of the fourth century at least, those who were liable for eisphora usually attended the assembly in significant numbers and showed much less interest in the law-courts. There are other indications of the prominence of poorer citizens in the law-courts. Aristophanes in the 420s and Isokrates in the 350s both depicted the dikasts as poor and dependent on the three-obol payment for the necessities of life.[83] Account must, of course, be taken of the effects of comic exaggeration by the playwright, while in the 350s financial difficulties seem to have beset many individual Athenians as well as the polis itself. Nevertheless, there is little reason to doubt that poorer citizens were in general prominent in the Dikasteria, as is clear from a speech composed in the years soon after 403, claiming damages for assault against a rich, young man. Isokrates in his speech *Against Lokhites* exploited popular antagonism towards the wealthy and the arrogant, sought sympathy for a poor man, but was careful to depict the jurors as not as impoverished as the victim, but as belonging to the mass or general run of the citizens.[84]

Associated with the factor of 'poverty', and perhaps more important than poverty alone, was the factor of age. The 'wasps' or dikasts depicted by Aristophanes in his play *The Wasps* (produced in 422) were not only poor but old: if anything, it was their age rather than their poverty which Aristophanes highlighted.[85] During periods of high military activity, it is true, younger men

---

[80] Dem. 24. 198 and see 24.193 for the identification of the jury with the majority (*hoi polloi*).

[81] Dem. 21.83, 95.

[82] Dover 34–5, Adkins 119–26, 140, Rhodes (1980A) 317, Markle (1985) 286–7.

[83] Ar. *Wasps* 300–13, Isok. 7.54, 8.130, 15.152.

[84] Isok. 20, especially 15–21; cf. *AP* 27.4, Dem. 21.182, 24.123.

[85] Ar. *Wasps* 548–51, and 1091–1101: the old dikasts recall their feats as rowers, implying that they were mainly from the thetic class, but Philokleon seems to allude also to fighting at Marathon as a hoplite with sword in hand (711–14; cf. *Akh.* 677–8 and 692–701; *Knights* 781, 1334). While it can hardly be said that the family was so poor that Philokleon was completely dependent on the three obols for the necessities of life (see Dover 35), he was now dependent on his son's goodwill, and for anything beyond the necessities he may well have needed the jury pay. See also Aiskhin. 1.88. Cf. Hom. *Il.* 18.503–6.

would have been available in smaller numbers than at other times, so the age distortion may have been greater during the Arkhidamian War and was thus reflected in *The Wasps*. The same image is to be found in Khremylos in *Ploutos* (produced in 388) – an old man in need of jury pay for the necessities of life.[86] The old juror may, of course, have been something of an Aristophanic type, but he may well have corresponded to a continuing, general reality. Older citizens, who had handed over the management of the *oikos* to their sons and who were no longer independent as they had been, may well have been inclined to feel (or liked to express the feeling) that they were poor and were dependent on the three-obol pay. Beyond the comic stage, we should hardly expect to find specific indications of the age of jurors – for example, in the speeches of the orators: their silence cannot, therefore, be used to rule out the possibility that a considerable proportion, perhaps a majority, of the jurors were old men.

The prominence of older citizens in the courts would not be surprising in so far as able-bodied men were able to be gainfully employed elsewhere. There were, of course, other important factors which influenced the decision of citizens of all ages whether, or when, to participate in the courts (or in other polis activities), but even in economic terms the decision would have entailed subjective considerations. Still, the necessities of life had to be provided. Citizens preferred to work for themselves, but if they did not have land to work, or wealth, slaves or other resources to exploit, or if they were not self-employed, they would have had to seek paid employment in the service of other individuals or in the service of the polis. It is likely that able-bodied men could earn up to about a drakhme a day in the latter part of the fifth century: the citizens (and metics and slaves) who completed the building of the Erekhtheion in the years between 409 and 406 are recorded as receiving up to a drakhme. While only limited numbers of citizens appear to have been engaged on that project, their pay may give a broad indication of general rates at the time.[87] In the same period, large numbers of thetes would, in the course of the sailing season, have served in the Athenian navy and would have received 3 obols a day, with the possibility of plunder from a successful campaign. And, despite the desperate financial situation of Athens in the last years of the Peloponnesian War, a two-obol payment was introduced in 410, probably as a measure of poor relief for those who were in financial distress through the war and who received no other payment from the polis, and was continued until 405/4, though it is likely that the rate was temporarily reduced to 1 obol in 406. Even payment for jury service may have been affected in the last stages of the Peloponnesian War.[88]

---

[86] Ar. *Plout.* 28–9, 972, 1164–7.

[87] See Appendix 2c and ch. 2.2 with n. 32.

[88] See ch. 3 n. 37, but see in general Dem. 57.40–2 on the possibility of serious financial effects for the family of a citizen absent on military service; *AP* 28.3 (and *CAAP*), Ar. *Frogs* 138–41 (and scholiast), *IG* II².1686B.59–60, Buchanan (1962) 35–48.

In the case of all those options involving daily payments, allowance has to be made for the fact that the pay had to provide also for days not 'worked', though on certain festival days those who could and did attend festivals received sustenance from the distribution after the sacrifices. By the early 380s the habitual juror might receive in addition 20 drakhmai if he attended 40 meetings of the Ekklesia as well. But even with that, it would be a lucky or indeed a canny citizen who received in state pay the equivalent of 2 obols for every day of the year. For the number of court days a year was probably between 150 and 200, and somehow he would have to manage to be allotted to jury service for 200 days in a year.[89] Consider, on the other hand, the citizen who did not have land or other resources and who eschewed jury service or had not been selected by lot among the 6,000 dikasts for the year. He could by no means assume that paid work could always be found, but he would have needed paid work for only 144 days (at 5 obols a day) or 120 days (at one drakhme) to have the same amount as our lucky juror for the year. He might, of course, be engaged in paid employment for as many as 260–300 days in a year. For all but the aged or invalids, some combination of activities would, of course, have been possible and common, *provided* that inclination, selection as a dikast, place of residence, and other factors favoured the several activities.

For the citizen with a family, it would seem, an average of 2 obols a day throughout the year would barely have sufficed. However, quite apart from the fact that individual Athenians had different ideas of what constituted a minimum to live on, the fragmentary evidence on prices and cost of living has made it very difficult for scholars to reach much agreement about the cost of maintaining a family.[90] Most Athenians lived frugally, and it may be suggested that a family of four may have managed to subsist on about $2\frac{1}{2}$ obols a day for food and somewhat less than $3\frac{1}{2}$ obols for all their basic needs.[91] Perhaps poorer Athenians lived more frugally than those estimates allow. In any case, it is reasonable to believe that to the poor of whatever age jury pay had its attractions. To the younger citizen with a family, however, jury pay would be a useful source of support, but not a sufficient means of livelihood in itself. He was, moreover, likely to receive up to twice as much (or more) from paid work, if it was available. To the older citizen, who had less chance of gainful employment, jury pay was much more attractive: 120 days in court would give

---

89 See Appendix 2A; Ar. *Plout.* 1164–7.
90 Lys. 32.20, 28 (a little less than 3 dr. a day for 2 boys and a girl, with an attendant and a maid, in the last decade of the fifth century), Dem. 27.36 (about 2 dr. a day for the young Demosthenes, and his sister and mother, or 4 obols each a day in the 370s and 360s); cf. [Dem.] 42.22; cf. public payments to invalids (1 obol a day early in the fourth century (Lys. 24.13), 2 obols in the 320s (*AP* 49.4)) and to epheboi (4 obols a day in the 320s for maintenance (*AP* 42.3)); see Ehrenberg (1951) 230–1.
91 See, most recently, Markle (1985) 271–81, 293–7, who argues for no increase in cereal prices, except for temporary fluctuations, from the late fifth century to the 320s and on the other hand tends to under-estimate the cost of non-cereals; see also Glotz (1926) 285–7, Tod (1927) 20–2, Jones 135 n. 1, Kluwe (1976) 329.

him an obol for every day of the year. If need be, he could probably support himself on about an obol a day, but most elderly citizens would themselves in varying degrees have been supported by their families. Bdelykleon would not have been alone in wishing that his father would live a life of noble ease, supported by his son, rather than acting the dikast. But Philokleon clearly enjoyed this activity *and* the measure of independence which jury service and pay provided.[92]

In the century from Kleon's time to the 320s jury pay was not increased. Yet assembly pay was increased from 3 obols at the end of the 390s to 6–9 obols by the 320s, thus roughly keeping pace with the inflation of wages for building workers, if we may regard the rates in the Erechtheion accounts and the Eleusinian accounts as indicative of wage levels towards the end of the fifth century and in the 320s.[93] The readiest explanation – that jury service continued to be generally popular, while the assembly encountered problems – is given some support by a recent study of the bronze allotment plates (*pinakia*) used by dikasts in the allotment process. The bronze pinakia which came into use about 378 and were replaced by wooden pinakia for the jurors about 350 seem to have frequently changed hands, suggesting that there was competition for jury service, with a constantly changing body of dikasts, not a relatively stable, life-long body of jurors.[94]

There are, however, some indications of a shortage of citizens available for, or interested in, jury service. Aristophanes in the *Ploutos* referred to the practice of enrolling in a number of dikastic panels.[95] This practice may reflect a shortage of citizens resulting from the cumulative effects of war and plague losses during the Peloponnesian War. It may, however, also be the result of the diminished activity of the courts following the collapse of the Athenian empire and thus the diminished chances of receiving the 3 obols. Multiple enrolment would increase the chances of being selected. Secondly, problems of the availability of men for jury service as well as military needs may lie behind changes in the organisation of the Dikasteria, in particular the change from the allotment of citizens at the beginning of their term to a jury panel (which was then allotted each day to a particular court) to the allotment of individuals each day from those dikasts who presented themselves. Other factors, such as the problems of the bribing of jurors, must be recognised in these changes.[96] Both

---

[92] Ar. *Wasps* 340–64, 503–631 (especially 503–18, 605–15).

[93] See ch. 2.2 with n. 32.

[94] Kroll 71–83. Since the sample of pinakia is very small and subject to chance factors in survival and discovery (cf. *Phoenix* 28 (1974) 274), deductions about the dikasts should be regarded as tentative. This is particularly true in regard to the socio-economic background of the dikasts – see Kroll 261–3, where he notes that well over half of the holders of dikastic allotment plates are either unknown themselves or from unknown families and argues that the poorer citizens predominated among the jurors.

[95] Ar. *Plout.* 1166–7 (388 B.C.); cf. Lys. 19.11 for economic difficulties in the 380s.

[96] See ch. 3.5; Kroll 5–7, 81–3 and MacDowell 35–40.

multiple enrolment and the more flexible system of individual allotment may, however, suggest a shortage of dikasts. Perhaps this shortage was largely confined to the generation after the restoration of democracy in 403 and the demographic problems may have been less severe by the 370s when the system of individual allotment was probably introduced. In general, however, the problems would seem to be demographic and manpower problems rather than problems of apathy.

In the following decades, there were times when the activities of the law-courts were curtailed or suspended. At one point at least in the years between 370 and 362 the courts heard only public actions, and not private ones. Apollodoros resorted to bringing a (public) charge of *hybris* (arrogant or outrageous conduct) against Phormion, while other citizens involved in disputes which did not allow such alternatives had presumably to be content with the decisions of the public arbitrators. This curtailment was ascribed to 'the war' (that is, against the Thebans).[97] Later, a taxiarch was to claim that in 348 he was unable to press immediately a charge of desertion because pay was not provided for the Dikasteria.[98] Financial difficulties (in 348, after the Euboian campaign) and the absence of Athenians on service abroad may be held to have been largely responsible for these interruptions to the activities of the courts.

It must be noted that if, as seems likely, the system of individual allotment was introduced in the 370s and one of the major objectives was to overcome the problems raised by the manpower needs of war, the system did not always achieve this. It must also be added that the new system should have largely removed the need for very large numbers of citizens presenting themselves on about one day in two throughout the year, as would seem to be inherent in the earlier systems. Though we do not know how the arrangements of any of these systems were made in detail on a day-to-day basis and we have no evidence for how many courts or how many jurors were sitting on particular days, it is improbable that anything like 6,000 dikasts would be required for a day, certainly under the new system.[99] It must also be borne in mind that not a few of the matters over which ordinary Athenians found themselves in dispute are likely to have been minor and to have been settled in the fourth century by the Forty or by arbitrators, not the Dikasteria.[100] The Dikasteria are, in short, unlikely to have required the high concentrations of citizens inherent in the quorum provisions for the successful transaction of some business in the assembly.

---

[97] [Dem.] 45.4; cf. Dem. 21.45–6, MacDowell 129–32, Buchanan (1962) 20 n. 2. See Lys. 17.3 for the suspension of private lawsuits in the course of the last years of the Peloponnesian War; cf. Thuc. 6.91.7 (and *HCT*).

[98] [Dem.] 39.17.   [99] Cf. MacDowell 35–40.

[100] Appeal to the Dikasteria against an arbitrator's decision would tend to be limited to disgruntled citizens with some confidence in their own ability to convince the dikasts or with sufficient wealth to hire a professional speech-writer to draft a speech for them to deliver. See ch. 3.5.

If, as is generally believed, jury service had a strong appeal for Athenian citizens, what was the basis of that appeal? To acknowledge their reputation for litigiousness is not to explain that appeal.[101] It is, of course, clear that the fate and fortunes of individuals rested in the hands of the citizen jurors. A sense of power and importance was felt by the jurors: it was depicted, with heightened vividness, by Aristophanes in Philokleon and the chorus of wasps, who revelled in their power and in the attention paid them by the powerful and the wealthy. To Bdelykleon the dikasts were suffering from a delusion in thinking that they were masters of the state, but in their own eyes they had the power of kings.[102] All the state officials were required to pass a scrutiny of their activities, but the dikasts alone were not subject to scrutiny and against their decision there was no appeal.[103] As a member of the assembly, the citizen might find the routine nature of much of the business and the intricacies of other matters tedious or lacking in appeal, and, more than that, he might vote for a proposal, only to find that it was blocked by a prosecution on the grounds that the proposal was unconstitutional. That prosecution was pursued in the law-courts, where the dikast could rule against the assembly's decision. In the fourth century the prosecution against an illegal proposal was used with increasing frequency, partly because political leaders attempted to bypass the cumbersome processes involved in changing the laws, and partly as a weapon in political warfare.[104] In so far as the assembly's decision could be blocked for a time or even overthrown, the dikasts acquired an important role in the processes of decision-making. Furthermore, their role in the legislative process had been enhanced by the introduction in about 403 of set procedures for the revision of laws, for the nomothetai who, after debate in the assembly, were left to examine and to approve new laws or changes to existing laws, were drawn by lot from the dikasts. On some occasions in the fourth century the recruitment of nomothetai from dikasts alone appears to have been ignored.[105]

Charged with these powers as well as their general judicial functions, the dikasts would clearly have felt some sense of acting decisively and with final authority. Or, as the author of the *Athenaion Politeia*, writing in the 320s, observed with hindsight when assessing Solon's institution of the right of appeal to the Heliaia, 'when the Demos are masters of the vote (in the courts), they become masters of the State'. By the end of the fifth century the power of the dikasts was increasingly apparent, and in the course of the fourth century there may have been a significant shift in the balance of power to the Dikasteria.[106]

Perhaps even more than in the assembly, where there was at least the regular invitation for any one to address the meeting, the citizen in the law-courts could play a passive role and not expose his inexperience or lack of detailed

---

[101] Ar. *Clouds* 206–8, *Wasps* 87–124, *Birds* 40–1, Xen. *Mem.* 3.5.16; cf. Thuc. 1.77.1, Meiggs 228–33, cf. Winton (1980) 89–97.   [102] Ar. *Wasps* 515–631, 1102–13.

[103] Ar. *Wasps* 587; cf. Dem. 24.73, 152.   [104] See ch. 6.5; cf. Hansen (1974) 22–65.

[105] See ch. 4.2.   [106] *AP* 9.1, 41.2; Hansen (1974) 61; Rhodes (1980A) 320–3.

knowledge and understanding. Moreover, in the Dikasterion he had the weapon of the secret ballot; as Philokleon declared, the dikast, though moved by the entreaties of the accused, was free to do none of the things he said he would.[107] In the mid-fourth century Isokrates depicted one of his associates warning him of the brutalising effects of envy and poverty which led some men to destroy, if they could, those whom they envied, and that not through ignorance but through deliberate intent and because they did not expect to be found out.[108] In a similar vein, Aristotle alleged against the demagogues of his own day that they used the Dikasteria to court the favour of the Demos and he urged that the abuse be checked by transferring confiscated property to the sacred treasury, not to the public treasury.[109] Earlier, in the 390s or 380s, Epikrates and his associates, so Lysias claimed, had sought to secure unjust verdicts by warning the jurors that state pay would not be forthcoming unless they convicted the defendants. Yet in the same speech Lysias also claimed that it was common for juries to convict but then to impose no penalty.[110] In general, however, it may be admitted that the rich entertained fears that their property was vulnerable to confiscation by the courts.

5.5 The assembly or the courts?

Despite the power of the courts, the taxpayers were apparently more inclined to attend the assembly than serve in the courts. Why? For them, Aristotle's notion of preoccupation with private affairs may have been a critical factor. In discussing the importance of holding few meetings of the assembly and few sittings of large courts, Aristotle observed that 'the men with resources are not willing to be away from their private affairs for many days, but are willing to be away for a short time'.[111] In terms simply of the number of days, then, the well-to-do would have been inclined to show greater interest in the assembly than in the courts. Allied to this was the unpredictability of being selected by lot. Jurors had to present themselves at the courts to take part in the allotment procedures, which alone would have been time-consuming and irksome.[112] The old or the poor, those with few or no alternative forms of employment, had time on their hands to take their chance. Unless on a particular day very few dikasts presented themselves, the outcome would have been quite unpredictable, especially after the introduction of individual allotment each day, though perhaps the day-to-day organisation of the courts minimised this. And the well-to-do would hardly relish the prospect of being passed over by lot and seeing a poor man selected. Furthermore, most of the wealthiest citizens may have been content to

---

[107] Ar. *Wasps* 560–1.   [108] Isok. 15.142–3.   [109] Arist. *Pol.* 1320a5–17.
[110] Lys. 27.1 (but cf. 27.16); see 19.11, 61–2, 21.13–14, 30.22; Ar. *Knights* 1358–61, Dem. 10.44–5, Arist. *Pol.* 1320a17–22; cf. Hyp. 4.33–7.
[111] Arist. *Pol.* 1320a17–29.   [112] See Dow (1939) 32–3.

lead comparatively private lives and show some enthusiasm in the performance of liturgies; others could take the risks as well as the benefits of a prominent role in the public life of Athens. However, in the assembly vital decisions were made which directly affected *all* the well-to-do – in particular a vote for war (or for the rejection of peace overtures) which, while affording some of them further opportunities, might require from all of them levies of property tax or the performance of trierarchies.[113]

Such pragmatic reasons for inclining to the assembly were probably reinforced or closely associated with reasons of tradition and history. The Dikasteria were not only fundamentally popular in their function and composition (in contrast to the situation in most other states), but they had also, in the view of conservative citizens, been corrupted and tainted by the introduction of state pay (*misthos*) in the mid-fifth century.[114] Participation in the assembly was probably more 'respectable' than participation in the courts. The comments attributed to 'the boys with the battered ears' about the corrupting influence of Perikles' introduction of jury pay may be regarded as typical of the views of men of property in general.[115] The chorus in the *Ekklesiazousai* lamented that in the days of the 'noble Myronides' in the first half of the fifth century, no one would have stooped to take money for attending the assembly and managing the city's affairs.[116] Those sentiments, albeit stated in exaggerated terms, reflected the views of the well-to-do not only in Myronides' time but also, in essence, in the 390s. Even after the introduction of assembly pay these attitudes to what was an older, more traditional institution (albeit not immune to change) than the courts with their clearly changing character and extended business remained strong. Taxpayers at any rate still seem to have recognised that attending the assembly was important for safeguarding their own interests.

These considerations and the amount of the payment strongly suggest that it was the poorer citizens who were the main target of the financial inducement to attend the assembly.[117] The pay of 1, 2 or 3 obols and even the increases in the interval between the 390s and the 320s would not, in themselves, have been a tempting bait to the well-to-do. Perhaps in the 390s there was a feeling that a wider range of citizens needed to be involved in the assembly to minimise the risks of a repetition of the political turmoil of the late fifth century.

To summarise, leisure (deriving from the possession of a measure of wealth or the provision of state pay) and economic considerations were critical factors in activating an Athenian's interest in the affairs of his polis and leading him, for example, to attend the assembly or serve on the juries. Family tradition and individual interest and ambition were also important. Among other variables, place of residence would have been for the poor a more critical factor than for

---

[113] Cf. Pl. *Rep.* 565b.　　[114] Cf. *AP* 27.4.

[115] That is, those with pro-Spartan sympathies: Pl. *Grg.* 515e.

[116] Ar. *Ekkl.* 303–5.　　[117] Cf. the typical comments of Plato in *Rep.* 565a.

the rich, while the influence of the urban poor is generally presumed to have been much greater than their rural cousins' with comparable economic resources.[118] Many of the poor may well have been attracted to the courts in the fifth century by the payment which was offered, and perhaps the old in particular. Increasingly in the fourth century, the jurors' sense of power and importance may have been a crucial factor in the perceptions of the poor. Any shift in the balance from the assembly to the courts may help to explain the continuing attraction of jury service.

[118] Cf. Arist. *Pol.* 1319a24–38; Hansen 136–7, Kluwe (1976) 295–333 and (1977) 45–81; on the identification and analysis of the variables see Sinclair (n. 76 above). See Hansen (1983B) 151–80 and (1983C) 227–38 for a valuable collection of material regarding the relationship between deme registration and (1) active participation as a *rhētōr* (orator) or strategos (see ch. 6) and (2) jury service. Hansen's analysis (228–9) reveals a remarkable correspondence between the bouleutic quotas for the three areas (City, Coast and Inland) and *known* dikasts and *known* rhetores/strategoi. He argues strongly that too little weight has been given to daily mobility and suggests a greater willingness on the part of Athenians to participate in public life, even when living at what would now be considered more than a reasonable walking distance from the city, than is usually accepted. While he also acknowledges a considerable migration from country to city, he does not give this sufficient weight in his analysis. If, for example, we take together the 63 rhetores and strategoi who are known to have been registered in city demes, the 4 who were registered in non-city demes but who are known, mainly through the exigencies of political speeches, to have owned houses in Athens or the Peiraieus, and the 9 for whom the provenance of tombstones suggests that they lived in or near Athens though they were registered in non-city demes (see 234–5), the remarkable correspondence is slightly disturbed but, more importantly, the smallness of the sample and our lack of evidence (both admitted by Hansen) and the limited value of deductions are underscored. Similarly, the small sample of dikastic pinakia and the limited excavations undertaken in rural Attike must be taken into account when considering the view of Kroll 9 n. 2 and 83 n. 21 that most jurymen were city-dwellers; see n. 94 above.

6 The hazards of leadership

6.1 The role of individuals

The functioning of the Athenian democracy depended on the support of large numbers of citizens willing to attend meetings of the assembly and to act as jurors. The space on the Pnyx could not, however, accommodate anything like the whole citizen body, and though the composition of the Ekklesia was not constant, there were undoubtedly not a few who, being unable or unwilling, rarely or never entered the assembly – or the courts.[1] The effective functioning of the Athenian polis depended also on the interest of citizens who were not simply content with listening and voting in the Ekklesia and the Dikasteria. These citizens could undertake one of the large number of offices of state which were determined by use of the Lot. Some experience would be gained in those offices, and some honour especially in the arkhonships. But collegiality, annual tenure and the prohibition of a second term limited their power, while the use of the Lot deprived them of any real significance in terms of political standing.[2]

The ambitious individual would seek rather to gain experience in the Boule or to be elected as a member of an embassy dispatched on a particular mission or as a member of a special committee appointed to investigate a specific matter. Or he would seek one of the elected offices – in particular, to be elected as a strategos or (in the mid-fourth century) as a Festival Fund Commissioner. The citizen could exploit the knowledge, experience and reputation gained in either of those offices to enhance his capacity to persuade the assembly. For the highest opportunity for many an ambitious man (*philotimos*) was afforded by the equal right of speaking. He might, with or without supporting argument, move a decree in the Boule or in the Ekklesia, he might (in the fourth century) propose a law before the nomothetai, or he might initiate a public prosecution in the Dikasteria. He might express his view or give advice to the council or the assembly or, as an advocate (*synēgoros*), address a court. In addressing any of these bodies the citizen was, in a legal sense, a *rhētōr* (speaker or orator). In general usage in the Attic Orators, however, rhetores were those who spoke frequently

---

[1] Pl. *Ap.* 17d, Isok. 15.38; cf. Thuc. 2.40.   [2] See ch. 4.1.

or habitually, especially in the assembly.[3] Rhetor was, furthermore, a term which might evoke different responses among Athenians. Demosthenes was well aware of this and in particular of the fact that the word could be used as a reproach, for he thought it important, in his attack on Meidias, to foreshadow the possibility that Meidias would say about him: 'This man is a rhetor.' Demosthenes countered:

If a rhetor is one who gives you such counsel as he thinks will be to your advantage, but stops short of pestering or bullying you, I would not disclaim . . . that title. But if a rhetor is one of those speakers that you and I sometimes see, men who are shameless and have grown rich at your expense, I cannot be one, for I have never received anything from you and I have spent on you all but a fraction of my fortune.[4]

Democracy, then, required energetic participation by citizens who were ready and able to devote a significant part of their time to public affairs, and over a period of some years, and thus provide an element of continuity as well as leadership.[5] Yet there is much detailed evidence to suggest that the risks as well as the rewards of leadership were high.[6] In the third quarter of the fifth century, political and military leadership had continued to be closely associated. By the 420s, the need for the capacity to persuade or win over the assembly was becoming more apparent and we see the first indications of specialisation in warfare and in public speaking and of a split between political and military leadership. That separation emerged more clearly in the first half of the fourth century and in the third quarter may be regarded as typical, though not universal. In the mid-fourth century the Commissioners of the Festival Fund emerged.[7] Despite the diminishing political activity of strategoi, in the fourth century they may be linked with the leading rhetores and – from the later 350s – the Festival Fund Commissioners (and other major financial officials) as constituting the 'political leaders' in Athens.[8]

---

[3] Hyp. 4.8–9; Perlman (1963) 327–55, Hansen (1983A) 39–42, 46–9. See ch. 5.1 for *rhētores* and *hoi legontes* with the sense of political activists who dominated the Boule at the expense of the ordinary members.

[4] Dem. 21.189 (Loeb tr. adapted). See Hansen (1983A) 46–7 on the range of connotations of other terms which may designate political activists: *politeuomenos* (one who engages actively in the life of the polis), *symboulos* (adviser, counsellor), *dēmagōgos* (leader of the Demos), *politikos* (statesman). *Dēmēgoros* (public speaker, popular orator), not found in the Attic Orators though related nouns and verbs are frequently used (Lys. 16.20 (cf. 14.45), Isok. 8.76, Dem. 18.60 (cf. 21.202), Aiskhin. 1.64, 195, Dein. 1.31), is used by other fourth-century writers, commonly in a pejorative sense (especially by Plato (*Grg.* 520a–b)), but also in a good or neutral sense (Xen. *Mem.* 6.2.15; cf. *Hell.* 6.3.3). Mention may also be made of *hoi ta tēs poleōs prattontes* (those who engage in the affairs of the polis, public men) (Lys. 18.16, 27.7, Xen. *Mem.* 3.7.2–3). *Prostatai* or *prostatai tēs poleōs* (leaders of the polis) is used with particular reference to earlier leaders (that is, of the fifth century) (Isok. 8.54, Aiskhin. 3.154; cf. Xen. *Mem.* 3.6.1, *AP* 28 (and *CAAP*)). For *prostatai tou dēmou* (protectors or leaders of the Demos) and terms used in the later fifth century, see Connor 108–19.

[5] See ch. 2.3.1.   [6] See below, especially n. 71; Roberts 14–29.

[7] See ch. 2.3.1–3; Plut. *Phok.* 7.3; cf. Dem. 18.212.

[8] Hansen (1983A) 33–55 (especially 49–53), (1983B) 151–80 (including a useful list of rhetores and strategoi).

Most officials – such as the Secretary of the Boule and the Receivers (of public moneys) (*apodektai*) – are not to be reckoned among the political leaders. They and the public slaves constituted a secretariat in the rudimentary sense of recording decisions and financial transactions, but in no sense did they approximate to the large bureaucracies or civil services of modern states, which at times seem to possess an autonomy of their own. And though the Boule was a much more important body in the discussion and formulation of policy than has sometimes been acknowledged, its annual tenure and constantly-changing membership, as well as its relationship with the assembly, rule out any comparison with 'the Government' of a modern state. The board of generals and the Festival Fund Commission might at times have been in a position to exercise a strong influence. Yet it was the vote of the assembly which was decisive – and decisive in a much more real sense than the vote of a parliament where in varying measure party discipline commonly makes the voting a formality.[9]

6.2 Leaders, 'occasional proposers' and ordinary citizens in the fourth century

Initiatives therefore seem to have come largely from prominent individuals. Yet it is notorious that these men were severely dealt with if their performance or their policies fell short of Athenian expectations. What precisely were these hazards and why did individuals aspire to leadership? How did they endeavour to maintain their position?

Much of our detailed evidence comes from the fourth century, while the revision of the laws in the years from 410 to 403 and developments in the character of, and avenues for, leadership make the fourth century distinctive in various respects.[10] Our examination will therefore be directed to the eighty years after the restoration of democracy in 403 and to the prominent individuals who devoted all or most of their time to public life. In particular, there were citizens who were very active in the assembly and the courts: in that sense, like the professional generals, they may be regarded as 'professional leaders'. They are probably to be numbered in single rather than double figures at any one time. In any prytany a Kephalos, a Kallistratos, an Aristophon or a Demosthenes might well speak in at least one of the assembly meetings.

Was leadership in public life, however, as highly individual and personal as ancient writers seem to suggest? These writers in general, and not only the biographers like Plutarch, tended to emphasise the role of the individual. And, given the scale and the character of Athenian life, the individual may well have

---

[9] See ch. 2.3.2–3 and ch. 4.5.
[10] Rhodes (1980A) 305–23, MacDowell 47–52; see ch. 2.3.2–3.

been, or may well have felt, more influential than individuals in large, technological societies. Yet the social, economic, cultural and political parameters within which individuals operated were important in Athens, though our limited evidence does not often enable us to delineate them with precision. However, some ancient writers also specifically indicated the importance of the supporters of a political leader. At the simplest level, they employed phrases which are literally translated 'those around [or, with] (Thrasyboulos)' or idiomatically 'the supporters of (Thrasyboulos)' or '(Thrasyboulos) and his supporters'.[11] These supporters did not constitute a 'party' in the modern sense of a political party with a more or less clearly defined platform and a high degree of internal organisation and discipline. They were essentially personal supporters of the leading figures.

These leading figures might share some similar attitudes: in 396, for example, 'Thrasyboulos, Aisimos and Anytos and their supporters' were more cautious in their attitudes towards Sparta than 'Epikrates and Kephalos and their supporters'.[12] A political leader might therefore cooperate on a continuing basis with other political leaders, and in particular those who were primarily engaged in military affairs were likely to find the support of rhetores in the assembly vital. Rhetores also gained from association with successful commanders. The value of such mutual support can be clearly demonstrated from the years 373 to 367, when Kallistratos, Khabrias and Iphikrates seem to have cooperated, in particular against Timotheos in 373. Such cooperation or working arrangements, which have for the sake of convenience been called 'alliances', were based on similar responses to the major questions of the time and the consequences for the individuals' influence in Athens.[13] Questions of foreign policy were frequently critical. These personal alliances were remarkable for the ease and rapidity with which they changed rather than for their durability. It could hardly be otherwise in view of the personal, competitive character of leadership and the absence of a strict party organisation. The career of Iphikrates, as will be seen, may be regarded as typifying the personal, fluid character of political relations.[14] Khares and Kharidemos and professional commanders in general, being so much away from Athens, had to rely heavily on rhetores to look after their interests, and it was said of some of them that they bought this support.[15]

It is perhaps all too easy to see political ties. The fact that Timotheos was elected to the board of strategoi for 378/7 along with Kallistratos and Khabrias need not mean that at this point all three had close political ties (and subsequently drew apart). In 378 the threat of Sparta was serious and the

---

[11] *Hell. Oxy.* 1.2; Xen. *Hell.* 1.7.8; Thuc. 8.65.1, 67.1, 90.3; Arist. *Pol.* 1305b25–7; cf. Dem. 57.59.
[12] *Hell. Oxy.* 1.2, 2.2 (and Bruce *Commentary*).
[13] Sealey 133–63; Finley 51.   [14] See ch. 7.1.
[15] Dem. 23.146–7, 185–6; cf. 51.16–22; Theopomp. *FGrH* 115 F213; Aiskhin. 2.71; cf. Dem. 2.29; see, however, Arist. *Rh.* 1364a19–23.

Athenians may well have decided to elect all three, whatever their relationships with one another. After all, in selecting strategoi the Athenians did not baulk at electing men with quite different attitudes. The most celebrated case was the selection as joint commanders of Alkibiades, the chief advocate of the Sicilian expedition, and Nikias who strongly opposed it, along with the 'professional' general Lamakhos. Similarly, among the envoys who went to Sparta in 371 to discuss peace were the Spartan proxenos Kallias, the anti-Spartan Autokles, and Kallistratos who is represented by Xenophon as espousing a neutralist attitude towards relations with Sparta and Thebes.[16] Nor were the ten envoys who were sent in 346 to discuss peace and later to receive the oaths from Philip II all of the same mind: certainly in 343 Demosthenes and Aiskhines were anxious to point up differences between them.[17] If anything, we should perhaps begin with the hypothesis that the members of a board or an embassy were likely to cover a diversity of viewpoints rather than that they shared similar views or were cooperating fully in a political sense.

It is clear, moreover, that there were many other citizens active in the assembly and other bodies besides the most prominent figures such as Thrasyboulos of Steiria, Androtion or Lykourgos. Some citizens, because of limited political ability or because they devoted less time to public life or for other reasons, did not reach the pre-eminent position of a Kallistratos. Such men may be identified as a second broad group in the continuum of political activity, though the distinctions between the two groups are not neat but rather blurred.[18] These two broad groups of political activists were in terms of contemporary usage 'the rhetores' – the citizens who spoke frequently in the assembly. They may together have numbered 20 to 30 at any one time.[19] The willingness to offer advice or a view to the assembly or to move a motion, however, was by no means limited to these two broad groups. At any meeting of the assembly where 6,000 citizens were present, the number of citizens who had spoken in at least one earlier meeting would, it may reasonably be assumed, have been of the order of 200 or 300, and perhaps in excess of that estimate, as Hansen has argued.

Any figure is at best an estimate, for our evidence is very fragmentary. Even from the comparatively well-documented period from 355 to 322, for example, we have only some 181 decrees where the name of the proposer is preserved. In all, some 82 citizens are thus known by name as proposers, with Demosthenes moving 39 decrees and Demades 21, but, equally important, with as many as 64 proposers with only 1 known decree. If, on an estimate of 9 decrees passed at each meeting, we assume a minimum of 13,000 decrees during the period, the

---

[16] Xen. *Hell.* 6.3.2–17; Mosley (1962) 41–6, Ryder (1963) 237–41, Tuplin (1977) 51–6.

[17] Dem. *On the Embassy*, Aiskhin. *On the Embassy*; Cawkwell (1963B) 120; cf. Mosley (1973) 55–62.

[18] Cf. 'the lesser rhetores' contemptuously dismissed by Hypereides (5.12) as 'masters only of noise and shouting'.   [19] Cf. Hansen (1984) 154 (suggesting 10–20).

preserved decrees would represent less than 1.5% of all proposals passed by the assembly.[20] If we had the complete record of assembly decrees, the number of proposers would clearly be much higher, though allowance has to be made for very active political leaders and for the possibility that lesser or unknown figures may have been more active than might have been expected. Whatever the number of citizens who proposed motions, however, it is clear that, though a rather limited number of rhetores probably tended to play a conspicuous part in the proceedings of the assembly, the number of citizens who had ventured at least once to address the assembly ran into hundreds at any one time. Apart from the political activists, some of them will have been councillors moving a recommendation on behalf of the council, some will have been supporters of political leaders, and some might with fuller evidence emerge as important public figures in their own right. Many or perhaps most of them, however, may well be regarded essentially as ordinary citizens (*idiōtai*) and were rhetores only in the legal sense of those who addressed the assembly, not in the political sense of regular or frequent speakers. The activity of this third group is an impressive indication of the readiness of Athenians to do more than vote and to take advantage of the opportunities afforded by the democracy of contributing to assembly debates and the formulation of decisions, though this readiness had presumably grown in the course of our period and was much more pronounced in these thirty years of the fourth century than the twenty or thirty years after 450. The stability and continuity in Athenian policy owed much to these 'occasional proposers' whom Aiskhines represented as characteristic of democracies, and to the citizens at large who, in making the decisions of state, were presumably more aware than most citizen bodies of the issues before them and of the potential and limitations of Athens.[21]

6.3 Networks in public life

Now, it may be asked to what extent the more active citizens acted in a concerted fashion in support of the leading figures. About the middle of the fourth century Demosthenes referred, in the speech to be delivered against Meidias, to 'the comrades who support [literally, are around] Meidias' (*hoi peri Meidian hetairoi*).[22] In Athens it had long been customary for *hetairoi* – 'comrades' of similar age and social position – to meet or dine together from

---

[20] Hansen (1984) 123–55, especially 132–5 (details of 82 proposers), 140–4 (on extrapolating from the accidental sample), 144–50 (evidence about politically active citizens, though not known as proposers in 355–322), 154 (estimate of 300–600 potential proposers at any one meeting – cf. the more cautious suggestion (152) that they must be counted by the hundred rather than by the score).

[21] Isok. 12.248, Aiskhin. 3.220–1; for the countryman who rarely attended the assembly but (partly because of that) made a great impact when he spoke, see Eur. *Or.* 917–22.

[22] Dem. 21.20; cf. 21.139, 208, 213; cf. Plut. *Per.* 14, 16; Dem. 57.59–60.

time to time. In periods of heightened political conflict, the political potential of such social gatherings might come to the fore. Such groups of hetairoi or *hetaireiai* in the sense of 'political clubs' played an important, if shadowy, role in public life in our period. In the 440s, as we have seen, Thucydides, the opponent of Perikles, had his supporters sit together in the Ekklesia to give them more weight, and within the wider group of his supporters Plutarch identified what he called a hetaireia consisting of his closest supporters.[23] But it was particularly in the turmoil after the Sicilian defeat and in the manoeuvres leading up to the overthrow of the democracy that the hetaireiai played a decisive and patently public role. Under the influence of Antiphon and other extreme oligarchs the hetaireiai became instruments of revolution. As they moved over to conspiracy and violent action, the hetairoi came to be regarded as oligarchic conspirators.[24] After 411 the hetaireiai were commonly associated with oligarchic factions. In the fourth century the political tendencies of the clubs are less clear. They are usually associated with wealthy and influential men, and there seems to have been a suspicion and general prejudice against such clubs in the fourth century, sufficient for Demosthenes to exploit in his attacks on Meidias and his wealthy friends.[25]

It might be thought, then, that hetaireiai in the sense of political clubs were the real, underlying forces in Athenian public life throughout our period and the means by which political leaders organised support. And it is true that other terms – *epitēdeios* (intimate acquaintance) and *philos* (friend) – seem to be used occasionally as synonyms for, or in close association with, hetairos.[26] But these and other terms could be used without implying political clubs of the type outlined, and rather than assuming that most supporters of political leaders belonged to hetaireiai, it seems better to postulate that all political leaders needed supporters who might or might not meet in more or less regular fashion and who, if they did meet, did not necessarily operate as the hetairoi are represented as doing. Friendships developed in the gymnasion and at symposia might be invaluable.[27]

In considering the role and the activities of a leader's supporters, we need not, therefore, postulate a degree of clear organisation, though where it existed, political objectives might more easily be achieved. Support could range from informal talk with neighbours and other citizens to concerted action in the courts, in the deliberations of the assembly and in elections. It could take the

---

[23] Plut. *Per.* 11, 14; see ch. 2.3.1.

[24] Thuc. 8.48.2–4, 54.4, 65.2; Lys. 12.43; Calhoun 7–9, Sartori (1957) 101–26. Cf. Thuc. 3.82.6; Plut. *Arist.* 2.

[25] Dem. 21.20, 139, 208–13; cf. [Dem.] 46.25–6; see Hyp. 4.8; Longo (1971) 41–156, especially 151–6. [26] Lys. 13.19; Plut. *Lys.* 21; cf. Thuc. 5.76.2.

[27] *AP* 34.3 shows that, in 404, even among 'the notable people' (*hoi gnōrimoi*) not all were members of hetaireiai; Connor 25–32; cf. Calhoun 22–3, who implies, on the basis of Pl. *Ap.* 36b, that the majority of Athenians belonged to political clubs; Aiskhin. 3.255, Humphreys (1978) 101–2.

form of gossip and rumour – and the Athenian citizens were, after all, a relatively small community[28] – or of appeals to the dikasts. The assertion that at the allotment of the jurors attempts had been made to influence them appears to be something of a regular argument (*topos*) or ploy. And though the fact that Demosthenes made this claim in a speech which was never delivered does not prove that the practice was very common, it does reflect the probability that it was by no means unknown in important cases and that in preparing the speech Demosthenes could therefore expect that such a claim would be credible.[29] The allegation was, moreover, very hard to counter, let alone disprove: as the potential dikasts gathered, there would no doubt be discussion about the cases to be heard that day. The frequency and the effectiveness of this practice and particularly of other practices about to be considered should not be over-estimated. Philokleon was by no means exceptional in feeling free, as a dikast casting his secret vote, to do none of the things he said he would.[30] In the second half of the fourth century, concentrated attempts against a panel, and especially against the large panels hearing serious charges, were hardly feasible, since the panels were not determined until the day of the trial. Similar caution should be exercised in considering the repeated allegations of the corruption of dikasts. Changes in the organisation of the jury system minimised the chances of wholesale corruption such as Anytos was said to have accomplished in 409.[31] Yet in 388 – that is, after the introduction of the allotment of a particular panel to a particular court on the day – Lysias alleged that Ergokles' associates went around saying that they had bribed as many as 2,100 dikasts, though he added that it had all been to no avail: Ergokles had been condemned to death.[32] An individual was named by Isokrates in *c.* 402 as an agent ready to suborn jurors, while in 345 Aiskhines reminded the jury of the conviction and execution of a number of men on charges of bribing the assembly and the courts.[33] In court, the Friend of Rascals portrayed by Theophrastos helped rascals by remarking to those sitting beside him 'The man is the people's watchdog, for he wards off those who do wrong' or by sitting together with groups in the support of bad causes. Applause, shouting and interruptions, individual or concerted, might have had some effect.[34]

Friends or associates might undertake the prosecution of an opponent of a political leader or of his supporters. In the virtual absence of a public prosecutor in Athens, this was all the more important.[35] Take the case of the poet Xenokleides. In 369 he had spoken in the assembly against Kallistratos' proposal to help the Spartans. Xenokleides did not go on that expedition, because he was entitled to exemption, having purchased the right to collect the 2% tax on

---

[28] Dem. 24.15–16, cf. 57.64.
[29] Dem. 21.4, 19.1, Aiskhin. 3.1; Calhoun 74 n. 2.   [30] See ch. 5.4.
[31] *AP* 27.5; cf. [Xen.] *AP* 3.7; see ch. 3.5.   [32] Lys. 29.12–13.
[33] Isok. 18.11, Aiskhin. 1.86–7; cf. Dem. 24.150, [Dem.] 46.25–7, Calhoun 67 n. 6.
[34] Theophr. *Char.* 29.5–6; cf. [Dem.] 25.40–1.   [35] Dem. 18.249; see also R. Osborne 3–6.

grain. Subsequently Stephanos, who was said to be an underling of Kallistratos, prosecuted Xenokleides on a charge of avoiding military service: the poet was convicted and deprived of his civic rights.[36] In other cases, a counter-suit by an associate or hired agent against an accuser or likely accuser might be launched, and indeed the allegation of such tactics became a standard argument. Demosthenes, for example, claimed that Meidias trumped up a charge of military desertion against him and hired a sykophantes, Euktemon, to lay the charge for the sole purpose of having the charge posted up for all men to see: 'Euktemon of the deme of Lousia has indicted Demosthenes of the deme of Paiania for desertion.' Such an allegation was likely to be very damaging. In the event, Euktemon did not proceed with the indictment and, as Demosthenes put it, 'disfranchised himself': more precisely, Euktemon presumably lost the right to bring another charge of desertion and was fined 1,000 drakhmai, though failure to pay the fine would have resulted in total loss of civic rights.[37] Financial assistance or one's own money might be directed to help in hiring a professional speech-writer or to hire witnesses and accusers; such help might supplement (or replace) pressure or intimidation to dissuade intending prosecutors or to convince prosecutors to drop a case.[38] Friends or associates might also testify or refuse to testify, or induce others not to testify, or they might commit perjury to help a friend or harm an enemy. Allegations of perjury, as may be suspected from their very frequency, were easy to make and should not all be taken at face value. In order to discourage perjury, loss of civic rights followed three convictions.[39] Men might, of course, resort to prosecution or to perjury for non-political motives: Demosthenes speaks for example of a 'gang of sykophantai' whose purpose was to make money.[40] Finally, a citizen, preferably of standing and influence, or of experience or ability in speaking, might speak in support of a friend or associate in the courts. In 343 Aiskhines called on Euboulos to speak on his behalf against the charge of misconduct on the embassy to Philip II in 346, while professional commanders needed the assistance of friendly rhetores.[41]

Most of the methods, whether legitimate or corrupt, that could be used in the courts could also be used in the assembly. Praxagora, for example, was warned in the *Ekklesiazousai* (Assembly Women or Women in Power) about the problem of interruptions, but the women of Athens in Aristophanes' comedy

36 [Dem.] 59.26–7, 43.
37 Dem. 21.103, 105–6, but cf. 139; cf. Aiskhin. 2.148; cf. [Dem.] 58.22–3, 36. On *atimia* (loss of civic rights or the active rights of citizenship), see Hansen (1976) 54–98, especially 59 and n. 23, 63–5, MacDowell 64–5; cf. Harrison 2.83, 169–76.
38 Andok. 1.132–5; cf. Lys. 29.1; Dem. 21.3, 215; cf. Aiskhin. 3.52; cf. Isok. 18.10.
39 Dem. 21.139, 37.48, 39.18; cf. Xen. *Mem.* 2.9.5–8; Lys. 12.43–7, Lykourg. *Leok.* 20; [Dem.] 49.19; Isok. 18.51, Lys. 29.7, Dem. 30.3, 54.33, [Dem.] 45–6; cf. Aiskhin. 2.154–5; see Dem. 29.22–3 on the motives for perjury; Andok. 1.74.
40 Dem. 39.2; [Dem.] 40.9.
41 Aiskhin. 2.184; Andok. 1.150, Isok. 21.1, Lys. 5.1, 12.86, Dem. 21.112, 22.40, 32.31–2, Aiskhin. 3.196; cf. [Dem.] 46.26; see n. 15.

had laid their plans well for seizing control of the assembly – getting to the Pnyx by day-break before the men arrived and thus 'stacking' the meeting, carefully selecting the spokeswomen, working out tactics in regard to applause, interruptions and dealing with insults.[42] In the play the tactics, despite some lapses, were very successful. In the real world of Athens, canvassing and bribery, before and during the meeting, were also possible, and were likely to meet with some success since, in contrast to the courts, most of the voting was by show of hands.[43] It was natural for friends and associates to congregate in one area on the Pnyx, and political leaders could exploit this and organise their supporters to sit together; shouting, interjections and interruptions could thus be concerted.[44] Demosthenes claimed in 343 that, three years earlier, he had been prevented from replying to Aiskhines' optimistic report of the embassy to Philip.

> I rose and said that this was news to me, and attempted to make the report which I had made to the Boule. But Aiskhines and Philokrates stood on either side of me – shouting, interrupting, and finally jeering. You would not listen to me and you did not want to believe anything except what this fellow had reported. And I must say that your feeling was quite natural. For how could anyone, filled with anticipation of these wonderful benefits, be patient of a speaker who said they would never eventuate or who denounced the conduct of these men?

From the same occasion Demosthenes also reported Philokrates' 'supercilious remark': 'No wonder, men of Athens, Demosthenes and I do not have the same opinion. He drinks water, I drink wine.' 'You all laughed', Demosthenes added.[45] Friends or supporters or (to accept that there was something behind the contemporary allegations) hired agents might also make proposals or support them, or might attack the proposals of opponents: in this area cooperation between rhetores and commanders could be particularly fruitful. In short, it was not only in a negative or destructive sense that supporters made a vital contribution, nor only in the actual meeting. They could assist, for example, in collecting information and in building up support for policies among their friends and neighbours. In the important deliberations of the Boule, too, friends or supporters could be invaluable, whether in the processes of the selection of individuals as envoys or for other positions or in proposing or supporting a measure.[46]

---

[42] Ar. *Ekkl.* 17–25, 116–284, 398–402, 427–33. For 'stacking' the Ekklesia, see Lys. 12.75–6, Dem. 18.143; cf. Thuc. 6.13.1, Xen. *Hell.* 1.7.8.

[43] Cf. Thuc. 6.13.1; for elections, see Lys. 12.43–4, Pl. *Tht.* 173d, Xen. *Symp.* 1.4, Dem. 18.149 (cf. Thuc. 8.54.4, Ar. *Lys.* 574–8), and for allegations of electoral irregularities (as with other allegations, not always convincing) Aiskhin. 1.106–7, Aiskhin. 3.3, 62, 73 (cf. Isok. 17.33–4, Dem. 39.12) and cf. *AP* 62.1; Theopomp. *FGrH* 115 F213, Aiskhin. 1.86–7.

[44] Dem. 2.29–30, 18.143, cf. Plut. *Per.* 11; Dem. 8.38, 19.15, 21.14, [Dem.] 25.64, 95, 59.43, Aiskhin. 1.34, 81–4, Plut. *Phok.* 9; cf. Ar. *Akh.* 37–9, Thuc. 6.25.1, Plut. *Nik.* 12.

[45] Dem. 19.23–4, 45–6 (Loeb tr. adapted).

[46] Isok. 8.129–30, Dem. 20.132, 23.146, 24.3, 66, 201, 203, [Dem.] 25.40–1, 59.43, Aiskhin. 3.159, 242; cf. Plut. *Per.* 7.5, Thuc. 8.68.1–2; Plut. *Per.* 14, Thuc. 6.29.3; see n. 15; Aiskhin. 2.18–19, 3.125–6; Finley 51.

6.4 The risks faced by military commanders

While there were extensive networks within Athenian public life, the 'political leaders' very largely supplied the elements of initiative as well as continuity and they were the chief objects of attack in the law-courts and the assembly. For the citizens of Athens were clearly ready to concur in the view expressed by Deinarkhos in his attack on Demosthenes in 323 that the good (and the bad) fortunes of a polis were attributable to a single cause – its leaders: its strategoi (Konon, Iphikrates, Khabrias and Timotheos were adduced as examples of brave generals) and its counsellors (Arkhinos and Kephalos (leaders in the restoration of democracy in 403) as examples of good counsellors – contrast Demosthenes).[47]

We may first consider strategoi. Often the exact charges brought against commanders are not specified in the surviving evidence. Failure to comply with the instructions of the assembly or action that seemed to exceed instructions or to affect adversely the interests of Athens were in some cases at the heart of prosecutions of commanders. In 379/8, for example, two strategoi who were stationed on the Boiotian border sent troops in response to the request of Theban exiles who then proceeded to force the Spartan garrison to withdraw from the Kadmeia. The strategoi presumably expected that the Demos would at least condone their actions, but the Athenians were not yet ready for an open breach with Sparta and, under pressure from Sparta, they condemned both generals: one was executed, the other, who realised the danger he faced, opted for exile.[48] Initiatives, however, had to be taken on campaign, not least when strategoi or mercenary commanders in the pay of the Athenians but operating far from Athens had, as was commonly the case, inadequate funds to sustain their campaigns and to pay the men under their command. Commanders 'requested' support from Athenian allies in the area of operation or acquired supplies, often by force, from other states. Back in the assembly, rhetores were wont to lament or to attack such activities as being detrimental to Athenian interests or contrary to the decisions of the Demos.[49] And at times the initiatives taken might seem to indicate that the military commanders were a law unto themselves, but an analysis of the relations between the Demos and the commanders reveals that the assembly sought, and largely managed, to exercise supervision of the strategoi and to a lesser extent of the mercenary commanders in its employ.[50]

The Athenians, however, expected more of their strategoi than compliance with the assembly's instructions. They also expected success. Somewhat prone to entertaining high hopes, the Athenian citizens were far from generous when faced with failure or defeat. Success or past services might or might not be

---

[47] Dein. 1.72–7; cf. [Dem.] 26.1–4; Finley (1974) 16–17.
[48] Xen. *Hell.* 5.4.9–12, 19; cf. D.S. 15.25.1–26.4, Dein. 1.38–9; Sinclair (1978) 42–3.
[49] See ch. 3.3.   [50] Pritchett 2.34–116.

allowed to weigh: they were by no means a guarantee against conviction.[51] Strategoi who in the fourth century appeared to have failed or to have been incompetent as well as those who did not carry out the assembly's instructions could be dealt with by methods employed in the fifth century. As office-holders they could, for example, be deposed at any time during their term of office, as Timotheos was in 373 for delay in carrying out his commission to sail to Kerkyra, or Autokles in 361 on the grounds of 'betraying' Miltokythes.[52] But a strategos who was deposed was normally required to stand trial before a Dikasterion, though in the period before 360–355 impeachments could be determined by the Ekklesia: if he was acquitted, he might (but, it would seem, did not automatically) resume his command, but if he was convicted, the jurors assessed what he should suffer or pay.[53] Failure could arise from, or be attributed to, *prodosia*. The word is usually translated as 'betrayal' or 'treason'. In essence *prodosia* denoted the action of giving up beforehand, abandoning or forsaking in need, and one of the grounds on which an *eisangelia* (impeachment) could be laid was 'if anyone betrays a city or ships or a land or naval force'.[54] While prodosia might result from calculated treachery, lack of will, circumstances beyond a man's control or other causes, it would appear that the Athenians were loath to accept reasons or excuses why a commander had given up a position, but they judged rather by the actual result. And in the course of the fourth century, many strategoi were charged with prodosia, with which other charges might be associated. Prodosia, misappropriation and taking bribes were, as we have seen, the grounds on which Ergokles was charged, condemned to death and his property confiscated in 388.[55]

Strategoi were vulnerable at any time during their year of office, for at the main meeting in each prytany not only did they have to be confirmed in office but they could also be impeached.[56] Eisangelia was, therefore, particularly useful when an urgent matter had to be resolved. The matter was determined by either the Ekklesia or the Dikasteria, but after *c.* 355 probably only by the Dikasteria.[57] Moreover, a citizen might more readily contemplate using the impeachment process, since the citizen laying the charge was, for almost all of

---

[51] Cf. Dem. 24.133–6, Dein. 3.17. Apart from fourth-century cases discussed in this chapter, see the condemnation of Phormion (probably in 428) (Androtion *FGrH* 324 F8, Westlake (1968) 54–9).   [52] Dem. 23.104, [Dem.] 50.12; Dem. 36.53.

[53] *AP* 61.2 (see MacDowell 169–70; cf. *CAAP* 683), [Dem.] 58.27–8.   [54] Hyp. 4.8.

[55] See Xen. *Kyr.* 6.3.27, Thuc. 6.103.4 (and *HCT*), and (for Ergokles) ch. 5. See Harrison 2.173, 178–9, 186, 212–17 on confiscation of property as a penalty in combination with the death penalty or loss of political rights (cf. Tod 123.55 – for proposing any amendment to the 'charter' of the Second Athenian League), as a penalty in itself or as a means of executing a judgement.   [56] *AP* 43.4 (and *CAAP*).

[57] On the basis of known and likely cases of eisangeliai, more cases were decided by the Ekklesia than the Dikasteria in the period from 403 to 362, but none by the Ekklesia in the years from 361 to 324, and Hansen (1975) 53–5 has argued convincingly that all impeachments were transferred to the Dikasteria by changes which were introduced between 360 and 355 and were probably induced in large measure by financial difficulties of the time.

our period, not liable to any penalty as opposed to those who brought indictments (*graphai*) and failed to gain a fifth of the votes.[58]

In the 81 years from 403/2 to 323/2 we know of some 27 strategoi who were probably prosecuted on serious charges: some 30 cases in all, since Timotheos was prosecuted three times and Khabrias probably twice. Most of the strategoi were probably charged by means of eisangelia, but euthynai, graphai or indictments and other procedures were also used or available.[59] In the 81 years there would have been 810 annual terms, though the actual number of individuals who held the strategia would have been much less. Khabrias, Timotheos, Iphikrates, Khares and Philokles, for example, are each known to have held the office more than ten times, quite apart from the 45 terms attributed to Phokion by Plutarch. Even so, it is a measure of the deficiencies in the evidence that we know the names of less than 80 strategoi and it would be idle to suggest that we have anything like a full record of prosecutions.[60] Any speculation based on extrapolations from such limited evidence is hazardous, but the suggestion that, on average, one or even two strategoi out of every board of ten in the years from 432 to 355 were subjected to eisangelia (quite apart from other charges) hardly seems plausible when we allow for the high rate during the Peloponnesian War.[61] Despite our lack of evidence, it seems unlikely that there was more than an occasional prosecution on a serious charge in years of little or no military activity – in the years, for example, from 403 to 395 or from 386 to 379.[62] Due account must be taken of areas as well as periods of special difficulty. The Thracian Khersonesos and the Hellespont, for example, constituted a particularly sensitive and difficult area for the Athenians, as Demosthenes emphasised in his speech *On the Embassy*. He proceeded to name strategoi who had been sentenced to death or had a heavy fine imposed on them for offences in the area – Ergophilos (362), Timomakhos (360), Kephisodotos (359) and 'in old times' Ergokles (388), Dionysios (387) 'and others'.[63] It is possible that 'others in old times' may include three of Dionysios'

[58] After *c.* 333 (or 330 at the latest) prosecutors who gained less than a fifth of the votes were, however, liable to a fine of 1,000 dr. (contrast graphai (see ch. 3) – fine *and* the loss of the right to bring the same type of charge again): Poll. 8.52–3, Harrison 2.51, Hansen (1975) 29–31.

[59] See n. 71 which includes prosecutions listed in the Catalogue in Hansen (1975) 87–111, 116–20 (and, for analysis, 58–65); the Catalogue includes all possible cases of eisangelia though some of the cases probably involved other processes and in particular euthynai (see 37 n. 2, 40 (at n. 28), 44–8, 66 for the degree of confidence in regarding cases as examples of eisangelia). The procedure known as *apophasis* (report of investigation) was used in the case of Philokles who in 324 allowed Harpalos to enter the Peiraieus: see Dein. 3.7 and nn. 111–12 below.

[60] For the years 403/2 to 323/2 some 74 full names (if we identify Ktesikles of 393/2 with the general of 374/3 and include Thrasyboulos of Steiria who is listed under 410/9 (the year of his first known strategia) and Antiphilos who is listed under 322/1 but who was elected after the death of Leosthenes in mid-323/2) are listed by Davis 162–5. A few might tentatively be added: e.g., in 403/2 Rhinon (*AP* 38.4) and perhaps Anytos (Pl. *Men.* 90b), perhaps Philon 361 (Hyp. 4.1–2) and another Philon 329/8 (*IG* ii².1672.271–2), while it is doubtful if some of those listed were strategoi (for example, Antiochos 353/2 and Athenodoros in 352/1).

[61] Hansen (1975) 60–1.   [62] Sinclair (1978) 40–3, 47–52.   [63] Dem. 19.180.

colleagues, though 'and others' was a common figure of speech, while from *c.* 360 we may add Theotimos who, after the loss of Sestos, went into exile and was sentenced to death in his absence.[64] These six, not surprisingly, form an important element in the 30 cases. The chronological dimension must also be considered. The late 360s and the early 350s witnessed a veritable rash of prosecutions which should probably be interpreted not as typical of the whole period but as a sign of the growing frustration of the Athenian Demos with the continuing failures of Athenian operations in Thrace and the north Aegean, not least in the abortive attempts to regain Amphipolis. These failures were keenly felt following Timotheos' success at Samos and the revival of Athenian ambitions in the mid-360s. In that climate the over-zealous Apollodoros, embittered by his experiences as a trierarch, brought prosecutions against Timomakhos, Menon, Autokles, Timotheos, a trierarch and 'many others' (presumably none of the 'many others' were strategoi). Demosthenes (in the speech which he wrote to support Phormion's defence against a charge of fraudulent appropriation of 20 talents brought by Apollodoros) described Apollodoros as a sykophantes, 'maliciously trumping up these public charges'.[65] Other strategoi who seem to have come to grief in the late 360s and the early 350s included Kallisthenes, Leosthenes (who, according to Aiskhines, was ranked by some as next to Kallistratos in ability as a speaker and who, when he went into exile, was condemned to death and had his property confiscated) and Philon, as well as Ergophilos, Kephisodotos and Theotimos who have already been named in regard to the Thracian Khersonesos and the Hellespont.[66]

It is, therefore, important to recognise the factors involving personalities and critical periods in these cases. This is not to deny that there were other Athenians at different times who took on the unenviable role of prosecutor – or indeed that this role was sought by not a few, particularly the opponents of strategoi.[67] It was not empty rhetoric when Demosthenes in 355 declared about one of Athens' most successful strategoi:

> If he had lost a single city or as few as 10 ships, these men would have impeached him for prodosia, and if he had been convicted, he would have been ruined for all time. But since on the contrary he took 17 cities, captured 70 ships and 3,000 prisoners, paid 110 talents into the treasury, and set up so many trophies, in that case will not his rewards for these services stand good? Moreover, men of Athens, it will be seen that Khabrias during his life-time did everything in your behalf, and that he met death in no other service.[68]

Rhetoric or not, there can be no doubt about the vulnerability of unsuccessful strategoi nor about the readiness of opponents or others to seek to exploit this.

---

[64] Xen. *Hell.* 5.1.26, Pritchett 2.10, n. *k*; Hyp. 4.1–2.

[65] Dem. 36.3, 53 (which asserts that the charge against Timotheos was a public suit – and therefore different from Apollodoros' suit (= [Dem.] 49) for the recovery of a private debt; but see [Dem.] 49.47 on Apollodoros' ties with Kallistratos, and Dušanić (1980) 116–17); cf. Bonner (1927) 130–1, Roberts 111–12.   [66] See Aiskhin. 2.124 and D.S. 15.95.3 for Leosthenes.

[67] See ch. 3.5.   [68] Dem. 20.79–80 (Loeb tr. adapted).

We must also note that Khabrias had indeed met his death fighting for Athens – in the battle of Khios in 356 – but as a trierarch, not as a strategos; and the erasure of his name from the list of strategoi to take the oaths from the Euboian cities in 357/6 indicates that he had been deposed from the board of generals of 357/6.[69] A cautionary tale.

In short, we have some evidence about the frustrations and difficulties of the decade after 365 and some evidence about the areas of particular difficulty for Athenian strategoi in the 81 years after 403. In the decade after 355 the Athenians were again less adventurous in their foreign policy, and in the years from 338 to 323 the superiority of Makedonian arms must have had the consequence of allowing few opportunities for prosecuting Athenian strategoi. Our evidence for the 81 years, however, *is* fragmentary and particularly in respect of prosecutions on lesser charges and unsuccessful prosecutions, even if we decline to accept Demosthenes' claim that 'as things are . . . every general is tried two or three times for his life in your courts, but not one of them dares to risk death in battle against the enemy; no, not once'.[70] It may be suggested that, whatever the average number of prosecutions for every board of 10 strategoi (and it was perhaps well below 2, even when we take into account all procedures and not only eisangelia), there were periods of high concentration.

But there are two more important questions – how high was the conviction rate and how heavy were the penalties? Our evidence about successful prosecutions on serious charges would seem, in very broad terms, to coincide with the unsuccessful periods or episodes in Athens' external history. This is not surprising on general grounds and in so far as evidence of convictions largely derives from the Attic Orators, for the orators would stress these and assemble relevant precedents in order to build up their case. It is not to be suggested, however, that there were no other successful prosecutions, but it is probably the case that our evidence is less seriously deficient in regard to the number of convictions on the most serious charges. Yet unless that evidence is more fortuitous than seems to be the case, one of the most striking aspects of the attacks on strategoi was the extremely high danger of prosecution and conviction during certain times when Athens most needed or most used her resources of military leadership, not least the 360s and 350s. Also striking are the high conviction rate and the severity of the penalties. Of the 30 known probable prosecutions of strategoi on serious charges, 5 probably resulted in acquittal and the verdict in 3 is unknown. Of the other 22, Timotheos (in 373) and Thrasyboulos of Steiria (388) and probably Khabrias (357/6) were deposed without further penalty, and the penalty imposed on 5 is unknown or uncertain. The death sentence was carried out on 4, and 5 did not await the

---

[69] Dem. 20.82 (cf. D.S. 16.7.3–4), Cawkwell (1962B) 34–40; Tod 153.20.

[70] Dem. 4.47. See Hansen (1975) 64 n. 52 for a list of strategoi known to have died in action in the period 432 to 355: 3 in the years 404–355 and 21 during the Peloponnesian War. See D.S. 18.13 for Leosthenes (323/2).

verdict but opted for exile. Fines were imposed on 3 (and perhaps 2 more): one was Kephisodotos who in 359 escaped the death penalty by only 3 votes and was fined the not inconsiderable sum of 5 talents, another was Timotheos who in 356/5 incurred the crippling fine of 100 talents and withdrew to Khalkis where he died within 2 or 3 years.[71]

Strategoi, in short, had to accept not only the honour and other benefits that derived from success, but also the heavy consequences of failure or of policies or actions that lost, or failed to win, general support. This situation was not novel to the fourth century. Miltiades in 489, Perikles in 430 and Thucydides in 424 are well-known examples from the fifth century. Nikias in 413 was very conscious of the likely consequences if he and his fellow strategoi withdrew their forces from Syracuse without orders, and he argued that many of the soldiers who cried out that they were in desperate straits at Syracuse would, on their return to Athens, cry out the opposite, that the general had been bribed to betray them and withdraw.[72] The condemnation of the Arginousai strategoi in 406 was remembered in 376 by Khabrias in the moment of victory off the island of Naxos: if he had pressed on with pursuit he could have annihilated the Peloponnesian fleet, but he turned aside to pick up the shipwrecked and the dead.[73] Nor were the Athenians exceptional in their treatment of unsuccessful or independently-minded leaders. In the space of a hundred years, we know of seven major figures who were brought to trial in Sparta – Kleomenes in c. 494, Leotykhidas in 476, Pausanias twice in the 470s, Pleistoanax in 445, Agis in 418, Gylippos in 405, Pausanias in 403 and 395. Some were condemned to death, some were exiled, some were fined, some were acquitted. In 382 Phoibidas, who on his own initiative placed a Spartan garrison in the Kadmeia at Thebes, was deposed and fined, while two of the three harmosts who surrendered the Kadmeia in 379 were condemned to death and the other was fined.[74] In 378

---

[71] The evidence is noted here only when the case is not included in Hansen's Catalogue (1975). *Acquittal*: Thrasyboulos of Kollytos (387) (probable), Khabrias (366/5), Iphikrates and Menestheus (356/5), Khares (probable – implied in Dem. 19.332 and Aiskhin. 2.71). *Verdict unknown*: Autokles, Timotheos and Menon (360). *Deposed*: Timotheos (373), and probably Thrasyboulos of Steiria (388 – Lys. 28.5–8 asserts that but for his death at Aspendos he would have been brought to trial as Ergokles had been) and Khabrias (357/6 – see n. 69). *Penalty unknown or uncertain*: Adeimantos (if prosecuted in 393/2 by his colleague Konon re strategia of 405/4), Dionysios (387), Hegesileos (349/8 – Dem. 19.290 with scholia), Proxenos (if in connection with strategia of 347/6 –guilt implied by Dem. 19.280–1), Philokles (323 – Dein. 3.11–15 and Hansen (1975) 43 n. 47). *Death penalty*: Ergokles (388), strategos of 379/8, Kallisthenes (362), Lysikles (338). '*Exile*': strategos of 379/8, Leosthenes (361), Philon (361, if a strategos), Timomakhos (360) and Theotimos (c. 360). *Fine*: Ergophilos (362), Kephisodotos (359), Timotheos (356/5); possibly Pamphilos and Agyrrhios (if in connection with strategiai of 389/8 and 388/7 and if a fine and not simple repayment of money belonging to the polis – [Dem.] 40.20, 22; Dem. 24.135). Cf. Dem. 24.127 (Melanopos is said to have been fined 3 talents for prodosia).

[72] Hdt. 6.136; Thuc. 2.65; Thuc. 7.48 (cf. 4.65.3), cf. Plut. *Nik.* 6, Paus. 1.29.12.

[73] D.S. 15.35.1; Roberts 178–9.

[74] For details and ancient references, see de Ste Croix (1972) 350–3 and Pritchett 2.4–33, including the table of Trials of Hegemones (5–10): the punishment of unsuccessful leaders was common to Greek poleis and to other ancient states.

Sphodrias who, in time of peace, had invaded Attike with a view to seizing the Peiraieus was arraigned on a capital charge; the cynical acquittal of Sphodrias embarrassed even Xenophon.[75]

6.5 The indictment for making an illegal proposal

Apart from men whose talents lay in the military field, ambitious citizens tended in the late fifth century, and increasingly in the fourth, not to seek office as annual magistrates or officials and consequently could not so readily be challenged. The graphe paranomon, or indictment for an illegal proposal, was one means of dealing with the citizen who proposed decrees in the assembly but did not hold an official position, and it was one way of applying to the rhetores the general principle of personal responsibility for public acts.[76] This was all the more important, for in the fourth century there was an increasing tendency, though perhaps not as universal as Demosthenes would have us believe, for orators to leave themselves a way of retreat in case anything happened. According to Demosthenes, none of the great rhetores before his own time – and he named Kallistratos, Aristophon, Kephalos and Thrasyboulos –

ever devoted himself to any public business from beginning to end; the man who proposed a motion would not go on the embassy, and the man who went on an embassy would not move the proposal. For each of them used to leave himself some relief, and at the same time a loophole, in case anything happened.[77]

Thus the political leader might endeavour to protect himself by participating either in decision-making or in execution of policy, but not both.

Demosthenes dismissed the obvious objection that he seemed to be claiming that he was so much stronger and bolder than others that he could do everything by himself, and said he ignored his personal safety because of the grave danger overhanging Athens. Aiskhines saw it rather differently: Demosthenes, he suggested, 'contrived such domination (*dynasteia*) for himself that he came forward to the platform and declared that he was going as envoy wherever he chose, whether you sent him or not . . .'.[78]

Even though Demosthenes was over-stating the extent of the loophole approach, it must be admitted that the role of envoy could be hazardous. This was particularly so when Athens was not in a strong negotiating position and envoys were likely to return to Athens with proposals or reports that were

---

[75] Xen. *Hell.* 5.4.20–33, D.S. 15.29.6, Plut. *Ages.* 24.6.

[76] Arist. *Pol.* 1255a8–9, Dein. 1.100–1. See ch. 3.5 and, for the indictment for proposing an unsuitable law, see n. 87.

[77] Dem. 18.219 (three of the four are known to have acted in both capacities, though not, on present evidence, on the one matter of public business); Isok. 8.54–5, Arist. *Rh.* 1364a19–23; cf. Thuc. 5.46, Tod 123.7, 76, Dem. 19.10–12, Aiskhin. 2.18, 3.63–4.

[78] Dem. 18.220, Aiskhin. 3.145–6.

disappointing or unacceptable to the citizen body. Demosthenes himself, when he was prosecuting Aiskhines for misconduct on the mission to Philip II in 346, reminded the jurors of the penalties determined on two occasions in the previous half-century. In 392/1 Andokides, Epikrates, Kratinos and Euboulides were prosecuted by Kallistratos for disobeying instructions and taking bribes on their mission to Sparta to discuss peace: they were condemned to death in absence.[79] In 367 two Athenians sent as envoys to Susa had failed to convince the Persian king to modify the terms of the Peace of Pelopidas, which required the Athenians to lay up their fleet. On their return to Athens, Leon, probably induced in part by motives of self-preservation, accused his colleague Timagoras of refusing to associate with him, of acting in collusion with Pelopidas and of accepting *dōra* ('gifts') from the Great King. The capital penalty was imposed on Timagoras.[80]

Another important factor in the tendency for the graphe paranomon to be used was the cumbersome procedure in the fourth century for the revision of the laws. As rhetores attempted to bypass this procedure, their opponents had recourse to the indictment for an illegal proposal. At times it was little more than a blocking device. Indeed, if the proposal attacked was a probouleuma which had not yet been passed by the assembly, a graphe paranomon could thwart the proposal altogether, since decisions of the Boule had effect for only the year. Thus proposals by Aristokrates to honour Kharidemos (352/1) and by Ktesiphon to honour Demosthenes (336) were blocked.[81] The graphe paranomon came to be used as a major weapon in political warfare and the frequent recourse to it was one of the reasons why the law-courts became a common battleground of Athenian politics by the mid-fourth century. There is ample evidence besides Aiskhines' speech *Against Ktesiphon* and Demosthenes' speech *On the Crown* that the technical grounds of an indictment for an illegal proposal were very likely to be less important than the jurors' political judgement – of the situation, of a man and his policies not only in the past but also in the present, and of the political consequences of conviction or acquittal – and that in general the political equation was important in the various types of public cases heard by the dikasts as well as those determined by the assembly. Indeed, the real object of many graphai paranomon was not the proposer, but a prominent individual who was being honoured by the decree under attack – whether a rhetor like Demosthenes or a strategos like Khabrias.[82]

The frequency with which political activists exploited the graphe paranomon is implicit in the boast of Aristophon (as reported by Aiskhines) that he had been acquitted 75 times of the charge of making an illegal proposal. At the other end of the spectrum was Kephalos, who claimed that although he had proposed more measures than anyone else, he had never been indicted for an

[79] Dem. 19.276–80, Philoch. *FGrH* 328 F149; cf. Perlman (1976) 230–1, Roberts 88–93.
[80] Xen. *Hell.* 7.1.33–8 (no mention of bribery), Dem. 19.31, 137, 191, Plut. *Pel.* 30.6; cf. Perlman (1976) 228–9.   [81] Dem. 23.92–3, 18.8–9.   [82] See ch. 3.5.

illegal proposal. Aiskhines claimed that this was all the more a matter for pride because in those days indictments were brought not only by political rivals but also by friends, if one had committed any error against the state.[83] But we should not accept the rhetoric. And, as Demosthenes with some justice retorted, why should a man who has been often accused but never convicted be the more justly open to reproach?[84] We should also observe that, whatever the reasons for Kephalos' immunity from such prosecution, his political career – which like that of Aristophon began about the turn of the fourth century – seems to have lasted into the 370s, while Aristophon was still active in the 340s.[85] The resort to the graphe paranomon appears to have become more frequent after the end of Kephalos' participation in public life. Indeed, Aiskhines himself complained in 330 that the graphe paranomon had lost its effectiveness.[86] But the hesitation which Demosthenes and his supporters showed in contemplating measures which might contravene the law regulating the disposal of state surpluses is in part a measure of the effectiveness of this type of indictment, and not merely of the unpopularity of a proposal that diverted money from the Festival Fund.

Conviction on the charge of proposing an illegal decree could result in a penalty with disastrous financial and political consequences. It is true that we know of no examples of the death penalty being imposed and there are only hints that it might be an appropriate penalty, though a certain Eudemos (otherwise unknown) is said by Demosthenes to have been put to death in 382/1, when he was convicted on the analogous indictment of proposing an unsuitable law.[87] Those who initiated a graphe paranomon seem to have aimed at convincing the Dikasterion to impose a heavy fine. And preferably, it would seem, a fine so heavy that the defendant could not pay it and, in consequence, would lose his civic rights as well as having the fine doubled. For then the defendant lost the active rights of citizenship and was in a generally vulnerable position.[88] The jurors, if they had convicted a proposer of a decree, listened to the penalties suggested by the prosecutor and the defendant. They might even be content with a token fine, for the fine of 25 drakhmai imposed on Polyeuktos (330–324) must be so regarded.[89] But that was probably rare. The well-to-do

---

[83] Aiskhin. 3.194.
[84] Dem. 18.251.
[85] See Appendix to this chapter, p. 162.
[86] Aiskhin. 3.191–2.
[87] Dem. 22.69, [Dem.] 25.87; Dem. 24.138. The indictment for proposing an unsuitable law seems to have been used much less frequently than the graphe paranomon, reflecting in large measure the fact that many more decrees were proposed than laws. Some 6 probable cases are known. In addition to the execution of Eudemos, Dem. 24.138 says that a certain Philippos escaped death by a narrow majority and that the jury accepted his assessment of the penalty, a heavy fine. In the other cases the outcome is uncertain or unknown: Lys. fr. 86–7, Dem. 20.1, 92,96, 144 (Leptines, 355), Dem. 24.1, 17, but cf. 24.3 (Timokrates), Aiskhin. 1.34. See *AP* 59.2, Wolff (1970) 28–44 and Hansen (1974) 44–8.
[88] Dem. 18.15; [Dem.] 59.6–8. See Aiskhin. 2.14 for a proposed penalty of 100 talents. For loss of civic rights, see Hansen (1976) 56–60 (vulnerability) and 90–4 (various graphai or indictments for offences punishable with atimia).
[89] Hyp. 4.18, see n. 93 below for the fine of 1 dr. reported to have been imposed on Thrasyboulos.

Apollodoros expressed his gratitude to the jurors who in 349/8, though they had ruled that his proposal for the assembly to decide whether the surplus funds should be paid into the Military Fund or the Festival Fund was illegal, had at least fixed the penalty at 1 talent and rejected Stephanos' proposal of a fine of 15 talents. That proposal, Apollodoros complained, was a deliberate attempt to deprive him and his children of their civic rights, for his property was worth less than 3 talents. We need not believe the latter claim; it was predictable that he would also claim that it was with difficulty that he had paid the fine.[90] A fine of 5 talents was imposed (335–330) on Aristogeiton, who was a notorious, rather than a leading, figure in the 330s and 320s and was called 'the watchdog of the Demos (or the democracy)'; being unable to pay, he lost his civic rights.[91] In 323 Demades was fined 10 talents in connection with his decree proposing that Alexander (the Great) should be acknowledged as a god; if, as seems likely, he was charged with making an illegal proposal and not with impiety, this was one of the three graphai paranomon on which he was convicted and in consequence lost his civic rights.[92]

We do not know of any other prominent rhetores who themselves were seriously and directly affected by being convicted of making an illegal proposal. Thrasyboulos' proposal for granting citizenship to those who helped in the restoration of democracy in 403/2 was overruled: he is reported to have been fined one drakhme. Hypereides' proposal in 338 to give citizenship to metics, free slaves and restore rights to disfranchised citizens was upheld by the dikasts. Both proposals involved a relaxation or an abandonment of traditional and fundamental attitudes about the character of Athenian society and they would doubtless have been indicted, no matter who had proposed them. In the case of Thrasyboulos, Aiskhines' assertion of friendship between Thrasyboulos and Arkhinos, who launched the indictment against his comrade-in-arms in the restoration of democracy, may be accepted, even if we reject the 'good-old-days' rhetoric. If, as a scholiast reported, Thrasyboulos was fined only a drakhme, that may have been the penalty proposed by Arkhinos, determined to block the proposal but content with that. Aristogeiton's attack on Hypereides' proposal smacks strongly of a desire to attack the proposer as much as, or more than, the proposal.[93] Certainly reasons of political rivalry were to the fore in the attack on Androtion's proposal in 356/5 to crown the outgoing council and in

---

[90] [Dem.] 59.6–8; cf. *APF* 438–42.

[91] [Dem.] 25.40, 60–7, [Dem.] 25. *hypoth.* 2–3, Dein. 2.12; Sealey 186–99. For fines of 10 talents, see [Dem.] 58.1–2, 30–2, 66; Dem. 21.182. Cf. [Dem.] 58.43.

[92] Ath. 251b, Ail. 5.12; D.S. 18.18 and Plut. *Phok.* 26, noting also the restoration of Demades' civic rights by the Demos in the desperate situation of 322. See Hyp. 2.11–12 for the pro-Makedonian Philippides who was convicted on at least two occasions of making an illegal proposal.

[93] *AP* 40.2, Aiskhin. 3.187, 194–5 (and scholiast, though we need not accept all his details such as Thrasyboulos' proposal of the death penalty in order to shame the Athenians), [Plut.] *Mor.* 835f–836a; see ch. 2.1.

Hypereides' attack on Demades' proposal to honour an Olynthian.[94] Two more prosecutions launched by Hypereides between 361 and 343 – against Aristophon and Diopeithes – were probably graphai paranomon: whether indictments or impeachments, we do not know the substance of these prosecutions, but we may presume they were at least motivated in part by the desire to challenge a political opponent. The result in Diopeithes' case is not known. Aristophon was acquitted – by a margin of 2 votes.[95] In the unsuccessful indictment of Hypereides' proposal to honour Demosthenes (338) and in the successful indictment of Demades' proposal to acknowledge Alexander as a god (323), both the proposer and the honorand were clearly under attack.[96]

Objections to a decree no doubt ranged from fundamental objection to its contents to a sheer desire to score politically, and any prosecutor was likely to have a number of motives for undertaking his indictment. In many of our known cases of graphe paranomon, the primary object of attack would appear to have been the indirect one – that is, the intended recipient of the honours proposed. Thus in the 370s three highly successful generals received special honours, but not without the decree being challenged by a graphe paranomon in one and probably all three cases. Like the decrees honouring Khabrias (376/5), Timotheos (375/4) and Iphikrates (371/0), a decree honouring Phokion (in or before 322) was upheld by the courts, while we do not know the result of a challenge to a decree honouring Kharidemos (352/1).[97] Aiskhines' target in his indictment of Ktesiphon in 336 was clearly his old rival Demosthenes, the intended recipient of the honours, while Polyeuktos was aiming at Demades (*c.* 335) and Hypereides at the honours proposed for Euboulos (343–330).[98]

6.6 The dangers of impeachment

But the graphe paranomon contained a risk for the prosecutor as well. Lykinos (in 348) and Aiskhines (in 330), for example, failed to win a fifth of the votes and incurred a fine of 1,000 drakhmai, as well as the loss of the right to bring another graphe paranomon. It may well be that Aiskhines was unwilling, rather than unable, to pay the fine, but in any case, whether he was able to pay or not, he had clearly failed in his primary purpose of discrediting Demosthenes and his

[94] See ch. 5.1; Hyp. fr. B.19 (=fr. 76, Jensen).
[95] Hyp. 4.28–9 (stating that he had 'brought to trial' (cf. 4.27) Aristophon, Diopeithes and Philokrates, but specifying an eisangelia only against Philokrates), fr. B.15, but cf. Hansen (1975) 99; Hyp. fr. B.17 (cf. fr. 40–4, Jensen; cf. Hansen (1974) 31).
[96] Dem. 18.222, Hyp. fr. B.20; see n. 92; cf. Hyp. 4 (Hypereides in 336 indicted the pro-Makedonian Philippides, with his sights on a decree honouring the king of Makedonia).
[97] Dem. 20.146 (states that Leodamas indicted the grant to Khabrias), Aiskhin. 3.243 (says 'the jurors' made the grants to all three; see Hansen (1974) 30–1); Hyp. fr. B.22 ([Plut.] *Mor.* 850b, cf. Plut. *Phok.* 4); Dem. 23.   [98] Lykourg. fr. c.14, Hyp. fr. B.21.

policies – and humiliated he withdrew from Athens.[99] For almost all of our period, however, a failed impeachment did not entail any disadvantage other than the fact of defeat. Moreover, with an eisangelia the death penalty was an option that the prosecutor could propose. And while more eisangeliai seem to have been directed against strategoi, they could be used to bring serious charges also against rhetores or against any Athenian (or metic). It is likely that in the fifth century there had been considerable latitude as to the acts which could be the subject of eisangelia, but probably in the years 410–403 (and certainly by the mid-fourth century) a law was passed specifying the types of offences. Some latitude may well have continued, or perhaps it developed and by the 330s amounted to a stretching of the law.[100] In his defence of Euxenippos in the years between 330 and 324, Hypereides quoted the circumstances in which impeachments should be used.

If anyone [the law states] tries to overthrow the democracy of the Athenians, or if he meets with others in any place for the purpose of overthrowing the democracy, or forms a political club (*hetairikon*); or if anyone betrays a city or ships or a land or naval force; or being a rhetor makes a speech contrary to the best interests of the Athenian Demos, receiving money (and gifts from those working against the Athenian Demos).[101]

While strategoi could be charged on the second ground of military treason, advice contrary to the interests of the Demos induced by corruption was the charge laid against Kallistratos in 361, and probably in 366/5. In 366/5 Khabrias as the strategos who acquiesced in the occupation of Oropos by Boiotian forces pending arbitration and Kallistratos who proposed this (interim) response faced prosecution over the loss of Oropos, but they were both acquitted.[102] Not so Kallistratos in 361. His withdrawal from Athens prevented, or rather delayed, the execution of the death penalty: when he miscalculated the general mood and returned to Athens in 355, he was seized and put to death.[103] In 343 Hypereides impeached Philokrates on the grounds of his services to Philip against Athens and secured his conviction: withdrawal prevented the execution of the death sentence.[104] Eisangelia was probably used against Thrasyboulos of Kollytos for (allegedly corrupt) advice given at the time of the Spartan occupation of the Kadmeia in 382, but he was probably acquitted.[105] One is left

---

[99] Aiskhin. 2.14; cf. Dem. 18.103, 222.

[100] For discussion of the law and other offences subject to eisangelia, see MacDowell 169–70, 183–6, 198–201, 210; Harrison 2.50–9, Rhodes 162–71 and (1979) 103–14, and Hansen (1975) especially 12–20 and (1980A) 89–95. See nn. 54–8.

[101] Hyp. 4.7–8, 29, 39. 'Deceiving the people by false promises' ([Dem.] 49.67) is probably a specification of the third ground, but may be a fourth ground.

[102] Arist. *Rh.* 1364a19–23, 1411b6–10, Plut. *Dem.* 5, Dem. 21.64.

[103] Hyp. 4.1–2, Lykourg. *Leok.* 93.

[104] Hyp. 4.29–30; see *Hesperia* 5 (1936), 399–400, lines 46–50, 110–15 for the sale of Philokrates' confiscated property.

[105] Lys. 26.23, Dem. 24.134. See also in Hansen's Catalogue (1975) nos. 116 (Pytheas, 336–323), 126 (Menesaikhmos, before 325) and 130 (Himeraios, 336–322).

with the impression that rhetores were not only less frequently attacked via eisangelia but were also more successful in defending themselves than strategoi. It was presumably difficult to obtain firm evidence of corruption and to convince the dikasts that the advice given by the rhetor had been affected by the acceptance of 'gifts'. Moreover, the failure of a strategos was demonstrable.

Eisangelia, like the graphe paranomon, seems to have been abused increasingly in the third quarter of the fourth century. Prosecutors used eisangelia in the 330s and 320s, if not before, to bring charges which required some stretching of the law to represent them as offences under the law relating to the use of eisangelia. Admittedly, it suited Hypereides' defence of Euxenippos to exaggerate the contrast between 'the serious and notorious crimes, which (c. 360) led to impeachment' (of Kallistratos and four strategoi) and what he depicts as the practice of the 320s of bringing 'frivolous charges which have nothing to do with the impeachment law'. Euxenippos had been charged with having accepted 'gifts' and having made a report about a dream against the best interests of the Demos. Hypereides sought to deny the definition of rhetor as any person who spoke in the Ekklesia and argued that Euxenippos was an ordinary citizen (*idiōtēs*), not a rhetor or habitual speaker against whom an eisangelia could properly be directed.[106] This was special pleading. Eisangelia was intended to cast a wide net to enable speedy action and certainly to encompass all Athenians. Prodosia in the sense of betraying a city was clearly a ground for impeachment, and in 338 when he was prosecuting Leokrates for leaving Athens after the disastrous defeat at Khaironeia, Lykourgos was at pains, for a variety of reasons, to argue that it was proper to invoke eisangelia against this (private) individual and to represent his departure as constituting prodosia − betrayal of Athens.[107] All in all, there appears to have been something in what Hypereides said about the abuse of eisangelia, particularly if we accept his statement that a citizen and a metic had been impeached on the grounds that they had hired out flute-girls at a price higher than that fixed by law (and perhaps could be represented as flouting the law and thus endangering the democracy, though the grounds for impeachment may have been wider than Hypereides indicated).[108] That case belongs to the same period as the Euxenippos case, and is all the more interesting in the light of an attempt to check the abuse of eisangelia which may be dated to c. 333. For it was then laid down that a prosecutor who gained less than a fifth of the votes was liable to a fine of 1,000 drakhmai, but not to any loss of civic rights.[109]

However, the temptation to abuse eisangelia and the graphe paranomon

---

[106] Hyp. 4.1–2, 4, 8–9.

[107] Lykourg. *Leok.* 1–10, 59. For other eisangeliai or possible eisangeliai (most of them against men who are not known to have been strategoi or rhetores or envoys), see Hansen's Catalogue (1975) nos. 79 (treasurers of Athena and the other gods), 99, 103–8 (thesmothetai of 344/3), 111, 113–15, 117–19, 122, 125, 127, 140–4.

[108] Hyp. 4.3.   [109] See n. 58.

should not obscure the fact that political leaders, in particular rhetores but also (often indirectly) strategoi, were deeply and frequently involved in the law-courts as well as the assembly and the fact that death, 'exile', confiscation of property, loss of civic rights or a heavy fine, not to mention loss of honour, might follow conviction. For while eisangelia and the graphe paranomon were the most frequency used devices, and could indeed be represented as the special means by which a rhetor protected the Demos against political actions detrimental to its interests, political leaders could also be brought to account by other methods.[110] The procedure known as *apophasis* (report of investigation), for example, could be employed against those suspected of treason or taking bribes or (probably) of attempts to overthrow the democracy.[111] The most famous use of apophasis was in 324/3 against those who were suspected of receiving money from Harpalos, the fugitive treasurer of Alexander the Great. Some 350 talents appeared to be missing from 700 talents believed to have been deposited by Harpalos in the Akropolis under the charge of specially appointed commissioners, including Demosthenes. Even without internal political rival-ries, the Athenians could not turn a blind eye and ignore the interest of Alexander of Great in the money with which his treasurer had absconded. After investigation the Areiopagos published a list of names with a sum of money imputed to each: 20 talents, for example, to Demosthenes. The Dikasterion of 1,500 condemned Demosthenes, who was the first to come up for trial. Demosthenes, unable to pay the fine of 50 talents, was imprisoned but presently escaped: on the death of Alexander a few months later, Demosthenes was recalled. Demades, who was also condemned, stayed in Athens.[112] Other processes which could be used for political purposes against opponents included *probolē* (lodging of a complaint to the Ekklesia) and *endeixis* (laying of information – allowing, but not requiring, the prosecutor to effect an arrest). Though support of a complaint (*probolē*) in the assembly might be valuable if the matter was subsequently pursued in the courts, probole was not very useful for political purposes (and seems to have been used rarely). For the lodging of a complaint was restricted, at least in the 320s, to the main meeting of the sixth prytany each year. It enabled action against sykophantai (as against the prosecutors of the Arginousai strategoi in 406), against offences at festivals (as by Demosthenes against Meidias and, despite Demosthenes' disclaimer, it could have political implications), or against 'anyone who has not done what he

---

[110] Dein. 1.100–2; cf. Lykourg. *Leok.* 7–10.

[111] Probably introduced *c.* 350, *apophasis* denoted strictly the report of the preliminary investigation by the Areiopagos made to the Ekklesia. Those 'named' by the investigation would be put on trial in the Dikasteria. See Dein. 1.1, 2.1; Hansen (1975) 39–40, MacDowell 190–1.

[112] Hyp. 5, Dein. 1–3; see n. 59. For other cases of apophasis, see Dem. 18.132–3, Dein. 1.56–8, 62–3, *P. Oxy.* 2686.

promised the Demos' (as used apparently by Euboulos against Aristophon).[113] As for endeixis, it could, for example, be employed against individuals who, in disregard of their loss of civic rights (often, as state debtors), undertook public activity: this information was laid against Theokrines for prosecuting in public suits, against Polyeuktos for being a member of the Boule, and against Aristogeiton for addressing the assembly and acting as a prosecutor.[114] Though apparently little used, *dokimasia tōn rhētorōn* (scrutiny of rhetores) was put to effective use by Aiskhines when he removed Timarkhos as a potential prosecutor of his own conduct on the embassy to Philip in 346.[115] And in the case of Athenian officials and envoys, euthynai was an important means of taking action, though there are surprisingly few cases which can be so identified with certainty.[116]

6.7 Were the stakes high?

Influence and political success depended to a large extent on a rhetor's success in the courts, whether as prosecutor or as defendant or in support of the prosecutor or the defendant. Among the leading political figures of the fourth century Aristophon, Kallistratos, Demosthenes, Hypereides and Demades were certainly involved in numerous political trials.[117] Contests in the law-courts appear to have become a more frequent component of political life. Nor was it only the great ones who were involved. The success rate in prosecution is difficult to estimate and evaluate, not least because of the limited evidence available. As far as rhetores are concerned, the less than 40 cases of the graphe paranomon about which we have some information presumably constitute a quite small sample: among these we have some information about the outcome of a little more than half, and in this smaller group the courts overruled slightly less than half of the proposed decrees. In some ways it may seem surprising that the jurors were apparently convinced that the assembly had (in most cases quite recently) erred, since it was not uncommon for speakers to identify citizens in the courts with citizens in the assembly. But their overall composition was by no means identical. Moreover, the prosecutor's aim in these and other cases was to convince the jurors that they and others in the assembly had been misled by clever or corrupt rhetores.[118] And rhetores were liable, as we have seen, to other

---

[113] *AP* 43.4–5, Xen. *Hell* 1.7.35, Dem. 21.8–10, 218 (and scholiast); Harrison 2.59–64, Hansen (1975) 38–9.

[114] [Dem.] 58, Dion. Hal. 651. *Dein.* 10, Dein. 2.12–13, [Dem.] 25–6. For endeixis, *apagōgē* (the offender was 'arrested' by the prosecutor) and *ephēgēsis* (the offender, having been denounced by the prosecutor, was arrested by the officials), see Hansen (1976) 90–8, Harrison 2.221–32.

[115] Aiskhin. 1, especially 28–30, 64; cf. Lys. 10.1 and Hansen (1983B) 153 n. 8.

[116] See ch. 4.1, ch. 6 n. 59 and Hansen (1983A) 42 n. 32.

[117] See the individual entries in *PA* (see ch. 2 n. 57) and Hansen (1983B) 159–79.

[118] See Hansen (1974) 29–43, 49 nn. 4–5, 53–4; see ch. 3.5; Lys. 20.20, Dem. 22.32, 23.4–5, 95–7, 146–7, [Dem.] 59.91, Aiskhin. 1.173–6, 178–9, 3.5, 16, Dein. 1.100–1.

processes, including impeachment on serious charges. Kallistratos, Philokrates, Demosthenes and Demades are witness to the range of processes and the severity of penalties. Of 30 known probable prosecutions of strategoi on serious charges, only 5 seem to have escaped unscathed and probably 3 more (Timotheos, Thrasyboulos of Steiria and Khabrias) were deposed without further penalty: 9 were executed or opted for exile instead of death.[119]

Indicative of the severity of the penalties are the crippling fine imposed on Timotheos and the execution of Kallistratos. Both belong to the difficult mid-350s when the Athenians were in desperate straits as their allies sought to break away, but death sentences and heavy fines (albeit less punitive than the fine imposed on Timotheos) are known from every decade in the 80 years after the restoration of democracy in 403. It may be added that Phokion was put to death in 318 during a period when democracy was briefly restored: past services were no protection in themselves, and in any case past 'services' were viewed differently by different individuals. Attitudes to Sparta, Thebes or Makedonia were far from static throughout the period and an individual's leanings might prove later to be a severe handicap. The frequency of 'exile' is another indication that the stakes were high and that the fundamental criterion was success. And for some Athenian envoys the chances of negotiating terms acceptable to the Demos were limited, though it should be added that scores of embassies would have been sent in the course of the years from 403 to 322, almost all of them, it is true, with easier briefs than those of 392 and 367.[120]

The prosecution, conviction and punishment of political leaders raise several questions. What effect, for example, did this situation have on the ongoing careers of political leaders in the fourth century – on men like Kallistratos or Timotheos? Or we might share the puzzlement of the Oligarchic Man whom Theophrastos depicted among his *Characters*. Full of complaints about Athens, the Oligarchic Man was wont to remark: 'I marvel why men take up public affairs.'[121] Why did they? Both of these questions will be considered in the next chapter, when the benefits of active participation are examined, as will another question: what were the bases of the support that prominent individuals enjoyed? For while public life, when viewed from the standpoint of the ambitious Athenian, seems to have been much concerned with individual rivalries and with relationships between leading individuals and the Demos, underlying these and interwoven with them were the perceptions of other Athenians – their perceptions of the policies being advocated in the assembly or the trials in the law-courts and the impact of these on Athens and on individuals.

---

[119] See n. 71 and Knox (1985) 132–61.   [120] See ch. 6.5 above.
[121] Theophr. *Char.* 26.5.

APPENDIX: A NOTE ON ARISTOPHON[1]

Oost (1977) 238–42 argues for the possibility that Aristophon (born *c.* 435, died *c.* 335) retired from active politics for some 40 years after 403/2, and certainly there is no evidence for the 40 years and most of our evidence comes from the 20 years beginning in 363/2. There is, however, no reason to doubt that Aristophon was very active in public life in and after 363, if not before, as rhetor in the assembly and the law-courts and as strategos (363/2) (Hansen (1983B) 161–2), while the large number of acquittals suggests he enjoyed widespread support among the citizens. His general record in the courts was the subject of jokes (schol. Aiskhin. 1.64). Whether Aristophon himself used the number 75 when he boasted about the number of times he had been acquitted of the charge of making an illegal proposal or whether Aiskhines (3.194) used that number in reporting Aristophon's claim, it would seem that Aiskhines (and probably others) may well have fancied the number 75 as indicating a huge number: Oost cites Aiskhines' claim (2.70) that Khares had lost 75 cities (!) won over to the Second Athenian League by Timotheos (cf. Isok. 15.113, Dein. 1.14, 3.17). But Aristophon was undoubtedly prosecuted very many times for making an illegal proposal, even if scepticism is aroused by the mention (schol. Dem. 19.297 (=8.445, Dindorf)) of 70 graphai, most or perhaps all of which were presumably graphai paranomon. That scholiast and also the scholiast on Dem. 18.70 (=8.287, Dindorf) affirm that Aristophon was never condemned, but that may have been inferred from the statements of Aiskhines and Demosthenes. For Demosthenes (18.251), when he made his rejoinder to Aiskhines' reference to Kephalos' claim, spoke of 'a man who has often been accused but never been convicted of wrongdoing', without naming Aristophon. That seems to imply that Aristophon had never been convicted. If, however, we accept the text of the scholia to Aiskhin. 1.64 (see Hansen (1974) 31), Aristophon *was* convicted when Hypereides brought a graphe paranomon against him in connection with affairs in Keos in 363/2. If he was convicted in 363/2, Aristophon may have been forgetful when he made his claim – presumably in the 340s or 330s towards the end of his long life. Or, more likely, he was presuming on the forgetfulness of the jurors or their willingness to accept the essential point of repeated acquittals, or possibly he was speaking tongue-in-cheek. 'Acquitted on "75" occasions', he said (and not necessarily in boast), and many did not remember or even know of the '76th' graphe, while for those who did Aristophon may perhaps have been making a point now lost to us. If he was convicted in 363/2, was it perhaps the first graphe paranomon lodged against him?

---

[1] See p. 154, n. 85.

7 The rewards of leadership

7.1 The rewards and the hazards: three contemporaries

Compared with the hazards of active participation in the public life of Athens, what benefits accrued to the individuals themselves or to the Athenian community of citizens from such participation? At the individual level, it may be useful first to identify the rewards and the hazards by a consideration of the careers of three ambitious Athenians who were near-contemporaries and, in particular, by an examination of the means employed by them to advance themselves and to protect themselves against attack. Their probable dates of birth were: Iphikrates *c.* 418 (but perhaps as late as 413), Kallistratos not later than 415, and Timotheos 414 or earlier. And all three had achieved some public fame in their twenties – at an early age by Athenian standards.[1]

Iphikrates was the son of a shoemaker and was conscious of his humble origins.[2] Kallistratos was the nephew of Agyrrhios, who in the 390s proposed the introduction of pay for attending the assembly, had been active in public affairs since at least 405, and was a strategos in 388/7. Kallistratos' wealth was such that in the 360s, and probably well before, he was liable for liturgies and served as a trierarch. In 392/1 Kallistratos took his first known political step when he successfully prosecuted the envoys who were sent to Sparta to discuss peace. Agyrrhios' public debt and imprisonment may have played a part in the lull in political activity by Kallistratos in the 380s, if the silence of the sources may be so interpreted.[3] Timotheos had an 'inheritance' of great potential value for an ambitious young man. First, he was the son of a man who had been a strategos. That in itself might assist in early ambitions, but Timotheos was exceedingly fortunate. He was the son of the great Konon who had (in conjunction, it is true, with the Persian satrap Pharnabazos) liberated the Aegean states from Spartan control after the naval victory off Knidos in 394 and who had made an important contribution to the refortification of Athens and the revival of Athenian naval power. Moreover, when in his twenties,

---

[1] See ch. 2 n. 57; for detailed references in the sources to Iphikrates see *PA* 7737, *APF* and Pritchett 2.62–72, 117–25; Kallistratos *PA* 8157 and *APF*; Timotheos *PA* 13700 and *APF*; see Sealey 133–63, Longo (1971) 60–81, Dušanić (1980) 111–44.

[2] Plut. *Mor.* 186f, *APF* 248.

[3] See, however, *IG* ii².84.9–10 (uncertain date), Dem. 24.134–5 and *APF* 278.

Timotheos had accompanied his father on his victorious cruise throughout the Aegean: statues were erected in his and his father's honour at Samos and Ephesos.[4] One of the great Athenian heroes of the 390s, Konon was honoured with a bronze statue set up in the Agora of his native city – the first man so honoured since the tyrannicides Harmodios and Aristogeiton – but he did not long remain an active force in Athens, for he was arrested by the Persians in the late 390s when on an embassy. From Konon's estate Timotheos received (*c.* 389) property worth not less than 17 talents. Such wealth could be an invaluable asset in the pursuit of honour and power.[5]

Meanwhile Iphikrates, who was probably in his twenties when the Corinthian War broke out in 395, was during that war the commander of a force of peltasts or light-armed infantry: his most spectacular success was the destruction of a Spartan detachment near Corinth in 390. Whether he was, as is probable, a strategos in 389/8 and the next two years or not, he could hardly have escaped without some share in the disgrace of the Athenian strategoi who in 387 lost control of the Hellespont to the Spartan admiral Antalkidas. In any case, with no military opportunities in Athenian service in the aftermath of the King's Peace of 387/6, Iphikrates entered the service of the Thracian prince Kotys in 386. He married into Kotys' family and apparently served Kotys for a few years.[6] In or after 380/79 he was sent by the Athenians, at the request of the Persian Pharnabazos, to assist the satrap against Egyptian rebels, but in 373 he was back in Athens. The return of such an experienced commander would have increased the competition for appointment to major expeditions. In that year we find him cooperating with Kallistratos. The latter had played an important role in attracting Aegean states to join the Second Athenian League which was established in 378, was one of the strategoi in 378/7, and in the mid-370s (and beyond) was one of the leading political figures in Athens. This collaboration between professional commander and rhetor was particularly important for someone like Iphikrates who lacked important family connections.[7]

Timotheos, too, had been elected one of the strategoi for the year 378/7. Since then he had won honour for himself by his military successes, especially his victory over the Spartan fleet at Alyzeia in 375. His standing in Athens may be measured by the erection of a statue next to his father's in the Agora and the inauguration of a festival of Peace which Isokrates associated with his victory and the peace which the Spartans were constrained to accept in 375/4.[8] In the mid-370s he was one of the two most popular strategoi in Athens. The other was Khabrias. Khabrias had played a conspicuous role in the resistance to Sparta in 378/7, showing calculated contempt for the forces led by Agesilaos against

[4] Paus. 6.3.16; for Konon see *PA* 8707.
[5] *APF* 508–10, and compare the career of Khabrias – see *PA* 15086, *APF* 560 and Table II, Pritchett 2.72–7.
[6] Davies *APF* 249–50 argues strongly that Iphikrates married Kotys' sister, not a daughter, and in 386, not later.
[7] See ch. 6.2.   [8] Tod 128; *SEG* 16.55, 29.88; Isok. 15.109–10.

Thebes. In 376 he won a decisive naval battle off Naxos – a victory which removed the threat to the import of Athenian grain supplies and which was to make Athens for the next half-century the strongest naval power in the Aegean, albeit a pale reflection of her fifth-century supremacy. Khabrias' achievements were honoured by the award of a gold crown, a statue in the Agora (which depicted his confrontation with Agesilaos' forces), and exemption from liturgies.[9] The honorary decrees for both Khabrias and Timotheos were, as we have seen, unsuccessfully challenged on the grounds of illegality.[10] Between the two leaders there was intense rivalry.

In 373 Timotheos had been instructed by the Demos to prepare a relief expedition for Kerkyra, but he first sailed to various Aegean islands to gain crews and support for his expedition. His prolonged cruise in the Aegean and his delay in carrying out instructions gave his opponents their opportunity. Timotheos was deposed from his command and was prosecuted by Kallistratos and Iphikrates for treason on the grounds that he had, by his delay, betrayed Athens' ally Kerkyra.[11] It is interesting to notice that his successor manned the ships expeditiously and obtained from the Athenians some 70 ships to enable him to set out forthwith for Kerkyra.[12] Yet there is no reason to doubt that lack of funds and associated problems had been important factors in Timotheos' decision to seek support in the Aegean. For it seems to have required considerable forcefulness on Iphikrates' part to get things under way: he is said by Xenophon to have compelled the trierarchs to do their duty and to have obtained adequate numbers of ships from the Athenians by holding out the prospect of sending back many ships if the Kerkyra campaign was successful. And there are clear indications that adequate funding was not available or was still not provided for the expedition. An early success in capturing ten Syracusan ships brought in more than 60 talents from the sale of the crews, and it was with these funds that Iphikrates paid his forces. Subsequently he maintained his sailors for the most part by having them work for the Kerkyraians on their lands, and in 372 he sailed to Kephallenia to collect money, in some cases with the consent of the people, in others against their will.[13] The campaign continued to be limited by shortage of funds.

It is probable, however, that in 373 Timotheos had been concerned not only about inadequate funds and had been intent on reaffirming or securing support among Aegean states not simply for Athens and for the Kerkyra expedition, but more particularly for himself so that he could match the prestige of Khabrias.

[9] Dem. 20.75–7. For the statue see D.S. 15.32.5, 33.4, Nepos *Chabrias* 1.2–3, Burnett and Edmonson (1961) 74–91, Anderson (1963) 411–13, and Buckler (1972) 466–74.
[10] Aiskhin. 3.243; see ch. 6.5.
[11] [Dem.] 49.9, 13, Lys. fr. 228; cf. D.S. 15.47.2–3; Tuplin (1984) 538–41, cf. Gray (1980) 315–17.
[12] Xen. *Hell.* 6.2.11–14.
[13] Xen. *Hell.* 6.2.14, 33–8, D.S. 15.47.7; see ch. 3.3. For Iphikrates' zeal in training his forces en route, see Xen. *Hell.* 6.2.27–30 (see also Nep. *Iph.* 2 and Polyainos 3.9.35) and for his successful use of light-armed troops Pritchett 2.117–25.

For Khabrias had followed up his victory off Naxos in 376 by securing many new members for the Second Athenian League, and there is clear evidence that Khabrias was casting himself in the role of Konon's successor in his achievements in the Aegean.[14] The Aegean cruise was thus intended to counter the great and increasing influence of Khabrias and Kallistratos and to enhance Timotheos' own influence, as well as to secure the means for the expedition around the Peloponnese. But his delays irritated sufficient numbers of Athenians to bring about his deposition, but not enough to secure his condemnation.[15] His treasurer Antimakhos was less fortunate or lacked the powerful friends at home and abroad (including Alketas, king of the Molossians, and Iason of Pherai, who were allies of Athens) whom Timotheos called in: he was punished with death and his property was confiscated.[16] Timotheos left Athens and, following the example of his father after Aigospotamoi, served as a mercenary commander abroad.

Xenophon especially commended Iphikrates for inducing the Demos to appoint Kallistratos and Khabrias as commanders to accompany him on the Kerkyra expedition. Whether the initiative came from him or not, the combination of the rhetor who was influential in the assembly (and who, we may add, was an expert in finance), Khabrias 'who was regarded as a very good general', and Iphikrates, the forceful general, won strong support for the expedition. But hitherto, according to Xenophon, there had been no political ties between Iphikrates and his two colleagues, and in fact Kallistratos is said to have been not very friendly with Iphikrates.[17] Close ties are hardly to be expected, for Iphikrates had been away from Athens assisting foreign powers for most, if not all, of the years since 386. Both may have had ties in the 390s with Konon, but even if this were so it would probably be true of a great many Athenians at the time of Konon's pre-eminence.[18] But either the ties of Kallistratos and Iphikrates with Konon were never close or the lapse of almost 20 years had weakened the ties between the two men. In the midst of the changing alignments of personalities in Athenian politics, however, Kallistratos, Khabrias and Iphikrates appear to have worked together for the next six or seven years, and, if we may judge from the military commands, to have exercised considerable, but by no means unchallenged, influence in Athens.

Successful at Kerkyra in 372, but then beset by shortage of funds, Iphikrates approved of Kallistratos' proposal to obtain more funds or to work for peace. The Athenian people now desired an end to the war with Sparta, and Kallistratos played a key role in the conclusion of peace which followed in 371. In 371/0 a decree awarding Iphikrates a bronze statue, free meals in the Hall of the Prytaneis and other honours survived the challenge of a graphe para-

---

[14] Davies (1969) 323 n. 85.
[15] See ch. 6.4; Tuplin (1984) 566–8; cf. Roberts 40–5.   [16] [Dem.] 49.10.
[17] Xen. *Hell.* 6.2.14, 39, though Xenophon leaves it an open question whether they were adversaries.   [18] See Sealey 137–9; cf. *APF* 249.

nomon.[19] In 370/69 it was Kallistratos who proposed help for the Spartans threatened by the Theban invasions of the Peloponnese in the wake of the Spartan defeat at Leuktra in 371, while Iphikrates was the commander of the mercenary force used by the Athenians against the Thebans. From 368 to 365 Iphikrates commanded Athenian forces in Thrace and the north Aegean until he was replaced by Timotheos as commander to Amphipolis and the Khersonesos. He then raised troops for Kotys and assisted the Thracian king, giving advice, for example, on raising revenue, but when, perhaps two or three years later, Kotys' designs on the Khersonesos clashed with Athenian aims, he left Kotys and retired to Antissa, then to Drys in Thrace.[20]

After his deposition in 373 Timotheos was away from Athens for several years, but his years of command in Egypt in the service of the Persians enabled him to repair his fortunes. This was vital, for in 373 Timotheos had mortgaged his property in order to gain funds to launch the expedition which he had been assigned. And, according to Isokrates and other writers, Timotheos received no public funds for the expedition against Samos in 366 and he presumably had to use his own funds again to initiate his commission.[21] His successful reduction of Samos made him once again one of the most influential figures in Athens – about the time when the loss of Oropos (366/5) gave Leodamas, the very able orator who had indicted the honorary decree for Khabrias in 376/5, the opportunity to prosecute Khabrias and Kallistratos over their role in the affair. The prosecution seems to have been damaging for their influence, even though they were acquitted. Kallistratos was said to have owed his acquittal to the brilliance of his speech, which was heard and greatly admired by the young Demosthenes.[22]

In the years between 365 and 362 Timotheos won many successes, in particular gaining Sestos and Krithote in the Thracian Khersonesos and bringing over to Athens many towns in the Khalkidike. His triumphant return early in 362 must have disturbed power relationships within Athens. He seems, however, to have been caught up himself in the failure to satisfy the high hopes entertained by the Athenians of recovering Amphipolis and extending their power in Thrace; at least he was prosecuted in 360 by Apollodoros who was zealous at this time, as has already been noted, in his prosecution of unsuccessful strategoi.[23] The result of that prosecution is not known, but another of the

[19] Dem. 23.130, Aiskhin. 3.243, Dion. Hal. *Lys.* 12.
[20] Dem. 23.129–32, 149; cf. Kallet (1983) 244–52.
[21] Isok. 15.111; see ch. 3 n. 54.
[22] See ch. 6.6; Roberts 69–73; Tod 131.35–49 on the misgivings of Mytilene in 369/8 about Athenian policies, and Sealey 147–50 on the problems faced by Kallistratos in his attempt to achieve a balance between Sparta and Thebes (including the failure of Timomakhos – who at some time in the 360s married Kallistratos' daughter – to stop the Thebans crossing the Isthmos in 367); Plut. *Dem.* 5.
[23] See ch. 6.4; see [Dem.] 50.6 for interference by Byzantion with the passage of grain ships bound for the Peiraieus in 362/1.

generals prosecuted by Apollodoros opted for exile. That was Timomakhos, the son-in-law of Kallistratos. A year or so earlier, Kallistratos, who had retained some influence in the assembly after his acquittal in 366/5, had been convicted on a charge of speaking against the best interests of the Demos. So ended the public career in Athens of a man whose personal habits, like those of other political leaders in the fourth century as well as the fifth, were subject to public comment by playwrights. A butt of jokes in the comic poets, Kallistratos was depicted as given up to pleasures by the historian Theopompos of Khios – a writer by no means averse to reporting scandal in Athens or anywhere else, though he acknowledged that Kallistratos was nevertheless attentive in public affairs. The Athenian leader delayed the execution of the death penalty until 355.[24]

In or possibly before 362, and perhaps as early as 365, Iphikrates' son Menestheus married Timotheos' daughter, signalling an accommodation between Iphikrates, whose military talents had enabled him to rise from obscurity and poverty, and his rival Timotheos.[25] Among the strategoi of 356/5 were Timotheos, Iphikrates and Menestheus. With Khares they were in command of the Athenian naval forces operating against the rebellious allies in the eastern Aegean. At Embata Khares engaged in battle with the enemy, but because of stormy weather his colleagues refused to engage. Khares sent a dispatch to Athens charging his colleagues with prodosia: self-preservation might well suggest such a course. The charges were taken up by the rhetor Aristophon, who had perhaps been cooperating with Khares for some years.[26] He prosecuted Timotheos for treason and for having been bribed by the Khians and the Rhodians, Iphikrates for treason, and Menestheus for the administration of the money paid out to the fleet.[27] Iphikrates and his son were acquitted. Timotheos was fined 100 talents and withdrew to Khalkis in Euboia. Both Iphikrates and Timotheos had died by 352.

Writing in 354/3, not long after the Embata trial, Isokrates was enthusiastic in his praise of his pupil Timotheos and his achievements, but he acknowledged Timotheos' partial responsibility for his condemnation and, more broadly, his refusal or failure, as he put it, 'to curry favour with the Demos' and 'to cultivate the rhetores and the speakers who are effective in private gatherings'. Timotheos' proud bearing which was an advantage to a strategos, Isokrates argued, was out of place in dealing with men from day to day: 'he was by nature as inept in courting the favour of men as he was gifted in handling affairs'. And it is likely that what Isokrates described as Timotheos' proud bearing, and others regarded as arrogant and anti-democratic, played no small part in the decision of the jury to impose a fine beyond his ability to pay.[28] As for Iphikrates, while

[24] Eub. fr. 11, 107, Antiph. fr. 300, Theopomp. *FGrH* 115 F97.
[25] Cf. Kallet (1983) 239–41 (in or before 368); Dem. 21.62 (Iphikrates' wealth and influence).
[26] D.S. 15.95.1–3, Dem. 51.8–9.
[27] Isok. 15.129, Dein. 1.14, Dion. Hal. *Lys.* 12.   [28] Isok. 15.129–39 (Loeb tr. adapted).

he had not had the benefit of receiving instruction in public speaking from Isokrates, he was regarded as an effective speaker. His style, which was said to contain much vulgar army slang and to smack of the headstrong and boastful character of the soldier rather than the ready wit of the orator, may have assisted in his acquittal. Polyainos relates that Iphikrates intimidated the jurors at his trial by stationing young men near the court who let the dikasts see their concealed daggers. Whether or not there is any truth in the anecdote, Iphikrates may at times have shown less regard for Athenian laws and traditions than Demosthenes attributed to him in his relations with his enemy Diokles of the Pitthean deme.[29]

Military commanders, in short, survived most readily if they were successful. Ability, experience, reputation and wealth had a part to play. If they were not successful, they faced removal from office and prosecution by their enemies. In the face of these hazards, they sought protection by collaboration with rhetores, by marriage ties, or by withdrawing from Athenian service until the clouds had passed, their own talents were once more needed, or they had gained strong political associates. It is not surprising that men with military talents did not accept the greater hazards of the official position of strategos as readily or as frequently as Phokion apparently did, but that at times they preferred to continue as mercenary commanders, whether in Athenian service or in the service of a Thracian prince or a Persian king or satrap.

7.2 Was the Demos ruthless?

The careers of Iphikrates, Kallistratos and Timotheos might seem to confirm the rhetorical commonplace – the harsh treatment of leaders by the Demos.[30] What was the reality in our period?

We may perhaps begin with ostracism, which was one of the striking features of Athenian public life in the fifth century, though, as we have seen, it fell into disuse in the fourth. At first sight it might appear a ruthless weapon. A political leader had no opportunity to defend himself, for the procedure allowed for no open debate. Each year at a regular meeting of the assembly in the sixth prytany, approximately January, the Demos decided whether to hold an *ostrakophoria* (vote of ostracism). If the vote was affirmative, the ostrakophoria itself was held in the eighth prytany. The citizen inscribed on a potsherd – a piece of a broken vase (*ostrakon*) – the name of the person whom he wished to remove from Athens. Provided the quorum requirement of 6,000 was met, the individual with the largest number of ostraka cast against him was required to go into exile for ten years. At neither meeting was debate allowed. The interval, however,

---

[29] Lys. fr. 3 (Budé – cf. fr. 7), Dion. Hal. *Lys.* 12; Polyainos 3.9.15, cf. 3.9.29 – see Xen. *Hell.* 2.3.55 for intimidatory tactics by the oligarchs in 404; cf. Roberts 49; Dem. 21.62–3.
[30] Plut. *Arist.* 26, *Nik.* 6, *Dem.* 26, Dem. 4.47.

did allow for discussion among individuals; it is arguable whether such private discussion might lead to sounder decisions than public discussion in a large assembly. The procedural requirement of two meetings meant that the decision was not hasty.[31] But the interval also gave the opportunity for organising the vote. The ostracism of Hyperbolos was the most notorious instance of this, but there is reason to believe that the interval had long been so utilised. Indeed, since there was no discussion of the matter in the assembly, there was presumably some need to encourage attendance and to mobilise votes for what was an anti-election. In the first half of the fifth century the opponents of Themistokles on one occasion systematically manufactured ostraka inscribed with the name of Themistokles, as is clear from the discovery by the excavators in the Agora of a hoard of 191 ostraka so inscribed in some fourteen different hands. The intention of this concerted effort was apparently to distribute these ostraka at the right moment in order to facilitate a vote against Themistokles.[32]

Exile for ten years was admittedly a severe, though not always a fatal, blow for a political leader and his power. Yet investigation of the earlier alternatives to ostracism suggests that it was a milder alternative. It enabled the removal of a political opponent or a leader felt to be too powerful or divisive and thus a danger to democracy and its stability – without recourse to *stasis* (civil strife) or to murder.[33] In Athens in the archaic period, and in other Greek poleis, defeat in stasis was likely to result in the execution of opponents or in the banishment of whole families, the confiscation of property and permanent loss of civic rights. Ostracism succeeded in providing an institutionalised device for constraining the excesses of civil strife and may be held to have exerted a stabilising effect on Athenian political life in the fifth century. At the same time, ostracism was itself used as a weapon in political conflict. Paradoxically, an institution that was commonly regarded as a means of removing a leader whose power gave rise to fears of tyranny or whose policies were not popular might well have the effect of significantly strengthening the position of another. Perikles' hand certainly seems to have been greatly strengthened after Thucydides, son of Melesias, was ostracised in 443. Indeed this realisation may have led to what seems to have been a disinclination to resort to ostracism in the next twenty-five years, especially if the move for an ostrakophoria in 443 had been particularly supported by the opponents of Perikles fearful of his increasing influence. The demonstration in 417 (when Hyperbolos' opponents engineered his ostracism) that the institution could be circumvented or subverted encouraged the demise of a regular, annual opportunity for deciding against individuals whose policies might divide the state and for dealing with the over-ambitious and the subversive.[34]

[31] *AP* 22.3–6 and 43.5 (and *CAAP*), D.S. 11.55.1–2, Plut. *Arist.* 7, Philokhoros *FGrH* 328 F30; Raubitschek (1952–3) 113–22, Hignett 159–66, ML 21, Vanderpool (1970).
[32] Humphreys (1978) 101; Broneer (1938) 228–43.
[33] *AP* 22.6, Plut. *Arist.* 7.2–3, Thuc. 8.73.3, Arist. *Pol.* 1284a17–22, 1302b15–21.
[34] See ch. 2.3.1 and ch. 5.2.

In the fourth century, however, and in the fifth, political leaders might be, and were, punished with death and confiscation of their property. Was the Demos ruthless in these cases? Central to that question is the question whether the decisions of the Athenians were just, capricious or vindictive. Such implications seem to be inherent in the opinion expressed by Aristotle that the case of Ergophilos was an example of the fact that 'men grow mild when they have spent their anger upon another. For although they were more annoyed with him than with Kallisthenes, they acquitted him, because they had condemned Kallisthenes to death on the previous day.'[35] A full answer to this central question would depend on an assessment of each decision. Even within the fortuitous sample of those cases about which something is known it is rare to have sufficient evidence to make a proper assessment. The measure of 'guilt' in a narrow technical or legal sense is difficult or impossible for us to judge, except in so far as the evidence presented by the Attic Orators – evidence which was not subjected to cross-examination – and the verdicts may give some indications. Yet the verdicts were not, as we have seen, related simply to what in other politico-legal systems might be a question of a specific breach of a particular law, but to wider questions. To that extent, more so than in some other societies, the prosecutions and the verdicts were concerned with political rivalry, political advantage and political judgements.[36] And in that respect it is doubtful whether it is proper to speak simply of the ruthlessness of the Demos.

Occasionally, however, there is evidence and it seems to be unambiguous. Anger swept reason aside, according to Antiphon, in the hasty conviction of a board of Hellenotamiai who were accused, probably in the 440s, of embezzlement. Nine were executed, but one was saved when the true facts of how the money had disappeared were discovered.[37] In 406 many Athenian sailors lost their lives when 25 ships were sunk or disabled in a naval battle off the Arginousai Islands. The refusal of the Athenian assembly to try each of the Arginousai strategoi separately and to allow each the proper time for his defence was in contravention of the laws. The irregularities of that trial were pointed out by a few at the time. But, as Xenophon's vivid narrative shows, the atmosphere in the assembly was highly explosive. Explosive, because the failure to rescue the shipwrecked sailors had occurred at a time of a severe manpower crisis.[38] Explosive, because in the interval between the two meetings of the assembly the family festival of the Apatouria had been celebrated, heightening the sense of loss of kin. Theramenes and the other trierarchs, who had been assigned the duty of recovering the shipwrecked, presumably did not believe the assembly would accept the violence of the storm as the cause of the tragedy: at any rate they were anxious to put the responsibility on the strategoi for the heavy loss of life and, according to Xenophon, exploited the feelings aroused by the

---

35 Arist. *Rh.* 1380b10–13; cf. Loeb edition of Aiskhines 161 and the remarks of the Loeb editors of Demosthenes, vol. 2, 233 ('that unreasonable reaction from severity to indulgence, which was (and still is) characteristic of the Athenian populace, if not of democracy in general').

36 See Dover 292–5.   37 Antiphon 5.69–71.   38 Xen. *Hell.* 1.6.24, D.S. 13.97.1.

Apatouria. At the second meeting the Boule recommended that the assembly pass judgement on the strategoi collectively and without hearing further argument. The attempt to indict this proposal on the grounds of unconstitutionality was swept aside by the cry that 'it was monstrous if the Demos were not permitted to do whatever it wished' and by the threat to try those bringing the graphe paranomon by the same vote as the generals. Similarly, the refusal of some of the prytaneis to put the question to the vote in violation of the law was swept aside, with Sokrates alone persisting in his dissent.[39] To an Aristotle this trial would have represented a classic instance of the spirit of an extreme democracy which made it ready to sacrifice the rule of the law to the decrees of the assembly. Yet it was not only an extreme democracy that under stress might so disregard the laws. It was, of course, no consolation that the irregularities of the trial were subsequently acknowledged by the majority when the assembly voted that complaints be lodged against those who had deceived the Demos, including Kallixenos who had proposed to the council that the strategoi be judged collectively and without further argument. Because of the disturbed internal situation in the final years of the war and because of the amnesty after the restoration of the democracy, these complaints were in fact not pursued.[40]

With regard to the crippling fine imposed on Timotheos in 356/5, it is hard to escape the conclusion that it had an element of the vindictive: inability to pay meant indefinite imprisonment or exile to avoid that fate. But even Isokrates felt, or purported to feel, that there was a case to be made for Athens. In terms of pure justice, he argued, the treatment of Timotheos was cruel and abominable. But 'if you make allowance for the ignorance which characterises all men, for feelings of envy and for the confusion and turmoil of our times', the cause is to be found in human nature. Timotheos bore some of the responsibility for the mistaken judgements, Isokrates added, because of his proud bearing and his ineptness in courting the favour of men.[41] The case for the Athenians might be put more strongly. The general impression is that Athenian judgements, if severe, were mostly in conformity with their conception of the character and purpose of a public suit and the responsibility of public figures.[42] For the grounds of prosecution, even when stated in narrow technical terms in part, usually involved wider, more open questions such as the worthiness of the recipient of honours. Any assessment of Athenian justice must therefore take full account of the fact that public suits were commonly political in character, and that the stated terms of the charge were not necessarily the only question, or indeed the main question, in the minds of the Athenian citizens. To accept this is

[39] Xen. *Hell.* 1.7, 2.3.32, D.S. 13.101.1–4 (cf. Henderson (1927) 467–75); Pl. *Ap.* 32b–c; de Laix 161–2, Andrewes (1974) 112–22, Roberts 64–9, MacDowell 186–9, Hansen (1975) 84–6.

[40] See Arist. *Pol.* 1292a4–7; Xen. *Hell.* 1.7.35.

[41] Isok. 15.130–1 (Loeb tr. adapted).

[42] Cloché (1960) 80–95, Pritchett 2.12–27, Roberts 107–23, 161–8; cf. Hansen (1975) 63–5, Knox (1985) 132–61.

neither to accept nor to deny that the Demos was or could be capricious in its judgements. From the vantage point of a Thucydides, the Demos certainly seemed capricious, but the deposition of Perikles can also be seen as an appropriate response to the consequences of his policies. In their apparent interest in the fact of failure rather than the reasons for failure, we may again be affected to some extent by the bias of sources which tend to be more sympathetic to strategoi than to the Demos. The fact that reasons or extenuating circumstances were offered suggests that the Demos *could* be receptive to such pleas. Nevertheless, at certain times leaders were particularly vulnerable – in the late 360s and early 350s, for example, when Athenian ambitions had been revived but the serious shortage of finance and the comparative weakness of Athens prevented their realisation. And, as Plutarch mused in his *Life of Phokion*, the conduct of affairs is likely to be more dangerous when the affairs of a polis are at a low ebb.[43]

In considering whether the Demos was vindictive and whether the penalties were severe, it is proper not only to compare the practices of contemporary states such as Sparta, but also to apprehend the Athenian attitude to the appropriateness of the death penalty in general.[44] For in Athens the death penalty was prescribed not only in cases of premeditated homicide, but also for such offenders as a public debtor who held a public office, a prostitute who addressed the assembly and was convicted as a result of an indictment, or a thief who stole by night or who, in daylight, stole from a gymnasion or stole more than 50 drakhmai elsewhere or (in the case of public property from a harbour) over 10 drakhmai. Given the range and character of capital offences, the punishment of strategoi by death may not appear unduly severe.[45] It might also be observed that prosecutors, in an endeavour to encourage juries to take a stern view of the alleged offences of those who actively participated in public life, were wont to warn the jurors against leniency. Aiskhines, for example, in seeking to stress the serious nature of Timarkhos' offences reminded the jury that certain jurors unable to defend themselves against old age and poverty together had been led, he claimed, to accept bribes and for that offence had been put to death.[46]

Many Athenians, in particular strategoi, did not appear to stand trial but, as we have seen, opted for exile. That in itself does not imply certainty of conviction or vindictiveness on the part of the Demos, nor for that matter does it prove the guilt of the particular individuals. Timomakhos, however, in 361/0

[43] See Xen. *Hell.* 1.7.33 for Euryptolemos' plea at the Arginousai trial not to return a verdict of prodosia instead of helplessness (because of the storm); Westlake (1969) 118–37, Roberts 124–41; see ch. 6.4; Plut. *Phok.* 2.   [44] See ch. 6.4.

[45] Dem. 24.113–14, *AP* 52.1; Cohen (1983) 69–83; Harrison 178, 205, 225, 231; Dover 280–90; Hansen (1976) 54.

[46] Aiskhin. 1.87–8, Dein. 1.17, 22–3; Lys. 28.3, 11, Dem. 21.184, 24.51, 192–3, [Dem.] 25.87, 58.24, Hyp. 5.25.

may have been prudent to opt for exile if, as seems to be the case, he gave illegal assistance to his father-in-law, the exile Kallistratos: the diversion of a trireme to transport Kallistratos may have been one element in Apollodoros' charge that Timomakhos had betrayed the Thracian Khersonesos.[47]

A comparison with the history of the Roman republic in the second and first centuries B.C. might, however, suggest that the probability of conviction and the punishment of officials was directly affected by the composition of the juries. For in this respect the Athenians with their popular Dikasteria differed from the practice of the Roman republic. In Rome, for example, the courts investigating alleged abuses of power by provincial governors and officials became the focus of political struggles in the second and first centuries, and the composition of the juries changed from time to time. Before the time of Gaius Gracchus, a provincial governor was tried by members of his own senatorial class and there was a widespread belief, whether right or wrong, that governors were treated with undue leniency. In the next half-century the juries at different periods were composed of *equites* (or wealthy non-senators), senators and equites, or senators alone. In 70 B.C. mixed juries were reintroduced, with the senatorial order providing a third of the judges. While senators might be said to have 'appreciated' the problems of a Roman official, an appreciation of the problems was a source of difficulty as well as a virtue. By contrast, in Athens, despite the much wider involvement of citizens in public office, the strategoi and the leading public figures seem to have been drawn mainly from restricted groups, and the treatment which they received seems to have been less sympathetic than that normally received by Roman officials under the republic. Isokrates, as we have seen, believed that poverty led some men to destroy, if they could, those whom they envied, while Plutarch saw in ostracism a clear demonstration of his view that envy of leaders was an important factor in Athenian public life.[48]

But such suggestions do not tell the whole story. For envy was probably more intense among Athenian leaders themselves. It is apparent that in their attempts to gain or retain power and influence, Athenian leaders in the fifth and fourth centuries did not hesitate to use against their opponents the various devices which we have discussed and to suggest extreme penalties for their opponents.[49] Moreover, different types of processes were available for certain offences, and with different maximum penalties for each type.[50] A defendant prosecuted for bribery by an *apographē* (deposition) might simply have the bribe confiscated; if brought before the court by means of euthynai, he might be

---

[47] Dem. 19.180, 23.115, [Dem.] 50.46–52, Aiskhin. 1.56, Hyp. 4.1–2, Bonner (1927) 130–1, Roberts 111–12.

[48] Isok. 15.142–3 and see ch. 5.4; Plut. *Arist.* 7, *Them.* 22; cf. *Pel.* 4; Arist. *Pol.* 1284a17–22; Walcot (1978) 53–61. Cf. Dem. 20.139–42.

[49] See ch. 6.4–6.6, Dem. 19.102–5 and Aiskhin. 2.139; Finley (1974) 23–4, Finley 118–19.

[50] Dem. 22.25–8; Hansen (1975) 9; cf. Cohen (1983) 51 n. 56.

penalised with a tenfold fine; if convicted by means of an eisangelia, he might be punished with death. In so far as the circumstances of the case allowed a prosecutor an alternative, the readiness to resort to eisangelia may have some significance, though it is clear that in cases of eisangelia bribery was commonly associated with more serious charges which themselves made eisangelia the appropriate process.[51] Perhaps the loss of a severe alternative, as ostracism fell into abeyance in the fourth century, made the way rather more open to capital charges – and capital sentences. In any case, Athenian leaders displayed a spirit of rivalry which was reminiscent of the fierce bitterness with which the aristocratic leaders of the sixth century and the early fifth had vied for power. Though the social origins of political leaders changed considerably in the fifth and fourth centuries, the game continued to be played in a highly competitive spirit. And in the later fifth century, rivalry between leaders was given a sharper edge by the merciless attitude of the demagogoi towards incompetence, not least aristocratic incompetence. In the sixth century, of course, the struggle for political power had been mainly a struggle between the leading figures; in the fifth and fourth centuries, the assertion by the Demos of its political power became increasingly apparent, and the Demos in exercising its sovereignty and in insisting on the 'accountability' of officials and public figures showed little or no mercy for unsuccessful or unpopular leaders. But the Demos should not be regarded as solely responsible for the severity of the penalties imposed. In those penalties we cannot exclude an element of spontaneity on the part of the Demos nor an element of the exploitation of the Demos by political rivals.

Contemporary views on the relationships between the Demos and the political leaders may be exemplified by reference to two Athenians who in their very different ways sought influence and approval – the playwright Aristophanes and the orator Demosthenes. The power, real or apparent, of the Demos was selected by Aristophanes in 424 as the central theme for a comedy. In *The Knights* the playwright personified the Athenian people in the figure of Demos, an old man who appears gullible and easily misled by his slaves. Like demagogues, the Paphlagonian (Kleon) and the new aspirant for Demos' favour, the Sausage-Seller, strive to outbid each other in their attempts to delude Demos with flattery and paltry gifts and so win his favour and make him dependent. Demos admits that he has for long been deceived but also asserts that it was really he who carried off the deception, for he shrewdly watches his slaves plunder and steal and at the end secures their thefts for himself. After a bitter contest in the assembly, Demos is won over by the even greater blandishments of the Sausage-Seller. Then, rejuvenated through the help of his new adviser Agorakritos or Market-Wrangler (alias the Sausage-Seller), Demos comes to realise how old and witless he has become. But now he is revealed once more resplendent as king of the Greeks. The play thus puts the spotlight on the fierce

---

[51] Lys. 21.16, 21, 25; *AP* 54.2; see ch. 5.3.2 and ch. 6.4 for Ergokles.

rivalry among those who sought to win Demos' favour and support and are portrayed as apparently able to fool him as much as they liked.[52] Contrast the positive view of such rivalry as developed by Demosthenes in 355, when he sought to persuade the dikasts to reject Leptines' proposal for abolishing immunities from liturgies or exemptions which had been granted by the Demos as marks of honour. Demosthenes painted a contrast with the types of honours awarded in Sparta, in particular the election of deserving Spartans to the Gerousia which is said to be 'the master (*despotēs*) of the mass of the citizens'. In Athens, 'the Demos is sovereign (*kyrios*)' and, Demosthenes argued, 'the freedom of a democracy is guarded by the rivalry with which good men compete for the rewards offered by the Demos' – crowns, immunities, free maintenance, and similar grants.[53]

7.3 Honour and power

There were, then, rewards as well as hazards for Athenians who aspired to leadership of the polis. For, as Sokrates observed to Glaukon in Xenophon's *Memorabilia*,

if you achieve that objective, you will be able to get whatever you desire, you will have the means of helping your friends, you will lift up the house of your fathers and will exalt your native land, and you will make a name for yourself, first in the polis, then in Greece and perhaps, like Themistokles, also in foreign lands. Wherever you go, you will be a man of mark.

Sokrates then proceeded to cross-examine the young Glaukon – not yet twenty years old, inexperienced but ambitious – and to demonstrate that if he wished to be honoured he must benefit the polis and do good services. In the course of the ensuing discussion, Sokrates suggested that the concerns of the leader were the revenues of the polis, advice about war, the defence of the country, the revenue from the silver mines, the corn supply, and the ability to persuade the Athenians. Fundamental for Sokrates, but regrettably, in Sokrates' view, not for many of those who addressed the assembly, was the need for thorough knowledge in all these matters – in that way a man could win fame and admiration in the polis.[54]

Evidence from the classical period, whether speeches, plays, other literary works or epigraphical documents, leaves little doubt about the strength and the importance of the desire to excel or to be first and so to acquire and maintain honour (*timē*) in a society that was not only highly competitive but also placed great store on reputation or recognition of merit.[55] Whether this was keenly felt

---

[52] See, for example, Ar. *Knights* 710–23, 747–1263, 1325–1408.
[53] Dem. 20.107–8 (Loeb tr. adapted).
[54] Xen. *Mem.* 3.6; see also Arist. *Rh.* 1359b17–1360a37.
[55] Thuc. 2.46, Pl. *Rep.* 361b–363a, Dem. 20.15–17, cf. 22.76, 61.52; Dover 226–36.

by all Athenians is not certain. Aristotle described timē as what the majority (*hoi polloi*) desired, and to judge from the speeches of the Attic Orators, timē and its implications were matters of moment to most Athenians. Elsewhere in the *Nikomakhean Ethics*, Aristotle contrasted the conception of 'the majority and the most vulgar' that the Good is pleasure with the conception of 'men of refinement and affairs' that it is honour. For timē, Aristotle observed, may be said to be the end or goal of political life, though being himself uneasy with this superficial view of the Good, he argued that men's motive in pursuing honour seemed to be to assure themselves of their own merit (*aretē*) and that, therefore, the end of political life might perhaps be held to be arete. In the *Politics*, it is true, Aristotle did not discuss timē extensively, but the notion that timē was virtually the goal of political life would seem to be assumed rather than denied. Certainly his discussion of gain (*kerdos*) and honour as major causes of stasis or factional strife implies that he regarded timē as of fundamental importance in political life and the analysis of it.[56]

At the level of the life of the polis, the marks of timē varied greatly. In its simplest, and in some ways most powerful, expression, timē was intangible and closely related to good report (*phēmē*) and fame or reputation (*doxa*). 'All who are ambitious for public honour', Aiskhines declared, 'believe that it is from pheme that they will win doxa.'[57] Timē might also find tangible expression – not least through honorific decrees. In the course of the fourth century, these tangible marks, which seem to have been comparatively rare or at least more subtle in the fifth century, became more common, though we need not accept all that Aiskhines (or Demosthenes) alleged about the contrast and about the prodigality of his own times in awarding crowns and honours. Nevertheless, while individual responsibility had a long tradition, there does seem to have developed in the fourth century a somewhat greater tendency to attribute good (and bad) outcomes to individuals rather than to the polis of the Athenians at large, and to honour (or punish) individual leaders. And these rewards were offered not only to strategoi and other leading figures, but also to individuals like trierarchs. Thus a gold crown was voted for Demosthenes in 336 and also for the first three trierarchs to have their triremes ready to sail on an expedition to found a colony in the Adriatic in 325.[58] Precedence or seats of honour at the theatre or at other festival gatherings are known from the fifth century on, while the grant of maintenance at public expense in the Hall of the Prytaneis seems to have been a rare honour, at least until about the middle of the fourth century. The latter is known to have been awarded to Kleon after his military success at Pylos in 425, to Iphikrates in 371/0, and (in the 330s) to Diphilos and

---

[56] Arist. *Eth. Nik.* 1159a16–25, 1095b14–31; *Pol.* 1302a31–b18; see also 1283a16–22, *Rh.* 1361a28–b2; cf. de Ste Croix 80, 551 n. 30.

[57] Aiskhin. 1.129.

[58] Aiskhin. 3.177–89, Dem. 23.198; Dem. 18.118–20; Tod 200.170–204 (and 258–63: a gold crown for the Boule and the prytaneis for the supervision of the dispatch of the expedition), *IG* II².1953; cf. Dem. 51.

Demades.[59] Statues, too, were awarded to Diphilos and Demades, but in our period statues were typically granted to military heroes – Konon in the 390s was the first, followed by Timotheos, Khabrias and Iphikrates. Yet to the public figure the most important marks of recognition were election or re-election to the strategia and appointment to major commands, or the goodwill and support of citizens in the assembly and the law-courts and the readiness to accept his proposals or his arguments and to appoint him as an envoy. The cumulative and reiterative effects of such marks of general approval were in themselves important for timē.[60]

Any mark of honour won by the individual was likely to enhance the honour of his family, whatever form it took. Athenians held in high regard, for example, the descendants of those who had achieved prominence in advising the Demos and especially the descendants of those who had served as strategoi. Some honours, moreover, might be inheritable: exemption from liturgies, for example, was granted to Khabrias and his descendants and probably to the descendants of Konon.[61] The third level, honour accruing to Athens, was frequently asserted, but most forcefully in the words of Alkibiades as set out by Thucydides.

It belongs to me more than to others, Athenians, to have command – for I must begin with this, since Nikias has attacked me – and I think, too, that I am worthy of it. For those things for which I am abused bring fame (*doxa*) to my ancestors and myself, and also profit to my country. For the Greeks, who previously hoped that our polis had been exhausted by the war, conceived an idea of its greatness that even transcended its actual power by reason of the magnificence of my display as its representative at the Olympic Games, because I entered seven chariots, a number that no private person had entered before, and won the first prize and the second and the fourth, and provided everything else in a style worthy of my victory. For by general custom such things do indeed mean honour (*timē*), and from what is done men also infer power (*dynamis*). And again, although whatever display I made in the polis, by providing choruses or in any other way, naturally causes jealousy among my fellow townsmen, yet in the eyes of strangers this too gives an impression of strength. And that is no useless folly, when a man by his private expenditure benefits not himself only but also his polis. Nor is it unfair, either, that one who has a high opinion of himself should refuse to be on an equality with others, since he who fares ill finds no one to be an equal participator in his evil plight.[62]

A man's achievements brought not only honour but also power or the impression of power. And implicit in Sokrates' analysis, too, though less immediately obvious, are notions of dynamis – the power to exalt one's native land, but also to control the conduct of affairs and to help one's friends. Traditionally or in public, it would seem, an Athenian would lay claim to

---

[59] Ar. *Knights* 278–83, 573–6, 702, Dem. 20.120, 23.130, Dein. 1.43, 101; M. J. Osborne (1981) 159, 167–8.

[60] Lys. 26.20, Dem. 19.237, 23.197, Dein. 3.12.

[61] Aiskhin. 1.27; Dem. 20.69–72, 75.   [62] Thuc. 6.16.1–3 (Loeb tr. adapted); see Lys. 19.63.

honour rather than assert that he had power. Nevertheless, power was eagerly pursued, and it may well be that for most Athenian leaders honour was largely, or perhaps simply, a means of acquiring power or even a cloak for power, their real objective. In any case, there was a close association between honour and power – the capacity to influence decisions and policies or, in so far as it was possible, to dominate public life. Yet dynamis, especially if it might seem to amount to *dynasteia* (lordship, domination), laid a leader open to suspicions that he was aspiring to tyranny or sole power. Thus Aiskhines sought to bring odium on Demosthenes by speaking of his 'dynasteia' on the eve of the final confrontation with Philip II and representing his opponent as contemptuous of the wishes of the Demos and contemptuous of the democratic institutions in his alleged assertion that he would go as envoy wherever he chose. The influential leader might, of course, help to secure appointments not only for himself but also for his associates, his friends and his relatives. And in a variety of ways, as we have already seen, he could bring his dynamis to bear in assembly debates and in the law-courts: the structure and the operation of the democratic institutions permitted or indeed required the leadership of individuals.[63] The aristocratic traditions of an earlier Athens pointed in the same direction and were adapted to a situation where birth and (to a less extent) inherited wealth were no longer indispensable. A measure of wealth, however acquired, was necessary, but above all individual ability in political skills, speaking, financial management, or in the military field. Power in Athens, in so far as it resided with individuals, resided with rhetores, with strategoi and with financial officials such as the Commissioners of the Festival Fund, not with the other officials of the civil administration. Lot, rotation of office and collegiality had deprived them of any real power.

7.4 Material rewards in public life

To judge from comedy and the orators, there were also material rewards in public life and these might be considerable. It is a commonplace in the orators that men make money out of office (*arkhē*) and out of public life (*politeia*), and Aristophanes' depiction of demagogues like Kleon, bloated with the proceeds of embezzlement and with bribes from allies and foreign states, is well known.[64] Athenians who had dealings with foreigners were particularly vulnerable to charges of corruption, for they lived and operated in societies, especially the monarchies of Persia and Makedonia, where notions of guest-friendship (*xenia*)

---

[63] Aiskhin. 3.145–6; see ch. 6.2.

[64] Lys. 19.57, 25.9, 19, 27.10–11, 30.25, Dem. 3.29, 19.275, [Dem.] 58.35, Aiskhin. 3.173, Dein. 1.41, 77; cf. Lys. 28.9, 29.6, Ar. *Wasps* 669–77, *Plout.* 377–9, 567–70; cf. the typical 'good-old-days' comment of Isok. 12.145–7; Ar. *Knights* 438–44, 824–35, 930–3, 991–6, 1141–50, 1218–26; *APF* 319.

had a strong reciprocal element and embraced the expectation that gifts would be offered to, and accepted by, guests.[65] The offering of *dōra* (gifts) to envoys was therefore to be expected, though the size and purpose of the gift was a critical question. Members of leading families were most likely to have had ties, recently or in the past, with individuals in other states. And for this and other reasons (including the expense and other problems involved in absence as an envoy, despite a travelling allowance), Dikaiopolis was probably reflecting a real-life tendency in appointments of envoys when he complained in *The Akharnians* that such appointments went to members of leading families, not to ordinary citizens.[66] In general, service abroad on behalf of Athens presented opportunities and dangers: Timarkhos, for example, was alleged by Aiskhines to have bought the governorship of Andros for half a talent and exploited this ally of Athens, and to have embezzled funds when sent out as an inspector of the mercenary troops at Eretria.[67]

One of the common charges brought against officials was embezzlement of public funds, and in one of his speeches Lysias commented on the readiness with which some people claimed that a man had made many talents out of office. He cited the example of Diotimos, a strategos in 388/7. It had been alleged in the assembly that he had received forty talents more from shipmasters and merchants in return for protecting them than he himself admitted. Those allegations, Lysias noted, were made when Diotimos was serving abroad, but on his return the sykophantai were not ready to put the matter to the proof in the courts. Lysias quoted other examples and somewhat disingenuously argued that a man's estate refuted allegations of making money out of office.

You all know that Kleophon for many years had all the affairs of the polis in his hands and was expected to have got a great deal from his office, but when he died this money was nowhere to be found, but his relatives, both by blood and by marriage, to whom he would have left it, are admittedly poor (*penētes*).

And perhaps even more surprising, Lysias cited the case of the (extravagant) Alkibiades who 'left a smaller fortune to his children than he had inherited himself from his guardians'.[68]

The Orators are also full of allegations of bribery (*dōrodokia*), and at every level in Athenian life. We have already considered the charges of the corruption of dikasts and of deme officials.[69] Writing *c.* 430, the Old Oligarch noted that 'some people say that if a man has money in his hand when he approaches the Boule or the Demos, his business will be dealt with', and he agreed that much

---

[65] Dem. 19.166–7; cf. 18.50–2, 109, 284, 19.138–40; cf. Harvey (1985) 105–7; Perlman (1976) 224–6.

[66] Ar. *Akh.* 609–17 (cf. 65–7, 90), Dem. 19.158, Tod 129.10–13, *IG* ii².264.9–15, Adcock and Mosley (1975) 155–6; Dem. 24.112; Bonner 21, Perlman (1976) 223–33; see ch. 6.5 for the prosecution of envoys in 392 and 367.

[67] Aiskhin. 1.107, 113; cf. Tod 152 for the conduct of Androtion.

[68] Lys. 19.48–52 (Loeb tr. adapted). [69] See ch. 3.1, 3.5.

could be negotiated for money in Athens, though with uncharacteristic restraint he did not make much of this. Bribery, after all, was not unique to Athens, and Spartan leaders in particular could hardly be held up as models of incorruptibility. Nevertheless, it can hardly be denied that small inducements to prytaneis might well have proved effective in getting a matter aired, and more likely with sympathy at that.[70] Allegations of corruption were also commonly levelled at the leading public figures: the strategoi and the rhetores. There seems indeed to have been a certain readiness to explain the unpalatable failure of a military enterprise by attributing it to dorodokia and prodosia on the part of the strategoi, not to other factors.[71]

The assessment of charges of embezzlement and bribery is fraught with difficulty and has evoked marked differences of opinion.[72] In his study of the Lot in Athens, for example, Headlam tended to minimise the extent of corruption in Athens: he argued that the use of the Lot helped restrict corruption. He suggested, furthermore, that in societies where corruption is rampant among those who rule, it rarely becomes a matter of public knowledge and concern, and while accepting that there was a good deal of petty dishonesty, he argued with some plausibility that corruption was petty in character, because the high number and high turnover of officials (arising from the principles of collegiality and limited tenure) worked with the use of the Lot to create a very different situation from an entrenched bureaucracy.[73] But strategoi were hardly handicapped in this way and it was very largely against them and against rhetores and (elected) envoys that the more serious charges were made. Strict accounting of the spoils of war and protection money was likely to be difficult – a fact which also greatly facilitated allegations of irregularity.[74] A man's opponents might make allegations and even go so far as to procure witnesses, while the activity of sykophantai could also result in a leader being threatened or confronted with false charges of embezzlement and bribery. Bribery, in particular, being usually clandestine, was very hard to disprove – or to prove. There are very few instances in the surviving speeches of the actual appearance of witnesses in bribery cases, while in any case the appearance of witnesses, who were not subject to cross-examination, is of limited value to us in attempting to determine guilt.[75] Nor is the occasional report of a verdict of as much value as

---

70 [Xen.] *AP* 3.3; Ar. *Peace* 905–8 (and scholiast), *Thesm.* 936–8, *Frogs* 361–2, Lys. 21.16, 21, 28.9, Aiskhin. 1.107. For Sparta, see Thuc. 1.131, 2.21, 5.16, D.S. 13.106.8–10, Arist. *Pol.* 1270b6–13, 1271a3–6.

71 Ar. *Knights* 834–5, *Plout.* 377–9, 567–70, Dein. 3.2; Thuc. 4.65.3, 7.48; see ch. 6.4.

72 For three recent discussions see Wankel (1982) 29–53, MacDowell (1983) 57–78 and Harvey (1985) 76–117 (and 76 n. 4 for bibliography).

73 Headlam 175–7; see *AP* 54.2, 55.5, Dem. 24.112, 123; Cohen (1983) 49–51.

74 Thuc. 6.12.2, 15.2, [Andok.] 4.30–1; Pritchett 1.83–92, 2.126–32.

75 Cf. [Dem.] 58.32–3; for witnesses, see Lys. 27.3–4, Aiskhin 1.86–8, 114–15, 2.154–5 (a witness who according to Aiskhines had rejected Demosthenes' attempt to bribe him to give false testimony against Aiskhines), Dem. 21.104, 107 (a speech that was never delivered). Cf. Dem. 30.37 for the notion that free men may give false testimony but that the evidence of slaves (given under torture) is reliable; MacDowell 242–7.

might be expected. Demosthenes' report of a fine of 50 talents imposed on Kallias for bribery over a century earlier, for example, has geen generally rejected by scholars. A conviction, moreover, does not necessarily prove bribery, because commonly, as in the case of Ergokles, a bribery charge was associated with other charges, and in any case verdicts were likely to be in part at least political judgements; while an acquittal might simply mean that the dikasts had accepted the argument that a defendant's past services to Athens should induce them not to entertain charges of bribery (or embezzlement).[76]

Allegations of bribery and embezzlement, not infrequently supplemented by claims of extravagance and loose-living, were a standard element in political abuse. Typical is a long string of allegations by Deinarkhos against Demosthenes – based on the proposition 'are there any decrees or laws for which he has not received money?' but offering no witnesses. With regard to Demosthenes' trierarchic law of 340, Deinarkhos invited any of the Three Hundred made responsible for trierarchic service by the law to tell their juror neighbours about Demosthenes' bribery, and for the rest he asked rhetorically 'is there any need to call witnesses?' Nor should we uncritically accept Demosthenes' deduction of bribery from a leader's change of policy or a change in his material fortunes.[77] Allowance must therefore be made for exaggeration and invention in these allegations. Such allegations, moreover, appear to have been a conventional means of attacking leaders whose conduct was felt to be, or could be represented as being, culpable in any way. Consider the three strategoi who in 424 made peace with the Sikeliot cities and returned to an Athens which had, in their absence, become sanguinely optimistic after the success at Pylos. It was not difficult then to believe that the generals should not have made peace and to entertain the charges (as reported by Thucydides) that they had taken bribes to depart from Sicily when they could have subdued it. The strategoi may well have accepted dora from the Sikeliot allies but perhaps there was more to it. It is, however, interesting that, for whatever reasons, Eurymedon was fined, while Pythodoros and Sophokles were punished with exile, and, further, that this conviction did not cause irreparable damage to Eurymedon's career. For he is known to have been elected general again for 413/12 (and possibly for 414/13), though there is no evidence that his two colleagues were elected as generals again.[78]

Despite all the uncertainties, it is likely that it was not rare for political 'gifts' to be offered and accepted and for misappropriation of public funds to occur. 'Gifts' appear to have been a recognised element in public life, though it should be added that a reputation for incorruptibility was highly prized in Athens. Further, Thucydides' comment that among the Odrysian Thracians it was

---

[76] Dem. 19.273–5, *APF* 261, Harvey (1985) 96–8 and n. 70; Lys. 28.1, 29.2; Lys. 21.16, 21; see ch. 6.6 for the findings of the Areiopagos and the jury verdicts in the Harpalos affair.

[77] Dein. 1.41–7; Dem. 19.9–10, 114, 119–20; cf. Webster (1970) 26–31.

[78] Thuc. 4.65.3, 7.16.2 (and *HCT*); Westlake (1969) 118–22 and n. 67; cf. Pritchett 2.128.

impossible to get anything done without gifts would seem to imply that things were somewhat different in the Greek poleis.[79] In a strict legal sense, if Demosthenes is to be believed, Athenian law forbade the acceptance of dora absolutely. Yet the orator could not conceal the fact that the Athenians might adopt a lenient attitude, though there was general agreement, Demosthenes argued, that it was scandalous and deserving of deep anger to accept anything for acts which would harm the polis. Moreover, for all his misdeeds as an envoy in 346, Aiskhines accepted what Demosthenes described as gifts (*dōra*) *and* fees or pay (*misthoi*), clearly implying that misthoi were reprehensible. Wilful deceit of the Athenians was thus alleged by Demosthenes against Aiskhines in 343 in regard to the embassy to Philip II of 346. He declared that he was so reluctant to play the sykophantes that he would acquit Aiskhines and advise the jury to do the same, if his blunders were due to stupidity or naivety or any other sort of ignorance. Demosthenes added, nevertheless, that 'no man is required or compelled by you to undertake public business . . . If a man succeeds he will be honoured, and so far will gain an advantage over ordinary people; but if he fails, will he put forward pretexts and excuses?' 'But', Demosthenes went on, 'if Aiskhines through villainy accepted money (*argyrion*) and dora, and if that is clearly proved from the facts of the case, put him to death if possible, or, failing that, make him a living example to the rest.' This was not a case of Aiskhines being deceived by Philip, he argued, but of having sold himself and wilfully deceived the Athenians, of having betrayed them to Philip.[80]

In a society where guest-friendship involved the offering and acceptance of dora, it might well seem realistic not to enforce the prohibition on dora rigorously. But what of the difficult (and usually subjective) question whether the acceptance of the dora brought harm to the polis?[81] Hypereides sought to distinguish private individuals to whom Harpalos gave money for safe-keeping, from strategoi and rhetores who took it with some policy in view. According to Hypereides, the laws prescribed repayment of the simple amount for 'wrongdoers' but a tenfold fine for those who accepted bribes. Yet even with strategoi and rhetores, he added, 'through your tolerance and generosity you willingly allow them to reap substantial benefits – with one proviso, that what is received will be used to further your interests, not oppose them'. The proviso about detriment was apparently part of the law governing eisangeliai, and if a rhetor or a strategos was induced by money to act against the best interests of the Demos – to give advice in the assembly or in other bodies that was contrary to the interests of the Athenian people, or as a strategos or envoy

---

[79] *AP* 25.1 (and *CAAP*); Thuc. 2.65, Plut. *Per.* 16; Plut. *Phok.* 18, 30; see IG II².223A.4–5, 11–13, 457B.13; Thuc. 2.97.3–4.

[80] Dem. 19.7–8 (cf. 119), 102–10 (Loeb tr. adapted). See Dem. 24.192–3 on laws relating to private life and public life.

[81] The 'law' included in the manuscripts at Dem. 21.113 refers to bribery to the detriment of any individual citizen (as well as to the detriment of the Demos).

or in any official capacity to act against those interests – he could, as we have seen, be impeached.[82]

While there are no secure grounds for determining the validity of Demosthenes' charges of corruption against Aiskhines, it should be noted that thirteen years later in his speech *On the Crown*, Demosthenes went much further and blamed corruption for everything to do with the Peace of Philokrates and its results. Particularly but not only with the passage of time, bribery allegations could be made.[83] It may also be observed that money received by an Athenian leader from a foreign power was likely to have a double purpose – to encourage the Athenian by personal profit in his pursuit of a particular policy and to provide support for effective action. In most cases, too, it is likely that Athenian leaders were paid rather than bought – that is, the foreign money encouraged or enabled a policy or line of action which they already believed was in the best interests of themselves (and their political associates) or their country. And political leaders perhaps have a greater propensity than other individuals to identify these two interests completely. In 397 Epikrates and Kephalos and their supporters were already advocating anti-Spartan policies when the Rhodian Timokrates visited Athens. The Persian gold which was passed to Epikrates and Kephalos (and to political leaders in Thebes, Corinth and Argos) by Timokrates did not cause the hostility of these states or these leaders to Sparta, but it did encourage the hostility and helped it to take concrete form in the anti-Spartan coalition of 395.[84] Some Athenians in the 340s may have been induced by Philip's money to change their policies, but the attitudes of Aiskhines and others may be explained on the assumption that at times they took a very different view from Demosthenes of how Athens' interests were best served, just as leaders in Peloponnesian states might well believe, and not for traitorous reasons, that good relations with Philip rather than with Athens were in the interests of their states and that to accept assistance from Philip was justified.[85]

In the *Politics* Aristotle argued that it was important in every type of constitution that the legal, administrative and financial arrangements be such that office-holding was not a source of profit. In his elaboration of this, Aristotle discussed only embezzlement, and we are left with the impression here and elsewhere that he regarded bribery as a less serious matter for the well-being of a state than embezzlement. Aristotle was fully aware of the impact of bribery, but he seems to have regarded it as less serious in a democracy: he cited, for example, the venality of Spartan ephors and members of the Gerousia, and he argued that it was more difficult to corrupt the multitude (*plēthos*) than the few (though he also believed the poor were vulnerable) and that limited tenure of high office

---

[82] Hyp. 5.2, 24–5, Dein. 1.13, 2.22, 3.2, [Demades] 21, Dem. 19.293–5, 21.113; Lys. 21.22; see ch. 6.6.
[83] Dem. 18.20–49; see also Perlman (1976) 228–33 (see ch. 6 nn. 79–80).
[84] *Hell. Oxy.* 7.2, Paus. 3.9.8 (but cf. Xen. *Hell.* 3.5.2); Adcock and Mosley (1975) 67.
[85] Polyb. 18.14, cf. D.S. 16.54; Cawkwell (1963B) 204–5.

checked corruption. Perhaps he felt that bribery, whether or not he believed it was pervasive in a democracy, was a less destabilising factor than misappropriation of public funds for private gain. And, unless he had a blind spot about 'gifts' from Makedonian kings, his attitude would seem to suggest that the orators indulged in considerable exaggeration when they depicted the bribery of Athenian leaders as common and damaging.[86]

On a charge of embezzlement Melanopos is said by Demosthenes to have received a tenfold fine. Lysias, rightly or for the sake of his argument, maintained that it was because of his misappropriation of public funds that Ergokles (who was charged with prodosia, embezzlement and bribery) was condemned to death.[87] It is also probable that wild or exaggerated allegations about embezzlement were common in Athens. That, as we have seen, was the line of argument adopted by Lysias in one case. Yet the failure to pursue in the law-courts the allegations made in the assembly does not of itself prove Diotimos' innocence: evidence or proof may have been difficult to obtain, particularly if Diotimos had been careful to share some of the protection money. Perhaps Diotimos did quite well personally out of his year as strategos – and certainly the risks were high as his colleague Dionysios discovered when he was sentenced to death or fined heavily for betraying the Thracian Khersonesos.[88]

The question of 'making money in office and in public life' may perhaps be viewed in different ways. It was easy for men of inherited wealth, some of whom were perhaps practised in the use of older, more subtle methods of bringing influence to bear, to accuse others of accepting 'gifts' (*dōrodokia*) and embezzlement, and without some resources, inherited or acquired, it was extremely difficult for a citizen to devote most of his time to public affairs.[89] Men of poor family were thus particularly vulnerable to charges of embezzlement and bribery, and in the case of some – Demades for example – the material rewards of office would seem to have been considerable. Men from non-traditional backgrounds – especially the so-called demagogues such as Kleon – were also commonly the objects of such charges, but in the case of Kleon (and others) there would seem to be little doubt that they came from a background of reasonable wealth.[90] Men of wealth presumably did not require such perks to commit themselves more or less full-time to public life, but that does not mean they declined such perks. Deinarkhos, in his prosecution of Philokles, made a point of the fact that he had much property and no male heirs and yet had accepted bribes, while the well-to-do Demosthenes was accused by his

[86] Arist. *Pol.* 1270b6–13, 1270b35–1271a6, 1286a31–41, 1308b10–16, 1308b31–1309a25; Harvey (1985) 99.
[87] Dem. 24.127, Lys. 28.2, 29.2; Lys. 27.3; see Aiskhin. 1.56.
[88] Dem. 19.180.
[89] Xen. *Hell.* 2.3.48, *Mem.* 2.3.16, Arist. *Pol.* 1308b31–1309a20; Tuplin (1985) 370 and n. 76.
[90] Isok. 21.5, Dem. 29.22, Plut. *Phok.* 30; APF 100, 319, Connor 151–2.

opponents of corruption.[91] For a poor man – one who depended on his own labour or efforts for a living – some material benefits were necessary to maintain an active part in the public life of the polis. Such benefits, however, did *not* begin in the period of the emerging democracy, but may be traced back to the aristocratic leaders of archaic Greece. The vast increase in evidence for, or rather allegations of, bribery in the fourth century is to be traced to a general increase in evidence, and in particular in the 'evidence' of orators (as opposed especially to the early fifth century), rather than to a decline in the standards of public life. There seems little reason to accept without considerable reservations the typical 'good-old-days' comments of Isokrates or his contemporaries.[92] By countenancing such benefits or taking over earlier aristocratic attitudes to them, the Athenian Demos also gave an opportunity to men like Iphikrates to employ their military talents and thus to escape from poverty and satisfy their ambition to succeed. Through booty and foreign service Iphikrates acquired wealth: his son Menestheus is known to have been liable for trierarchic service.[93] Rhetores, too, had opportunities to advance their socio-economic position. Receiving no salary or misthos from the polis, some rhetores at least needed such opportunities in order to participate fully in public life. Hypereides and others may have largely sustained such participation by inherited wealth supplemented by other means, such as fees from speech-writing. However, while professional speech-writing may have assisted them in building up a reputation and in entering into public life, the receipt of misthos for speech-writing was not very highly regarded.[94] For all public figures, therefore, the maintenance or the acquisition of property power was important – in order to have the leisure for participation but also to use wealth for political purposes. Wealth represented, for most Athenian public figures, the opportunity for satisfying social–personal and political needs rather than the means of expanding their economic potential. The latter, no doubt, interested some Athenians – those, for example, who acquired slaves to be hired out, especially for working in the silver mines, and those who lent money for bottomry loans. But for most political leaders, wealth seems to have been a symbol of honour and power and a means of power and influence.[95]

7.5 Political networks

While there were opportunities for material rewards from public life, honour and power were for most Athenian public figures the important benefits of

[91] Dein. 3.18; Dein. 1.41–7, Aiskhin. 3.103–5 (but cf. Brunt (1969) 254–5); Dem. 21.215–16; *APF* 133–5, Cawkwell (1969) 176–7.
[92] Isok. 12.145–7, Dem. 9.36–49, 19.271–7, Aiskhin. 3.257–9, Dein. 1.37–40, 2.15–17, 24–6.
[93] Dem. 21.62; *APF* 250–1.
[94] Ar. *Plout.* 377–9, 567–70; Hyp. 3 (*Against Athenogenes*), 4.28; *APF* 518–19; Pl. *Phdr.* 257c–d, Aiskhin. 2.180, 3.173, Dem. 19.246, Hyp. 3.3, Dover (1968) 155–9.
[95] Finley (1951) 83–7 and (1981) 67–73, Humphreys (1970) 17–22; Xen. *Oik.* 14.10, Dem. 21.158–9, Arist. *Pol.* 1284a19–22.

leadership. And 'those in power' or 'the powerful' (*dynatoi*), influential rhetores or successful strategoi, were well placed to do in superior fashion what all Athenians expected to do – help their friends and harm their enemies. And this was the essential basis of the political networks in Athenian life.[96] The mutual assistance of leaders and close supporters displayed itself in the various ways that were examined in the last chapter, and not simply in the distribution of any material benefits.

The individual or personal relationships within these networks were central to them. In the mid-fifth century the nuclei of these relationships tended to be family and marriage ties, and though the importance of these diminished in the later fifth century and the fourth, they continued to play a varied role. Beyond these circles aspiring leaders would seek support in their own deme and beyond. At all times and especially in the latter period, such wider ties of friendship and support were the most important element in political networks. As the individual extended the basis of his support, vertical alignments were likely to become more important than horizontal dimensions. 'Abundance of friends' was rightly regarded by Aristotle as one of the key elements in dynamis.[97] Without the support, direct or indirect, of men with meagre or modest resources, the support of wealthy or powerful individuals, relatively few in number, was of limited value. And from the small meeting of the deme to the mass meeting on the Pnyx, the individual was prominent and the networks of support, based on the interaction of various factors, were fundamentally personal.

Support for a public figure was related not only to his ability, experience and influence, but also to his attitudes and policies. It was thus closely bound up with, and dependent on, perceptions of self-interests, perceptions of sectional or class interests, and perceptions of Athenian interests. And while in the fifth century leaders to some extent were supported or gave support on the basis of political or ideological views, after the excesses of 404/3 oligarchy was largely discredited and ceased to be a serious alternative in practical politics.[98] Mutual support might also have some relationship to class or sectional interests. The men of property, for example, are commonly represented as having different attitudes from the poor – in particular as being disposed to favour peace and thus minimise the burdens of the trierarchy and property tax, with the poor anxious for employment in the triremes.[99] In reality, the situation was more complex. While the poor may have had some interest in naval activity in the days of the Athenian Empire when pay was readily available, it was hardly true

---

[96] Lys. 9.13, 14.21, Pl. *Rep.* 362b, *Men.* 41e, Xen. *Mem.* 2.4.6, 2.6.25, 3.7.9, Connor 35–47, Dover 180–4, 304–6, Finley 51.

[97] Arist. *Pol.* 1284a19–22; see Connor, especially 3–84, 134–6; Whitehead 231–4, 305–26; see ch. 2.3 and ch. 6.3.　　[98] Cf. Lys. 25.8–10.

[99] For the relationship of political attitudes and groupings to economic factors, see for example Arist. *Pol.* 1297b6–12, *Hell. Oxy.* 6.2–3, D.S. 18.10, Perlman (1963) 336–40, Finley (1973) 48–9, (1974) and Finley 9–11, Austin and Vidal-Naquet (1977) 3–26, de Ste Croix 69–80, 91–6, 283–93, especially 290.

in the fourth century. Moreover, even in the fifth century, the farmers were said to be disposed towards peace because of the vulnerability of their lands to enemy invasion. Such fears cut across economic divisions and the poor farmer eking out an existence on his ancestral land would not be likely to favour war and its disruption.[100] Even the urban poor who are often accused of sabre-rattling would have found little benefit in war in the fourth century, and it must be recognised that it was particularly strategoi (who tended to be well-to-do) that would win honour and other benefits from war, and that the upper classes as well as the poor benefited from the fifth-century empire. Moreover, as we have argued earlier, Athenians did not conceive their attitudes on foreign or defence policies purely, or even predominantly, in economic terms.[101]

7.6 The harnessing of 'ambition'

Sokrates' comments to Glaukon reflected the view that honour in the polis derived from good services done for the polis. Yet the pursuit of honour as part of the ethos of aristocratic competition was a highly individualistic thing and this pursuit might, and sometimes did, conflict with the interests of the polis (and, for that matter, with the interests of the family). Indeed, the nature and desirability of *philotimia* (love of honour) was a matter for debate about the middle of the fifth century and continued so into the fourth. Just as the activity was not of itself necessarily good in the context of the community, so the word *philotimia* seems to have been ambiguous. The term could carry a pejorative connotation similar to that of the word often used to translate it, 'ambition', and this connotation is frequently found in contemporary writers. The deleterious effects of philotimia, whether because it was excessive, selfish or misdirected, or involved unacceptable means, are clearly stated in Thucydides' analysis of the policies of Perikles' successors.

In matters that apparently had no connection with the war the Athenians were led by private ambitions (*philotimiai*) and private interests to adopt policies which were bad both for themselves and for their allies; for these policies, so long as they were successful, merely brought honour or profit to individuals, but when they failed proved detrimental to the state in the conduct of the war.[102]

In the fifth and fourth centuries the Athenians (and other Greeks) seem to have endeavoured to subordinate the pursuit of timē to the interests of the polis or to harness it, and in particular the financial outlays involved, for the benefit of

---

[100] [Dem.] 50.6, 11–13, Dem. 51.11, see ch. 3.3; [Xen.] *AP* 2.14, Ar. *Peace* 551–9, *Ekkl.* 197–8.
[101] Thuc. 8.48.6; Finley (1978) 115–17, 121–4, de Ste Croix 604 n. 27; see ch. 3.3.
[102] Thuc. 2.65.7 (Loeb tr. adapted); see 3.82.8, 8.89.3; Pind. fr. 198; Eur. *Phoin.* 531–67, Lys. 14.21, Dem. 8.71.

the polis.[103] A deliberate attempt by the Athenians to democratise the concept of philotimia by defining it in terms of their collective profit may be discerned in the second half of the fifth century. The Old Oligarch, at any rate, perceived the trierarchy, the khoregia and other liturgies as the rich paying for the entertainment and support of the lower classes (*dēmos*), and the clear implication is that at least some Athenians as early as *c.* 430 felt that philotimia had already been democratised.[104] Demosthenes enunciated the orthodox public view of his own time when, with pride or indeed boasting, he told the dikasts in 330:

> When I came of age, I was in a position to provide a chorus, to undertake the trierarchy, to pay property-tax. I renounced no ambitions (*philotimiai*), either private or public, but sought to be useful to the polis and my friends. When I decided to engage in public affairs, the policies which I chose were such that I was frequently honoured with a crown both by my own country and by many other Greeks.[105]

The notion of reciprocity was clearly bound up in the concept of philotimia. One of Demosthenes' major objections to Leptines' proposal to abolish all immunities from liturgies (except for the descendants of the tyrannicides) and to make them illegal for the future was:

> you deprive the Demos of those who might seek after honour [or, in Vince's translation, would-be patriots] by proclaiming unmistakably that those who confer any benefit will gain no advantage from it.

> The result of honouring too many citizens is to encourage many to do you good service, but the result of not honouring any one, even if he is deserving, is to discourage all from emulation [or seeking after honour].[106]

About the middle of the fourth century philotimia, expressed as an abstract quality or by the use of adverbial phrases, seems to have emerged as the 'fashionable' quality in honorific decrees. These decrees, whether granting a crown or other marks of honour, made some reference to the services of the honoured citizen (or non-citizen). In the fifth century the statements typically had been brief and matter-of-fact; about the middle of the fourth century they became increasingly verbose. Over time other changes had occurred – both in regard to the services or qualities singled out for mention and in regard to a tendency towards abstract formulation. Thus the decrees moved from the simple statement (typical of the fifth and early fourth centuries) that *A* and *B* are

---

[103] Thuc. 2.44.4, Lys. 16.18–20; Whitehead (1983) 56–60. Honorific decrees underline the continued importance of liturgies and other services at deme and tribal level and their role in pursuit of honour and support: see Whitehead 241–52.

[104] [Xen.] *AP* 1.13; see Demokr. fr. 255; cf. Whitehead (1983) 59–64 who would date the democratisation of philotimia to the fourth century and finds in Thuc. 2.44.4 an embryonic stage in this development.

[105] Dem. 18.257; cf. 258–64 on Aiskhines; Lys. 26.3; Aiskhin. 1.11; Dover 230–6.

[106] Dem. 20.5, 103 (Loeb tr. adapted); see Lys. 21.22–5, Isok. 18.58–63, Isai. 7.35–6, Dem. 20.69, 42.25 ('useful and *philotimos* with his property and his person'), Arist. *Rh.* 1361a28–b2.

'good men (*andres agathoi*) in their dealings with the Demos of the Athenians', to an abstract formulation of the idea − *A* and *B* are rewarded 'for their *andragathia*'.[107] The philotimia decrees of the mid-fourth century specified, perhaps from the outset as a regular element, though in varied forms, that the decree would fulfil the important role of encouraging others to emulate the example of philotimia and of recording the readiness of the Demos to return favours.[108] This specific reference to philotimia as such and the encouragement of it are first securely attested in honorific decrees in the 340s and may well have originated about that time. If so, it would seem more than coincidence that it developed in the mid-fourth century. The expense involved in full-time participation in public life or in liturgies and other services to the polis may well have been more difficult to sustain in the fourth century with reduced opportunities for material rewards abroad and diminished prosperity as is clear from Xenophon's *Poroi*. The individual benefits of personal performance of the trierarchy in particular had largely evaporated and there were acute problems which led to the reforms of Periandros in 357.[109] This, the most expensive of the liturgies, had become rather anonymous, like the payment of property tax. And in general, the outlays on competitions, sacrifices and other forms of liturgical activity had probably come increasingly to be seen as a propitiatory offering to the poor to avert hostility, rather than a claim to honour.[110] It would seem, and not surprisingly, that the importance of philotimia and the notion of reciprocity were consciously or self-consciously emphasised when serious doubts had arisen among the well-to-do whether love of honour expressed in benefits to the polis still brought fitting rewards.

---

[107] *IG* II².223A.11–14, 300.2–5; see the navy lists for the first known triremes with the names Andragathia (*IG* II².1604.37 – the first extant list in the fourth-century series and dating to 377/6) and Philotimia (II².1611.242 – the list of 357/6); Whitehead (1983) 60–70; Tod 133.21–2, 30; Isok. 15.93–4; Dover 164.

[108] Whitehead (1983) 62–4.   [109] See ch. 3.4; see Davies 88–90.

[110] See the complaints in Isok. 8.128 (cf. 15.159–60) and Humphreys (1970) 12–13.

8 The critics of Athenian democracy

8.1 Factors in the extent of participation

In the course of the years from the introduction of jury pay in the middle of the fifth century to the overthrow of democracy in 322, participation became one of the hallmarks of Athenian democracy. It is, however, important to consider not only the degree but also the cost and the consequences of participation. Some factors encouraged the participation of citizens, others impeded it. And there was a cost; indeed, the Athenians have been charged with financing their own participation by exploiting their slaves and the subject states of the Athenian empire. Further, the consequences of participation have been viewed differently by the critics of Athenian democracy. Participation, for example, encouraged citizens, according to some, to be meddlesome; others have seen it as promoting a generally stable society.

'The majority of you do not exercise your right to speak.' This criticism was levelled not only against members of the Boule but also against citizens in the assembly, even though many ordinary Athenians, as we have seen, did accept the herald's invitation: 'Who wishes to speak?'[1] Not all citizens were eager to play an active role in public life at the level of the polis, nor even a passive role. Some were primarily interested in their own private affairs – farmers, for example, preoccupied with eking out an existence or simply wanting to farm and, like the farmer depicted in Aristophanes' *Georgoi (Farmers)*, 'willing to pay 1,000 drakhmai (!) if you let me off office', while many men of property are not known for any public activity beyond the performance of liturgies, and appear to be nonentities.[2] For some the affairs of their own deme continued to be all-absorbing, and a leading role in such activity was not necessarily a step on the road to prominence in the polis.[3] Individual and family circumstances and preferences would have been major determinants in attitudes towards participation in public life throughout our period.

Yet, even within families which had been strongly apolitical or, for that matter, strongly political, the tendency might be reversed. Iphikrates emerged from humble origins to become a very prominent Athenian, albeit as a military commander, while in later generations Demades and probably Aiskhines came

[1] Dem. 22.30, 36; see ch. 5.1 and ch. 6.2.
[2] Ar. *Georgoi* fr. 1.   [3] R. Osborne 88–9, Whitehead 305–26.

from poor families. Plato's uncle Kharmides who reached manhood *c.* 432, a few years before Plato's birth, was depicted by Xenophon as reluctant to enter public life because of his diffidence in addressing the mass assembly.[4] Plato's decision not to engage in public life despite a strong family tradition of involvement would seem to indicate something different and more general – a tendency among prominent families, in the years after the restoration of democracy in 403, to pursue private interests because of disenchantment with the conduct of public affairs. In part this may be attributed to the emergence in the previous thirty years of men like Kleon and Kleophon, challenging – successfully – the political leadership of the older families. In the two decades after Perikles' death, the implications of popular sovereignty, which had to some extent been obscured by Perikles' strong leadership in the 430s, became apparent, and many well-to-do citizens who had previously been content to work within, or 'use', the democratic system, felt a sense of alienation.[5] Oligarchy was tried as an alternative system of government, but the excesses of the oligarchic regimes of 411 and 404 destroyed the possibility of another resort to oligarchy in Athens. Again, the Demos' treatment of Athenian leaders such as the Arginousai generals may have disturbed the expectations of well-to-do Athenians. That men of ability may have been deterred from aspiring to leadership by the severe penalties imposed on leaders in Athens in these years, or at other times in the fourth century, cannot be denied. But analysts of Athenian democracy may be prone to exaggerate this, losing sight of the penalties imposed in earlier generations on unsuccessful leaders like Miltiades or the severity inherent in ostracism.[6] In so far as there was a tendency among members of prominent families to abstain from public life, it is to be traced in large measure to the leading role in the oligarchy of 404/3 of men like Plato's relatives Kritias and Kharmides. In 403 both had died fighting at Mounikhia against the democrats under Thrasyboulos. Whatever other considerations influenced Plato's decision not to engage in public life, the deadweight of his relatives' political record made any other decision very unlikely, while he himself, aged 28 at the time of Sokrates' condemnation in 399, clearly felt disillusioned and helpless. Indignant at the Thirty's attempt to involve Sokrates in their illegal actions against fellow citizens, Plato had, on the restoration of democracy, again been moved, though less strongly, to engage in public life. So he declared in a letter written some fifty years later, in which he also acknowledged the general moderation of the democratic exiles on their return. He was shaken, however, by the judicial attack on Sokrates, and his view of the men then conducting affairs and their methods convinced him of the difficulty of managing public affairs 'well'. In practical terms he recognised that it was impossible to engage in public life without friends and trusty companions (*hetairoi*). Those whom Plato could have enlisted would hardly have been active

---

[4] Xen. *Mem.* 3.7.
[5] See ch. 2.3.2 and Connor 175–94.   [6] See Knox (1985) 151–2.

in public life, while he would have found few or no supporters among those active in the restored democracy.[7] In this Plato would not have been unique. And it would seem that it was the lack of support for their political views and their recognition of this and other factors rather than fear of ruthlessness on the part of the Demos that determined the attitudes of men from the old families to active participation in public life.

For all its stress on equality of political rights, the Athenian democracy encompassed in practice various inequalities or impediments to participation. The greatest impediment was, for many Athenians, lack of leisure and lack of resources to enable a man to devote serious attention to public affairs. At deme level, if we may believe Euxitheos' admissions that his family was (or had been) 'poor', a man from a poor family might undertake the office of demarch, though the general impression from the limited evidence available is that demarchs tended to be men of moderate, but not great, wealth.[8] Nor were the poor necessarily denied the opportunity of holding office at polis level: whether for corrupt or honourable reasons, a well-to-do citizen gave financial support to a citizen of respectable but impoverished family to undertake the position of basileus.[9] The office of basileus, however, lasted for but one year and could not be renewed. A serious aspirant to leadership in Athens would seek rather to become a strategos or establish his reputation as a rhetor in the assembly and the law-courts. Active participation over a number of years was essential, and for that resources, inherited or acquired, were needed.

Associated with his family's economic circumstances were an Athenian's education and his experience, gained formally and informally and varying with the standing of his family. Some tuition in the art of persuasion from the professional sophists and teachers would be very useful for leadership ambitions in a polis where persuasion in public situations was central to the processes of decision-making. A poor family, however, could not afford the high fees demanded by sophists like Prodikos of Keos, the contemporary of Sokrates, nor even the fees charged by less distinguished men. In the fourth century Athenian fathers probably paid 1,000 drakhmai to Isokrates for tuition at his school of rhetoric, which over the years attracted about 100 pupils; that was the sum paid by a foreigner from Phaselis, though there was a tradition that Isokrates never *demanded* fees from a fellow citizen.[10] The inequality of wealth in Athens was thus strongly reinforced by the inequality of the poor in regard to formal and informal education. These associated inequalities were perhaps the most marked of the inequalities in democratic Athens and severely limited the potential of poorer men.

This is not to say that only those with a high level of formal education were effective as speakers. A countryman might intervene all the more effectively

---

[7] Pl. *Ep.* 7.324b–326b.
[8] Dem. 57.25, 35–6, 45, 52; R. Osborne 84–5.
[9] [Dem.] 59.72; see ch. 5.1 and n. 13.
[10] Dem. 35.15, 42; [Plut.] *Mor.* 837d–e, 838e–f.

because he rarely did so or because he spoke simply and directly.[11] For there was in Athens a suspicion of 'clever' speakers and it was common to seek to stir up prejudice against an opponent by warning the assembly or the court not to be misled by clever arguments. At the assembly convened to reconsider the punishment of the rebel Mytilenaians in 427, Kleon warned against the speaker who, 'confident in his ability as an orator, would struggle to prove that what had been finally agreed had not been decided, or, being bribed, would compose an elaborate speech and try to mislead the assembly'.[12] These warnings, of course, might well be given by men who themselves were skilful speakers and adept in turning arguments to their own advantage.

At a passive level of participation inequality in terms of education and experience was a less serious limitation. Political knowledge, judgement and being informed about public affairs are not closely related to 'higher education', particularly in an oral society, which the Athenian polis essentially was. It may be assumed, however, that the ability to read was an advantage – to read for oneself the agenda for assembly meetings, proposed changes to the law, or assembly decisions inscribed on stone or bronze in public places. It was useful also to be able to write, but others could assist an illiterate man, even if we regard with scepticism Plutarch's story of Aristeides obliging an illiterate countryman by inscribing the name of Aristeides on an ostrakon. By the last quarter of the fifth century, a basic literacy seems to have been more or less general.[13]

Another inequality, the physical inequality between various parts of Attike, also had a differential impact related to wealth. A wealthy man could not only afford prolonged absence from his distant fields, but in many cases he owned a house in Athens or the Peiraieus. For him a term as a member of the Boule was less burdensome than for a poorer bouleutes. Active participation as a rhetor or a strategos over a number of years was even more dependent on a measure of wealth. The constraints of residential location also operated at the level of passive participation. The composition of jury courts with their meeting days on roughly one day in every two would have been more affected by the jurors' places of residence than the assembly with its meetings of the order of 40 a year. There is good reason to believe that at most times the predominant element in the courts was urban, and more particularly the old and the poor. However, the concentration of the rural population in the city for prolonged periods during the Peloponnesian War, while partly offset by the demands of men for military and naval expeditions, may have affected the overall composition of the courts (and the assembly).[14]

---

[11] Eur. *Or.* 917–22.   [12] Thuc. 3.37–8.
[13] Plut. *Arist.* 7, Ar. *Knights* 188–9, Ath. 454b–e. On the disputed questions of the level and the extent of literacy in Athens in our period, see in particular Harvey (1966) 585–635; see also Turner (1952) 8–10, 21–3, Woodbury (1976) 349–57, Burns (1981) 371–87; cf. Havelock (1971) 34–61.   [14] See ch. 5.1, 5.2, 5.4; R. Osborne 184–5.

The impediments to participation and the inequalities of opportunity should not, however, blind us to the extent to which the humbler and the inexperienced citizens participated in public affairs at polis level, even beyond attendance in the assembly and the courts. The participation of large numbers of them in office-holding was encouraged by the extensive use of the Lot and the limited responsibilities attached to the sortitive offices. The use of the Lot carried with it the implication that all citizens were competent to hold these offices and that no special qualifications or experience were required, while the limited responsibilities, which were, moreover, mostly shared with colleagues on a board of ten, made that implication credible. A high level of participation was indeed made necessary by the large number of offices (several hundreds at home apart from bouleutai) and in particular the size of the Boule, and by the fact of annual tenure and the prohibition on re-election to any of the sortitive offices or, in the case of the Boule, the restriction to two terms.[15]

Quite different were the offices of substantial power, in particular the strategia, in which selection was based on voting. While the strategoi were members of a board of ten, all with equal legal standing, one or more were commonly appointed to the command of particular expeditions and thereby given particular responsibility, and in any case their duties in general carried far higher levels of responsibility than the offices determined by lot. Wealth and its associated advantages gave a citizen dignity and prestige if he sought, and after he gained, election as a general.[16] In tangible terms, the rich man would have gained experience as a trierarch in command of a trireme or as a hipparch in charge of cavalry, while taxiarchs or commanders of the hoplite infantry would have been of zeugite status or above. Thus merit and reputation rather than wealth as such were the crucial qualifications in securing election to the strategia. What constituted merit and reputation would have changed with the changing character of the office which we have earlier noted, with different weighting, at different times and for particular individuals, for military skill, capacity and experience as a leader, political standing, experience in dealing with other states, and private resources to activate an expedition. And there is good reason to accept Plutarch's view that the Athenians chose their strategoi seriously and with good sense.[17]

The wealthy to a large extent monopolised leadership at polis level and the initiative associated with it, but these groups were not self-perpetuating as they tended to be in Rome under the republic. The family dynasties of the sixth and fifth centuries and the claims of aristocratic birth seem to have weakened with the growing recognition of the need for individual ability in speaking, in war, in financial management, and in the arts of leadership. And in so far as leadership continued to be monopolised by elite groups, popular participation was limited

---

[15] See ch. 3.5.   [16] Plut. *Alkib.* 21; see Thuc. 6.16 and ch. 7.3.
[17] See ch. 2.3.3 and ch. 7.1, Isok. 15.115–25, Xen. *Mem.* 3.4.1–5, Plut. *Phok.* 8.

in its political power and effectiveness, yet it was far from an empty shell. Any citizen could make a proposal in the assembly and not a few took their opportunity as we have seen, while the knowledge and experience gained by large numbers of citizens in the Boule should have made a critical difference to the extent to which the assembly was informed and experienced. It is perhaps reasonable to assume that in any decade some 4,500 different individuals were elected to the Boule – a little less than 1 in 4 of the citizens over the age of 30 when the adult male citizens numbered 30,000 (or less than 1 in 5 when they numbered 40,000).[18]

8.2 The cost of participation – exploitation of others?

But if Athenian citizens, or large numbers of them, did participate and exercise their rights as citizens, was it at the expense of others and through the economic exploitation of others – slaves, women, or the subject states of the Athenian empire? Athenian women enjoyed no political rights and played no direct part in the political life of the city, but, as we have already seen, they made a crucial contribution to the maintenance of the *oikos*.[19] Adult male citizens thereby had less demands to meet. Even so, among the poorer citizens it is doubtful whether, with the exception of older men, many of them had much opportunity to participate in the life of the polis. For those citizens who did have sufficient leisure and those for whom state pay made participation possible – whether in fact individuals from either group did participate or not – the work of women was a critical factor in providing the opportunity to share in the life of the polis.

Whether the ability to exercise citizen rights was dependent on slave labour has been much debated. The limited evidence available permits widely differing views about the number of slaves and the degree of the citizens' dependence on their slaves. Such evidence as there is relates very largely to wealthier citizens and metics, while little or nothing is known about the number of slaves owned by ordinary Athenians, the productivity or efficiency of slaves, or the proportion of slaves to citizens in any particular activity. Some slaves were owned by the polis. These state slaves included the 1,200 Skythians armed with bows and charged with keeping order in the assembly, the courts and in other public places, and with attending upon various officials.[20] Slaves were also used to keep public records and accounts, and some were employed in the mint. But

---

[18] See ch. 2.3.3 and ch. 6.2. Those over 30, constituting according to model life tables (see Appendix 1C) 62.8% of the total adult male population, would number almost 19,000 in a total of 30,000 adult male citizens (or 25,000 in a total of 40,000). If we assume that 500 or 600 of the 5,000 bouleutai served twice within the decade, a little less than 1 in 4 of citizens over 30 (when the overall total was 30,000) would have served on the Boule in that decade. In the unlikely event that as many as 1,250 served twice *within the decade* (see ch. 3 n. 82 and ch. 4 n. 61), the 3,750 individuals would represent about 1 in 5 of those over 30.

[19] See ch. 3.1.   [20] Andok. 3.5, 7, Aiskhin. 2.173–4 (300 originally).

the number of public slaves was slight compared with the numbers owned by Athenian citizens and by metics, and it is the exploitation of the privately-owned slaves which is said to have enabled the development and the maintenance of democracy in Athens. The total number of slaves (of all ages) increased from perhaps 30,000–40,000 in *c.* 480 (a suggested figure out of an estimated total population of 120,000–150,000) to a high point *c.* 431 (perhaps 80,000–110,000 out of 215,000–300,000).[21]

As well as total numbers, the areas in which slaves were employed and the distribution of slaves among citizen owners must be considered. The largest concentrations of slaves were employed in the silver workings at Laureion. In the fifth century, at the high point of the exploitation of the mines, a few owners like Nikias were believed to have hired out hundreds of slaves. We hear of a mine lessee in 347 owning 30 slaves. Slaves undoubtedly provided a very high proportion of the labour in one of the most important fields of economic activity. When Xenophon advocated in the 350s an intensification of silver mining, he argued that the mines could employ more than 10,000 slaves which he said was the case in the period before the Spartan occupation of Dekeleia in 413. These mining slaves probably constituted a large proportion of the more than 20,000 slaves who deserted during the occupation of Dekeleia from 413 to 404.[22] The rich silver deposits of Laureion which had enabled the expansion of the Athenian navy in the 480s were the means of the fine silver coinage which was accepted throughout the Aegean. In so far as the silver mines were the basis of an Athenian surplus and also boosted the capacity to import grain, they could be held to point to Athenian dependence on the slave labour which worked the mines. Yet the mines went out of production in the last years of the Peloponnesian War, and production does not seem to have revived fully until the 340s. An inscription of 367/6 recorded 17 mining leases and payments into the state treasury of 3,690 drakhmai – that is, over 6 talents during the year, if payments were made each prytany. A fragmentary inscription of probably 342/1 listed more than 62 leases and perhaps as many as 141: the receipts have been estimated at 160 talents (or 16 talents, if the payments were annual). For much of the fourth century, therefore, the Athenian polis did not benefit greatly in a direct way, but even with the reduced activity the lessees sometimes did very well.[23]

There were smaller concentrations of slaves in workshops. The largest known workshop was the shield factory of the metics Lysias and Polemarkhos. Presumably the majority of the 120 slaves owned by the brothers worked in this

---

[21] Ehrenberg (1969) 31; see also Gomme 20–6, Lauffer 2 (1956) 152, Jones 76–9.
[22] Lauffer 1 (1955) 5–13, Jones (1960) 4–6; Xen. *Poroi* 4.4, 14–26 (a popular report that 1,000 slaves were owned by Nikias for hiring out – rejected by Westermann (1960B) 81–3); Dem. 37.4–6; [Dem.] 42.20; Thuc. 7.27; Jones 17.
[23] Ar. *Frogs* 721–5; Xen. *Poroi* 3.2, 4.11; Crosby (1950) 202–6, 244–54, 286, 289–90; Hopper (1953) 237–54 and (1979) 175–89.

factory, which would have expanded during the Peloponnesian War. Moreover metics, since they could not own land though they could rent it, perhaps invested money in slaves more readily than citizens did. Xenophon has Sokrates refer to several Athenians who in his time lived well on their slaves' earnings, and there are references to other well-to-do citizens who owned about ten slave craftsmen. Demosthenes' father had almost half his fortune of 14 talents invested in two workshops, one employing '32 or 33' knife makers and the other 20 bed makers. The production of manufactured goods, however, was also carried out by citizens, though only guesses can be made at the proportion of citizen and slave production. But it is clear that large numbers of citizens worked on their own as craftsmen, for, as Poverty asserted in *The Ploutos*, they had to work for a living. Some slaves were employed in the construction industry – for example in the building of the Erekhtheion, where they worked side by side with metics and citizens and at the same rates of pay.[24]

Overall the largest number of slaves were probably 'household' slaves, working alongside their masters or, in the case of female slaves, assisting in the domestic duties. The prestige attached to having slaves, and not merely production, was important for many wealthier citizens. But for most citizens production was the paramount consideration. And it would seem that it was 'household' slaves that made a fundamental and extensive contribution to agriculture, the basic economic activity in Attike in our period. The fact that surviving 'mortgage-pillars' refer to slaves in connection with workshops but not (with one exception) in conjunction with land may be indicative. In any case 'household slaves', rather than specialists such as vine dressers, probably provided most of the labour for agricultural pursuits. Certainly there was no pattern of vast estates or large plantations, though the wealthiest landowners probably relied on slave labour supervised by an overseer who would normally be a slave or a freedman.[25]

But most farmers probably had to work their land themselves, assisted by their family, by slaves or, at harvest times, also by their neighbours or by hired labour. Aristotle, in explaining one of Hesiod's verses, declared that the ox serves instead of a servant for the poor (*penētes*), and elsewhere argued that those without resources (*aporoi*), having no slaves, are forced to use their wives and children as assistants. Citizen women might be forced by poverty to work in the harvest, or slaves might be hired as need arose.[26] Yet a litigant who owned three or more slaves represented himself to the jurors as a man of small means. That was intended to retain the sympathy of the jury, but it is hazardous to generalise

---

[24] Lys. 12.19, Xen. *Mem.* 2.7.3–6, Aiskhin. 1.97, Lykourg. *Leok.* 23, 58; Dem. 27.9; Ar. *Plout.* 510–34, *IG* l³.476.5–45; Jones 14–16.

[25] Theophr. *Char.* 22.10; Lys. 7.16, 19, 31 (a trierarch); [Dem.] 47.52–3 (a trierarch); Dem. 55.31–2; Xen. *Oik.* 7.35–6, 12.2–4 and 19, 13.9–12; Jones 13–14, Mossé 54–8, Jameson (1978) 132–41, de Ste Croix 505–6; cf. Finley (1951) 73.

[26] Arist. *Pol.* 1252b12, 1323a5–6; Dem. 57.45, [Dem.] 53.19–21.

about the spread of slaves from such statements; after all, this man could presumably afford to have Demosthenes write his speech for him. Again, we may doubt whether Khremylos, who is described in Aristophanes' *Ploutos* as 'poor', burdened by toil like his farmer neighbours, and yet (on a literal interpretation) as owning three or more slaves, may be taken as typical of 'poor' farmers in Attike.[27] It is indeed open to serious doubt whether the poorer citizens, be it in the rural districts or in Athens and the Peiraieus, owned any slaves. Once acquired, a slave who was a serious helper to the master could be expected to produce more than the cost of his maintenance, while state pay would cover the cost of maintaining a slave, or of hiring one if one was available. But the real question was the cost of acquiring a slave. Some indication of the prices for slaves is provided by the records of the sale (in 414) of property confiscated from those who were condemned for the mutilation of the Hermai: the prices of slaves ranged from 72 to 301 drakhmai, with a median price of 157 drakhmai.[28] An Athenian would therefore require land or resources sufficient to accumulate a surplus or to assist in repaying a debt if he borrowed some money for the purchase of a slave.

In short, the proportion of citizens who owned slaves is a matter for speculation, not proof. The 1,200 richest families no doubt owned a disproportionately high number of the slaves and the numbers decreased in relation to family wealth. But when Jones suggested that two-thirds to three-quarters of the citizen population did not own any slaves, he would seem to have underestimated the spread of slave ownership. Most subsequent discussions, however, would seem to overestimate the spread. Perhaps somewhat more than half of the citizens owned a slave or slaves. But even those scholars who would push the ownership of slaves to the lower limits of the scale of wealth accept that slavery did not relieve most Athenians of the need to work with their hands, though it may still be argued that it was the availability of slaves which gave most citizens sufficient leisure to participate in public life. But it is yet another matter to suggest that a family could live off state pay alone, and there is every reason for doubt, where a citizen's participation was limited to attending the assembly and serving in the courts.[29]

As for the wealthiest citizens, their wealth gave them the opportunity to hire labour or to own labour, and in so far as they largely or exclusively used slave labour, their ability to play an active role in the life of the polis depended on their slaves and the surplus they produced. In so far as such men constituted an elite providing the initiative and the leadership element in Athenian democracy, the exploitation of slave labour may then be said to be of critical importance for

---

[27] Dem. 55.31–2, 35; Ar. *Plout.* 26–9, 223–4, 254.

[28] Jameson (1978) 140; ML 79.34–49, Pritchett (1956) 276–7; Jones (1960) 5.

[29] Jones 14, 17; Jameson (1978) 122–45 (with bibliography), de Ste Croix 505–6; see Finley (1960) 53–72; cf. Ehrenberg (1951) 165–91 especially 190–1, Jones 10–19, Starr (1958) 17–32; see ch. 5.4.

the workability of the democratic system.[30] Modern democracies, it might be rejoined, are based on the 'exploitation' of wage-labour. The wage-labourer, however, is legally or theoretically free to do what he wishes to do, to live where he wishes and to go where he wishes. The slave of the citizen or the metic was not.[31]

Athenian democracy did rely to a significant degree on slave labour, as did other societies in the ancient world. But the recency of the formal abolition of slavery in modern western society, like the recency of universal suffrage and the even more recent extension of the suffrage to women, underlines the need to examine such questions within the context of the social structure as a whole. The same is true of the incontrovertible fact that only a fraction of the population of Attike had, or exercised, political rights. For whatever view is taken of the extent to which Athenian citizens played an active role in the life of their polis, those with full civic rights represented a select group within the total population. Most estimates at different points in our period assume or imply that slaves constituted perhaps 30%–37% of the population, persons of metic status 10%–15%, citizens and their families 50%–55%, with only 14%–17% of the total – the adult male citizens – in possession of full political rights (and among them considerable numbers, at various times, were not living in Attike).[32] This should not be forgotten, but what was remarkable for a society in the ancient world or, for that matter, for a society in the modern world until comparatively recent times, was the extension of political rights and the direct participation of large numbers of citizens. Whether democracy could have developed and continued so strongly in a larger, less exclusive, and less cohesive political community may be another question. Yet the exclusivity of Athenian citizens with respect to other Greeks carried its own cost, as it prevented the Athenians – in contrast to the Makedonians and the Romans – from engaging the support of others.

The oft-repeated charge that democracy was parasitic on the subject states of the Athenian empire would seem to be undermined by the fact that, despite the interposition of the Spartan-backed Thirty, the democratic system ultimately survived the loss of empire, and state pay for public service continued into the fourth century and, despite the loss of empire, was extended to attendance in the assembly.[33] Yet state pay, one of the outstanding features of Athenian democracy, was made possible by the population growth and the increasing level of prosperity in Athens in the mid–fifth century and that prosperity was closely related, at least in part, to the growth of Athenian power.[34] That power, as we noted in the first chapter, was based on several factors – the exploitation of the silver at Laureion, the growth in the confidence of the Demos in the first half

[30] de Ste Croix 52–3.
[31] Westermann (1960A) 25–30.
[32] See Appendix IA, D, E.
[33] Jones 5–9; see ch. 5.2; Hansen (1979A) 5–22.
[34] Arist. *Pol.* 1293a1–6. On political pay outside Athens, see de Ste Croix 602 n. 24 and (1975) 48–52.

of the fifth century, the development of the Peiraieus as a port. In addition to those factors and closely interwoven with some of them, there was the growth of Athenian naval power, due in no small way to the reluctance of the allied members of the Delian League to serve on expeditions themselves and their willingness to commute their obligations into money payments. Thus the Athenians undertook a greater share in the expeditions and, by this and other methods, increased their power in the Aegean and their external revenue.

At the outbreak of the Peloponnesian War in 431, the imperial revenues of Athens, including tribute, amounted to some 600 talents a year, while the building of the Parthenon (447–432) and other projects in Athens and Attike had been financed from the tribute payments which had accumulated over the years to the tune of 9,700 talents and which in 431 stood at 6,000 talents. State pay for jury and other service may well have come from internal revenues, which in 431 were of the order of 400 talents a year.[35]

How much money would have been expended on state pay? When it was first introduced for dikasts, pay of 2 obols would have totalled $8\frac{1}{3}$ talents a year for every 1,000 dikasts on the basis of some 150 sitting days.[36] That sum is probably of about the right order of magnitude for the payment of dikasts in the mid-fifth century. If anything, it may be on the high side, but even if we allow an average of 2,000 dikasts for as many as 200 sitting days, the total of 22 talents is not a huge amount in terms of internal revenue of perhaps 300 talents in the mid-fifth century. Nevertheless, this revenue had to meet other needs of the Athenian polis, and the introduction of state pay would have been difficult without a rising revenue or heavier imposts on the wealthy. Indirectly at least, therefore, the fact of empire and the material benefits, whether direct or indirect, had some influence on the development of democracy. The tribute of the allies, the import and other dues at the Peiraieus which was now the greatest trading-post in the Aegean, the provision of goods and services in the Peiraieus, the benefits of Athens as the capital city of the empire, the consequences of the widespread use of Athenian coins, the payment of reparations by allies who had tried to secede – all these enhanced the resources at the disposal of the Athenian citizens. Moreover, the empire encouraged the boost in their confidence and in their political expectations.[37] It must also be added that the empire brought other benefits. The lower classes gained, for example, not only through their employment in the Athenian navy and associated industry but also through their acquisition of land in klerouchies and settlements abroad. The upper classes too, but perhaps mainly through private acquisition, obtained land in allied states. They had enhanced opportunities as Athenian strategoi or as

---

35 Thuc. 2.13.3 (and *HCT*), Xen. *Anab.* 7.1.27; cf. Ar. *Wasps* 656–60 (for 422 – after the trebling of the assessment of tribute) and [Dem.] 10.37–8.
36 See Appendix 2A; cf. Jones 5–6.
37 Meiggs 255–72, Finley (1978) 103–26; Pečírka (1975) 307–11 and (1982) 117–25; see ch. 1.3–1.4.

officials in allied states and they were likely to be called upon less frequently to help finance Athenian activities and had greater resources when called upon, for example, to act as trierarchs.[38]

The combination of all these factors created a set of circumstances which made participation in the political life of Athens feasible for a widening circle of citizens, particularly when the polis could afford to pay jurymen, bouleutai and state officials, quite apart from the hoplites and the sailors. In short, the development of democracy in the mid-fifth century was associated with the growing dominance of Athens over her allies, for this dominance (and other factors) permitted that development to be stable and acceptable to the wealthier citizens. State pay would have been much more difficult to finance from internal revenues and would have caused even greater opposition if it required heavier imposts on the wealthy, or confiscations.[39] Nevertheless, it would seem rash to argue that Athenian democracy – which was not a new growth in the mid-fifth century but had its origins in the sixth, particularly in the reforms of Kleisthenes – could neither have developed nor been sustained without the empire, but equally rash to argue that it would have developed so strongly or so rapidly without the resources and the mood which derived from the empire.

8.3 The consequences of participation

8.3.1 Contemporary views

What were the consequences of democracy and the participation of large numbers of citizens? This aspect of Athenian democracy, perhaps more than any other, reveals, or conceals, the basic assumptions and prejudices of critics, both ancient and modern. The difficulties of a balanced evaluation, let alone the illusory search for a purely 'objective' judgement, may be illustrated by reference to some of the ancient writers.

The criticisms of these writers and their evaluative comments cluster around two main aspects: fundamental consideration of democracy as a political system and comments on democracy in practice, both in respect of inherent tendencies and in respect of a particular situation. In so far as these two aspects were distinct, philosophers were largely concerned with the first. Plato, with his insistence on the need for expert knowledge, the rigorous education of the most talented individuals and the specialisation of functions in a community, had little sympathy with democracy. Though not alone in his belief that in a democracy freedom is abused and every man lives and acts as he likes, Plato took a very serious view of this as destroying harmony in the polis. The *Republic* and *Laws* were utopian or reforming in purpose, and while Plato was

---

[38]   [Xen.] *AP* 1.2, 13–20, *IG* I³.46 (ML 49).39–42, Jones 168–77, Brunt (1966) 71–92; Thuc. 8.48.6, *IG* I³.422.375–8, de Ste Croix 604 n. 27.   [39]   Arist. *Pol.* 1320a17–35.

clearly most conversant with Athenian democracy, his criticisms were directed at democracy as such.[40] Aristotle's discussion of political systems in the *Politics* was analytical and more utilitarian in its overall approach, and while not sympathetic with the lower classes but favouring a balance between oligarchy and democracy or rather a broadly-based oligarchy, he was generally judicious in his analysis. Though Aristotle illustrated his general observations with references to Athens, his observations about democracy, especially the extreme form found in large, prosperous poleis, do not always fit well with our other evidence about the Athenian system in the fourth century.[41] The comment in the *Athenaion Politeia* that 'the Athenians seem to have been well governed under the regime of the Five Thousand (in 411/10), when they were at war and political rights were vested in the hoplites' is indicative of the disinclination of the writer to consider the importance of naval power and the common people (though elsewhere he acknowledges both) and his preference for 'the better people'.[42]

Frankly polemical was the *Athenaion Politeia*, written around the beginning of the Peloponnesian War. Convinced of the baseness, ignorance and indiscipline of the lower classes, the writer nevertheless argued that the Athenian system was most efficient in ensuring the rule of the Demos. For him widespread participation meant that 'the vulgar fare better than the good' and, in particular, that participation gave the common people the opportunity to satisfy their desire for profit by filling the paid offices of state.[43] In the fourth century Isokrates affected an acceptance of democracy or at least the democracy of Solon, for like Plato and others he believed in 'the kind of equality which gave each man his due', not 'the kind which makes the same award to all alike'. The offices of state were therefore not to be filled by lot from all the citizens, but the best and the ablest for each function were to be selected. Isokrates' yearning for the good old days make his comments about the fourth century (and also about the fifth) of dubious value, unless they are corroborated by other sources.[44]

Playwrights, too, might consider the merits and demerits of the democratic system. Take, for example, the fiery exchange in *The Suppliants* between the loud-mouthed Theban herald and Theseus, the legendary king of Athens but depicted very much as a constitutional monarch carrying out the wishes of the Athenian people. Into the mouth of the herald Euripides puts some of the common criticisms of democracy – rule by the mob; men who flatter the mob,

---

[40] Pl. *Rep.* 496a–e, 557a–558c, 562b–563e, *Laws* 701a–b; see Arist. *Pol.* 1310a25–36, 1317a40–18b3, Isok. 7.20, 37, 12.131; cf. Lys. 2.18–19, 64.

[41] Arist. *Pol.* 1273b35–74a21, 1291b.20–5, 1293a1–10, 1303b10–12, 1304a20–4, 1318b27–19a6, 1319b19–27; cf. *Nik. Eth.* 1180b29–81a24.

[42] *AP* 33.2 (see Thuc. 8.97.2), cf. 26.1, 27.1, 4.   [43] [Xen.] *AP* 1.

[44] Isok. 7.15–27 (cf. 3.14–15); on arithmetic and proportionate (or geometric) equality see also Pl. *Rep.* 558c, *Laws* 756e–758a, Arist. *Pol.* 1301a25–35, Vlastos (1964) 18–33, Harvey (1965) 107–22, 126–9.

seek their own advantage and evade the consequences of their own mistakes by accusing others; the lack of education of the Demos; the poor prevented by their work from attending to public affairs; the resentment of the better people when a nobody with a ready tongue gains a hold on the Demos.[45] But in the fifth century the comedians in particular probed the tendencies of the democracy in operation. The question of the relationship between the Demos and the demagogoi was taken by Aristophanes, as we have seen, as the central theme for *The Knights*, and the consequences of the judicial system for *The Wasps*. Beneath the comic exaggeration and the dramatic needs of the play, serious criticisms may be discerned.[46]

Of the historians, Thucydides was intensely interested in the political aspects of the Peloponnesian War. He approved of the strong leadership which he believed Perikles provided and he maintained that it was the bitter struggles of his successors to win the favour of the Demos that were the root cause of Athens' defeat in the war in 'that they handed over the control of the affairs to the whims of the Demos'. The best government in Athens in his lifetime, Thucydides declared, was the rule of the Five Thousand: political rights were based on a property qualification – the ability to arm oneself as a hoplite – or, as the historian put it, 'there was a moderate blending of the few and the many'. The conservative predilections of Xenophon, the country gentleman who lived for most of his life outside his native Athens and who had close ties with Agesilaos and other Spartans, may be inferred from the conversations attributed to Sokrates in the *Oikonomikos* and the *Memorabilia*, rather than from his history of Greece (*Hellenika*).[47]

The validity and strength of the arguments and claims of the Attic Orators, who were themselves active in the Ekklesia and the Dikasteria, are in many ways the most difficult to assess. While speakers might find fault with their audience for past errors of policy or contrast the slowness of the Athenians with the speed of Philip in making and executing decisions, they took the democratic system for granted and implied their commitment to it. At the end of the day, they had to convince the Ekklesia, the Dikasterion, or the Boule. In pursuit of that goal the orators devoted conscious thought to the types of arguments likely to win the minds and hearts of their listeners. We have already had occasion to note some of these stock arguments, while the collections of *prooimia* (introductions) with their general arguments which could be adapted to a particular occasion are a further indication of the need for caution in drawing inferences. Yet, while recognising that they were sometimes engaged in seeking a reputation for eloquence, we cannot, on that basis alone, dismiss their criticisms.[48] Exaggerated though their assertions may sometimes be, they had to

---

[45] Eur. *Suppl.* 399–441; see Hdt. 3.81.   [46] See ch. 5.4 and ch. 7.2.
[47] Thuc. 2.65, 8.97.2; see, for example, Xen. *Oik.* 6.5–17, *Mem.* 3.5.15–20.
[48] See, for example, Dem. 18.235, 19.185–6; *Prooimia* 9.

retain enough plausibility not to run a serious risk of being rejected out-of-hand by the majority of the audience.

8.3.2 *The conduct of the assembly and the courts*

What precisely, then, were felt by contemporaries to be the major consequences of widespread participation in the political–judicial life of Athens? To some the very fact of a higher level of participation was in itself deleterious, for they would have agreed with Aristotle's preference for low levels of participation or politicisation. Thus, while recognising the value of certain democratic institutions such as popular election of officials, the accountability of officials to the Demos, or the hearing of lawsuits by the citizens at large, Aristotle argued that an agricultural democracy was the best form (for the farmers did not have leisure but put the law in control and held the minimum number of assemblies necessary) and the worst was the most extreme form in which, according to him, pay enabled the lower classes to dominate the affairs of the polis.[49] A polemical writer like the Old Oligarch might specifically characterise the lower classes as vulgar, ignorant, uneducated and disorderly, while other writers enunciated the view that the work of artisans, market-traders and the wage-earning class was degrading and that men of that sort should either be excluded from citizenship or full political rights, or be given few opportunities by limiting the number of assemblies. The orators recognised the prejudice that could easily be provoked against the poor and against certain occupations such as market-traders.[50]

It is therefore not surprising that, when in practice the Athenians allowed, encouraged, or indeed achieved, the participation of these 'baser' elements, many writers found the consequences undesirable. Undesirable because of the attitudes and the conduct of those who sat in the assembly or the courts, undesirable because of the individuals who then emerged as demagogoi, leaders of the Demos, and undesirable in the interaction of these two. This is not to say that the ancient criticisms were without foundation, but to indicate one of the elements underlying them.

The demagogoi of the late fifth century were attacked on the grounds of their origins ('from the base people'), their qualifications ('uneducated'), and their style and methods of leadership ('the most violent of the citizens and by far the most influential with the Demos at that time').[51] They appealed directly and

---

[49] Arist. *Pol.* 1292b25–93a10, 1317b38–41, 1318b6–19a38.
[50] [Xen.] *AP* 1.4–5; Pl. *Rep.* 495c–496a, Arist. *Pol.* 1319a24–30, cf. 1328b33–29a2; see Appendix 2C; Dem. 57.30–6 and see ch. 5.3.1 and n. 54.
[51] Ar. *Knights* 178–93, 733–40, *Frogs* 727–37, Arist. *Pol.* 1274a14–15, *AP* 28, Thuc. 3.36.6, Connor 158–75.

unashamedly to the Demos. With their glib tongues they could mislead the assembly with their promises and the jurors with their deceitful arguments. And when one of the demagogoi, Kleon – in his endeavour to dissuade the assembly from reversing its decision about the punishment of Mytilene – charged the assembly with being 'at the mercy of your ears', he echoed the often-repeated charges about the Athenians' delight in clever arguments.[52] In 415, when the Athenians were debating the proposed expedition to Sicily, Nikias sought to counteract the enthusiasm aroused in large part by Alkibiades and urged the older men not to be intimidated by the presence of Alkibiades' supporters into voting for war. But because of the excessive enthusiasm of the majority, Thucydides commented, the few who were opposed to the expedition were afraid of appearing unpatriotic by holding up their hands to vote against it, and therefore kept quiet.[53]

Furthermore, by their conduct the political leaders of the fourth century as well as those of the later fifth were held to have contributed to disorder and rowdiness in the assembly and the courts. By organising applause and interruptions they might hope to influence debates and trials. While much of our testimony for disorder comes from the speeches of Demosthenes and Aiskhines *On the Embassy* (343 B.C.) and in the trial of Ktesiphon (330 B.C.) and Aiskhines' speech *Against Timarkhos*, applause and interruptions were not confined to those moments of high drama in that difficult period, when the Athenians sought to establish policies appropriate to the power of Makedonia.[54] Dikaiopolis, all set to interrupt and abuse the speakers if anything other than peace was discussed, was not in this respect a figment of Aristophanes' imagination, as is clear from Thucydides' account of the Mytilene debate and the reported treatment handed out to the young, inexperienced Glaukon and to Demosthenes. Many assembly debates, especially those on controversial issues, were undoubtedly lively affairs. Sometimes, too, disorder arose in the Boule – not only the democratic council but also, if Andokides' account is to be believed, in the oligarchic council of 410 B.C. Sometimes disorder in the assembly might impede serious or rational deliberation. But even if it is accepted that there may be some tendency, though not an inevitability, for disorder and rowdiness to increase with the size of a meeting, rational discussion is not the sole prerogative of smaller groups nor is the possibility of rational discussion necessarily enhanced by smaller groups.[55] Again, the assembly of 407 seems to have been as impervious or hostile to any opposition to the appointment of Alkibiades as was the assembly of 370 to any opposition to the

---

[52] See ch. 2.3.1. Cf. Ar. *Knights* 837, Thuc. 3.38.   [53] Thuc. 6.13.1, 24.4.

[54] Aiskhin. 3.1–4; Bers (1985) 1–15. It is far from certain that there was an increase in the fourth century in boisterous conduct in the Ekklesia as suggested by de Laix 83 and n. 143.

[55] Ar. *Akh.* 37–9, 59–64; Thuc. 3.38.6; Xen. *Mem.* 3.6.1, Plut. *Dem.* 6; Aiskhin. 1.80–4; Aiskhin. 3.1–4, Andok. 2.15; see Dem. 5.2–3 and [Dem.] 13.3 implying that proper discussion could be impeded, cf. Pl. *Rep.* 492b–d; see ch. 6.3.

proposal to help Sparta, or the assemblies that Demosthenes said did not want to hear him, or the assemblies that Plutarch says Phokion had to wrestle with. It might be that sometimes a political leader made such assertions later, in order to explain his earlier failure to carry the assembly or his earlier reticence.[56] On the other hand, uproar from the assembly crowd, spurred on by speakers, could prevent Demosthenes from manoeuvring to stop a motion being put to the vote, though it could also intimidate the presiding officials and frighten them into procedures contrary to the laws, as happened at the hearing of the charges against the Arginousai strategoi. Yet, while there was no doubt potentially a tension between the rule of law and the will of the people, there are no other indications of the anger of the moment so seriously overriding the laws of Athens.[57] In the fourth century the graphe paranomon, used and abused though it was as a weapon in political warfare, but now assisted in some respects by the careful procedures for the revision of the laws, may have helped to reduce the tension.

Athenian juries were not like the silent juries of many modern courts. But in courts where no cross-examination was possible and a prosecutor could only counter an argument by anticipating it, interjections might help to discourage outrageous claims. Or speakers might warn jurors not to be misled by deceitful advocates or might alert them to specific questions to which they should demand an answer.[58]

The extent of the impact of oratorical displays and clever arguments is difficult to gauge. Large gatherings are, however, not the only meetings where speakers may be inclined to say what their hearers want to hear. Such flatterers were in fact compared with the flatterers of a tyrant. Nor are small deliberating bodies immune to arguments of immediate self-interest as opposed to the long-term good of the community (in so far as these are or can be distinguished by participants at the time).[59] Yet it may be that the very openness of the Athenian Ekklesia and the large number of citizens made extravagant promises and expectations more likely. But more influential in the decades after the death of Perikles was the circumstance, as reported by Thucydides, that his successors were more on a level with one another and in the attempt to establish their supremacy they were drawn to outbid each other.[60] In the last decade or more of his career Perikles, while he had confronted more opposition than is sometimes supposed, had not faced such a situation.

Another consequence of the interaction of widespread participation and demagogoi, it might be argued, was an increased vulnerability of the rich and

---

[56]   Xen. *Hell.* 1.4.20, 6.5.49; Dem. 19.23–4, 45–6 (cf. 19.15, 113); Plut *Phok.* 9. D.S. 17.15.2; Dem. 18.143.

[57]   Aiskhin. 2.84, Dem. 20.166; Xen. *Hell.* 1.7.12–13; see ch. 3.5 and ch. 7.2 and n. 39; Jones 50–4 and de Ste Croix 76, cf. Arist. *Pol.* 1292a4–37.

[58]   Dem. 19.75, 20.131, 23.95–9, 33.35–6, Aiskhin. 2.4, 153, 3.205–6, 244, Bers (1985) 9–14.

[59]   Dem. 6.3, Isok. 8.3–8; Arist. *Pol.* 1292a11–23, 1313b32–42.   [60] Thuc. 2.65.

their wealth. The determination of Athenian foreign and domestic affairs and the dispensation of justice were now in varying degrees in the hands of ordinary Athenians. The harnessing of individual wealth to the benefit of the polis was interpreted by the Old Oligarch as the rich paying for the Demos to take part, whether through choral performances, athletic contests, or the trierarchy. As we have also seen, one of the means for financing war in the late fifth century and in the fourth was the levying of property tax on the well-to-do: these levies do not seem in themselves to have been excessive, though being unpredictable they might cause temporary embarrassment and in some cases might conceivably result in the confiscation of an estate because of default.[61] In so far as ordinary Athenians predominated in the assembly, we might have expected more 'milking' of the rich if the clash of class interests was the chief determinant in Athenian life. But, despite some complaints by the rich, there is little to suggest that the assembly in its decisions sought in a vindictive way to exploit their wealth.[62] In any case well-to-do citizens had traditionally borne the responsibility for the security of the state: the question was whether their efforts in this regard, now shared by the thetic rowers in the fleet, would still achieve some recognition, even if different in kind from the past.

The expectations of the poorer citizens in Athens can easily be exaggerated. There was probably much truth in Aristotle's view that 'even when the poor do not share in honours they are willing to remain quiet, provided no one treats them arrogantly or deprives them of any of their property'. The willingness of poorer citizens to accept wide disparities in wealth was perhaps encouraged also by their sense of cohesion as against the slave population, which enjoyed no or few possessions and lacked freedom, and by their tendency to absorb aristocratic values and attitudes.[63] Birth (and wealth) could still open doors, as we have seen in the case of Alkibiades.[64] Nor should we expect, in practice, equally strong penetration of egalitarian concepts into all areas of Athenian life. In the structures and procedures of Athenian institutions conservative attitudes may be discerned. In the administration of justice, for example, the popular courts did not take over dealing with acts of violence. Acts of deliberate homicide and wounding, for instance, were left in the hands of the Areiopagos whose members held office for life, while the Eleven (the gaolers and executioners) had the right to execute without trial any thief or robber caught in the act.[65]

The treatment of men of property was also one of the common complaints

61 [Xen.] *AP* 1.13 and see ch. 7.6; see ch. 5.3.2, Lys. 29.9, Dem. 22.50–4.
62 Xen. *Mem.* 1.2.45, Isok. 8.128; Cloché (1951) 231–41, Jones 55–8; cf. Pl. *Rep.* 565a–b; see ch. 5.3.2.
63 Arist. *Pol.* 1297b6–8; de Ste Croix 290; see Vlastos (1953) 352–6; see Adkins (1976) 319 and (1972) 119–26, and Appendix 2C.   64 Thuc. 6.16, Plut. *Alkib.* 8, 10, see ch. 7.3.
65 Hansen (1976) 7–8; cf. 118–21 on other aspects including the tendency to absolute liability independent of intention or negligence; see ch. 7.2 on the treatment of leading figures.

levelled at the Dikasteria (and the Ekklesia when it heard impeachments). Some wealthy men entertained fears about the confiscation of their property or heavy fines, because they perceived, and it could be suggested by prosecutors, that such exactions would benefit the poor or even would be necessary to ensure jury pay. In times of financial stringency such as the early years of the fourth century, such suggestions may have influenced the verdict of some citizens. For the most part, however, the fears of the well-to-do were probably exaggerated. Certainly the well-to-do who led private lives had far less to fear under the democracy than under the rule of the Thirty. For in 404/3 the oligarchs engaged in wholesale confiscation of the property of wealthy men: in many of those cases the victims also lost their lives and their only offences seem to have been their wealth and their refusal to give active support to the Thirty.[66] In some cases involving public figures, as we have seen, fines were ruinously heavy, but the motivation seems to have been political rather than economic, relating to perceptions of the character and success of the leadership of a Timotheos. A popular jury, or a large assembly, and the overall character of Athenian democracy clearly made public life much more hazardous in democratic Athens than in oligarchic regimes, but not all will go so far as some recent judgements on this aspect of the Athenian system.[67] Nevertheless, it is clear that in the difficult balance between holding leaders responsible for their policies and actions and sympathetic understanding of their difficulties, the Athenian Demos were hard masters.

Furthermore, the rich might be subjected to attacks in the law-courts by prosecutors motivated by personal financial gain. Such attacks were indeed a consequence of the virtual lack of a public prosecutor in Athens and the reliance on individual initiative to prosecute wrongdoers. The sykophantes might argue, as he did in Aristophanes' *Ploutos*, that he was in charge of all matters, both public and private, and that he was a virtuous patriot whose activities benefited the polis. Yet benefiting the polis in this way might be, and was, seen by others as being a busybody.[68] And the scourge of sykophantia is to be related to two wider phenomena: the restlessness or meddlesomeness (*polypragmosynē*) attributed to Athenians and the notorious litigiousness of Athenians. Cor-inthians and others perceived the Athenians to be 'busy about many things' or 'meddlesome' – ever active, disinclined to keep quiet themselves or to leave others to be quiet. In external affairs this restlessness or meddlesomeness lay at the heart of their dynamic imperialism in the mid- and late fifth century.[69] Within the Athenian community the various devices encouraging or requiring the participation of large numbers of Athenians could be seen as intensifying the

---

[66] Lys. 27.1 (but cf. 27.16); see ch. 5.4 and n. 110; *AP* 35.4, Xen. *Hell.* 2.3.21.
[67] See ch. 6.5 and ch. 7.2; Hansen (1975) 11, Knox (1985) 143–52.
[68] Ar. *Plout.* 898–923; cf. *Akh.* 824–33, Aiskhin. 2.145; compare the dependence of police and public prosecutors in modern times on information (voluntary or 'paid').
[69] Thuc. 1.70.8–9, 2.63.2–3, 6.18.7, 87.3, Plut. *Per.* 20–1; Ehrenberg (1947) 46–67.

propensity always to be active and alert or, as some saw it, to be busybodies, and in turn the devices themselves were feasible in practice because of this Athenian characteristic.[70]

The heightened awareness by increasing numbers of Athenians of political and judicial processes does seem to have helped promote recourse to litigation.[71] The extensive use of the law-courts may, however, also be attributed to other powerful factors. Apart from the election of military officials and a few others, the selection of officials did not provide an arena for deciding between political rivals. And though elections of strategoi were presumably keenly contested, even these were less critical in Athens than in modern elections which not only determine 'the rulers' for the next few years but also implicitly confirm the continuing delegation of power and sovereignty to the elected representatives. Rather, political rivalries erupted in the debates in the assembly and, with a greater finality in a sense, in the law-courts, where assembly proposals could be overturned by means of the graphe paranomon and political leaders could be brought to trial. Impeachments, too, heard by the assembly or the courts, likewise contained the double element of rivalry between leaders and the 'accountability' of officials and advisers to the Demos.[72] Moreover, Athenian courts were regularly called on for services that have no parallel in modern states – the dokimasia of officials (whether by appeal or in the first instance), the euthynai, appeals against the assessment of tribute and other matters arising from the Athenian empire, and disputes regarding liability to perform liturgies. In the absence of a police force to ensure enforcement of court decisions, such enforcement might require action by voluntary prosecutors.[73] Litigiousness may, in short, have been encouraged by the desire of the Demos to control the polis and the administration of public affairs.

The participation of large numbers of citizens in the Dikasteria induced allegations about the corruption of these courts. Such allegations, which have already been considered, were based on the notion of the corruptibility of the poor. Yet the popular courts could also be defended on the grounds that 'the few are easier to corrupt than the many, whether by money or favours'. At the same time we must note the various modifications of the jury system which seem in part to have been directed against potential or actual bribery.[74] The widespread participation of citizens in the administration of justice may also be held to explain in part several features which have been criticised in modern times. No appeal from a verdict was normally allowed. In Athenian eyes the involvement of large numbers of citizens and the whole procedure for selection would presumably have contributed to the view that the decision of the dikast

---

[70] Cf. Thuc. 2.37.

[71] See, for example, Ar. *Clouds* 206–8, *Wasps* 87–124, *Birds* 40–1; cf. [Xen.] *AP* 3.4–6; see ch. 5.4; see Isok. 15.230–1 on the effects of rhetorical training.

[72] See ch. 4.1 and ch. 6.5.   [73] Bonner 39–45.

[74] See ch. 3.5 and ch. 5.4; *AP* 41.2 (cf. 27.4–5); Lys. 27.14–15; Aiskhin. 3.52.

was, and should be, final, with no provision for any appeal. Secondly, there was no provision for a pardoning power such as exists in many modern states, yet actual cases show that in arguments about an appropriate penalty, special or extenuating circumstances (including appeals to consider the family of the defendant) were frequently advanced.[75] It would have been a diminution of the sovereignty of the Demos to suggest that there should be an authority above the Dikasteria to give (further) attention to such considerations. Thirdly, the dikasts were not experts in law and had to rely on the adversarial guidance on matters of law offered by litigants. Athenian laws, however, were far less complex than laws in modern technological societies, and the lack of expertise was the price paid for the Athenian system of entrusting the dispensation of justice to large numbers of individuals drawn from the whole citizen body – or at least from those over 30. It may be added that while jurymen in modern times not only are guided on questions of law by an expert judge but also (with benefit or otherwise) deliberate among themselves before reaching their verdict on the question of fact, there was no formal discussion among Athenian dikasts before each dikast cast his secret vote. Fourthly, each Dikasterion has been said to be a law unto itself with precedents having psychological, but no legal, effect.[76] With a popular court and with no right of appeal it could hardly be otherwise. Yet the criticism, valid though it may be, is rather a reflection of the character of Athenian public trials which, as we have seen, commonly had a strong political element. The judgement was likely to be based on current perceptions of a political leader and his policies rather than a decision about a technical or substantial infringement of the law. Modern superior courts by contrast have perhaps sometimes been preoccupied with precedents and literal interpretation of the law in the apparent belief that law is apolitical. Finally, the size of Athenian juries, it has been argued, made them more susceptible to oratorical skills. Yet, 'masterpiece of splendid oratory' though Demosthenes' *On the Crown* may be, it does not necessarily follow that it was the orator, not the statesman, that convinced the dikasts.[77] For whatever complex reasons, sound or otherwise, the dikasts may have felt a greater sympathy with Demosthenes' past policies, even though they had failed to stem the advance of Makedonian power. The few, if they are experienced and well-informed, may perhaps be less susceptible to the charms of oratory, though their judgement may be affected by other considerations such as narrow self-interest.

8.4 Did Athenian democracy work? Amateurs and experts

Athenian democracy may be said to have 'worked', not least in the sense that Athens for most of our period remained one of the most powerful states in the

---

[75] See ch. 3.5 and ch. 5.4; Pl. *Ap.* 34b–c, Lys. 20.34, Aiskhin. 2.179.
[76] Bonner 45–6.   [77] See Bury and Meiggs (1975) 493.

Greek world. The critics of Athenian democracy have, however, argued that this external situation obtained despite democracy, not because of it. And while the confidence and the vitality of the Athenian people, enhanced by the opening up of the life of the polis, should not be underestimated, it is clear that Athenian power was based on the development of the silver deposits at Laureion, the exploitation of the opportunities afforded by leadership of the Athenian alliance, and other developments in the first half of the fifth century. Thucydides went so far as to attribute the disasters suffered by Athens to political problems – to such factors as rivalry between demagogues after the firm leadership of Perikles. Ironically the very strength of Perikles' leadership may have created a vacuum after his death.[78] The Sicilian Expedition did prove disastrous, yet Athenian ambitions had in an earlier generation led to the large-scale Egyptian expedition (which was to end in disaster for Athens and especially her allies) and also to moves against Aigina and against Boiotia while they were thus engaged in distant Egypt.

More generally, it has been argued that at all times the democratic system was dependent for its viability and for success on the leadership of the Athenian elite. In the early fifth century the elite had largely been drawn from aristocratic families, but with the diminishing importance of aristocratic birth the composition of the elite changed in the course of our period. With the growth of specialisation and changes in the situation of the Athenians, the critical areas for leadership also varied. The need for competent leadership in war had always been recognised: the selection of strategoi continued to be by vote, not by lot, but also in the fourth century strategoi tended to be specialists or 'professionals'. In the fourth century the problems of financial resources, particularly in comparison with the third quarter of the fifth century, were acute. In the 370s and 360s Kallistratos made his contribution not only in terms of advice to the assembly as a powerful speaker, but also through his skill in financial management.[79]

With the Social War, however, the fragility of Athens' resources was dramatically exposed. Less ambitious policies abroad were promoted by rhetores like Euboulos, but the financial problems also led to the recourse to an institutionalised remedy in *c.* 354. The Festival Fund Commission was established to control any surpluses which were automatically, even in time of war, to be paid into the Festival Fund. The commissioners were to be elected by vote and could be re-elected (or possibly were elected for a term of four years). The Festival Fund Commission acquired considerable control of the whole administration of the state. This may well have developed from its probable involvement with the boards of financial officials: in contrast to the Boule with its large, constantly-changing membership of citizens selected by lot, the elected commissioners who might serve for a number of years were in a position to gain

---

[78] See ch. 1.3 and ch. 2.3.1; Thuc. 2.65, cf. Jones 62–4. [79] See ch. 2.3.2.

a mastery of financial affairs, and in so far as they supervised the control of surplus moneys which would be crucial for any sudden or extraordinary expenditure, they could exercise great influence.[80] That is, the Athenians in the difficult years after the Social War recognised the need for experts. On the elitist interpretation of Athenian democracy the real dependence of the democracy on a few men of ability was once more revealed. And it must at least be conceded that the Athenians turned their backs on the use of the Lot and rotation with their strong egalitarian assumptions, and also that overall financial supervision was passing from the democratic, 'amateur' Boule to men of ability and experience. Greater efficiency may also have been the paramount consideration in 366/5 in the changes in the character of the secretaryship concerned with the recording of decrees. But if so, the change in tenure (from a prytany to a year) seems to have been counterbalanced by a change from election to sortition.[81] The responsibilities of the Festival Fund Commissioners were vastly more complex and important than those of the secretaries, and it was the crucial importance of finance which now brought this area of specialisation into the same method of selection as the strategoi. The changes towards expert financial management do not seem to have worked well or to have been completely acceptable. For Hegemon's law in the 330s introduced modifications, including perhaps a new limit of four years for the tenure of officials elected to supervise the public finances. A new office concerned with overall financial supervision seems to have emerged in the mid-330s: the influence of Lykourgos in financial matters and the general trends of the 330s and 320s suggest a continuing priority for efficiency and a strengthening of the reliance on experts.[82]

Another indication that Athenians may have relied on a limited number of able individuals may be found in Demosthenes' reference to the appointment of Leodamas, Aristophon, and others as advocates to speak in support of Leptines' law about exemptions from liturgies in 355. According to Demosthenes, a second election as an advocate was forbidden by a law – a very sound law framed, he said, to prevent profit or blackmail.[83] The Athenians, in turning a blind eye to the legal restrictions, may have been showing good sense in recognising the value of making the best appointments in this particular instance, but we do not know whether such irregular appointments were common, nor indeed if Demosthenes was fully and accurately relating the legal position.

In the initiation of policy, in the advocacy and execution of policies, demagogoi were an inherent necessity in the structure of democracy, and Athenian leaders played a crucial role. That could, of course, appear differently

---

[80] Aiskhin. 3.24–5, *AP* 43.1 (and *CAAP*), 47.2; Buchanan (1962) 53–60, Cawkwell (1963A) 47–8, 54–61, Rhodes 105–8, 235–40, Develin (1984) 133–8.   [81] See Appendix 3A.

[82] [Plut.] *Mor.* 841b–c, D.S. 16.88.1, Mitchel (1962) 213–29, Rhodes 107–8, 219–20, *CAAP* 515–16.

[83] Dem. 20.146, 152–3; see Dem. 18.149 on lack of alertness in the assembly.

to some Athenians or could be so represented: 'the people have surrendered the control of affairs to a few – to the rhetores'. Rhetores who did not have, had lost, or wished to arouse, popular support were prone to make such claims.[84] And though most, if not all, Athenian leaders may have shared to some extent Timotheos' feeling of superiority without showing as much contempt for the ordinary people, there is little or no reason to regard them as conspiring against the interests of the Demos. Political leaders did cooperate with others with similar views on particular issues. At times some might even work together to 'cover up'. But we should not accept at face value, nor draw general inferences from, Deinarkhos' allegations that the leaders and the demagogoi had colluded in their attempts to mislead and manipulate the Athenian people – 'in the assemblies they abuse one another, but in private they are united'.[85] The Harpalos affair itself and other incidents reveal how eagerly political leaders might seize their opportunity to attack opponents: witness Hypereides' attack on Demosthenes in 323 despite their cooperation in the past.

It was hardly a case of the demagogues like the Sausage-Seller manipulating Demos, nor of Demos being the servant of the political leaders. For, though the Athenian people may not always have been as shrewd as the Demos of Aristophanes' *Knights* declared himself to be, the Demos could not be taken for granted, as numerous depositions from the strategia and penalties imposed on rhetores demonstrate.[86]

Ordinary Athenians were not blind to the crucial role of leaders, while opponents, especially when prosecuting, found it useful and indeed necessary to attribute the good and bad fortunes of a polis to its leaders. Some criticism of the Demos – for apathy or past omissions – might be offered by orators, but for the most part they had to adopt the attitude that we have seen was commonly adopted by those who brought a graphe paranomon. The method of attack was to convince the jurors not that the citizen assembly had been foolish in its decision but that their fellow-citizens (and they themselves) had been misled by clever or corrupt speakers.[87] And when the Athenians changed their mind, contemporary critics detected a fickleness on the part of the Demos and a readiness to seek out those who had deceived it, while Aristophanes might detect a readiness on the part of the Athenians to discard one adviser for another. The Old Oligarch noted a tendency to be found in any sovereign body: if some policy or action turns out well, he declared, the Demos takes the credit, but if badly the Demos resorts to accusing a few individuals of acting against its interests.[88]

Yet while the number of prominent leaders was limited, it was not as restricted as has sometimes been supposed, and due account must be taken of

---

[84] [Dem.] 13.15; Aiskhin. 3.233–4, Dem. 3.31–2.   [85] Dein. 1.99.

[86] Dem. 23.109; see ch. 6.4–6.6.   [87] See ch. 6.4, 6.7.

[88] *AP* 28.3, Thuc. 2.59.1–2, 61.2–3, 65.3–4, 3.36.4, 38.1, 43.4–5, 8.1.1, Xen. *Hell.* 1.7.35, Ar. *Ekkl.* 191–203, [Xen.] *AP* 2.17.

lesser rhetores.[89] Nor should the contribution of leaders to the workability of Athenian democracy obscure the role of Athenians in general in the Boule, the Ekklesia and the Dikasteria. In the Boule, as we have seen, there was a certain apathy or passivity and men like Androtion could exercise great influence. Nevertheless its activities, wide-ranging and crucial in the functioning of democracy, did depend on the contribution of large numbers of Athenians, and the Boule does seem to have been effective in promoting knowledge and experience of polis affairs. Nor could the decision of the Ekklesia be assumed. The recommendations of the Boule had to be approved by the Ekklesia which was far from acting like a rubber-stamp. The contemporary critics of the democracy also testified to the power of ordinary Athenians in the assembly.[90]

Aristotle, albeit somewhat reluctantly, recognised the importance of the many in the sound functioning of a constitution. Thus he reserved the highest offices for men with some claim to distinction:

it is not safe for the mass of the citizens (that is, those who are not rich nor possessed of any distinguishing excellence at all) to participate in the highest offices, for injustice and folly would inevitably cause them to act unjustly in some things and to make mistakes in others.[91]

Nevertheless, for reasons of political necessity or expediency, Aristotle acknowledged the desirability of allowing the many to share in the deliberative and judicial functions, so that the many would not be alienated. Yet how, he asked, could the sovereignty of the multitude be preferred to that of the few 'best' men? How could one believe in the discernment and justice of the many and in the notion of the collective superiority of the many compared with the few good men? Aristotle found great difficulty in accepting this notion, but did concede that it might conceivably be true about some particular multitude, but not about all. The arguments which he noted (though with an apparent lack of enthusiasm or conviction) in support of the notion were presumably the arguments of those who advocated or defended democracy.

It is possible that the many, though not individually good men, yet when they come together may be better, not individually, but collectively, than those who are good men . . . for where there are many, each individual, it may be argued, has some portion of virtue and wisdom, and when they come together . . . the multitude becomes one personality as regards the moral and intellectual faculties. This is why the many are better judges of the works of music and those of the poets, for different men can judge a different part of the performance, and all of them all of it.[92]

To those who found difficulty with the concept of the collective superiority of the many Aristotle suggested two other lines of argument. One dealt with

---

[89] See ch. 6.2.   [90] See ch. 4.4.3, 4.5 and ch. 5.1; see Finley 140.
[91] Arist. *Pol.* 1281b21–8 (Loeb tr. adapted); cf. Thuc. 2.37.1, Pl. *Menex.* 238c–d.
[92] Arist. *Pol.* 1281a40–b38 (Loeb tr. adapted); Thuc. 6.39.1; cf. Pl. *Laws* 700e–701a; see Larsen (1954) 4–5, 9.

the view that it was 'absurd for the base to be in control of more important matters than the respectable'. Aristotle suggested that it could be argued that it was just for the many to elect the officials and control their euthynai because 'the assessed property of all those members collectively is more than that of the officials holding great offices individually or in small groups'. The second argument is more convincing. The view that 'to elect rightly is a matter for experts' is countered by the notion of collective wisdom and by the argument that 'about some things the man who made them would not be the only or the best judge in the case of experts whose products come within the knowledge of laymen also'. 'A house, for example, can be judged not only by the man who built it, but in fact the man who uses the house (that is, the householder) judges it better.' In another section of the *Politics* Aristotle seems more enthusiastic about the collective wisdom of the masses and declares that 'in many cases a crowd judges better than a single person'. He adds that the multitude is more incorruptible, and in particular that it is difficult for all the people to be roused to anger and go wrong together.[93]

The dilemma about amateurs and experts showed up clearly in the assembly. Plato and others never tired of contrasting the Athenian practice of seeking advice on technical questions from experts (for example, from shipwrights on ship construction) with their willingness to listen to anyone on matters relating to the government of the polis. But, as we have seen, the assembly was also intolerant of ill-informed speakers in regard to larger questions. Moreover, while there was probably a kernel of truth in Plato's contrast, Isokrates noted that in deliberations about most important matters 'those who are thought to be the wisest sometimes miss the appropriate course of action, whereas now and then some chance person from among those who are deemed of no account (*phauloi*) hits upon the right course and is thought to give the best advice'.[94]

In the final analysis, however, each Athenian in the assembly was called upon to exercise his own judgement, relying in varying measure on the advice of experts and political leaders. And ordinary Athenians appear to have believed that all men, or at least all Athenian citizens, were characterised by a measure of justice (*dikaiosynē*) and good sense (*sōphrosynē* – a virtue claimed particularly by men of conservative views). They would have accepted the implications of a myth told by Protagoras in Plato's dialogue named after that fifth-century teacher. Zeus, according to the myth, feared that mankind was in danger of utter destruction for, while each man had been allotted different talents to survive, men's attempts to band together against the dangers from wild beasts by founding cities had failed. They did wrong to one another because they did not possess the civic virtue – the art of sharing in the life of the polis. Zeus therefore sent Hermes to distribute to men respect for others and a sense of

---

[93] Arist. *Pol.* 1281b38–82a41 (Loeb tr. adapted), 1286a28–35; see *AP* 49.3.
[94] See ch. 2.2; Isok. 12.248 (Loeb tr. adapted).

right, but not differentially as had happened with the arts. 'Let all have their share, for cities cannot exist if only a few have a share of these as of other arts.' Hence, argued Protagoras,

> men and especially the Athenians think that a few should share in offering advice on matters of artistic excellence or good craftsmanship . . . but when they meet to consult about civic capacity, where they should be guided throughout by justice (*dikaiosyne*) and good sense (*sophrosyne*), they naturally allow advice from everybody, on the grounds that everyone should partake of this excellence, or else poleis could not exist.

The art of sharing in the polis, Protagoras argued, could be taught and developed, and the Athenians 'have good reason for accepting the advice of a smith or a shoemaker in public affairs'.[95]

Similar assumptions underlie the assertions made by Perikles, as reported by Thucydides, on the occasion of the public oration to commemorate those Athenians who had died in the service of Athens in the first year of the Peloponnesian War. As might be expected, Perikles waxed eloquent on Athens, her institutions and her citizens.

> We find it possible for the same people to attend to private affairs and public affairs as well, and notwithstanding our varied occupations to be adequately informed about public affairs. For we are unique in regarding the man who does not participate in these affairs at all not as a man who minds his own business, but as useless. We ourselves decide matters or submit them to proper consideration, taking the view that debate is not harmful to action, but rather not to be informed through discussion before we proceed to take the necessary action.[96]

There were, however, other attitudes to participating in polis affairs. Indeed the Greek term for 'minding one's own business' (*apragmosyne*) was regularly used in a complimentary sense, and peace and quiet were frequently praised – not only by Athenians from aristocratic or wealthy families who would oppose, or at least deprecate, any disturbance to the political and social status quo or who concentrated their energies on private pursuits, but also by Athenians generally, desirous of being left alone, of keeping away from the courts or of avoiding a term as an official.[97] Demosthenes wrote in his speech *Against Meidias* about the reasons why those who had suffered at the hands of the wealthy Meidias did not seek redress in the courts: 'I suppose you all know the stock excuses for shirking the duty of self-help [by going to court] – want of leisure, a distaste for affairs (*apragmosyne*), inability to speak, lack of means and a thousand such reasons.' Those reasons or excuses were also likely to deter many citizens from acting like the Athenians of Perikles' speech, more particularly from engaging in the more

---

[95] Pl. *Prt.* 319a–324d (Loeb tr. adapted).
[96] Thuc. 2.40.2 (and *HCT* for textual problems and interpretation).
[97] Pl. *Ep.* 7.324b–326b, *Rep.* 433a; [Xen.] *AP* 2.18, Ar. *Clouds* 1007, *Georgoi* fr. 1, Eur. fr. 193, Lys. 24.24, Isok. 15.98–9, Dem. 21.141, 40.32, 47.82; Adkins (1976) 301–27.

active forms of sharing in the life of the polis. Demosthenes, it may be added, decided to drop his case against Meidias.[98]

8.5 Factors in the support for democracy

The contemporary critics of Athenian democracy tended to point, by way of contrast, to the blending of monarchical, oligarchic and democratic elements in Sparta and the stability and durability of Spartan institutions.[99] The Athenians, however, avoided the rigidity, limitations and stagnation of many aspects of the Spartan polis, and democracy in Athens in fact displayed a remarkable stability and durability, especially in comparison with other poleis. The tensions within the Athenian citizen body were for most of our period accommodated to a sufficient degree to avoid revolution and bloodshed. At times of military difficulty or defeat, conservative and oligarchic elements or sentiment might come to the fore. In the 340s, for example, this was one factor in Demosthenes' recourse to the Council of the Areiopagos for support against his opponents, though the revived importance of that council was to rebound on Demosthenes over the Harpalos affair.[100] In 411 the democracy succumbed in the wake of the Sicilian disaster, as it did in 404 after defeat and surrender to Sparta and in 322 after the abortive attempt to assert Athenian independence against Makedonian power. In 404 and 322 the role of Sparta and Antipater in overthrowing the democracy was central. Social and economic tensions also seem to have been contained, though less effectively in times of financial stringency.[101] Hypereides in c. 330 had to concede that well-to-do citizens including mine operators had been afraid of judicial attacks on their property, but he sought to impress upon the jury the magnanimity of the Athenian Demos by referring to recent court decisions to demonstrate that the Demos did not entertain malicious accusations and did not show a blind hatred of the rich.[102]

Our evidence about democracies elsewhere is slight, but there is little to suggest that they were as durable as in Athens or that they developed as strongly. Syracuse, for example, the largest polis in Sicily, experimented with democracy in the period from 466 to 405. But while larger poleis may have accumulated greater resources to sustain radical democracies and to minimise the social and political consequences of natural disasters and protracted war, disturbed external conditions and instability within Syracuse made democracy fragile and facilitated the seizure and retention of power by Dionysios from 405

---

[98] Dem. 21.141 (Loeb tr. adapted), but see Aiskhin. 3.52, Plut. *Dem* 12.
[99] Xen. *Lak. Pol.* 10.8, 14, Arist. *Pol.* 1265b33–41, 1333b12–26.
[100] Dem. 18.132–6, Dein. 1.61–3, *SEG* 12.87, Plut. *Dem.* 26, Rhodes (1980A) 319–20.
[101] Perlman (1967) 161–9; see also Perlman (1963) 355 on political leaders' social links (which Perlman overestimates) and their views on social and economic problems.
[102] Hyp. 4.33–7; see ch. 5.4.

to 367.[103] Smaller, largely agrarian communities like Mantineia had democratic regimes in the fifth and fourth centuries, but it was vulnerable to intervention by Sparta or other powers.[104] Khios, which had a popular or broadly-based boule as early as the sixth century, seems to have enjoyed political stability in the fifth century until 412, but the political arrangements in the fifth century appear to have constituted a blend of oligarchic and democratic elements – in essence perhaps an oligarchy with some democratic features.[105]

Both the stability and the degree of democratic development were dependent on factors peculiar to each polis as well as general factors operating in our period. And if, as has been suggested, important elements in democratic developments in Athens were economic development and the empire, what factors contributed to stability in Athens?

Large poleis were freer from stasis in the view of Aristotle, who explained this by noting that the middle class was numerous and that polarisation into rich and poor was thus avoided. He also argued that democracies were more secure and more long-lived than oligarchies, since the middle class was more numerous and had a larger share of the honours in democracies than in oligarchies.[106] And there can be little doubt that the growth of Athens and improved economic conditions played a part in increasing the number of zeugitai and, in other ways, in consolidating and fostering a commitment to democracy in the second half of the fifth century. The tensions between rich and poor were blunted, so that ordinary Athenians appear to have been largely satisfied with political equality – inherent at deme level and in the Boule, the Ekklesia and the Dikasteria, and no matter how much circumscribed in practice – and to have acquiesced in economic inequality. Increased prosperity and the opportunities afforded by klerouchies and colonies helped to dampen any tendency (feared in other Greek poleis) to demand redistribution of property. Poorer citizens might have more to do with poorer metics than with rich citizens, but in the final analysis they recognised their affinity with rich citizens as against metics and slaves. State pay and many other factors encouraged quiescence and political stability.[107]

Even with the loss of prosperity in defeat at the hands of the Spartans, democracy was able to re-emerge in 403 – partly because the Thirty, by their violent actions against the persons and the property of more than 1,500 people (and not only their political opponents), had undermined oligarchy as a practical alternative.[108] An important element in the reconciliation of the factions was the provision for an amnesty or general pardon for all past acts: 'no

[103] Arist. *Pol.* 1293a1–6, 1320a17–b4; D.S. 11.68.5–6, 87, 13.34–5, 94–6, Arist. *Pol.* 1304a27–9; Finley (1979) 58–73; Finley 60.　　[104] Arist. *Pol.* 1318b21–7, Xen. *Hell.* 5.2.1–7.
[105] ML 8c, Thuc. 8.24.4, Quinn (1969) 22–6, O'Neil (1979/80) 66–73.
[106] Arist. *Pol.* 1296a9–32. On the stability and durability of the oligarchic regime in Corinth, see Salmon (1984) 231–9, 354–62, 384–6.
[107] Jones 166–9, French (1964) 107–62, Finley 31–4, 108–11; Eur. *Suppl.* 404–8; see ch. 2.2.
[108] *AP* 35.3–4, Aiskhin. 3.235.

one is to remember the past misdeeds of anyone, except the Thirty, the Ten, the Eleven and the governors of the Peiraieus, and not even of these if they render an account of their office (*euthynai*)'. The Athenians thus sought to limit the consequences of the bitterness of the civil war. The execution of a man who moved to ignore the amnesty seems to have had a generally salutary effect. Although some prosecutions were launched, none is known to have been successful. Not that all could be, or was, forgotten: a man's allegiance in 404/3, for example, might be, and was, adduced in hearings before the courts or the Boule, especially in regard to dokimasia, when a citizen's career and attitudes came under review. Overall the response of the Athenians to their past misfortunes, both personal and as a community, was acknowledged by the author of the *Athenaion Politeia* as better and more public-spirited than that of any other people.[109] The influence of the occupying power (tempered by the moderate, low-profile attitude of King Pausanias) should not be overlooked, though it must be added that the Athenians rejected a proposal favoured by Sparta – the proposal by Phormisios in 403 to restrict citizenship to those who possessed land. Enough landholders, small or great, valued the sense of community with their landless fellow-citizens to defeat the limitation of democracy. The landholders declared their preference for democracy.[110]

While economic conditions were important, the earlier consolidation of democratic sentiment was critically dependent on political and social factors. The fundamental reforms of Solon and the encouragement of unity by the Peisistratids were noted in the first chapter. Above all Kleisthenes disturbed the old patterns of aristocratic influence and reorganised the citizen body in such a way as to develop alternative foci for loyalty, especially the demes and the new tribes. Yet the new political structure left the leading families with a major outlet for their experience and influence in the strategia, while ostracism provided a means of removing, with a minimum of disruption, any leader who might seem to be a threat to the citizen community. This safety valve of democracy greatly minimised the danger of civil war and permitted the gradual, but surer, development of democratic sentiment in the first half of the fifth century. The circumvention of ostracism in 417 and the disenchantment with the demagogoi and the conduct of the war were exploited by oligarchs, as we have seen, to engineer the revolution of 411.[111]

Of other political factors contributing to the stability of Athenian democracy two may be mentioned here. One, obedience to the laws, was commonly regarded as a characteristically conservative attribute. This was of the essence of *eunomia*, with which the characteristic of democracy, isonomia, was contrasted. The praises of eunomia had been sung by Solon, and democrats contrasted the rule of law with the arbitrary rule of tyrants and some oligarchic regimes. There

---

[109] *AP* 39.6, Andok. 1.90–1, Isok. 18.20; *AP* 40.2–3, *CAAP* 471–2, Lys. 16, Xen. *Hell.* 2.4.40–3, Isok. 18.31–2. [110] Xen. *Hell.* 2.4.35–8, *AP* 38–9; see Xen. *Hell.* 2.4.20–1.
[111] See ch. 1.1, ch. 7.2 and ch. 2.3.1.

would have been general agreement with the sentiment expressed by Euripides – 'the power that keeps cities of men together is goodly observance of the laws'.[112] The determination of Athenians to enforce the rule of law and obedience to the laws was one element in their propensity to resort to litigation: even so, in the interests of reconciliation in 403 they could agree to forget much, but not all, of the recent past. And while individual Athenians had to work within the laws, the Ekklesia for all its claims to 'sovereignty' was not exempt. There was, it is true, also a contrary current in Athenian thinking which found its expression in the assertion that 'the Demos has it in its power to do whatever it wishes' and in the decision to condemn the Arginousai generals *en masse*. But the graphe paranomon and the procedure of nomothesia provided clear mechanisms for ensuring that assembly decisions and decisions of the nomothetai conformed to existing law. In so far as these principles were upheld (and rivalry among rhetores tended to see that disregard of the principles at least did not go unchallenged), the assembly acted under the rule of law. Nomothesia meanwhile permitted the assembly to initiate change, but change which had to be duly considered.[113] Other indications of a sense of balance and perspective may be found. Athenians at large, for example, seem to have been content with the possession of power and with the exercise of it in ways that enabled them to employ the talents of ambitious individuals while keeping their leaders under close scrutiny, and in ways, too, that would not undermine the holding of private property with all its inequalities.

These various indications of good sense and a desire for continuity and stability must also be related to a second factor – the various structural features of Athenian institutions which have been examined in earlier chapters and which in themselves constituted the basis for democracy and contributed to the support for democracy. The use of the Lot with its notion of equality and the principle of rotation, for example, helped to restrict the potential for bitterness, divisiveness and disorder in elections. Or again, and more fundamentally, the right of all citizens to participate, actively or passively, in the assembly and the courts and in particular the right to vote on any issue whenever they chose (or were able) to do so provided the opportunities for the development of democracy and the legitimation of democratic institutions. Yet the Athenians managed, it would seem, to cope with a high level of politicisation and not to be overwhelmed by the need for continuing discussion and decision-making.[114]

Structural features such as the use of the Lot and annual tenure in many ways worked against continuity, stability and efficiency. Yet despite the charges of

---

[112] Thuc. 8.64.5, Xen. *Lak. Pol.* 8, Hdt. 1.66; Solon fr. 3 (Diehl); Eur. *Suppl.* 312–13, 429–41; Thuc. 2.37.3, 3.37.3, Lys. 2.18–19, Xen. *Mem.* 3.5.16–18, Dem. 24.5, 36, 75–6, [Dem.] 25.20–7, Aiskhin. 1.4–6, 177–8, 3.6–7, Lykourg. *Leok.* 4, Hyp. 4.5; cf. Xen. *Mem.* 1.2.40–6; see ch. 3.1 and n. 2 and Hansen (1974) 47–8.

[113] See ch. 3 n. 91, ch. 4.2 and ch. 7.2; on the 'revision of the laws' initiated in 411 and completed by 400/399 see Thuc. 8.97.2, Andok. 1.81–9, Clinton (1982) 27–37, Sealey (1982) 293–6, 301–2.

[114] See ch. 3.5 and ch. 4.1; Finley 82–3.

their critics, Athenians achieved considerable continuity and stability. In part this may be traced to the continuing leadership both of rhetores in the assembly and the courts and of elected strategoi, certain financial officials and envoys. Individual leaders and their personal power and influence provided an element of continuity. That, however, usually fell far short of the continuity which may be provided by a 'government' or cabinet ministers or a bureaucracy or an independent, permanent judiciary. In Athens continuity and stability were also achieved by the interest and participation of Athenian citizens – not only by the activities of prominent political leaders, but also by the 'occasional proposers' and the citizens at large. For the citizens at large acted as minor officials and in particular were party to the discussions in the Boule and the Ekklesia, they served in the Dikasteria and they directly exercised the sovereign power of the Demos.[115]

[115] Cf. [Xen.] *AP* 1; see ch. 6.2.

Appendix 1 The population of Athens

(A) On the vexed question of the population of Athens, see the fundamental studies of Beloch (1886 and (1923) 386–418) and Gomme. For the fifth century, see Thuc. 2.13.6–8 (and *HCT*) (for 431) and other evidence examined by Gomme 1–35 and Gomme (1959) 61–8, Jones 161–80, Patterson (1981) 40–81, Strauss (1979) 72–118, Whitehead (1977) 148–9, Jameson (1978) 141, Duncan-Jones (1980) 101–9, Hansen (1981) 19–32, Garnsey (1985) 62–75. For convenient tabulations of estimates of the total population and of the citizen, metic and slave components at different times from *c.* 480 to 313, see Gomme 26, 29, Ehrenberg (1969) 31 and Ruschenbusch (1979A) 146.

(B) The rate of population growth has been much debated. Aristotle (*Pol.* 1265a38–65b17) seems to indicate some increase in citizen populations in Greek cities, for he represents Plato's failure (in the *Laws*) to control the birth rate as based on the assumption of a sufficiently stationary population, 'because that is thought to be the case now in the poleis'. Aristotle, however, appears to believe that in fact there was some population growth both in the mid-fourth century and earlier – sufficient to require the attention of lawgivers. Throughout the period from the mid-fifth century to 322, a natural growth of not less than $\frac{1}{2}$% in the Athenian citizen population may be suggested. Before 451, when Perikles' restrictive law (see ch. 2.1) made the citizen body a 'closed population', the rate may have been somewhat higher. For in the years immediately after Salamis the demes may have accepted some foreigners as fellow Athenians, as suggested by Patterson (1981) 68–71, but if so the numbers are likely to have been much lower than she suggests. Patterson's estimate (68) of *c.* 40,000 citizens by the early 450s would seem to be rather high.

(C) On general problems of historical demography and historical method, see most recently Hansen (1986) 7–25, including 10–11 on the appropriateness of demographic models based on population patterns in Europe in the period from *c.* 1500 to *c.* 1750 and computerised model life tables (e.g. Coale and Demeny (1966) or *U.N. Model Life Tables* published by the United Nations in the series of *Population Studies*). The use of these tables involves different (but still unverifiable) assumptions such as the (reasonable) selection of Model West, males, mortality level 4 (life expectancy at birth of 25.26 years) and annual increase of $\frac{1}{2}$% as reflecting the characteristics of the adult male citizen population of Athens.

(D) For the fourth century, see D.S. 18.10.2, 11.3 (Athenian forces in the Lamian War in 323/2), 18.18.5 (9,000 full citizens in 322 after more than 22,000 had been disfranchised: G. T. Griffith (by letter) made the attractive suggestion that the figure of 'more than 12,000' in Plut. *Phok.* 28 was the number of disfranchised who went to Thrace or the disfranchised who stayed in Attike and that Plutarch (or his source) reported one of these two figures as the total number of disfranchised: compare the 21,000 citizens in the census of Demetrios of Phaleron in 317–307 as reported by Athenaios 6.272c) and other evidence examined most recently by Hansen (1986) 26–69; see also Gomme 1–35, Gomme (1959) 67–8, Strauss (1979) 72–118, Rhodes (1980) 191–201, Williams (1983) 241–5, Hansen (1985) 172–89; cf. Jones 76–9, Ruschenbusch (1981A), (1981B), (1984) for 21,000 as the number of adult male citizens before the disqualification of 322.

(E) On the distinction between the number of Athenian citizens usually living in Attike (including those on not infrequent military expeditions) and the total number of Athenian citizens (including klerouchs, men serving as mercenaries in foreign armies, Athenians living abroad – privately or as officials – and foreigners awarded citizenship who did not move to Athens), see Beloch (1923) 402–3 and Hansen (1986) 8–9, 70–2. The difference in numbers would have been most marked in the third quarter of the fifth century and in the middle third of the fourth century and was reduced to a minimum after the forced repatriations by Lysander at the end of the Peloponnesian War. For our investigations of participation by citizens those resident in Attike are particularly relevant. A few klerouchs, for example, may have served on the Boule and attended the assembly in the same year (Hansen (1986) 56–7), but it is otherwise highly unlikely that, as long as their usual place of residence was outside Attike, klerouchs participated in the working of the Boule, the Ekklesia or the Dikasteria, though klerouchs made their contribution to Athenian defence and foreign policy, especially in the area where the klerouchy was located, but also occasionally by serving on Athenian expeditions in other areas (Thuc. 3.5.1 and *HCT*, 4.28.4, 5.8.2, 7.57.2, Jones 174–7, Hansen (1986) 70–2).

Appendix 2 'Working days'

(A) The demands made by service on the Boule and the jury panels may be deduced from the following exclusions from an ordinary year of 354 days.

(1)   *Annual festival days*: normally no sittings of the Boule, jury courts or Ekklesia (Ar. *Thesm.* 78–80, [Xen.] *AP* 3.8, schol. Ar. *Wasps* 660–3, Lys. 26.6): at least 75 days.

(2)   *Monthly festival days*: normally the Ekklesia did not meet, but the Boule did. These were days 1–4 and 6–8 of each month – that is, 84 in a year, but 9 coincided with annual festival days: 75 days.

(3)   *'Impure' days* or days of ill omen: days involving the purification of the polis – by the rites of the Plynteria (Thargelion 25) when the garments of Athena's statue were washed, or by the hearing of homicide cases by the Areiopagos Council to rid the polis of the pollution of murder. The Areiopagos Council could judge homicide cases only on the 27th, 28th and 29th days of each month but would presumably not have done so on the major day of the Panathenaia (Hekatombaion 28) nor on the day of the Theogamia (Gamelion 27): of the somewhat less than 36 days thus available, perhaps about 15 might be postulated as 'impure' in any year. These days were probably not used by the Boule or by courts or by the Ekklesia. See Mikalson (1975A) 19–27.

(4)   *Days on which the assembly met*: Dikasteria were not convened (Dem. 24.80) – 40 regular meetings of the assembly each year in the 320s (*AP* 43.3).

The incidence of meetings in the 320s may be estimated to have been:

(a)   The Boule was convened on every day except 'days of recess (or dismissal)' (*AP* 43.3 – usually translated 'holidays' or 'festival days'), that is, every day except (1) and (3). About 260 days a year. (One of 24 attested meetings was, however, held on an annual festival day, 11 on monthly festival days). See ch. 3.5.

(b)   The Dikasteria did not meet on (1), (3), and (4). The thesmothetai, therefore, had up to 220 days on which they could set sitting days for the courts (cf. *AP* 59.1), but they might have tried to make sparing use of (2). The total number of days in any year would depend on the amount of business coming before the courts and probably fell between 150–160 and about 200. 150 talents would be required each year – as alleged by Bdelykleon in Ar. *Wasps* 660–3 (see scholiast) – if 6,000 dikasts received 3 obols for each of 300 court days, but both 6,000 (receiving pay for each court day) and 300 are inflated figures.

(c)   The Ekklesia did not normally meet on (1), (2), and (3). Some meetings, however, are known which were apparently held on festival days: of these one (in 346 B.C.) was specifically noted as exceptional (Aiskhin. 3.66–7; cf. Dem.

24.26 for a meeting of Nomothetai in 352), one may have been held in the course of the City Dionysia (Thuc. 4.118.11–13; for two later examples see *Hesperia* 7 (1938), no. 31.1–7 of 319/18 B.C. and *Hesperia* 5 (1936), no. 15.1–4 of 196/5 B.C.), while two after our period were held on the days of festivals celebrated exclusively by women (the Theogamia, *IG* II².849.1–4 of 206/5 B.C. and the Thesmophoria, *IG* II².1006.50–1 of 122/1).

See Mikalson (1975B) 127–9, 186–204 and Hansen 35–72, 131–4.

(B) Such were the 'working days' for the major institutions of the Athenian polis. Festival days were, however, not necessarily non-working days for all the population of Attike. A gang of ten men working on the temple at Eleusis in 329/8 was paid for 40 consecutive days, working not only on monthly festival days but also on annual festival days including even the Panathenaia. During the same period, however, three bricklayers and their assistants worked 25 days and a stone-dresser and a plasterer only 17 days – at least at the temple (*IG* II².1672.26–34). Work patterns no doubt varied with such factors as the type of work and the socio-economic status of the men involved, the availability of work and its location. The architect at Eleusis received a salary amounting to 2 dr. a day, as compared with 2 and 2½dr. for skilled workers (*IG* II².1672.11–12, 26–8, 31–2, 110–11, 177–8; 1673.59–60): his skill and responsibility were, however, recognised by the fact that his salary covered every day, whether he worked or not. The clear presumption is that men who were hired on a daily basis did not usually work every day. Perhaps they might have expected to work about the same number of days as the Boule met (some 260) or 300 days, if work was abundant and the weather favourable.

But there is good reason to believe that in many years in our period the demand for labour for building purposes was not high. The two decades after 450 were the high-point in temple and other building in Athens and Attike generally, while the two decades after 338 witnessed an upsurge in building for public purposes. From the intervening years we know of a range of projects, including the building of the temple of Athena Nike in the mid-420s and the Stoa Basileios *c.* 420, the completion of the Erekhtheion in the last years of the Peloponnesian War, the remodelling of the Pnyx and the building of the New Bouleuterion about the end of the fifth century, work at Eleusis in the 350s (and 320s) and the building of a temple of Asklepios about 350. But such (known) construction work as was available in the intervening years mainly related to utilitarian purposes including defence works such as the rebuilding of the fortifications and the Long Walls in the 390s (a considerable undertaking), and work on the dockyards in the 340s. (See *IG* II².244 and 1654–85; Burford (1969) 25–35 and Boersma (1970) 65–104.) A worker, whether unskilled or skilled, might therefore frequently have had to seek employment in seasonal or other work. If he managed to receive 1 dr. (a daily rate known from the Erekhtheion accounts from the last years of the Peloponnesian War: *IG* I³.475–6) for as many as 260 days from whatever source, he would have had available slightly less than 4½ obols a day to support himself and his family throughout the year (or some 5 obols, if employed for 300 days), and in the 320s amounts proportionate to the daily rates of 1½, 2 and 2½ dr. known from the Eleusinian accounts (*IG* II².1672–3).

(C) The number of days of paid employment may, for many of those Athenian citizens who offered or had to offer their labour for hire, have been considerably less than 260 days. Much of the 'hired labour' would have been slave labour or metic labour, but there is very little evidence, and little agreement, about the extent of hired labour and in particular citizen hired labour (see de Ste Croix 179–86, 188–91, who regards the latter as comparatively insignificant).

The indications in the literary sources of strong prejudice against manual labour (and against trade) present a partial picture of Athenian attitudes. The attitudes expounded in the generalisations of Aristotle and (in stronger terms) Plato were desirable or proper attitudes as they saw them: the citizen should be concerned with the pursuit of *aretē* (virtue or excellence) and with participating in public life and in holding office (Pl. *Laws* 846d–847b, Arist. *Pol.* 1328b33–29a39). Other activities were to be avoided. Yet agricultural pursuits are commonly represented by ancient writers as acceptable (Xen. *Oik.* 4.4; cf. Arist. *Pol.* 1318b6–17, 1319a24–30), and in Athens these 'proper' attitudes were far from being upheld in practice by all the well-to-do in our period, either in respect of the activities pursued or in giving high priority to participating in public life.

Nevertheless wealthy citizens did not need to work with their hands (or body (*sōma*) as the Athenians put it). It was different for the *penētes* (see ch. 5.3.1). Poorer Athenians worked their own land, with or without the assistance of slaves. Others worked as craftsmen or as labourers, sometimes working side by side with metics and slaves. The literary sources, however, indicate that craftsmen or artisans were generally not held in particular esteem: indeed the term *banausos* which is used as a descriptive term for their work came to acquire the sense of 'illiberal' or 'vulgar' (see Hdt. 2.167, Soph. *Aj.* 1120–1, Xen. *Oik.* 4.2–3, Arist. *Pol.* 1328b33–29a2; cf. Pl. *Ap.* 22c–d; Whitehead (1977) 116–20). Those who engaged in trade in the Agora, particularly because of the common association with doubtful or dishonest practices, were the butt of jokes and were much despised (Ar. *Knights* 128–44, 738–40, 1009, 1257–8, *Clouds* 639–40; Ehrenberg (1951) 114–15, 119–20, Hopper (1979) 64–7). Those who worked as hired labourers (*thētes*), wage-earners or wage-labourers (*misthōtoi*), were not to be envied (Eur. *El.* 201–6, Isai. 5.39, Pl. *Rep.* 371c–e). For a free man should not live in dependence on others like a slave, but should work for himself (Xen. *Mem.* 2.8, Arist. *Rhet.* 1367a28–32). And while it is no doubt true that Athenians in general preferred to work for themselves, and not to work for a wage (*misthos*) and thus be at the beck and call of any man, for many Athenians the reality was quite different and they had to offer their labour to others – or to sell goods or services (Xen. *Mem.* 3.7.6; Ehrenberg (1951) 113–36, Hopper (1979) 61–70, 126–41).

The snobbish attitudes depicted in Plato, Aristotle and the 'country gentleman' Xenophon, and in particular the prejudice against those who traded in the Agora, are not absent from speeches intended to convince dikasts in the law-courts. Demosthenes' sneers about the family of Aiskhines are notorious but not unique, while it is of interest that in order to counter certain statements by his opponent about his mother, Euxitheos saw fit to cite a law which he said provided that anyone who reproached any male or female citizen with carrying on business in the Agora was liable to the penalties for slander (Dem. 57.30–1, 33–6; see ch. 3.1).

For many ordinary Athenians there was probably some discrepancy between the reality of their lives and their public attitudes. Yet, even in the limited evidence that we have about poorer Athenians, there are indications of a pride in their craft or occupation (Pl. *Ap.* 22c–d, *IG* I².473, de Ste Croix 274). It may well be that their values and attitudes were not fully apprehended by well-to-do Athenians or, if they were, were not acknowledged by those who provide most of our literary and epigraphical evidence.

Appendix 3 Notes on three constitutional matters[1]

(A) Variation in the recording of decrees may in part be traced to the character of the secretaryship concerned with the recording of decrees. Until 367/6 **'the Secretary of the Boule'**, who was the official directed to publish decrees, held office for one prytany. In and after 366/5 the secretary concerned (known sometimes by the same title) held office for a year (*AP* 54.3 and *CAAP*). The longer period of tenure should have led to greater efficiency and uniformity of practice (and in many respects decrees from the 350s and later display less variation in formulation, though other factors as well as the secretariat were working in this direction).

It would seem probable, however, that it was at the same time in the 360s that the method of selecting the secretary was changed from voting to sortition, and it is likely that he was no longer selected from among the bouleutai (Rhodes 135 n. 11; cf. de Laix 77). The uncertainty of these two aspects makes hazardous the deduction of reasons for the change to an annual secretary. On the basis of the observation of *AP* 54.3 that previously the most distinguished and trustworthy men were selected, it has been argued that the change was designed to downgrade the importance of the secretary by the introduction of sortition with its egalitarian assumptions. It should, however, be noted that the author of *AP*, if (as is likely) he is not Aristotle himself, shares with Aristotle a disposition to explanation in terms of anti-aristocratic attitudes in democracies. Nevertheless, it may be that these were the paramount considerations in this case. If so, the extension of the term may have been intended in the interests of efficiency to counteract some of the consequences of the use of the Lot. Moreover, the character of the duties was such that only those with an interest and some competence in the duties were likely to offer themselves for election. The fundamental motivation would then be consistent with the general tendency for the Athenians to give a higher priority to egalitarian aspects of appointment to office than efficiency. Yet the demands made on the secretary, especially if (as the prescripts and general formulation of decrees seem to suggest) the Athenians were displaying somewhat more interest in their records, may have been increasing. It is possible (and perhaps more likely), then, that a desire to have one person giving full attention to this (and not concerned with bouleutic duties) over a period of a year was the paramount consideration with those who sponsored the change, but that the position was not deemed so vital or demanding as to warrant the continuing use of election and that the Lot was introduced to counteract any increase in the importance of the position. See Rhodes 134–8, de Laix 76–7, 128 n. 53, and Alessandri (1982) 7–70.

(B) In the later fourth century **non-probouleumatic decrees** used the enactment

---

[1]   (A) see p. 86; (B) see p. 89; (C) see p. 103.

formula 'it was resolved by the Demos' and the motion formula 'be it resolved by the Demos', while **probouleumatic decrees** had the enactment formula 'it was resolved by the Boule and the Demos' and a probouleumatic formula. In the 50–60 years before 405/4 motion formulas are not found, while the standard enactment formula for all assembly decrees was 'it was resolved by the Boule and the Demos'. In the first half of the fourth century the two types of enactment formula were used and motion formulas began to appear, but there seems to have been a tendency to continue to use the fifth-century enactment formula with any enactment of the Demos. For the arguments in support of this analysis see Rhodes 64–81, 244–83 and (1974) 233 arguing for a transitional stage in the first half of the fourth century.

The inconsistency (see ch. 4 n. 76) and the carelessness of secretaries of the Boule may explain some of the instances from the early fourth century which do not conform to the later differentiation, but it may be doubted whether such a distinction was recognised in the earlier fourth century, even though by the mid-century the distinction seems to have been accepted and the corresponding formulas customarily applied. For a different interpretation of the epigraphical evidence and its implications for the role of the Boule, see de Laix 87–142, and for the inconsistency and carelessness of secretaries or masons see IG II².243.5–6 (336 B.C. – Boule and Demos are in the reverse order in the enactment formula) and IG II².672.4 (280/79 B.C., but a sobering example as this stone and a copy of the decree – *Hesperia* 10 (1941), 338–9 – must have had different enactment formulas) and Rhodes 77–8.

(c) The methods for selecting **presiding officials** for the Boule and the Ekklesia were changed at some time after 399 and before 379/8 (see Lys. 13.37 (399 B.C.), *CSCA* 5 (1972), 164–9 (379/8 B.C.), Tod 123.6 and 124.6–7 (378/7 B.C.), Smith (1930) 250–76, D.M. Lewis (1954) 31–4 and Rhodes 16–27, 218).

The fifty prytaneis selected their chairman (*epistatēs*) by lot from their own number. In the second half of the fifth century the prytaneis presided in the Boule and the Ekklesia, while their chairman, who served for one day only (probably in his life-time – see *CAAP* 531), acted also as chairman in the Boule and in the Ekklesia if it met on his day of office. Thus an individual had very limited opportunity for exercising a chairman's influence and for 'organising' the business discussed by the Boule or the Ekklesia. The prytaneis, however, had the potential, though for a limited period, through their preparation of the agenda and their functions as presiding officials to influence discussions in the Boule and the Ekklesia (cf. Dem. 24.22, Ar. *Akh.* 169–73, IG I³.34 (ML 46).35–7, I³.71 (ML 69).28–38, Thuc. 6.14, Xen. *Hell.* 1.7.14–15).

It was perhaps to minimise this potential, though practical considerations of spreading workloads may have been paramount, that a new system of *prohedroi* (presiding officials) was introduced at some time after 399. When the prytaneis summoned the Boule or the Ekklesia, their chairman (selected by lot and serving for only one day as before) appointed by lot nine prohedroi, one from each tribe, except the tribe holding the prytany at the time, and he selected (by lot) one of them as their chairman (*epistatēs*). A councillor could be one of the prohedroi once in every prytany, but no one could be chairman more than once in the year (*AP* 44.1–3). The possibilities of collusion in the preparation of the agenda and in the conduct of meetings of the Boule and Ekklesia were thus diminished and so, too, the chance of small groups dominating the Boule or the Ekklesia by exploiting such possibilities.

Bibliography

1 Abbreviations

For the sources the system of abbreviations of the *Oxford Classical Dictionary* has been followed (with the exception of Aristotle (?) *Athenaion Politeia* which is abbreviated to *AP*), and for the titles of periodical journals the system of *L'Année philologique*.

The following abbreviations have also been employed:

APF   J. K. Davies, *Athenian Propertied Families 600–300 B.C.* Oxford, 1971

ASI   E. Badian (ed.), *Ancient Society and Institutions: Studies presented to Victor Ehrenberg.* Oxford, 1966.

ATL   B. D. Meritt, H. T. Wade-Gery and M. F. McGregor, *The Athenian Tribute Lists.* 4 vols. Cambridge, Mass., 1939–53

CAAP   P. J. Rhodes, *A Commentary on the Aristotelian Athenaion Politeia.* Oxford, 1981

Crux   P. A. Cartledge and F. D. Harvey (edd.), *Crux. Essays presented to G. E. M. de Ste Croix* (= *History of Political Thought* 6.1–2, 1985)

FGrH   F. Jacoby, *Die Fragmente der griechischen Historiker.* Berlin/Leiden, 1923–58

HCT   A. W. Gomme, A. Andrewes and K. J. Dover, *A Historical Commentary on Thucydides.* 5 vols. Oxford, 1945–81

HMA   G. F. Hill, R. Meiggs and A. Andrewes, *Sources for Greek History between the Persian and Peloponnesian Wars* (2nd ed.). Oxford, 1951

ML   R. Meiggs and D. M. Lewis, *A Selection of Greek Historical Inscriptions to the End of the Fifth Century B.C.* Oxford, 1969

PA   J. Kirchner, *Prosopographia Attica.* 2 vols. Berlin, 1966 (reprint of 1901–3 ed.) (see ch. 2 n. 57)

Tod   M. N. Tod, *A Selection of Greek Historical Inscriptions*, vol. 2: *From 403 to 323 B.C.* Oxford, 1948

2 Modern Discussions

(A) Select Bibliography
(Works to which frequent reference is made in the notes and which are cited by author's name only.)

Bonner, R. J. *Aspects of Athenian Democracy.* Berkeley, 1933
Calhoun, G. M. *Athenian Clubs in Politics and Litigation.* Rome, 1964 (reprint of 1913 ed.)
Connor, W. R. *The New Politicians of Fifth-Century Athens.* Princeton, 1971

Davies, J. K. *Wealth and the Power of Wealth in Classical Athens*. New York, 1981
Dover, K. J. *Greek Popular Morality in the Time of Plato and Aristotle*. Oxford, 1974
Finley, M. I. *Politics in the Ancient World*. Cambridge, 1983
Gomme, A. W. *The Population of Athens in the Fifth and Fourth Centuries B.C.*
  Oxford, 1933
Hansen, M. H. *The Athenian Ecclesia*. Copenhagen, 1983
Harrison, A. R. W. *The Law of Athens*, vol. 1: *The Family and Property* and vol. 2:
  Procedure. Oxford, 1968 and 1971
Headlam, J. W. *Election by Lot at Athens*. 2nd ed. revised by D. C. MacGregor.
  Cambridge, 1933
Hignett, C. *A History of the Athenian Constitution to the End of the Fifth Century B.C.*
  Oxford, 1952
Jones, A. H. M. *Athenian Democracy*. Oxford, 1957
Kroll, J. H. *Athenian Bronze Allotment Plates*. Cambridge, Mass., 1972
Laix, R. A. de *Probouleusis at Athens: A Study of Political Decision-Making*. Berkeley,
  1973
MacDowell, D. M. *The Law in Classical Athens*. London, 1978
Meiggs, R. *The Athenian Empire*. Oxford, 1972
Mossé, C. *La fin de la démocratie athénienne*. Paris, 1962
Osborne, M. J. *Naturalization in Athens*. 4 vols. Brussels, 1981–3 (see ch. 2 n. 9)
Osborne, R. *Demos: The Discovery of Classical Attika*. Cambridge, 1985
Ostwald, M. *Nomos and the Beginnings of the Athenian Democracy*. Oxford, 1969
Parke, H. W. *Festivals of the Athenians*. London, 1977
Pritchett, W. K. *The Greek State at War*. 3 vols. Berkeley and Los Angeles, 1971–9
Rhodes, P. J. *The Athenian Boule*. Oxford, 1972
Roberts, J. T. *Accountability in Athenian Government*. Wisconsin, 1982
Ste Croix, G. E. M. de *The Class Struggle in the Ancient Greek World*. London, 1981
Sealey, R. *Essays in Greek Politics*. New York, 1967
Staveley, E. S. *Greek and Roman Voting and Elections*. London, 1972
Thompson, H. A. and Wycherley, R. E. *The Athenian Agora, XIV: The Agora of
  Athens*. Princeton, 1972
Traill, J. S. *The Political Organization of Attica: A Study of the Demes, Trittyes and
  Phylai, and their Representation in the Athenian Council* (*Hesperia* Suppl. 14),
  1975
Whitehead, D. *The Demes of Attica 508/7–ca. 250 B.C.* Princeton, 1986
Wycherley, R. E. *The Athenian Agora, III: Literary and Epigraphical Testimonia*.
  Princeton, 1957

(B) Other works
(Works cited by author's name and year of publication.)

Accame, S. (1941) *La lega ateniese del secolo IV a. C.* Rome
Adcock, F. A. and Mosley, D. J. (1975) *Diplomacy in Ancient Greece*. London
Adeleye, G. (1983) 'The Purpose of the *Dokimasia*', *GRBS* 24.295–306
Adkins, A. W. H. (1972) *Moral Values and Political Behaviour in Ancient Greece*.
  London
    (1976) '*Polupragmosune* and "Minding one's own Business": A Study in Greek
    Social and Political Values', *CPh* 71.301–27

Bibliography

Alessandri, S. (1980) 'IG ii².140 (Una proposta di lettura)', ASNP 10.1131–61
    (1982) 'Alcune osservazioni sui segretari ateniese nel IV sec. a. C.', ASNP 2.7–70
Amit, M. (1965) Athens and the Sea: A Study in Athenian Sea-Power. Brussels
Anderson, J. K. (1963) 'The Statue of Chabrias', AJA 67.411–13
Andrewes, A. (1956) The Greek Tyrants. London
    (1962) 'The Mytilene Debate: Thucydides 3.36–49', Phoenix 16.64–85
    (1974) 'The Arginousai Trial', Phoenix 28.112–22
    (1977) 'Kleisthenes' Reform Bill', CQ 27.241–8
    (1978) 'The Opposition to Perikles', JHS 98.1–8
    (1981) 'The Hoplite Katalogos', in G. S. Shrimpton and D. J. McCargar (edd.),
        Classical Contributions: Studies in Honour of M. F. McGregor (New York), 1–3
Andreyev, V. N. (1974) 'Some Aspects of Agrarian Conditions in Attica in the
    Fifth to Third Centuries B.C.', Eirene 12.5–46
Austin, M. M. and Vidal-Naquet, P. (1977) Economic and Social History of Ancient
    Greece: An Introduction. London
Badian, E. (1971) 'Archons and Strategoi', Antichthon 5.1–34
Barron, J. P. (1964) 'Religious Propaganda of the Delian League', JHS 84.35–48
Beck, F. A. G. (1964) Greek Education 450–350 B.C. London
Beloch, K. J. (1886) Die Bevölkerung der griechisch-römischen Welt. Leipzig
    (1923) Griechische Geschichte (2nd ed.), 3.2. Berlin and Leipzig
Bers, V. (1985) 'Dikastic Thorubos', in Crux 1–15
Billheimer, A. (1938) 'Amendments in Athenian Decrees', AJA 42.456–85
Bishop, J. D. (1970) 'The Cleroterium', JHS 90.1–14
Boardman, J. (1975) Athenian Red Figure Vases: The Archaic Period. London
Boegehold, A. L. (1963) 'Toward a Study of Athenian Voting Procedure', Hesperia
    32.366–74
Boersma, J. S. (1970) Athenian Building Policy from 561/0 to 405/4 B.C. Groningen
Bonner, R. J. (1927) Lawyers and Litigants in Ancient Athens. Chicago
Bonner, R. J. and Smith, G. (1930–8) The Administration of Justice from Homer to
    Aristotle. 2 vols. Chicago
Bourriot, F. (1982) 'La famille et le milieu social de Cléon', Historia 31.404–35
Bradeen, D. W. (1955) 'The Trittyes in Cleisthenes' Reforms', TAPhA 86.22–30
Briant, P. (1968) 'La boulè et l'élection des ambassadeurs à Athènes au IVᵉ siècle',
    REA 70.7–31
Broneer, O. (1938) 'Excavations on the North Slope of the Acropolis, 1937',
    Hesperia 7.228–43
Brunt, P. A. (1952) 'Thucydides and Alcibiades', REG 65.59–96
    (1966) 'Athenian Settlements Abroad in the Fifth Century B.C.', in ASI 71–92
    (1969) 'Euboea in the Time of Philip II', CQ 19.245–65
Buchanan, J. J. (1962) Theorika: A Study of Monetary Distributions to the Athenian
    Citizenry during the Fifth and Fourth Centuries B.C. Locust Valley, N.Y.
Buckler, J. (1972) 'A Second Look at the Monument of Chabrias', Hesperia
    41.466–74
Burford, A. (1969) The Greek Temple Builders at Epidauros. Liverpool
Burnett, A. P. and Edmonson, C. N. (1961) 'The Chabrias Monument in the
    Athenian Agora', Hesperia 30.74–91

Burns, A. (1981) 'Athenian Literacy in the Fifth Century B.C.', *JHI* 42.371–87

Bury, J. B. and Meiggs, R. (1975) *A History of Greece* (4th ed.). London

Buxton, R. G. A. (1982) *Persuasion in Greek Tragedy: A Study of Peitho.* Cambridge

Cargill, J. (1981) *The Second Athenian League: Empire or Free Alliance?* Berkeley

Caven, B. (1976) Review of Hansen (1974) and (1975) (see below), *JHS* 96.227–8

Cawkwell, G. L. (1962A) 'The Defence of Olynthus', *CQ* 12.122–40

    (1962B) 'Notes on the Social War', *C & M.* 23.34–49

    (1963A) 'Eubulus', *JHS* 83.47–67

    (1963B) 'Demosthenes' Policy after the Peace of Philocrates', *CQ* 13.120–38,
        200–13

    (1969) 'The Crowning of Demosthenes', *CQ* 19.163–80

    (1981) 'Notes on the Failure of the Second Athenian Confederacy', *JHS*
        101.40–55

Clairmont, C. W. (1983) *Patrios Nomos. Public Burial in Athens during the Fifth and
    Fourth Centuries B.C.* Oxford

Clinton, K. (1980) 'A Law in the City Eleusinion concerning the Mysteries',
    Hesperia 49.258–88

    (1982) 'The Nature of the Late Fifth-Century Revision of the Athenian Law
    Code', *Studies in Attic Epigraphy, History and Topography* (*Hesperia* Suppl. 19)
    27–37

Cloché, P. (1951) *La démocratie athénienne.* Paris

    (1960) 'Les hommes politiques et la justice populaire dans l'Athènes du IVe
    siècle', *Historia* 9.80–95

Coale, A. J. and Demeny, P. (1966) *Regional Model Life Tables and Stable
    Populations.* Princeton

Cohen, D. (1983) *Theft in Athenian Law.* Munich

Connor, W. R. (1974) 'The Athenian Council: Method and Focus in some recent
    Scholarship', *CJ* 70.32–40

Connor, W. R. and Keaney, J. J. (1969) 'Theophrastus on the End of Ostracism',
    AJPh 90.313–19

Cooper, A. B. (1978) 'The Family Farm in Greece', *CJ* 73.162–75

Crosby, M. (1950) 'The Leases of the Laureion Mines', *Hesperia* 19.189–292

Daux, G. (1963) 'La Grande Démarchie: un nouveau calendrier sacrificiel
    d'Attique', *BCH* 87.603–34

    (1983) 'Le calendrier de Thorikos au Musée J. Paul Getty', *AC* 52.150–74

Davies, J. K. (1967) 'Demosthenes on Liturgies: A Note', *JHS* 87.33–40

    (1969) 'The Date of IG II^2.1609', *Historia* 18.309–33

    (1975) Review of Connor (see above), *Gnomon* 47.374–8

    (1977/8) 'Athenian Citizenship: The Descent Group and the Alternatives', *CJ*
    73.105–21

    (1978) *Democracy and Classical Greece.* Glasgow

    (1979) 'A Reconsideration of IG I^2.847', *LCM* 4.151–6

Develin, R. (1984) 'From Panathenaia to Panathenaia', *ZPE* 57.133–8

Dickie, W. W. (1973) 'Thucydides 1.93.3', *Historia* 22.758–9

Dinsmoor, W. B. (1933) Review of *Hesperia* vol. 1 (1932), *AJA* 37.180–2

Dover, K. J. (1960) 'ΔΕΚΑΤΟΣ ΑΥΤΟΣ ', *JHS* 80.61–77

    (1968) *Lysias and the Corpus Lysiacum.* Berkeley

Dow, S. (1937) *Prytaneis. A Study of the Inscriptions Honoring the Athenian Councillors* (*Hesperia* Suppl. 1)

    (1939) 'Aristotle, the Kleroteria and the Courts', *HSCP* 50.1–34

    (1968) 'Six Athenian Sacrificial Calendars', *BCH* 92.170–86

Duncan-Jones, R. P. (1980) 'Metic Numbers in Periclean Athens', *Chiron* 10.101–9

Dušanić, S. (1980) 'Plato's Academy and Timotheus' Policy, 365–359 B.C.', *Chiron* 10.111–44

Ehrenberg, V. (1947) 'Polypragmosyne: A Study in Greek Politics', *JHS* 67.46–67

    (1950) 'The Origins of Democracy', *Historia* 1.515–48

    (1951) *The People of Aristophanes* (2nd ed.). Oxford

    (1969) *The Greek State* (2nd ed.). London

Eliot, C. W. J. (1962) *Coastal Demes of Attika*. Toronto

Evans, J. A. S. (1979) 'Herodotus' Publication Date', *Athenaeum* 57.145–9

Finley, M. I. (1951) *Studies in Land and Credit in Ancient Athens, 500–200 B.C.* New Brunswick

    (1960) 'Was Greek Civilization Based on Slave Labour?', in M. I. Finley (ed.) *Slavery in Classical Antiquity* (Cambridge), 53–72

    (1968) *Aspects of Antiquity*. London

    (1973) *The Ancient Economy*. London

    (1974) *Studies in Ancient Society*. London

    (1975) *The Use and Abuse of History*. London

    (1978) 'The Fifth-Century Athenian Empire: A Balance Sheet', in P. D. A. Garnsey and C. R. Whittaker (edd.), *Imperialism in the Ancient World*, (Cambridge), 103–26

    (1979) *Ancient Sicily* (2nd ed.). London

    (1981) *Economy and Society in Ancient Greece*. London

Fisher, N. R. E. (1976) *Social Values in Classical Athens*. London

Fornara, C. W. (1971A) *The Athenian Board of Generals from 501 to 404 B.C.* (*Historia* Einzelschriften 16)

    (1971B) 'Evidence for the Date of Herodotus' Publication', *JHS* 91.25–34

    (1981) 'Herodotus' Knowledge of the Archidamian War', *Hermes* 109.149–56

Forrest, W. G. (1960) 'Themistokles and Argos', *CQ* 10.221–41

    (1966) *The Emergence of Greek Democracy*. London

French, A. (1964) *The Growth of the Athenian Economy*. London

Frost, F. J. (1964) 'Pericles, Thucydides, son of Melesias, and Athenian Politics before the War', *Historia* 13.385–99

Fuks, A. (1971) *The Ancestral Constitution*. Westport (reprint of 1953 ed.)

Gabrielsen, V. (1981) *Remuneration of State Officials in Fourth Century B.C. Athens.* Odense

Garnsey, P. D. A. (1985) 'Grain for Athens', in *Crux* 62–75

Glotz, G. (1926) *Ancient Greece at Work*. London

Gomme, A. W. (1937) *Essays in Greek History and Literature*. Oxford

    (1959) 'The Population of Athens Again', *JHS* 79.61–8

    (1962) *More Essays in Greek History and Literature*. Oxford

Gray, V. J. (1980) 'The Years 375 to 371 B.C.: A Case Study in the Reliability of Diodorus Siculus and Xenophon', *CQ* 30.306–26

Green, J. R. and Sinclair, R. K. (1970) 'Athenians in Eretria', *Historia* 19.515–27

Griffith, G. T. (1935) *The Mercenaries of the Hellenistic World*. Cambridge

    (1966) 'Isegoria in the Assembly at Athens', in *ASI* 115–38

Guthrie, W. K. (1969) *A History of Greek Philosophy*, vol. 3. Cambridge

Hammond, N. G. L. (1967) *A History of Greece to 322 B.C.* (2nd ed.). Oxford

Hansen, M. H. (1971–80A) 'Athenian *Nomothesia* in the Fourth Century B.C. and Demosthenes' Speech against Leptines', *C & M* 32.87–104

    (1971–80B) 'Perquisites for Magistrates in Fourth-Century Athens', *C & M* 32.105–25

    (1974) *The Sovereignty of the People's Court in the Fourth Century B.C. and the Public Action against Unconstitutional Proposals*. Odense

    (1975) *Eisangelia*. Odense

    (1976) *Apagoge, Endeixis and Ephegesis against Kakourgoi, Atimoi and Pheugontes*. Odense

    (1979) 'Misthos for Magistrates in Classical Athens', *SO* 54.5–22

    (1980A) 'Eisangelia in Athens: A Reply', *JHS* 100.89–95

    (1980B) 'Seven Hundred *Archai* in Classical Athens', *GRBS* 21.151–73

    (1981) 'The Number of Athenian Hoplites in 431 B.C.', *SO* 56.19–32

    (1981–2) 'The Athenian *Heliaia* from Solon to Aristotle', *C & M* 33.9–47

    (1983A) 'The Athenian "Politicians", 403–322 B.C.', *GRBS* 24.33–55

    (1983B) '*Rhetores* and *Strategoi* in Fourth-Century Athens', *GRBS* 24.151–80

    (1983C) 'Political Activity and the Organization of Attica in the Fourth Century B.C.', *GRBS* 24.227–38

    (1984) 'The Number of *Rhetores* in the Athenian *Ecclesia*, 355–322 B.C.', *GRBS* 25.123–55

    (1985) 'Demographic Reflections on the Number of Athenian Citizens 451–309 B.C.', *AJAH* 7.172–89

    (1986) *Demography and Democracy: The Number of Athenian Citizens in the Fourth Century B.C.* Herning

Hansen, M. H. and Mitchel, F. W. (1984) 'The Number of Ecclesiai in Fourth-Century Athens', *SO* 59.13–19

Hanson, V. D. (1980) *Warfare and Agriculture in Ancient Greece*. (Stanford University dissertation; University Microfilms)

Harding, P. A. (1976) 'Androtion's Political Career', *Historia* 25.186–200

Harrison, A. R. W. (1955) 'Law-Making at Athens at the End of the Fifth Century B.C.', *JHS* 75.26–35

    (1959) Review of Jones (see above), *CR* 9.60–2

Harvey, F. D. (1965) 'Two Kinds of Equality', *C & M* 26.101–46

    (1966) 'Literacy in the Athenian Democracy', *REG* 79.585–635

    (1985) '*Dona Ferentes*: Some Aspects of Bribery in Greek Politics', in *Crux* 76–117

Havelock, E. A. (1971) *Prologue to Greek Literacy*. Cincinnati

Henderson, B. W. (1927) *The Great War between Athens and Sparta*. London

Henry, A. S. (1977) *The Prescripts of Athenian Decrees* (*Mnemosyne* Suppl. 49)

Hoffman, R. J. (1975) 'Epigraphic Notes on *IG* I².71', *CSCA* 8.92–104

Hopper, R. J. (1953) 'The Attic Silver Mines in the Fourth Century B.C.', *BSA* 48.200–54

Bibliography

(1957) *The Basis of the Athenian Democracy*. Sheffield

(1979) *Trade and Industry in Classical Greece*. London

Humphreys, S. C. (1970) 'Economy and Society in Classical Athens', *ASNP* 39.1–26

(1978) 'Public and Private Interests in Classical Athens', *CJ* 73.97–104

Jacoby, F. (1944) '*Patrios Nomos*: State Burial in Athens and the Public Cemetery in the Kerameikos', *JHS* 64.37–66

Jameson, M. H. (1955) 'Seniority in the *Strategia*', *TAPhA* 86.63–87

(1978) 'Agriculture and Slavery in Classical Athens', *CJ* 73.122–45

Jones, A. H. M. (1960) 'Slavery in the Ancient World', in M. I. Finley (ed.) *Slavery in Classical Antiquity* (Cambridge), 1–15

Jordan, B. (1975) *The Athenian Navy in the Classical Period*. Berkeley and Los Angeles

Kallet, L. (1983) 'Iphikrates, Timotheos and Athens, 371–360 B.C.', *GRBS* 24.239–52

Keaney, J. J. and Szedegy-Maszak, A. (1976) 'Theophrastus' *De Eligendis Magistratibus*: Vat. Gr. 2306, Fragment B', *TAPhA* 106.227–40.

Kearns, E. (1985) 'Change and Continuity in Religious Structures after Kleisthenes', in *Crux* 189–207

Kelly, D. H. (1978) 'The Athenian Archonship 508/7–487/6', *Antichthon* 12.1–17

Kennedy, G. (1963) *The Art of Persuasion in Greece*. London

Kinzl, K. H. (1978) 'ΔΗΜΟΚΡΑΤΙΑ: Studie zur Frühgeschichte des Begriffes', *Gymnasium* 85.117–27 and 312–26

Kluwe, E. (1976) 'Die soziale Zusammensetzung der athenischen Ekklesia und ihr Einfluss auf politische Entscheidungen', *Klio* 58.295–333

(1977) 'Nochmals zum Problem: Die soziale Zusammensetzung der athenischen Ekklesia und ihr Einfluss auf politische Entscheidungen', *Klio* 59.45–81

Knox, R. A. (1985) '"So Mischievous a Beaste"? The Athenian *Demos* and its Treatment of its Politicians', *G & R* 32.132–61

Koerner, R. (1974) 'Die Entwicklung der attischen Demokratie nach dem Peloponnesischen Kriege in Verfassung, Verwaltung und Recht', in E. C. Welskopf (ed.), *Hellenische Poleis* (Berlin), 1.132–46

Kourouniotes, K. and Thompson, H. A. (1932) 'The Pnyx in Athens', *Hesperia* 1.90–217

Krentz, P. (1980) 'Foreigners against the Thirty: IG 2².10 Again', *Phoenix* 34.298–306

Lacey, W. K. (1968) *The Family in Classical Greece*. London

Laing, D. R. (1965) *A New Interpretation of the Athenian Naval Catalogue, IG II².1951* (University of Cincinnati dissertation; University Microfilms)

Laqueur, R. (1927) *Epigraphische Untersuchungen zu den griechischen Volksbeschlüssen*. Leipzig and Berlin

Larsen, J. A. O. (1948) 'Cleisthenes and the Development of the Theory of Democracy at Athens', in M. R. Konvitz (ed.), *Essays in Political Theory presented to G. H. Sabine*. Ithaca

(1954) 'The Judgement of Antiquity on Democracy', *CPh* 49.1–14

(1955) *Representative Government in Greek and Roman History*. Berkeley and Los Angeles

Lauffer, S. (1955–6) *Die Bergwerkssklaven von Laureion*. 2 vols. Wiesbaden

Lewis, D. M. (1954) 'Notes on Attic Inscriptions', *BSA* 49.17–50

    (1959) 'Law on the Lesser Panathenaia', *Hesperia* 28.239–47

    (1963A) 'Cleisthenes and Attica', *Historia* 12.22–40

    (1963B) Review of Eliot (1962) (see above), *Gnomon* 35.723–5

    (1973A) 'Themistocles' Archonship', *Historia* 22.757–8

    (1973B) Review of Reinmuth (1971) (see below), *CR* 23.254–6

    (1975) Review of Connor (see above), *CR* 25.87–90

    (1977) *Sparta and Persia*. Leiden

    (1982) Review of Gabrielsen (1981) (see above), *JHS* 102.269

    (1983) Review of Siewert (1982) (see below), *Gnomon* 55.431–6

Lewis, J. D. (1971) 'Isegoria at Athens: When did it Begin?', *Historia* 20.129–40

Lofberg, J. O. (1917) *Sycophancy in Athens*. Chicago

Longo, C. P. (1971) *"Eterie" e gruppi politici nell' Atene del IV sec. a. C.* Florence

Loraux, N. (1981) *L'invention d'Athènes*. Paris

McDonald, W. A. (1943) *The Political Meeting Places of the Greeks*. Baltimore

MacDowell, D. M. (1975) 'Law-Making at Athens in the Fourth Century B.C.', *JHS* 95.62–74

    (1976) Review of Hansen (1974) (see above), *CR* 26.231–2

    (1983) 'Athenian Laws about Bribery', *RIDA* 30.57–78

MacKendrick, P. (1969) *The Athenian Aristocracy, 399 to 31 B.C.* Cambridge, Mass.

Markle, M. M. (1985) 'Jury Pay and Assembly Pay at Athens', in *Crux* 265–97

Marrou, H. I. (1956) *A History of Education in Antiquity*. London

Martin, J. (1974) 'Von Kleisthenes zu Ephialtes. Zur Entstehung der athenischen Demokratie', *Chiron* 4.5–42

Meiggs, R. (1964) 'A Note on the Population of Attica', *CR* 14.2–3

Meritt, B. D. and Traill, J. S. (1974) *The Athenian Agora*, XV: *The Inscriptions – The Athenian Councillors*. Princeton

Michell, H. (1975) *The Economics of Ancient Greece* (2nd ed.). Cambridge

Mikalson, J. D. (1975A) *"Ἡμέρα ἀποφράς"*, *AJPh* 96.19–27

    (1975B) *The Sacred and Civil Calendar of the Athenian Year*. Princeton

    (1977) 'Religion in the Attic Demes', *AJPh* 98.424–35

    (1983) *Athenian Popular Religion*. Chapel Hill

Mitchel, F. W. (1962) 'Demades of Paeania and *IG* II².1493, 1494, 1495', *TAPhA* 93.213–29

    (1970) *Lykourgan Athens: 338–322* (Semple Lecture, Cincinnati)

    (1975) 'The So-Called Earliest Ephebic Inscription', *ZPE* 19.233–43

Morrison, J. S. and Williams, R. T. (1968) *Greek Oared Ships 900–322 B.C.* Cambridge

Mosley, D. J. (1962) 'The Athenian Embassy to Sparta in 371 B.C.', *PCPhS* 8.41–6

    (1965) 'The Size of Embassies in Ancient Greek Diplomacy', *TAPhA* 96.255–66

    (1973) *Envoys and Diplomacy in Ancient Greece* (*Historia* Einzelschriften 22)

Moysey, R. A. (1981) 'The Thirty and the Pnyx', *AJA* 85.31–7

Neil, R. A. (1909) *The Knights of Aristophanes*. Cambridge

O'Neil, J. L. (1979/80) 'The Constitution of Chios in the Fifth Century B.C.', *Talanta* 10/11.66–73

Oost, S. I. (1977) 'Two Notes on Aristophon of Azenia', *CPh* 72.238–42

Bibliography

Osborne, M. J. (1972) 'Attic Citizenship Decrees: A Note', BSA 67.129–58
    (1981) 'Entertainment in the Prytaneion at Athens', ZPE 41.153–70
Osborne, R. (1985) 'The Erection and Mutilation of the Hermai', PCPhS 31.47–73
Palagia, O. (1982) 'A Colossal Statue of a Personification from the Agora of
    Athens', Hesperia 51.99–113
Parke, H. W. (1933) Greek Mercenary Soldiers. Oxford
Patterson, C. (1981) Pericles' Citizenship Law of 451–50 B.C. New York
Pearson, L. (1962) Popular Ethics in Ancient Greece. Stanford
Pečírka, J. (1973) 'Homestead Farms in Classical and Hellenistic Hellas', in M. I.
    Finley (ed.), Problèmes de la terre en Grèce ancienne (Paris), 13–47
    (1975) 'Die athenische Demokratie und das athenische Reich', Klio 57.307–11
    (1982) 'Athenian Imperialism and the Athenian Economy', Eirene 19.117–25
Pélékidis, C. (1962) Histoire de l'éphébie attique. Paris
Perlman, S. (1963) 'The Politicians in the Athenian Democracy of the Fourth
    Century B.C.', Athenaeum 41.327–55
    (1967) 'Political Leadership in Athens in the Fourth Century B.C.', PP 22.161–76
    (1976) 'On Bribing Athenian Ambassadors', GRBS 17.223–33
Pickard-Cambridge, A. W. (1968) The Dramatic Festivals of Athens (2nd ed. revised
    by J. P. A. Gould and D. M. Lewis). Oxford
Piérart, M. (1974) 'A propos de l'élection des stratèges athéniens', BCH 98.125–46
Pomeroy, S. B. (1973) 'Selected Bibliography on Women in Antiquity', Arethusa
    6.125–57
    (1975) Goddesses, Whores, Wives and Slaves: Women in Classical Antiquity. New
    York
    (1982) 'Charities for Greek Women', Mnemosyne 35.115–35
Powell, C. A. (1979A) 'Religion and the Sicilian Expedition', Historia 28.15–31
    (1979B) 'Thucydides and Divination', BICS 26.45–50
Pritchett, W. K. (1956) 'The Attic Stelai, II', Hesperia 25.178–317
Quinn, T. J. (1969) 'Political Groups at Chios: 412 B.C.', Historia 18.22–30
Radin, M. (1927) 'Freedom of Speech in Ancient Athens', AJPh 48.215–30
Randall, R. H. (1953) 'The Erechtheum Workmen', AJA 57.199–210
Raubitschek, A. E. (1952–3) 'Athenian Ostracism', CJ 48.113–22
    (1962) 'Demokratia', Hesperia 31.238–43
Reinmuth, O. W. (1952) 'The Genesis of the Athenian Ephebia', TAPhA 83.34–50
    (1971) The Ephebic Inscriptions of the Fourth Century B.C. (Mnemosyne Suppl. 14)
Rhodes, P. J. (1974) Review of de Laix (see above), JHS 94.232–3
    (1979) 'ΕΙΣΑΓΓΕΛΙΑ in Athens', JHS 99.103–14
    (1980A) 'Athenian Democracy after 403 B.C.', CJ 75.305–23
    (1980B) 'Ephebi, Bouleutae and the Population of Athens', ZPE 38.191–201
    (1981) 'More Members Serving Twice in the Athenian Boule', ZPE 41.101–2
    (1982) 'Problems in Athenian Eisphora and Liturgies', AJAH 7.1–19
    (1985) 'Nomothesia in Fourth-Century Athens', CQ 35.55–60
Ridley, R. T. (1979) 'The Hoplite as Citizen: Athenian Military Institutions in their
    Social Context', AC 48.508–48
Roberts, J. T. (1980) 'The Athenian Conservatives and the Impeachment Trials of
    the Corinthian War', Hermes 108.100–14
Robertson, M. (1975) A History of Greek Art, vol. 1. Cambridge

Ruschenbusch, E. (1957) 'ΔIKAΣTHPION ΠANTΩN KYPION', *Historia* 6.257–74

(1958) 'ΠATPIOΣ ΠOΛITEIA', *Historia* 7.398–424

(1978) 'Die athenischen Symmorien des 4. Jh. v. Chr.' *ZPE* 31.275–84

(1979A) *Athenische Innenpolitik im 5. Jahrhundert v. Chr.: Ideologie oder Pragmatismus?* Bamberg

(1979B) 'Die soziale Herkunft der Epheben um 330', *ZPE* 35.173–6

(1979C) 'Die soziale Zusammensetzung des Rates der 500 in Athen im 4. Jh.', *ZPE* 35.177–80

(1981A) 'Epheben, Buleuten und die Bürgerzahl von Athen um 330 v. Chr.', *ZPE* 41.103–5

(1981B) 'Noch einmal die Bürgerzahl Athens um 330 v. Chr.', *ZPE* 44.110–12

(1984) 'Zum letzten Mal: Die Bürgerzahl Athens im 4. Jh. v. Chr.', *ZPE* 54.253–69

(1985) 'Ein Beitrag zur Leiturgie und zur Eisphora', *ZPE* 59.237–40

Ryder, T. T. B. (1963) 'Athenian Foreign Policy and the Peace-Conference at Sparta in 371 B.C.', *CQ* 13.237–41

Ste Croix, G. E. M. de (1953) 'Demosthenes' Timema and the Athenian Eisphora in the Fourth Century B.C.', *C & M* 14.30–70

(1963) 'The Alleged Secret Pact between Athens and Philip II concerning Amphipolis and Pydna', *CQ* 13.110–19

(1966) 'The Estate of Phaenippus (Ps.-Dem. 42)', in *ASI* 109–14

(1972) *The Origins of the Peloponnesian War.* London

(1975) 'Political Pay outside Athens', *CQ* 25.48–52

Salmon, J. B. (1984) *Wealthy Corinth. A History of the City to 338 B.C.* Oxford

Sartori, F. (1957) *Le eterie nella vita politica ateniese del VI e V secolo a. C.* Rome

Schaps, D. M. (1979) *Economic Rights of Women in Ancient Greece.* Edinburgh

Sealey, R. (1955) 'Dionysius of Halicarnassus and some Demosthenic Dates', *REG* 68.77–120

(1974) 'The Origins of *Demokratia*', *CSCA* 6.253–95

(1982) 'On the Athenian Concept of Law', *CJ* 77.289–302

Seltman, C. (1957) *Women in Antiquity* (2nd ed.). London

Siewert, P. (1977) 'The Ephebic Oath in Fifth-Century Athens', *JHS* 97.102–11

(1982) *Die Trittyen Attikas und die Heeresform des Kleisthenes* (Vestigia 33)

Sinclair, R. K. (1978) 'The King's Peace and the Employment of Military and Naval Forces 387–378', *Chiron* 8.29–54

Smith, S. B. (1930) 'The Athenian *Proedroi*', *CPh* 25.250–76

Starr, C. G. (1958) 'An Overdose of Slavery?', *JEcH* 18.17–32

Strauss, B. J. (1979) *Division and Conquest: Athens, 403–386 B.C.* (Yale dissertation; University Microfilms)

Stroud, R. S. (1963) 'A Fragment of an Inscribed Bronze Stele from Athens', *Hesperia* 32.138–43

(1971) 'Greek Inscriptions; Theozotides and the Athenian Orphans', *Hesperia* 40.280–301

(1974) 'An Athenian Law on Silver Coinage', *Hesperia* 43.157–88

Sundwall, J. (1906) *Epigraphische Beiträge zur sozial-politischen Geschichte Athens im Zeitalter des Demosthenes* (*Klio* Beiheft 4)

Bibliography

Taylor, M. W. (1981) *The Tyrant Slayers: The Heroic Image in Fifth Century B.C. Athenian Art and Policy*. New York

Thompson, H. A. (1937) 'Buildings on the West Side of the Agora', *Hesperia* 6.1–226

    (1982) 'The Pnyx in Models', *Studies in Attic Epigraphy, History and Topography* (*Hesperia* Suppl. 19) 133–47

Thompson, W. E. (1966) '*Τριττὺς τῶν πρυτάνεων*', *Historia* 15.1–10

    (1971) 'The Deme in Kleisthenes' Reforms', *SO* 46.72–9

    (1979) 'An Aspect of Athenian Public Finance', *AClass* 22.149–53

Thomsen, R. (1964) *Eisphora: A Study of Direct Taxation in Ancient Athens*. Copenhagen

Tod, M. N. (1927) 'The Economic Background of the Fifth Century', in *Cambridge Ancient History* 5.1–32

Traill, J. S. (1981) 'Athenian Bouleutic Alternates', in G. S. Shrimpton and D. J. McCargar (edd.), *Classical Contributions: Studies in Honour of M. F. McGregor* (New York), 161–9

    (1982) 'An Interpretation of Six Rock-Cut Inscriptions in the Attic Demes of Lamptrai', *Studies in Attic Epigraphy, History and Topography* (*Hesperia* Suppl. 19) 158–71

Travlos, J. (1971) *Pictorial Dictionary of Ancient Athens*. London

Tritle, L. A. (1981) 'Phokion Phokou Potamios?', *AJAH* 6.118–32

Tuplin, C. (1977) 'The Athenian Embassy to Sparta, 372/1', *LCM* 2.51–6

    (1982) 'Satyros and Athens: *IG* II².212 and Isokrates 17.57', *ZPE* 49.121–8

    (1984) 'Timotheos and Corcyra: Problems in Greek History, 375–373 B.C.', *Athenaeum* 62.536–68

    (1985) 'Imperial Tyranny: Some Reflections on a Classical Greek Political Metaphor', in *Crux* 348–75

Turner, E. G. (1952) *Athenian Books in the Fifth and Fourth Centuries B.C.* London

Tyrrell, W. B. (1984) *Amazons: A Study in Athenian Mythmaking*. Baltimore

Vanderpool, E. (1970) *Ostracism at Athens* (Semple Lecture) in *Lectures in Memory of L. T. Semple II* (1973, Cincinnati) 215–70

Vlastos, G. (1953) 'Isonomia', *AJPh* 74.337–60

    (1964) 'ΙΣΟΝΟΜΙΑ ΠΟΛΙΤΙΚΗ', in J. Mau and E. G. Schmidt (edd.), *Isonomia: Studien zur Gleichheitsvorstellung im griechischen Denken* (Berlin), 1–35

Walbank, M. (1978) *Athenian Proxenies of the Fifth Century B.C.* Toronto

Walcot, P. (1978) *Envy and the Greeks*. Warminster

Wankel, H. (1982) 'Die Korruption in der rednerischen Topik und in der Realität des klassischen Athen', in W. Schuller (ed.), *Korruption im Altertum* (Munich), 29–53

Webster, T. B. L. (1969) *Everyday Life in Classical Athens*. London

    (1970) *Studies in Later Greek Comedy* (2nd ed.). Manchester

Welwei, K.-W. (1974) *Unfreie im antiken Kriegsdienst*, vol. I. Wiesbaden

Westermann, W. L. (1960A, B) 'Slavery and the Elements of Freedom in Ancient Greece', and 'Athenaeus and the Slaves of Athens', in M. I. Finley (ed.), *Slavery in Classical Antiquity* (Cambridge), 17–32, 73–92

Westlake, H. D. (1968) *Individuals in Thucydides.* Cambridge
  (1969) *Essays on the Greek Historians and Greek History.* Manchester
Whitehead, D. (1977) *The Ideology of the Athenian Metic.* Cambridge
  (1983) 'Competitive Outlay and Community Profit: *philotimia* in Democratic
    Athens', *C & M* 34.55–74
Williams, J. M. (1983) 'Solon's Class System, the Manning of Athens' Fleet, and
    the Number of Athenian Thetes in the Late Fourth Century B.C.', *ZPE*
    52.241–5
Winton, R. I. (1980) 'φιλοδικεῖν δοκοῦμεν : Law and Paradox in the Athenian
    Empire', *MH* 37.89–97
Wolff, H. J. (1970) *'Normenkontrolle' und Gesetzesbegriff in der attischen Demokratie*
    (Sb. Heidelberg)
Woodbury, L. (1976) 'Aristophanes' *Frogs* and Athenian Literacy', *TAPhA*
    106.349–57
Woodhead, A. G. (1960) 'Thucydides' Portrait of Cleon', *Mnemosyne* 13.289–318
  (1967) 'ΙΣΗΓΟΡΙΑ and the Council of 500', *Historia* 16.129–40

Index

Index

Index

Pharnabazos, 163, 164
Philaids, 10
Philip II, 22, 27, 32, 58–9, 87, 123, 144, 145,
    157, 183, 184, 204
Philippides, 155 n.92, 156 n.96
Philippos, 154 n.87
Philodemos, 1 n.1
Philokleon, 127 n.85, 130, 132, 133, 143
Philokles, 148, 151 n.71, 185
Philokrates: (PA 14574), 124–6; (PA 14599),
    145, 156 n.95, 157, 184
Philon: (PA 14825; APF 274–5), 148 n.60,
    149, 151 n.71; (PA 14805), 148 n.60
philotimia, 58 n.39, 61, 134, 136–7, *188–90
Phokion, 33, 46, 91 n.61, 148, 156, 161, 169,
    207
Phormion: (PA 14951), 131, 149; (PA
    14958), 46, 147 n.51
Phormisios, 43, 220
phratries, *3
Phrynikhos, 25, 90–1, 92–3
phylarchs, *52, 61
Phyle, 'the men from – ', 26, 27 n.16, 43
pinakia, *130
place of residence, 12, 107–8, 114, 134–5, 194
plague, 116
Plataia, 5, 6, 26
Plato, 44, 123, 192–3, 202–3, 216, 223, 227;
    Sokrates in, 29, 33–4, 49, 50
plēthos, *17, 116, 121, 184; see multitude
plousioi, *121–2; see wealthy
Plutarch, 38 n.81, 39, 50, 115, 138, 148, 194,
    223–4; on operation of democracy, 33,
    142, 173, 174, 195, 207
Pnyx, 67, 116, 117–18, 136, 145, 187, 226
polemarch, 29, 31, *47
Polemarkhos, 29, 197
politeia: (citizenship), *77, see citizenship;
    (public life), *179
politēs, *50–1, 77; see citizens
political involvement, 14, 41 n.94, 65–9,
    136–7, 221; see also experience,
    participation
political rivalry, 20, 36, 142, 164–5, 170,
    174–6, 182, 210, 212; courts and, 132, 153,
    155–6, 171, 210; see also factions,
    supporters
hoi polloi, *15, 177; see multitude
Polyainos, 169
Polyeuktos: (PA 11928), 160; (PA 11946), 95;
    (PA 11947), 154; (PA 11950), 156
polypragmosynē, *209–10
poor: terms for, 15, *121–2, 198–9; attitudes
    of, 57, 59, 61 n.56, 124, 135, 187–8, 208,
    227; attitudes to, 121, 127, 185, 205; and
    courts, 71, 127, 129, 133, 134–5, 194; and
    public life, 66, 108, 109–10, 134–5, 193,
    196; see also poverty, rich vs poor

poor relief, 117, 128
popular will, 68, 172
population, 115, 223–4; elements in, 9–10,
    200; estimated numbers of citizens, 9–10,
    43, 110, 114, 115 n.32, 116, 196 n.18,
    223–4
Poteidaia, 57 n.37, 98
poverty, 21, 133, 173; and participation, 32,
    44–5, 47, 52, 106–8, 109–10, 120–3, 127–8,
    134–5, 193–4; see also poor
power, 44–5, 47–8, 64, 132, 135, 136, 178–9,
    187, 195
powerful, 14, 15, 187
Praxagora, 144
precedence, 31–2, 33, 81, 177
presiding officials, 33, 68, 81 n.13, 103, 109,
    207, 229; see also prohedroi, prytaneis
pre-vote, 100
priests, 26, 44
private affairs, 51, 121, 123, 133–4, 191,
    217–18
privileges, 30–4
probouleuma, *88–9, 112; see also Ekklesia
    decrees: probouleumatic and non-
    probouleumatic
probouleusis, *74, 84–5; see also decision-
    making
Prodikos, 193
prodosia, *147, 149, 157, 158, 168, 173 n.43
proeisphora, *63
professional, 40, 46, 48, 186, 193, 212
prohedroi, 103, 109, *229
prokheirotonia, *100
propertied classes, see wealthy
property, 63 n.70, 64–5, 122, 219, see also
    confiscation of property, wealth; -power,
    64–5; -qualification, 2, 19, 21, 32, 43–4,
    66, 106, 110–12, 204
property tax, 42, 59, 60, 113, 122, 123–4,
    125–7, 134, 208; organisation, 30, 46, 52,
    62–3, 115
prosecution, 43, 79, 146–51, 151–6, 156–60,
    173; voluntary – , 68, 72–3, 112, 143–4,
    149, 160–1, 210; see also sykophantēs
prostatai tou dēmou, *15–16, 37, 137 n.4
Protagoras, 216–17
protection money, 180
proxenos, *35, 93 n.71
Proxenos, 151 n.71
prytaneion, *88, 177
prytaneis, 33, 74, 88, *103, 180–1, 229; and
    assembly, 33, 81, 85, 103, 109, 172, 229
prytany, *67, 108
psēphismata, *84; see Ekklesia: decrees
psēphoi, *119; see secret ballot
public friend, 35, 90
public moneys, 38; see also embezzlement
public order, 196

Index

superiority, 13–14
supervision, 58 n.43, 74–5
supporters, 112, 124–5, 133, 139, 141–5, 170, 179, 187; see also political rivalry
Susa, 153
sykophantēs (pl. sykophantai), *73, 144, 159, 180, 181, 183, 209
symmoriai, *62, 122
symposia, 142
synēgoros (pl. synēgoroi), *72, 79, 136
syntrierarchs, 62
Syracuse, 26, 116, 151, 218

talent, 30, *61 n.59, 65
Tanagra, 9
tax contracters, 56
taxation, 11, 29, 30, 31, 62–3, 76, 78; see also property tax, taxpayers
taxiarchs, *52, 61, 195
taxpayers, 30, 60, 62–3, 122, 123–4, 125–7, 133–4
temples, 90, 113
Tenedos, 120
tenure of office, 19, 21, 66–7, 68–9, 80, 104; implications of limited – , 68–9, 102, 181, 213
Thasos, 6, 9, 10, 11, 35
Thebes, Athenian relations with: before 371 B.C., 26, 88, 98, 140, 146, 151, 161; after 371 B.C., 61, 63 n.71, 88, 161, 167
Themistokles, 8, 16, 36, 37, 170, 176
Theokrines, 160
Theophrastos, 45 n.111, 143, 161
Theopompos, 168
Theoric Fund, see Festival Fund
Theotimos, 149, 151 n.71
Theozotides, 27
Theramenes, 171
Thermopylai, 59
Theseus, 1, 5, 28, 203
thesmothetai, *79, 84, 225
thētes, *2, 10, 13, 56, 120, 127 n.85, 128, 227; and office, 2, 14, 17, 32, 66, 106, 110
Thirty, 43, 192, 200, 209, 219–20
Tholos, 103, 108
Thorikos, 107 n.5
Thrace, 6, 10, 45, 58–9, 149, 167, 182–3, 223
Thracian Khersonesos, 10, 11, 37; in fourth century, 59, 61, 148, 167, 174, 185
Thrasyboulos of Kollytos (PA 7305), 98, 151 n.71, 152, 157
Thrasyboulos of Steiria (PA 7310), 26, 44, 124–5, 139, 148 n.60, 150, 151 n.71, 155
Thrasyboulos (PA 7311), 91
three-obol payment (triobol), 61 n.59, 127, 129, see pay (political): dikasts; see also 59, 128 for two-obol payments

Thucydides (historian) (PA 7267), 3, 6, 8, 40, 151, 178, 182, 204; on Boule and Ekklesia, 82, 86, 102, 115, 206; on Demos, 79, 173, 204; on Perikles, 38, 39, 79, 204, 217; on Perikles' successors, 40, 41–2, 188, 204, 207, 212
Thucydides son of Melesias (PA 7268), 37 n.77, 38, 142, 170
Timagoras, 153
Timarkhos, 160, 180
timē, 57–8, *176–8, 188–90; see also honour
Timokrates, 126
Timomakhos, 148, 149, 151 n.71, 167 n.22, 168, 173–4
Timotheos, 44, 60, 107, 139, 163–8; and Demos, 46, 172, 214; 'failures', 147, 148, 149, 150, 151 n.71, 161, 163–8, 172; successes, 146, 148, 149, 156, 162, 163–8, 178
trade, 11, 29
tradition, 134, 192
traditional values, 41, 49, 134, 227
treason, 72, 157; see prodosia
tribes, 4, 52–3, 78 n.4
tribute, 7, 42, 74, 92, 97 n.84, 102, 201
trierarch/trierarchy, 134, 171, 177, 189, 190; liability, 30, *61–2, 64–5, 121, 122
triremes, 8, 23 n.82, 61–2, 120, 190 n.72; see also navy
trittyes, *4
Troy, 5
tyrannicides, 2–3, 6, 164
tyranny, 2–3, 13

unfit, 56, 129 n.90
unity, 3, 4, 52–3, 220

voluntary action, 110–12; see also prosecution: voluntary
voting: in Dikasteria, 20, 70, 119, 133; in Ekklesia, 16 n.59, 20, 47, 80, 119, 145; see also officials: elective offices, Lot

wage rates, 30, 109, 128–9, 130, 226–7
war, 57–8, 60–1, 123, 187–8
water supply, 80, 93 n.66
wealth, 8, 21, 188–90, 207–9; advantages, 1, 2, 40–1, 64–5, 113, 120; and public leaders, 18, 40–1, 44–5, 47, 60, 113, 164, 167, 179, 186, 195, 199–200
wealthy: terms for, 2, 15, 16, *121–2; attitudes of, 20, 133, 134, 185–6, 187–8, 190, 192, 209, 217; attitudes to, 124, 127, 142, 178, 207–9, 218; obligations of, 61–5, 122, 125, 190; and public life, 14, 44–5, 52, 106–8, 120–2, 133–4, 194, 195, 199–200; see also rich vs poor, wealth

103352

JC 79 .A8 S56 1988 c.1
Sinclair, R. K.
Democracy and participation
  in Athens

DATE DUE

NOV 0 5 2010	
OCT 2 9 2013	

Fernald Library
Colby-Sawyer College
New London, New Hampshire

GAYLORD   PRINTED IN U.S.A.